The **Rough Guide** to

Buenos Aires

written and researched by

Andrew Benson and Rosalba O'Brien

ROUGH
GUIDES

www.roughguides.com

Contents

Colour section — 1

Introduction 4
What to see............................... 6
When to go 10
Things not to miss 11

Basics — 17

Getting there........................... 19
Arrival 21
City transport.......................... 24
The media 28
Culture and etiquette 29
Travel essentials 31

The City — 43

1 Monserrat 45
2 San Nicolás.......................... 61
3 Puerto Madero 72
4 San Telmo 80
5 Boca 88
6 Retiro 94
7 Recoleta............................. 106
8 Palermo 120
9 The outer barrios.............. 138

Listings — 147

10 Accommodation............... 149
11 Cafés 158
12 Restaurants...................... 164
13 Bars, live music and clubs...177
14 The arts and
   entertainment.................. 185
15 Tango 191
16 Gay and lesbian Buenos
   Aires............................... 195
17 Shopping 198
18 Sports and outdoor
   activities........................... 209
19 Kids' Buenos Aires............ 216
20 Festivals and events 219

Out from the city — 225

21 San Isidro........................ 227
22 Tigre and the Paraná
   Delta 232
23 The Pampas..................... 239
24 Colonia del Sacramento
   (Uruguay) 245

Contexts — 249

History 251
Art... 262
Books 265

Language — 269

Argentine Spanish.................. 271
Pronunciation........................ 271
Useful expressions and
   vocabulary 272
An Argentine menu reader 276
A glossary of terms and
   acronyms 279

Travel store — 281

Small print & Index — 285

Building Buenos Aires
colour section
following p.82

Tango colour section
following p.178

Colour maps following
p.296

◄◄ Boys playing table football ◄ Puente de la Mujer

Introduction to
Buenos Aires

Seductive and cultured, beguilingly eclectic and in constant flux, Buenos Aires is the capital city to be in: it never bores, seldom sleeps and exerts a mesmerizing power over visitors. Often described as a subtle blend of Paris, Madrid, Milan and London, with a dash of Manhattan, it basks in a wonderful subtropical climate and has its own deeply entrenched traditions – such as drinking tea-like mate out of hollowed gourds. The city's fashion-conscious inhabitants, known as Porteños, are immensely hospitable and wildly extravagant, while delighting in an introspective melancholy that defines the city´s best-known product, tango. Despite the endless comparisons with Europe, and its often turbulent past, Buenos Aires is a fascinating Latin American city with a larger-than-life personality all of its own.

Buenos Aires – aka Capital Federal, Baires, BsAs or simply "BA" – is a supremely elegant metropolis, whose beneath-the-surface attractiveness lies in its heartfelt passions, its hidden facets and its bewildering variety. There are restaurants and nightclubs to suit every taste and pocket, plus a world-class opera house, myriad theatres, packed cinemas and splendid mansions, all of which reflect the city's attachment to the arts and its overriding sense of style. These qualities are also reflected in **tango** – although most locals live tango-free lives, there is a whole gamut of venues to choose from, be they seedy dives or smart theatres putting on breathtakingly sophisticated shows. Several of the city's **museums** feature the works of international artists, old and modern, some of which are on sale at countless cutting-edge **galleries**. Fascinating artefacts are also for sale in the city's many **antiques shops** and **flea markets**, including the crowd-pulling Feria de San Telmo. BA has a fascinating **history** featuring some captivating personalities; topping the bill is star icon **Evita**, whose devotion to her fellow working class citizens captured the world's imagination.

The city owes much of its character and, historically, its enormous **wealth** to its proximity to nature. During the city's heyday (1880–1920) thousands migrated from Europe and beyond to join the boom, which was almost entirely fed by agriculture: before the Great Depression, Argentina was the fifth wealthiest nation on earth, trading in wheat, salted meat, wool and leather. Today the city's stores and markets are full of reminders of the nearby **Pampas**, a vast verdant plain lapping at its western edges. Horseriding gear and leather goods make for impressive gifts, while flavour-packed fresh meat, fruit and vegetables will lure you with their incredible variety – one of the reasons why you can eat so well in BA.

Many **parks** and **gardens** also dot the city; there are thousands of native and imported **trees**, and in spring and summer, jacarandas and *ceibos* provide a riot of vibrant colour. This greenery attracts a huge number of **birds** – the ubiquitous kiskadees (*benteveos*) and squadrons of squawking parrots help visitors to forget that this is the world's twelfth largest conurbation – there are nearly 14 million inhabitants in the Greater Buenos Aires area. Many of these Porteños are notorious **sports** fanatics – get ready to say which football team you support or your favourite player. A complete trip to the city should undoubtedly include a **football** match, a horse race or even a **polo** game, even if it is only watching it on TV; the crazy commentators will stretch your knowledge of Spanish.

Buenos Aires never ceases to amaze, having resurrected itself time and time again from the deepest and nastiest of crises, not least the devastating economic and **financial meltdown** of 2001. Talk to the locals and they will complain bitterly about urban problems common to cities around the world. Chat further and they will admit that they have an excellent **quality of life**, particularly by Latin American standards, with a fabulous climate, and an endless supply of cultural and sporting events, many of them totally free.

▶ The Obelisco, Plaza de la República

Defining Porteños

"A Porteño is an Italian who speaks Spanish, lives like a Frenchman and wants to be English."

Anonymous

Inhabitants of Buenos Aires are known as **Porteños**, a term deriving from the full name of the original Spanish settlement: Puerto de Santa María del Buen Ayre. Most Porteños are still only second or third generation, and the overwhelming majority claim at least one grandparent born in the Old World: mixed descent is by no means exceptional. The main country of origin, however, is **Italy** – a glance through the city's telephone directories reveals page after page of surnames ending in -etti and -ini. Moreover, the city's distinctive accent – much the same "Rioplatense" version of **Spanish** spoken in Rosario and across the river in Uruguay – has the unmistakeably operatic lilt of Italian. *Lunfardo*, the local slang – a complex amalgam of underground neologisms and borrowed words – is peppered with Italian (such as *birra* for beer). On the other hand, Porteños have an almost old-fashioned love of afternoon tea (scones and all), shop for clothes at places called Windsor and Oxford and excel at polo and football (originally introduced by the **British**). Over the decades, however, they have tried to make their city look like a subtropical replica of **Paris** – copies of Wallace's Three Graces fountain, mansions inspired by Loire chateaux and mansard roofs abound. Porteños have a justified reputation for **good looks** and irresistible charm, though it has to be said that the surgeon's laser and endless hours spent in beauty salons play a major part in their aesthetic appeal.

▲ Porteños playing chess

Notwithstanding the city's shantytowns and other poor neighbourhoods, you will gain the rightful impression of a city moving ahead fast, with restaurants full every night until late, discos packed to the gills and museums that are mobbed every time a new exhibition opens.

What to see

Buenos Aires may look dauntingly **huge**, yet thanks to its **compact core** and the closeness of most of the main sights you won't have to travel far to gain a sense of the city's layout. Owing to the flat terrain aimless wandering is a real treat, while the fairly strict grid pattern inherited from colonial Spain makes orientation easy; the city proper is roughly in the shape of a fan, with the paddles stretching west from the caramel-hued sleeve of the Río de la Plata, the world's widest river estuary.

Of the city's 48 barrios, you will spend most of your time in the half-dozen most central. **Downtown** takes in the tiny but historic barrios of **Monserrat** and **San Nicolás** – busy and smoke-choked on weekdays, bustling with shoppers on Saturday mornings, but spookily quiet on Sundays – with their fair share of hotels, bars, banks and offices, plus the national parliament, pink presidential palace and some of the country's oldest public buildings. Offering a total contrast, nearby **Puerto Madero**, the city's newest barrio, runs along the former dockside, where warehouses and wharves have been transformed into deluxe apartments, hotels and a private university. It is glitzy rather than atmospheric, yet the huge expanses of water and adjacent **nature reserve** make it one of the most appealing areas to wander about.

The **south** of the city offers an alluring mix of tradition and popular culture. The narrow, often cobbled, streets of **San Telmo** are lined with some of the capital's finest architecture: late nineteenth-century townhouses with ornate Italianate facades. Once seedy but increasingly gentrified, it is the setting of the city's Sunday antique market and various tango haunts, and some of its formerly dilapidated houses have been converted into luxury B&Bs and

▶ Mural of Carlos Gardel

excellent-value youth hostels. Further south you can share the boisterous passion of resolutely working-class **Boca** on football match days, when it seems to drown in a sea of blue and yellow. The neighbourhood is so inextricably linked with its football team – Boca Juniors – that many buildings and even tree-trunks are painted those colours. Whatever you do, don't stray from tourist-filled streets and be especially careful at night, when Boca can be a real danger zone (take the usual precautions). The badly polluted **Riachuelo**, a tributary of the Río de la Plata that runs past the barrio, is infamously malodorous on hot days, so be warned.

Far more sweetly scented, the well-heeled, generally more sedate **north** of Buenos Aires begins at Avenida Córdoba. **Retiro**, **Recoleta** and **Palermo** are the leafiest and wealthiest barrios – you may well opt for one of their boutique hotels, head there to shop for designer clothes or souvenirs (such as a *mate* gourd or a leather belt) or dine in one of the many smart restaurants, serving anything from traditional Argentine cooking to Peruvian-Japanese fusion. Set off against feather-leafed *tipa* trees, the architectural styles of the barrios' aristocratic palaces are part Spanish and part British, but overwhelmingly French. The bulk of the city's **museums** lie here, too, with themes as varied as military hardware and Eva Perón – whose final resting place you will find in Recoleta's glorious cemetery, **La Recoleta**. A star among the city's sights, the burial ground is a magnificent and bombastic paean to the oligarchy's thwarted desire for immortality. Further north, incredibly wide avenues sweep past enormous **parks**, such as Parque 3 de Febrero, and major sports venues, where you can watch world-class polo, horseracing and tennis. Pockets of mid-nineteenth-century Buenos Aires remain, the most beguiling of all being **Palermo Viejo**, whose cobbled streets and single-storey houses contrast with the grandiose mansions and lofty apartment blocks that populate much of this side of the city.

Another three dozen mainly residential neighbourhoods stretch beyond central BA. These include the inner barrios of **Caballito** – a lower middle-class district with an old-fashioned natural science museum – and **Balvanera**, where you can find an Art Deco shopping mall, a museum dedicated to Carlos Gardel, the godfather of tango, and shops and canteens run by the city's Jewish and Andean communities. A hit with Argentine and foreign visitors alike is Gardel's shrine-like tomb in the huge cemetery of **Chacarita**. Another popular destination is the weekend gaucho fair in the far western barrio of **Mataderos**, which offers the unforgettable sight of dashingly dressed horsemen galloping through the city streets, plus smoky barbecues and a wide range of arts and crafts. The northern barrio of **Belgrano** is home not only to the more prosperous members of the Jewish community and middle-class Porteños of all ethnic origins, but also to a remarkable collection of Hispanic art housed in an equally fabulous Neocolonial mansion. Just across the border with adjacent **Núñez** stands the aptly named Monumental football stadium, where Boca Juniors' bitter rivals River Plate are based.

For all its bird-filled parks, Buenos Aires is nonetheless a very urban place and many visitors find it a relief to get away from the hectic ferment for a day or two. Beyond residential Belgrano, the genteel northern suburbs ("**Zona Norte**"), particularly **San Isidro**, have preserved a certain small-town charm, a mere forty-minute train ride from central Buenos Aires. North of here, the subtropical islets, steamy swamps and traditional stilted houses of the **Paraná Delta** could not be a more radical change from the capital. The focus of this intriguing watery landscape is **Tigre**, a kind of subtropical Venice, with an outstanding art museum, busy waterways and a colourful arts and crafts market. A little further afield, the beautifully preserved Portuguese colonial town of **Colonia**

▲ Busy shoppers in central Buenos Aires

del Sacramento in neighbouring Uruguay is but a short ferry ride across the Río de la Plata. Regarded by many Porteños (but not the Uruguayans) as the forty-ninth barrio of their city, the town sits on a deliciously tranquil sand-fringed protuberance of coast.

Over to the west, the flat **Pampas** stretch mesmerizingly for hundreds of kilometres across Buenos Aires Province, the fertile hinterland on which the capital built its wealth, and far beyond. These plains still host dozens of working ranches, or **estancias**, some of which, such as the ones near the rural market town of **San Antonio de Areco**, open their doors to visitors for idyllic days of horseriding and barbecue lunches or full-board accommodation in luxurious conditions formerly enjoyed only by the country's wealthiest denizens.

When to go

B uenos Aires' climate is a pleasant, subtropical one, making it fine to visit all year round. However, the city's relatively short **spring**, around October and November (the seasons are of course reversed from those in Europe and North America), may be the best time to go – temperatures are warm and the streets become a riot of colour, as thousands of trees burst into blossom. **Autumn** (March & April) also usually sees moderate temperatures. Statistically, March and October are the wettest months, but rainfall is spread throughout the year.

Summer (Dec–Feb) in the city is a mixed experience – cultural events and nightclubs move outdoors, but most theatres and some museums are closed in January, as the locals head off en masse to holiday elsewhere. The hot sunshine may appeal, but be prepared for the accompanying humidity, as temperatures soar well over 35°C, alleviated mercifully by sudden violent downpours (which can cause localized flooding).

The cool, damp days of deep **winter** (June–Aug) can be fairly miserable, as minimum temperatures can drop to freezing and sea fog can sweep in. However, it's rare to have wall-to-wall overcast skies or relentless drizzle – bright sunshine usually alternates with rain. Snow is extremely rare, although violent hailstorms are a hazard at any time of year – listen out for weather warnings.

Average monthly temperatures and rainfall

	Jan	Feb	Mar	Apr	May	Jun	Jul	Aug	Sep	Oct	Nov	Dec
Buenos Aires												
Max/min (ºC)	29/17	27/17	26/15	22/11	18/8	15/5	14/5	16/6	18/7	21/10	24/12	27/16
Rainfall (mm)	93	81	117	90	77	68	59	65	78	97	89	96

things not to miss

It's not possible to see everything that Buenos Aires has to offer in one trip – and we don't suggest you try. What follows is a selective taste of the city's highlights: engaging neighbourhoods, first-rate museums, historic architecture, exciting festivals and more. They're arranged in five colour-coded categories, which you can browse through to find the very best to see and experience. All highlights have a page reference to take you straight into the guide, where you can find out more.

01 Plaza de Mayo Page **45** • The city's modern heart and historical centre, from the cry for independence via the great Peronist rallies to the 2001 riots; the square is home to the Casa Rosada (presidential palace), the cathedral and the city hall.

02 **Bookshops** Page **201** • As befits one of the world's most literate cities, Buenos Aires is a paradise for bookworms: make sure to check out some of its truly magnificent *librerías*.

03 **Feria de San Pedro Telmo** Page **82** • Crumbly San Telmo is a great place to browse among antiques and jumble any day of the week, but Sunday's enthusiastically attended open-air market is the best.

04 **Feria de Mataderos** Page **143** • If you haven't the time to explore the Pampas, let the Pampas come to you in this authentic weekly celebration of traditional *criollo* culture inside the city limits.

05 **Tigre and the Paraná Delta** Page **232** • Visiting the lush Paraná Delta just outside the city limits is like taking a day-trip to the jungle – only there's a fabulous art museum, too.

06 **MALBA** Page **125** • See this fantastic collection of contemporary Latin American art in an equally fabulous contemporary building, proving that Buenos Aires is far more than faded grandeur.

07 **Green spaces** Page **79** • A huge amount of central Buenos Aires is given over to grass, trees and subtropical foliage in tastefully landscaped plazas, leafy avenues and vast parks.

13

08 Recoleta Cemetery Page **108** • This historic burial ground is a city within the city – extravagant masterpieces, ranging from Baroque sepulchres to Art Deco vaults, line its noble avenues and obscure passages.

09 Tango Page **191** & *Tango* **colour section** • No visit to the city is complete without time spent listening to tango or watching it being danced – take a few lessons and you might even pluck up the courage to join in at a milonga.

10 Parrillas Page **167** • Eating at Buenos Aires' fabulous steak houses is one of the great experiences on offer – vegetarians can sample salads and grilled vegetables but the beef is succulent, full of flavour and simply the best in the world.

11 **Palacio de las Aguas Corrientes** Page **141** • This architectural marvel, taking up an entire block and iced in Royal Doulton pottery, looks fit for the aristocracy but actually housed the city's first major waterworks.

12 **San Antonio de Areco** Page **239** • Spend a day out of the city in this charming town that celebrates its status as a centre of pampas culture – you can even stay over at a local estancia (ranch).

13 **Leather goods** Page **203** • Take advantage of cutting-edge designs – plus loads of traditional work – in the city's myriad leather-goods outlets.

14 **Café culture** Page **158** • An espresso in Buenos Aires is much more than just a small coffee – it's about *belle époque* decor and ceremonial service, including tiny glasses of water and little platters of biscuits.

15 **Boca** Page **88** • Boca's famous Caminito is on every visitor's must-see list, but other parts of the colourful barrio, including the Boca Juniors stadium, are well worth a visit too – just take special care.

16 **Teatro Colón** Page **69** • Catch up on some high culture at Argentina's grandest theatre, one of the world's great opera houses – the acoustics are rated in the global top five.

17 **Football** Page **209** • Silky skills, breathtaking goals, lively crowds and awe-inspiring stadiums – matches in Buenos Aires are an eye-opening experience for anyone, and unmissable for football fans.

Basics

Basics

Getting there 19

Arrival 21

City transport 24

The media 28

Culture and etiquette 29

Travel essentials.. 31

Getting there

Buenos Aires is Argentina's major transport hub. It's possible to fly to the inter national airport, Ezeiza, and sometimes to the domestic airport (Aeroparque), from cities on every continent, though you might have to go via São Paulo (Brazil), Santiago de Chile, Madrid or an airport in the US. Buses travel to the city from elsewhere in South America, while ferries run daily from Uruguay, across the Río de la Plata (see box, p.245).

In general, airfares to Buenos Aires are high, but they vary by routing and season. The highest fares are charged between December and February, around Easter and in July and August, while you'll get the best prices during the low season – March to June (not counting Easter) and September. Flying at weekends often hikes fares; price ranges quoted in this section assume midweek travel. You can reduce costs by booking your ticket online, through your chosen airline's website or a travel website, or by going through a discount flight agent (see p.21). The cheapest deals are generally airlines' APEX (Advance Purchase Excursion) fares, but these are not flexible: you need to pay for your ticket at least 21 days before departure, your trip needs to be a minimum of seven days and a maximum of three months and you are likely to be penalized if you change your schedule. Most cheap return fares offer no refunds or only a very small refund if you need to cancel your journey, so make sure you have travel insurance (see p.35) before you pay for your ticket.

Flights from the US and Canada

Several airlines offer daily nonstop flights **from the US** to Buenos Aires. Typical return fares start at US$1100 from New York in low season, US$1200 from Chicago or Washington DC, and rise by US$400 or so in the high season. Flying times to Buenos Aires are around eleven hours from New York and Chicago, and nine from Miami.

From Canada, Air Canada offers the only direct flight – from Toronto via São Paulo (with connections from other major Canadian cities). A more flexible itinerary might involve connecting flights with a US carrier. Direct flights from Toronto take around thirteen hours and prices start at Can$1200 in low season; from Vancouver the total journey time is around eighteen hours and fares start from around Can$1200.

Flights from the UK and Ireland

A dozen airlines offer regular scheduled flights **from the UK** to Buenos Aires. Most are via another European city or via the US (the latter trips can be marginally less expensive), although British Airways does a direct flight from London. It may be cheaper to book your flight through a **discount flight agent**. We've listed several on p.21, but check the travel sections of London's *Time Out* and the national Sunday newspapers, or phone the Air Travel Advisory Bureau (☎020/7636 5000) for a list. **Fares** from London to Buenos Aires range from around £700 in the low season to over £1000 in the high season. There are no direct flights **from Ireland** to Argentina. If you're trying to keep costs down, consider flying to London with an economy airline like Ryanair (@www.ryanair.com) and making a connection there, but you might be better off flying direct to New York or Miami and catching an onward flight.

Flights from Australia, New Zealand and South Africa

The best flight deals to Buenos Aires from **Australia** and **New Zealand** are offered by Aerolíneas Argentinas and LAN in conjunction with Qantas and Air New Zealand, either direct or with a stopover in Santiago. In

Australia, most flights to Buenos Aires leave from Sydney, though there are a couple each week from Brisbane and Melbourne. The most direct route to Buenos Aires from New Zealand is from Auckland and takes about seventeen hours. Flights from **South Africa** to Argentina leave from Cape Town and Johannesburg and go via São Paulo, taking sixteen or seventeen hours. Malaysia Airlines flights between Kuala Lumpur and Buenos Aires stop over in Cape Town, from where the last leg takes around ten hours.

Airfares depend on both the season and duration of stay. From Australia they normally start around Aus$1400 in low season, with flights from New Zealand costing around NZ$1800. The lowest return fares from Cape Town cost around ZAR8000.

Round-the-world flights

If Buenos Aires is only one stop on a longer journey, you might consider buying a round-the-world **(RTW)** ticket. Some travel agents can sell you an "off-the-shelf" RTW ticket that will have you touching down in about half a dozen cities (Buenos Aires is on many itineraries). Alternatively, you can have a travel agent assemble a RTW ticket for you; in this case the ticket can be tailored to your needs but may be more expensive.

By bus

There are frequent **bus** services to Buenos Aires from all of Argentina's neighbouring countries, including La Paz in Bolivia, São Paulo and Rio de Janeiro in Brazil, Santiago in Chile, Asunción in Paraguay and Montevideo in Uruguay, plus major destinations across the rest of the country. **Fares** vary enormously, being dependent on length of journey and month of travel, but in general, long-distance buses throughout South America tend to be both relatively cheap and comfortable.

Six steps to a better kind of travel

At Rough Guides we are passionately committed to travel. We feel strongly that only through travelling do we truly come to understand the world we live in and the people we share it with – plus tourism has brought a great deal of **benefit** to developing economies around the world over the last few decades. But the extraordinary growth in tourism has also damaged some places irreparably, and of course **climate change** is exacerbated by most forms of transport, especially flying. This means that now more than ever it's important to **travel thoughtfully** and **responsibly**, with respect for the cultures you're visiting – not only to derive the most benefit from your trip but also to preserve the best bits of the planet for everyone to enjoy. At Rough Guides we feel there are six main areas in which you can make a difference:

- Consider what you're contributing to the **local economy**, and how much the services you use do the same, whether it's through employing local workers and guides or sourcing locally grown produce and local services.
- Consider the **environment** on holiday as well as at home. Water is scarce in many developing destinations, and the biodiversity of local flora and fauna can be adversely affected by tourism. Try to patronize businesses that take account of this.
- Travel with a purpose, not just to tick off experiences. Consider **spending longer** in a place, and getting to know it and its people.
- Give thought to how often you **fly**. Try to avoid short hops by air and more harmful night flights.
- Consider **alternatives to flying**, travelling instead by bus, train, boat and even by bike or on foot where possible.
- Make your trips **"climate neutral"** via a reputable carbon offset scheme. All Rough Guide flights are offset, and every year we donate money to a variety of charities devoted to combating the effects of climate change.

Remember, though, that while bus travel won't destroy your budget, it will eat into your time – travelling from the Brazilian border to Buenos Aires, for example, takes the best part of a day and night.

Airlines, agents and operators

Airlines

Aerolíneas Argentinas ⓦwww.aerolineas.com
AeroSur ⓦwww.aerosur.com
Air Canada ⓦwww.aircanada.com
Air Europa ⓦwww.aireuropa.com
Air France ⓦwww.airfrance.com
Air New Zealand ⓦwww.airnewzealand.com
Alitalia ⓦwww.alitalia.com
American Airlines ⓦwww.aa.com
Avianca ⓦwww.avianca.com
British Airways ⓦwww.ba.com
Continental Airlines ⓦwww.continental.com
Delta ⓦwww.delta.com
Emirates ⓦwww.emirates.com
Gol ⓦwww.voegol.com
Iberia ⓦwww.iberia.com
LanChile ⓦwww.lan.com
Lufthansa ⓦwww.lufthansa.com
Malaysia Airlines ⓦwww.malaysiaairlines.com
Mexicana ⓦwww.mexicana.com
Qantas Airways ⓦwww.qantas.com
Ryanair ⓦwww.ryanair.com
Swiss ⓦwww.swiss.com
United Airlines ⓦwww.united.com

Agents and operators

Bridge the World UK ☎0870/443 2399, ⓦwww.bridgetheworld.com. Specializing in round-the-world tickets, with good deals aimed at backpackers.
Ebookers UK ☎0870/010 7000, ⓦwww.ebookers.com. Low fares on an extensive selection of scheduled flights.
North South Travel UK ☎&℻01245/608 291, ⓦwww.northsouthtravel.co.uk. Recommended travel agency offering competitive discounted fares worldwide. All profits are used to support projects in the developing world, especially the promotion of sustainable tourism.
South America Travel Centre Australia ☎1800/655 051 or 03/9642 5353, ⓦwww.satc.com.au. Big selection of tours and city accommodation packages throughout the region.
South American Experience UK ☎020/7976 5511, ⓦwww.southamericanexperience.co.uk. Mainly a discount flight agent, but also offers a range of tours, plus a very popular "soft landing package", designed to make arrivals pain-free.
STA Travel US & Canada ☎1-800/781-4040, ⓦwww.sta-travel.com; UK ☎0870/160 0599, ⓦwww.statravel.co.uk; Australia ☎1300/733 035, ⓦwww.statravel.com.au; New Zealand ☎0508/782 872, ⓦwww.statravel.co.nz. Worldwide specialists in independent travel. Also provide student IDs, travel insurance, car rental, rail passes etc.
Trailfinders UK ☎020/7938 3939, ⓦwww.trailfinders.com; Republic of Ireland ☎01/677 7888, ⓦwww.trailfinders.ie; Australia ☎1300/651900, ⓦwww.trailfinders.com.au. One of the best-informed and most efficient agents for independent travellers.

Arrival

Most people arrive in Buenos Aires by plane – the city is well served by numerous international and domestic flights. Bus services from other South American cities, as well as most towns and cities in Argentina, arrive at the main bus terminal, Retiro, while ferries from Uruguay arrive at Dársena Norte (see box, p.245).

By air

All international **flights**, with the exception of a few from neighbouring countries, arrive 35km west of the city centre at **Ministro** **Pistarini Airport** (☎011/5480-6111; ⓦwww.aa2000.com.ar) or – as it is usually referred to – **Ezeiza**, in reference to the outlying neighbourhood in which it is situated. Arriving at Ezeiza is relatively stress-free: touting for taxis has been banned and the tourist information stand (Mon–Fri 10am–5pm) has good information on accommodation in the city. Ignore the privately run exchange booths strategically placed by the arrivals exit – instead change money at the small branch of Banco Nación in the airport arrivals hall, where you will get a much better rate; there are also ATMs here.

Taxis into the city (around $120) are available at one of the official taxi stands immediately outside the arrivals exit. It is best to avoid the unofficial taxis, whose drivers loiter outside the terminal building; they are cheaper, but scams of various kinds have been reported. Good value for solo travellers in particular are the **shuttle buses** operated by Manuel Tienda León (every 30min during the day or every 60min at night; 40min journey; $45; ☎011/4314-3636, ⊛www.tiendaleon.com.ar), a quick and secure way to reach the central barrios. They drop you at the company's main terminal at San Martín and Madero; for an extra $5 you can get a transfer from there to anywhere in the centre or Retiro/Recoleta. Alternatively, there's **local bus** #86 ($1.75), which runs between Ezeiza and Calle Brandsen in Boca, entering the city via Avenida Rivadavia and continuing past Congreso, Plaza de Mayo and San Telmo; it takes about two hours, and leaves from just beyond the entrance to the airport. Make sure you have change for the ticket machines, as notes are not accepted, and be warned that it can become very full.

Buenos Aires' **domestic airport** is **Aeroparque Metropolitano Jorge Newbery** (same contact details as Ezeiza), usually known as Aeroparque, on the Costanera Norte around 6km north of the city centre. Most flights from within the country and some flights from Brazil and Uruguay arrive and depart from here. Manuel Tienda León runs a bus service from Aeroparque to its Terminal Madero in the centre (9am–midnight; $17), or there is the option of **local bus** #33, which will take you to Paseo Colón. There is a tourist information booth (daily 10am–5pm) at this airport as well. For anyone arriving at Ezeiza and making a domestic connection at Aeroparque, Manuel Tienda León also operates a shuttle between the two airports (9am–midnight; $50).

By bus

If you are travelling to Buenos Aires by **bus** from other points in Argentina, or on international services from neighbouring countries, you will arrive at Buenos Aires' huge long-distance bus terminal, the **Estación Terminal de Omnibus** (☎011/4310-0700, ⊛www.tebasa.com.ar), known as Retiro, at the corner of Avenida Antártida and Ramos Mejía in Retiro. There are good facilities here, including toilets, shops, cafés and left luggage. It's also centrally located – hotels in the Florida/Retiro area of the city are within walking distance. Alternatively, the Retiro subte station is just a block away, outside the adjoining train stations. There are also plenty of **local buses** leaving from stands along Ramos Mejía, though finding the one you want might be a rather daunting first taste of local bus transport. Buses #5 or #50 will take you to Congreso and the upper end of Avenida de Mayo, a promising hunting ground for accommodation if you haven't booked ahead. Try to avoid arriving at night and if you do, get a taxi: there is a shanty-town close by (see p.98) and it's not a safe place to linger after dark.

City transport

Buenos Aires may seem a daunting city to get around, but it's served by an extensive and inexpensive public transport service. The easiest part of the system to navigate is the underground or subte (short for subterráneo), which links the city centre to some of the places you might want to go, while buses are the only form of public transport serving the whole city. Taxis are both plentiful and reasonably priced, and you will probably find them the most convenient means of getting around, especially at night. Driving yourself is not encouraged, and the only decent train services are those serving to the northern suburbs and Tigre (see p.232). The short tram line running alongside Puerto Madero (see p.74) has more novelty value than real usefulness. One of the impressive features of public transport in Buenos Aires is that most passengers are polite, and will never hesitate to give up a seat to someone who needs it more; it is customary to queue at bus stops and on train platforms (not the subte). The useful website ⓦwww.xcolectivo.com.ar contains up-to-date information about fares, routes and times for the city's trains, underground, buses and even boats.

By subte

Buenos Aires' underground or **subte** (ⓦwww.metrovias.com.ar), inaugurated in 1913, is the oldest in the southern hemisphere and the Spanish-speaking world. It's reasonably efficient – you shouldn't have to wait more than 4–10 minutes during peak periods – and is a quick way to get from the centre to Plaza San Martín, Caballito, Plaza Italia (Palermo), Belgrano or Chacarita. The main flaw is the network's fork-like shape: journeys across town involve going down one "prong" and changing trains before heading back out to your final destination (often a bus will be faster). This will improve, however, as the network is being extended, with work well underway on new north–south lines as well as extensions to the existing lines. Trains are not especially comfortable, there is no air-conditioning and they get very crowded at rush hour. On most lines trains run from 5am until 10.30pm from Monday to Saturday and from 8am to 10pm on Sundays and public holidays.

Notwithstanding these inconveniences, using the subte is fairly straightforward. There are six **lines**: A, B, D and E run from the city centre outwards, while Line C (between Retiro and Constitución) connects them all; line H, partially inaugurated in 2007 and gradually being extended, is one of the new north–south lines. The lines (*líneas*) have different colours on the maps while directions to station platforms are given using the name of the last station on the line. Take note, too, that some stations on different lines but with the same name (such as Callao) are located some distance apart and have no direct connection between them.

You can purchase **tickets** from the **boleterías** (ticket booths) and machines at the stations. A single *viaje* ticket ($1.10) will take you anywhere on the system. Buying multi-trip tickets will save you time but not money. At ticket booths you can ask for free **maps** (*mapas*) of the system.

Don't miss the chance to travel on **Line A**, which runs between Plaza de Mayo and Caballito. It's the only line still using the original carriages, and travelling in one of the rickety wood-framed cars is like being propelled along in an antique wardrobe. They may not, however, be operative for much longer – there are plans to replace old rolling stock.

By bus

Buenos Aires' privately run **buses** (*colectivos*) – many of which are still rather

antiquated, though the fleet is being modernized gradually – are a useful way of getting to many of the outlying barrios if you're on a limited budget. This said, they can also be somewhat alarming: they are noisy, driven crazily and prone to belching out clouds of exhaust – standing, or even sitting, can be an ordeal, and is certainly an experience. They are also downright worthless during peak commuting hours, when it can be quicker to walk. Possibly the most daunting thing about them, though, is the sheer number of routes – almost two hundred in total. Invest in a combined street and bus-route map (see p.37), however, and you shouldn't have too much trouble.

Although journeys under 3km cost $1.10, most trips (3–6km) are $1.20; for the sake of simplicity it may be easier to pay the latter fare. If you're travelling outside the city, to San Isidro, for example, or Ezeiza, it is easier just to state your destination; the fare is $1.25 between 6 and 12km, $1.75 between 12 and 27km and $2 if over 27km. **Tickets** are acquired on board from a machine, which gives change for coins, though not for notes: as you get on you usually need to state your

fare ("*uno con diez/veinte*") to the driver before inserting your money in the ticket machine. Do not expect the driver to be helpful if you're not sure where you're going, or to wait for you to sit or get a grip before accelerating. Many services run all night, notably the #5 and the #86. Buses are generally safe but keep your eyes on your belongings, especially when buses are crowded.

By car

Driving in Buenos Aires demands nerves of steel – the volume of traffic is high and very fast-moving, and even a split-second hesitation is greeted by a fusillade of honking. Given the comprehensive public transport system and the abundance of taxis, there's really little point in renting a car simply to tour the city, though you may wish to take the plunge if you'll be exploring the outlying areas.

Should you decide to test your driving skills, the good news is that the city is a straightforward place to navigate once you've got the hang of the street system. With a few exceptions – notably avenidas 9 de Julio and del Libertador – the streets are one-way, with the direction (which mostly alternates street by street) marked on the street signs with an arrow; the micro-centro is closed to private traffic during the day. At intersections be prepared to give way if the other driver looks more determined and never take it for granted that a speeding bus will respect your trajectory.

Parking in the street is allowed wherever the curb is not painted yellow. However, car theft has risen sharply in recent years and you may prefer the relative security of a *playa de estacionamiento*, often shortened to *playa* (car park; not a beach). There are numerous places throughout the city centre that charge $3–4 an hour; look out for flag-waving dummies or scantily clad ladies marking entrances.

Many of the world's major **car rental companies** and several national companies operate in Buenos Aires, offering a range of vehicles. Be prepared to book some time ahead if you're planning to rent a car over a long weekend or holiday period.

Car rental agencies

Alamo ⓦ www.alamo.com
Avis ⓦ www.avis.com
Budget ⓦ www.budget.com
Dollar ⓦ www.dollar.com
Europcar ⓦ www.europcar.com
Hertz ⓦ www.hertz.com
National ⓦ www.nationalcar.com
Thrifty ⓦ www.thrifty.com

By taxi

The sheer volume of black and yellow **taxis** touting their business on the streets of Buenos Aires' city centre is one of the capital's most characteristic sights, and it's rare to wait more than a few minutes when flagging down a cab (you seldom need to find a rank). The meter starts at $5.80 and clocks up 58 centavos every couple of blocks (a twenty percent surcharge applies from 10pm–6am daily) – fares are hiked fairly regularly though remain far lower than in most comparable cities. Taxi rides can be white-knuckle affairs – drivers range from amiable characters full of anecdotes to maniacs who seem to want to involve you and others on the streets in a road-borne suicide pact, though the latter are mercifully rare. Regardless of road skills, however, drivers (known popularly as *tacheros*) are generally trustworthy, despite occasional reports of their using accomplices to rob passengers.

Radio taxis are regarded as more secure and better quality than the unaffiliated type – they are distinguished by the company name on the side and can be hailed in the street or ordered by telephone. **Remises** are plain cars that can also be booked through an office. They're slightly cheaper and usually more comfortable than taxis for getting to the airport (they tend to have larger boots).

Addresses

In Buenos Aires **addresses** are nearly always written with the street name only, followed by the number – thus, San Martín 2443; the only exception is with **avenues**, where the abbreviation Av or Avda appears before the avenue name – thus, Av Santa Fe 2443. Pasajes (Pje) and Bulevares (Bv) are far less commonplace. The word **calle** (street) and its abbreviation (c/) are seldom used by locals, written or orally, though in this guide we have sometimes used them for clarity. Many streets have had their names officially changed (from Canning to Scalabrini Ortiz, for example), but continue to be referred to by their former labels, even in written addresses. Blocks, or **cuadras**, go up in 100s, making it relatively easy to work out on a map where house no. 977 or a restaurant at no. 2233 is located. Two more useful words to know when it comes to finding a shop or business are **piso** (floor) and **oficina** (office). You enter buildings at the **planta baja** (ground floor; "PB" in lifts), and go up to the **primer piso** (first floor) and so on; there may be an **entrepiso** (mezzanine floor; "EP") in some hotels and other buildings. You will also sometimes see the ° symbol in addresses, which denotes number or locale (**local**) within a building. 2° usually means second (**segundo**) floor, etc.

Taxi companies

Ciudad ☎011/4923-7444. Generally reliable and with "mini-vans" (people carriers) that are useful if you are with a group or have lots of luggage. Reserve ahead.

Premium ☎011/4374-6666, ⓦwww .taxipremium.com. Good-quality cars, all with a/c and backseat seatbelts, at the same price as other taxis.

Remise companies

Del Sol ☎011/4702-8070.
Tres Sargentos ☎011/4312-0057.

Cycling

Cycling is increasingly popular in Buenos Aires, partly thanks to the introduction of new cycle paths, though these are limited in extent and locals are having trouble getting used to them. Cycling along most city streets is nightmarish and although you can take bikes onto trains (eg to Tigre), this is all but impossible at busy times such as morning rush hour or sunny Sundays. Some hotels and hostels have bikes to borrow or rent, while a number of companies offer bike rental or interesting two-wheel tours.

The media

In terms of newspaper circulation, Argentina is Latin America's most literate nation, with a diverse and generally high-quality national press. Its television programming is a rather chaotic amalgam of light-entertainment shows and sports.

Newspapers and magazines

Buenos Aires does not have a local newspaper as such, but in the evenings look out for *La Razón* (ⓦwww.larazon.com.ar), a freebie given out at subte stations and toll-booths. In any case, the Argentine national papers are inevitably somewhat Buenos Aires-centric; all are widely sold at pavement kiosks.

The *Buenos Aires Herald* (ⓦwww.buenos airesherald.com) is a long-running **English-language daily**, useful for getting the lowdown on current events in Argentina and for catching up on international news and sports, as it features stories from the wires as well as syndicated articles from the likes of the *New York Times* and Britain's *Independent*. If you have some Spanish, the most accessible and popular of the national dailies is *Clarín* (ⓦwww.clarin.com.ar), which is mass market but not lowbrow. *Clarín* also owns *Olé*, a paper dedicated solely to sports (mostly football). Argentina's major **broadsheet** is *La Nación* (ⓦwww.lanacion.com.ar). Conservative in some ways, it is also the most

international in outlook and arguably the best-written of the Spanish-language newspapers.

As far as **magazines** go, the Argentine market is mostly a mix of Spanish-language versions of well-known international titles – often produced in Madrid – and home-grown enterprises. Fashion magazines *El Planeta Urbano* (ⓦwww.elplanetaurbano.com) and *D-Mode* (ⓦwww.d-mode.com) are good for finding out which clubs and restaurants young, hip Porteños are heading to.

International publications such as *Time*, *The Economist*, the *Miami Herald* and the *Daily Telegraph* are sold at kiosks on Calle Florida, in Recoleta, and at the airports, as are some imported European and US magazines. However, they can often be long past their publication date; they are also usually so expensive that unless you're desperate you're probably better off with the *BA Herald*.

Television

There are five national **television** stations, mostly showing a mix of football, soap operas (*telenovelas*) and chat shows. There have been Argentine versions of international hits such as *Big Brother,* although on the whole there is less interest in "reality TV" than in Europe or the US. Syndicated foreign programmes are almost always dubbed. Even if you can't understand it, though, local TV can provide a glimpse into certain aspects of society, from the almost freakish plastic surgery of some presenters to the bouncy Saturday afternoon *cumbia* show *Pasion de Sabado*. Cable TV is common in many mid-range and even budget hotels; the channels you get depend on the cable provider, but they generally include CNN and/or BBC World, with myriad channels playing international movies, TV shows (usually subtitled rather than dubbed),

worldwide sports and music. Local c news channels include *Clarín's* TN (*Teler cias*) and the unique Crónica, a bu operation that provides live, unedited coverage of anything that happens in the city; indeed, it is said that the Crónica vans often arrive before the police do.

Radio

Argentina's most popular **radio** station, Cadena 100 (99.9FM), plays a fairly standard formula of Latin pop, whereas Rock y Pop (95.9FM) veers, as its name would imply, towards rock and blues. Neither the BBC World Service nor the Voice of America broadcast on shortwave to Argentina.

Culture and etiquette

Buenos Aires' mores reflect its overwhelmingly European ancestry; visitors from North America and Europe will find the culture much more familiar and easier to integrate with than in most Latin American cities. Apart from the language barrier, the biggest differences are in attitudes to rules and time-keeping.

Rules and regulations

Porteños' rather cavalier attitude towards **rules** and considerations of health and safety is probably the biggest culture shock many foreigners have to deal with; the most obvious example of this is the anarchy you'll see on the roads, but you will also likely come across things such as loose wiring in hotels and taxis lacking functioning seatbelts. A complaint will probably get you no more than a shrug of the shoulders.

Another difference is the Kafka-esque **bureaucracy** that you will bump up against if you're in the city for any length of time. Do not lose your temper if faced with red tape – it will have absolutely no benefit and quite possibly hinder your cause.

Additionally, the pace of life is altogether less stressed and attitudes to **time-keeping** are rather more relaxed than in Anglo-Saxon cities, though locals are far more punctual

than the stereotypical Latin and Buenos Aires does seem to be moving gradually towards the Northern European/North American model. Whereas siestas are common in the provinces they are seldom observed in the city.

Manners

When **greeting** people or taking your leave, it is normal to kiss everyone present on the cheek (just once, always the right cheek), even among men, who may emphasize their masculinity by slapping each other on the back. Shaking hands tends to be the preserve of businessmen or formal situations; if in doubt, watch the locals. One area of etiquette that will probably be new to you is the very Argentine custom of drinking **mate**, which comes with its own set of rules (see box, p.30), but foreigners will be given lots of leeway here, as in other areas of social custom – faux pas are more likely to cause amusement than offence. It's also worth noting that Buenos Aires is one of the few cities in the world in which people **queue** for buses and trains.

Drinking and smoking

Argentine attitudes to **drinking** tend to be similar to those in southern Europe: alcohol is fine in moderation, and usually taken with food. Public drunkenness is rare and frowned upon, but occurs more frequently among the young than it used to. **Smoking** is fairly common among both sexes and all classes (estimated at around thirty percent of adults), although in 2006 Buenos Aires passed a statute making it illegal to smoke in enclosed public areas, including public transport and offices, plus restaurants and bars – the latter may set aside a smoking area if they are big enough. So far compliance has been surprisingly high.

Public toilets

An everyday minor frustration is the general lack of **public toilets** (baños; men: caballeros, hombres, varones or señores; women: damas, mujeres or señoras). The toilets in the city's modern shopping malls tend to be spick and span, however, and are often the

---

Drinking mate

Mate, Argentina's national beverage, is brewed from the leaves of the evergreen tree, *Ilex paraguayensis*, a member of the holly family native to northeastern Argentina, Brazil and Paraguay. The herb contains mateine, a gentler **stimulant** than the closely related caffeine, which helps to release muscular energy, pace the heartbeat and aid respiration without any of the nasty side-effects of coffee. It's a tonic and a **digestive agent**, and by dulling the appetite can help you lose weight. Although its laxative, diuretic and sweat-making properties can be inconvenient, *mate* is very effective at purging toxins and fat, perfect after excessive *asado* binges.

The **vessel** you drink *mate* out of is also called a *mate*, or **matecito**, originally a hollowed-out gourd of the species *Lagenaria vulgaris*, native to the same region. It's dried, hollowed out and "cured" by macerating **yerba mate** inside it overnight. These gourds are still used and come in two basic **shapes**: the pear-shaped *poro*, traditionally used for sweet *mate*, and the squat *galleta*, meant for unsweetened *mate*. Many *mates* are works of art, sometimes intricately carved or painted, and often made of wood, clay or metal, though connoisseurs claim gourds impart extra flavour to the brew. The **bombilla** – originally a reed or stick of bamboo – is the other vital piece of equipment. Most are now straw-shaped tubes of silver, aluminium or tin, flattened at the end on which you suck, and with a bulbous or spoon-shaped protuberance at the other; this is perforated to strain the *mate* as you drink it.

If ever you find yourself in a **group** drinking *mate*, it's good to know how to avoid gaffes. The **cebador** – from cebar, "to feed" – is the person who makes the *mate*. After half-filling the *matecito* with *yerba*, the *cebador* thrusts the *bombilla* into the *yerba* and trickles very hot – but not boiling – water down the side of the *bombilla*, to wet the *yerba* from below. If asked "¿Como lo tomás?", answer "*amargo*" for without sugar, or "dulce" for sweetened; the latter's a safer bet if it's your first *mate* session. The *cebador* always tries the *mate* first – the "fool's *mate*" – before refilling and handing it round to each person in turn – always with the right hand and clockwise. Each drinker must drain the *mate* through the *bombilla*, without jiggling it around, sipping gently but not lingering or sucking too hard (it's not a milkshake), before handing it back to the *cebador*. Sucking out of the corner of the mouth is also frowned upon. A little more *yerba* may be added from time to time, but there comes a moment when the *yerba* loses most of its flavour (it is said to be *lavado*). The *matecito* is then emptied and the process started afresh. When the *cebador* has had enough, he or she "hangs the *mate* up". Saying "*gracias*" means you've had enough, and the *mate* will be passed to someone else when your turn comes round. The greatest honour comes when it's your turn to be *cebador*.

best place to head for. In bars and cafés the toilets are usually of an acceptable standard and not all establishments insist that you buy a drink. In less salubrious establishments, toilet paper, hot water and soap (*jabón*) are frequently missing.

Shopping

You will find no real tradition of **haggling** in Buenos Aires, although you can always try it. Expensive services such as excursions outside the city and car rental are obvious candidates for bargaining sessions, while hotel rates can be beaten down off season, late at night or if you're paying cash (*efectivo*). But try and be reasonable, especially in the case of already low-priced crafts or high-quality goods and services that are obviously worth every centavo.

Tipping

Tipping is not very common in Argentina, with a couple of exceptions. It's normal (though not expected) to round up taxi fares to the nearest 25 centavos (or peso if you are feeling generous), and you should add a gratuity of ten percent to restaurant bills if service is not included. The kids who hang around taxi ranks to open and close doors also appreciate a coin.

Travel essentials

Costs

High inflation (unofficially about twenty five percent) combined with a relatively stable exchange rate since 2002 means Buenos Aires can no longer really be considered a cheap destination for international visitors, and prices are rising all the time. However, the city still compares well cost-wise with Europe, the US or neighbouring Brazil, and the top quality of many things makes the occasional bitter pill of stiff prices much sweeter to swallow than in some other major cities. Roughly speaking, on average you'll need to plan on spending at least $1000/US$260/£160 a week on a tight budget (sharing a dorm, eating snacks, limiting other spending), double that if staying in budget accommodation but not skimping, while to live in the lap of luxury you could easily burn through $15000/US$5000/£1000 or more. If you're **travelling alone**, reckon on adding up to fifty percent to these prices. For advice on tipping, see above.

Generally speaking, **eating out** is particularly good value for money, as quantities are generous and the quality reliable; you can save money by having your main meal at lunch time – especially by opting for the set menu (usually called *menú ejecutivo*). Taxi costs are reasonable (see p.27), but with some exceptions manufactured goods tend to be expensive. Hotels, restaurants and big stores may request a hefty handling fee for credit-card payments (as high as twenty percent), while many businesses – and hotels in particular – will give you a fair-sized **discount** on the quoted price, for cash payments (*efectivo* or *contado*) though they may need prompting.

Be aware that some places operate **dual pricing** – one price for Argentine residents (including foreigners) and another, often as much as three times more, for non-residents. Hotels and other types of commerce, especially at the luxury end of the market, may charge foreigners in US dollars, rather than Argentine pesos, as a covert but perfectly legal way of charging more. Watch out also for IVA (sales tax, or VAT) which is a hefty twenty one percent – sometimes hotels and airlines quote prices without adding it on, but you'll still have to pay it.

Student cards

These are not as useful in Buenos Aires as they can be in other cities, as museums and the like often refuse to give **student discounts**. Some bus companies, however, do give a ten- to fifteen-percent discount for holders of **ISIC cards**, as do certain hotels, laundries and even one or two ice cream parlours. ASATEJ, Argentina's student travel agency, issues a booklet that lists partners. The international student card often suffices for a discount at youth hostels, though membership of Hostelling International may entitle you to even lower rates. Membership of the South American Explorers Club also entitles you to discounts of five to thirty percent on a range of local services – see p.40.

Crime and personal safety

In recent years Buenos Aires has somewhat lost the reputation it long enjoyed as a totally safe destination. However, any concerns you have should be kept in perspective – the actual likelihood of being a victim of **crime** remains small, and considering its size and social problems Buenos Aires is still one of South America's safest cities for visitors. Nonetheless, precautions should be taken, especially in the poorer barrios. Incidents of violence and armed robbery have dramatically increased here in recent years; this includes a wave of much-publicized "express kidnappings", in which victims are bundled into cars and forced to get money out at ATMs or held for ransom. Affecting wealthy locals far more than tourists, this practice seems anyway to be on the wane, although middle-class paranoia and a crime-obsessed media can make the situation seem worse than it is.

There are some **basic precautions** you should take regardless of where you are in the city: only carry what you need for that day, and conceal valuable items; be cautious when withdrawing cash from ATMs; and avoid bumbags (fanny packs). Don't leave valuables lying around; use the hotel safe if there is one, or take a padlock for hostel lockers. If you're coming from elsewhere in the country or continent, make sure you have a city-worthy outfit – nothing announces that you are a tourist more than hiking boots in the middle of Buenos Aires. Take a cab if you're not sure about the wisdom of walking somewhere – but call radio taxis or hail them in the street, rather than taking a waiting one. Don't wander around quiet areas, particularly after dark and on your own.

Pickpockets most commonly hang around the markets, busy subway stations and bus terminals (particularly Retiro), and on crowded trains and buses. If you should catch someone taking your belongings, get away from them fast and make as much noise as possible, shouting "thief!" ("*ladrón!*"), "police!" ("*policia!*") or for help ("*socorro!*"). If you are robbed or lose anything of value, you will need to make a report at the nearest police station for insurance purposes. This is usually a time-consuming but fairly straightforward process. Check that the report includes a comprehensive account of everything lost and its value, and that the police add the date and an official stamp (*sello*).

Noisy street **demonstrations** have long been a part of the fabric of Buenos Aires life, even more so since the 2001 recession. The chance of getting caught up in this kind of thing is very rare – tourists are not targets. Though usually peaceful, demonstrations have turned violent in the past, however, and if so the police do not hesitate to use tear gas, so it is best to keep your distance. Roadblocks by unemployed *piqueteros* are more of an annoyance in terms of traffic flow, and you should always allow plenty of time to arrive at your destination for this reason.

Emergency numbers

☏ 101 Police
☏ 107 Medical emergencies
☏ 100 Fire

The police in Buenos Aires are entitled to check your documents, but they have no right to inspect your money or travellers' cheques: anyone who does is a con-artist, and you should ask for their identification or offer to go to the police station (*gendarmería*). If you ever are "arrested", never get into a vehicle other than an official police car.

Should you be unlucky enough to be the victim of a petty crime, you can report it to the **Comisaría del Turista** (Tourist Police), where there should be English speakers, at Avenida Corrientes 436 (℡0800/999-5000 or 011/4346-5748). For emergencies, dial ℡101. If you feel you've been ripped off or treated badly, there is a "tourist ombudsman" in the Museo Quinquela Martín in Boca (see p.91; ℡011/4302-7816, Ⓔturista@defensoria.org.ar).

Electricity

220V/50Hz is standard. The sockets are two-pronged with round or slanting pins, but are different to two-pin European plugs. Adapters will probably be needed and can be bought at a string of electrical shops along Calle Talcahuano. Some, but not all, of the multi-adaptors on sale at airports will do the trick, so check the instructions.

Entry requirements

Citizens of the US, Canada, the UK, Ireland, South Africa, Australia and New Zealand do not currently need a visa for tourist trips to Argentina of up to ninety days. All visitors need a valid passport and will have to fill in a **landing card** (*tarjeta de entrada*) on arrival, when you will be given a stamp and leave to stay for ninety days (though sometimes much longer if you have to buy a visa – especially US citizens; see below). As of 2010 Argentina began to charge "reciprocal" entry fees to citizens of those countries which charge Argentine citizens – at the time of writing, this was the US (US$140, valid for several years), Canada (US$70, valid once) and Australia (US$100, valid once); the fee is charged at Ezeiza, but not at other ports of entry. If you are travelling alone with a child you may be requested to show a notarized, translated document certifying both parents' permission for the child to travel.

You can **extend your** [stay] ninety days by presenting [yourself at] the main immigration dep[artment], de Migraciones, Av An[…] 1350, Retiro (℡011/[…] 4317-0238). This costs $3[00 and is] done on weekdays betwee[n…] be prepared for a possible l[ong] wait and go at least ten days before your stay is up. You can get this extension, called a *prórroga*, once only. Alternatively, you could try leaving the country (the short hop to Colonia del Sacramento in Uruguay is a much-used option) and returning to get a fresh stamp. This usually works, but may be frowned on if done repeatedly, and the provision of an extra stamp is totally at the discretion of the border guards. If you do overshoot your stay, you pay a $300 fine at Migraciones, who will give you a form that allows you to leave the country within ten days (*habilitación de salida*).

Visas for work or study must be obtained in advance from your consulate. Extensive paperwork, much of which must be translated into Spanish by a certified translator, is required; allow plenty of time before departure to start the process.

Theoretically, visitors are legally obliged to carry their passport at all times but ID checks are virtually unheard of. You may need identification, though, to pay by credit card when shopping or to change money.

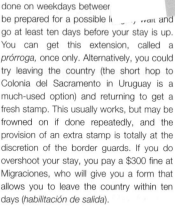

Argentine embassies and consulates abroad

Australia

Embassy John McEwan House, Level 2, 7 National Circuit, Barton ACT 2600 ℡02/6273-9111, Ⓦwww .argentina.org.au.
Consulate 44 Market St, Level 20, Sydney, NSW ℡02/9262-2933, Ⓦwww.argentinasydney.org.au.

Canada

Embassy 81 Metcalfe 7th floor, Ottawa, Ontario K1P 5B4 ℡613/236-2351; Ⓦwww .argentina-canada.net.
Consulates 2000 Peel St, 7th floor, Suite 600, Montréal, Québec H3A 2W5 ℡514/842-6582, Ⓦwww.consargenmtl.com; 5001 Yonge St, Suite 201, Toronto, Ontario M2N 6P6 ℡416/955-9075, Ⓦwww.consargtoro.ca.

...land

...ssy Allied Nationwide Finance Tower, _evel 14, 142 Lambton Quay, PO Box 5430, Wellington ☎ 04/472-8330, ⓦ www.arg.org.nz.

South Africa

Embassy 200 Standard Plaza, 440 Hilda St, Hatfield 0083 Pretoria ☎ 12/4303-527, ⓦ www .embassyofargentina.co.za.

UK

Embassy 65 Brook St, London W1K 4AH ☎ 020/7318 1300, ⓦ www.argentine-embassy-uk .org.
Consulate 27 Three Kings Yard, London W1K 4DF ☎ 020/7318 1340.

US

Embassy 1600 New Hampshire Ave, NW, Washington DC 20009 ☎ 202/238-6400, ⓦ www .embassyofargentina.us.
Consulates 245 Peachtree Center Ave, Suite 2101, Atlanta, GA 30303 ☎ 404/880-0805; 205 N Michigan Ave, Piso 42, Suite 4209, Chicago, IL 60601 ☎ 312/819-2610; 2200 West Loop South, Suite 1025, Houston, TX 77027 ☎ 713/871-8935; 5055 Wilshire Blvd Suite 210, Los Angeles, CA 90036 ☎ 323/954-9155; 1101 Brickell Ave, 9th floor, North Tower, Miami, FL 33131 ☎ 305/373-1889; 12 West 56th St, New York, NY 10019 ☎ 212/603-0400.

Embassies in Buenos Aires

Australia Villanueva 1400 ☎ 4779-3500 (Mon–Thurs 8.30am–5pm).
Brazil Cerrito 1350 ☎ 011/4515-2400 (Mon–Fri 10am–1pm).
Canada Tagle 2828 ☎ 011/4808-1000 (Mon–Thurs 2–4pm).
Chile Roque Saenz Peña 547, 2nd floor ☎ 011/4331-6228 (Mon–Fri 9am–1pm).
Ireland Libertador 1068, 6th floor ☎ 011/5787-0801 (Mon–Fri 9am–1pm).
New Zealand Carlos Pellegrini 1427, 5th floor ☎ 011/4328-0747 (Mon–Thurs 9am–1pm & 2–6pm).
South Africa M.T. De Alvear 590, 8th floor ☎ 011/4317-2900 (Mon–Fri 9am–noon).
UK Dr Luis Agote 2412 ☎ 011/4808-2200 (Mon–Fri 9am–1pm).
US Av Colombia 4300 ☎ 011/5777-4533 (call for times).
Uruguay Ayacucho 1616 ☎ 011/4807-3040 (Mon–Fri 9.30am–4.30pm).

Health

Travel to Buenos Aires doesn't raise any major **health** worries and special vaccinations are not needed. A bout of travellers' diarrhoea, as your body adjusts to local microorganisms in the food and water, is the most you're likely to have to worry about. It's best to ease yourself gently into the local diet – the sudden ingestion of generous quantities of red meat, beefy wine, strong coffee and sweet pastries can be very unsettling. The tap water in the city is generally safe to drink, if sometimes heavily chlorinated, but you may prefer to err on the side of caution. Mineral water is widely available.

Health facilities

Pharmacies in Buenos Aires are plentiful, well stocked and can be a useful port of call for help with very minor medical problems; the staff may offer simple diagnostic advice and will often help dress wounds, but if in doubt consult a doctor. You'll find a wider range of **medicines** available without prescription here than in many other countries; while the brand names will undoubtedly be different, if you have the packaging of the product you're looking for, take it along so the pharmacist can find you the local equivalent. Medicines and cosmetic products are fairly expensive, however, as they are mostly imported, so if you have room, take plenty of supplies.

The easiest way to get treatment for more serious ailments is to visit the outpatient department of a **hospital**, where treatment will usually be free. The Hospital de Clínicas, José de San Martín, Av Córdoba 2351 (☎ 011/4961-6001), is a particularly efficient place to receive medical advice and prescriptions; you can simply walk in and, for a small fee, make an on-the-spot appointment with the relevant specialist department – English-speaking doctors can usually be found. There are also many private hospitals, where treatment is often faster and of an international standard; two of the biggest and best known are the Hospital Británico, at Perdriel 74 in Barracas (☎ 011/4309-6400), and Hospital Italiano, at Gascón 450 in Almagro

(☎011/4959-0200). For a list of **English-speaking doctors**, contact the British, Australian, New Zealand, Canadian or US embassy in Buenos Aires.

Health hazards

HIV and AIDS cases have been climbing steadily in Argentina in recent years; according to national statistics, around two percent of the adult population between 15 and 49 years carry HIV. Some of the condoms on sale in Buenos Aires are of pretty poor quality, so it's wise to bring a reliable brand with you. You should take the sun seriously, as the summers can be very hot. During the warmer months avoid excessive activity between about 11am and 4pm; if you do have to be out in the sun, wear sunscreen and a hat, and drink plenty of liquids.

Insurance

It is a good idea to take out an **insurance** policy before travelling to cover against theft, loss, illness or injury. Before paying for a new policy, however, it's worth seeing whether you are already covered: some home insurance policies may cover your possessions when overseas, and many private medical schemes include cover when abroad. After checking out these possibilities, you might want to contact a specialist travel insurance company, or consider the travel insurance deal we offer (see box below).

A typical **policy** usually provides cover for the loss of baggage, tickets and – up to a certain limit – cash or cheques, as well as cancellation or curtailment of your journey.

Many policies can be changed to exclude coverage you don't need – for example, sickness and accident benefits can often be excluded or included at will. If you do take medical coverage, ascertain whether benefits will be paid as treatment proceeds or only after you return home, and if there is a 24-hour medical emergency number. When securing baggage cover, make sure that the per-article limit is adequate. If you need to make a claim, you should keep receipts for medicines and medical treatment, and in the event you have anything stolen, you must obtain an official statement from the police.

Internet

Buenos Aires has no shortage of places where you can access the **internet**. There's the odd cybercafé, but you'll mostly find access is via *locutorios* (see p.39). Rates vary considerably, from $3 to $15 an hour, with the highest rates at Ezeiza airport. Practically all hotels and hostels, and many cafés, offer wi-fi. The Spanish keyboard is prevalent (similar to the English QWERTY, but with some variations); if you have problems locating the "@" symbol (called *arroba* in Spanish), try holding the "Alt" key down and typing 64.

Laundry

Buenos Aires has a plentiful supply of **laundries** (*lavanderías* or *lavaderos*). Some laundries also do dry-cleaning, though you may have to go to a *tintorería*. Self-service places are almost unheard of; you normally leave your washing for pick-up later (if you speak some Spanish you can also often call

Rough Guides travel insurance

Rough Guides has teamed up with WorldNomads.com to offer great **travel insurance** deals. Policies are available to residents of over 150 countries, with cover for a wide range of **adventure sports**, 24-hour emergency assistance, high levels of medical and evacuation cover and a stream of **travel safety information**. Roughguides.com users can take advantage of their policies online 24/7, from anywhere in the world – even if you're already travelling. And since plans often change when you're on the road, you can extend your policy and even claim online. Roughguides.com users who buy travel insurance with WorldNomads.com can also leave a positive footprint and donate to a community development project. For more information go to ⓦ**www .roughguides.com/shop**.

aundry service and they will pick up from and deliver to your hotel; a tip is appreciated you use this free service). Laundry is either charged by weight or itemized, but rates are not excessive, especially compared with the prices charged by hotels. One important word of vocabulary to know is *planchado* (ironed). The Laverap chain has outlets throughout the city, including Suipacha 722 (☎011/4322-3458) and Av Córdoba 466 (☎011/4312-5460).

Living and working in Buenos Aires

If you decide to stay in Buenos Aires long term, you'll be in good company. There are lots of online forums and blogs catering to expats and explaining the bureaucracy of getting residency permits etc – try ⓦbaexpats.org or www.livinginargentina .com. The South American Explorers Club offers a home from home for both long-stay and short-stay residents (see p.40 for details), while Club Europeo (☎011/43119896, ⓦwww.clubeuropeo .com) is a more traditional outfit made up of various European expat clubs such as the Club Alemán and the Anglo Hurlingham Club.

Should you choose to stay, remember that tourist visas are usually only valid for ninety days; visa renewal means an encounter with immigration services (see p.33), as does the often-frustrating process of trying to obtain some form of residence permit (usually only granted if you have an Argentine spouse or child, or make a considerable investment in the economy). Many medium-term residents simply leave the country every three months to get a new stamp, but this approach might not be tolerated over many years.

There are plenty of outfits aimed at foreigners offering information in English and reservations for long-term accommodation in Buenos Aires, primarily in shared apartments, university residences and B&B type establishments; try ⓦwww.alojargentina .com, buenosaires.en.craigslist.org or the expat resources above. Apartments aimed at locals are advertised in newspapers or rented by *inmobiliarías* (estate agents) and are generally cheaper, but difficult to obtain,

as you need a local who owns property to be your guarantor, with two-year contracts the norm.

As far as **working** is concerned, remember Argentines themselves compete for the few jobs on offer and your entry into the employment market may not be entirely kindly looked upon; also, unless you are on a contract with an international firm or organization, you will be paid in pesos, which will inevitably add up to a pretty low salary by global standards. If you're determined anyway, many English-speaking foreigners do the obvious thing and **teach** English. Training in this is an advantage but by no means necessary; the demand for native English-speaking teachers is so high that many soon build up a roster of students via the odd newspaper ad and word of mouth. Working in **tourism** is another possibility – a fair proportion of agencies and hotels are run by foreigners. You might also consider translation if you have the language ability. If you just want to volunteer, contact the South American Explorers Club (see p.40), which always has a list of potential opportunities and doesn't charge a hefty fee, or try the organizations listed below.

Study, volunteer and work programmes

AFS Intercultural Programmes ⓦwww.afs.org. Intercultural exchange organization.
American Institute for Foreign Study US ☎1-866/906-2437, ⓦwww.aifs.com. Language study and cultural immersion, as well as au pair programmes.
Council on International Educational Exchange (CIEE) US ☎1-800/40-STUDY or ☎1-207/533-7600, UK ☎020/8939 9057, ⓦwww .ciee.org. Leading NGO offering study programmes and volunteer projects.
Insight Argentina US ☎01-646/472-5188, Argentina ☎011/5032-6424, ⓦwww .insightargentina.org. Organization offering both short- and long-term volunteering opportunities in Buenos Aires and the country's far-flung provinces.
Road2Argentina US ☎1-800/998-9251, Argentina ☎011/4826-0820, ⓦwww .road2argentina.com. Buenos Aires-based Spanish immersion programmes that link learning the language with opportunities such as volunteering and internships, and tango or cookery classes.

Lost property

Ezeiza airport (☎011/5480-6111) has a left-luggage office in Terminal A, which will also deal with reports of theft from luggage. Otherwise, you should report missing items to the police for insurance purposes (see p.33). Generally speaking, however, once it's gone, it's gone.

Mail

Argentina's privatized **postal service**, Correo Argentino, has improved greatly of late and while it remains relatively costly to send post to North America or Europe (starting at $10 for a postcard), at least mail now usually arrives at its destination, and surprisingly fast. Even so, if you want to **send mail abroad**, it is worth opting for the *certificado* (registered post) system (starting at about $20 for a letter). The safest way of sending a parcel is Correo Argentino's *encomienda* system (around $120 for a package under 1kg to Europe or the US), a **courier-style** service; if you are sending something important or irreplaceable, it is highly recommended that you use this service or a similar international one such as UPS (☎0800/2222-877) or DHL (☎0810/2222-345), though the latter are extremely expensive and not always that fast. For regular airmail, expect delivery times of a week or so. In accordance with customs regulations you are not permitted to seal envelopes with sticky tape: they must be gummed down (glue is usually available at the counter).

Receiving mail is generally more fraught with difficulties than sending it. Again, a courier-style service is a safer method; if not using this, make sure the sender at least registers the letter or parcel. All **parcels** go to the international office at Retiro opposite the bus station. You will receive a card at the destination address with the exact location and opening times for picking up the parcel; you will have to pay customs duties and should expect a long wait. Post offices keep **poste restante** for up to a year. Items should be addressed clearly, with the recipient's surname in capital letters and underlined, followed by their first name in regular script, then Poste Restante, Correo Central, 1000 Capital Federal, Buenos Aires. Bring your passport to collect items (Mon–Fri 10am–8pm).

The central post office, **Correo Central**, is at Sarmiento 189; there are also branch offices scattered throughout the city. Many *locutorios* (public call centres; see p.39), lottery kiosks and small stores deal with mail as well, so you don't usually have to go very far to find somewhere open.

Maps

The **maps** in this guide should be more than adequate for most purposes, but should you feel in need of further guidance, the street plans distributed for free at the tourist kiosks (see p.40) can be useful. Some cover just certain neighbourhoods such as San Telmo or Palermo, and others have specialist topics such as gay Buenos Aires or antique stores. However, they rarely cover the barrios outside the centre or have street indexes. If you are planning to stay in the city a while or explore off piste then it is worth investing in a more detailed fold-out street map of the capital, such as those produced by Automapa, widely sold at street kiosks and bookshops, or De Dios, which has a series of themed maps on topics such as shopping, restaurants and tango. An alternative, particularly if you will be using the buses, are the comprehensive combined **street map and bus guides** such as Guía Lumi or Guía "T". They are also sold at the kiosks and occasionally, at knockdown prices, from hawkers on the buses or trains.

Money

The currency of Argentina is the **Argentine peso$**, which divides into 100 centavos; notes come in 2, 5, 10, 20, 50 and 100

Currency notation

When you see the "$" sign in Buenos Aires – and throughout this book – you can safely assume that the currency being referred to is the **Argentine peso**. Where a price is quoted in US dollars, the normal notation in Argentina – and the notation we use – is "**US$**".

enominations (a new 200 peso note ...ed for 2011), while 1 peso and 5, 10, ... 50 centavo coins are in circulation. ...xchange rate has been stable at around four pesos to the US dollar for some time; you can check current exchange rates at ⓦ www.xe.net/currency.

Commission is rarely charged when **exchanging** cash and increasingly the more central places will exchange pounds sterling, euros and other currencies, although your safest bet is to have US dollars. There is an entire street of **bureaux de change** in the financial district, near the corner of San Martín and Sarmiento – rates are similar and opening hours are generally Monday to Friday 9am to 6pm. You'll also find the central **bank** branches in this area; they open similar hours. At other times, look out for the branches of exchange company Metropolis at Corrientes 2557, Florida 506 and Quintana 576, which are also open at weekends. When changing money ask for small denomination notes if possible, and break bigger ones at places where they obviously have plenty of change (busy shops, supermarkets and post offices). Sometimes people are loath to give change, as coins and smaller notes can be in short supply, so it's a good idea to have plenty of loose change on your person.

Using your **debit card** is usually the best method of getting cash in Buenos Aires. Make sure you have a card and personal identification number (PIN) that are designed to work overseas. **ATMs** (cajeros automáticos) are easy to find in the central barrios, harder in the outer areas. You can nearly always get money out with Visa or MasterCard, or with any cards linked to the Plus or Cirrus systems. Most ATMs are either Banelco or LINK – test the networks to see which works best with your card. Machines are mostly multilingual, though some of them use Spanish only, so you might need to have a phrasebook handy; use the "credit account" option for international debit cards. Note that ATMs are usually stocked with pesos only, not US dollars (despite what the screen may say).

Credit cards (tarjetas de crédito) are fairly widely accepted in Buenos Aires. Visa, MasterCard and American Express are all commonly used, while Diners is sometimes accepted. Remember that you might have to show your ID when making a purchase with plastic, and, especially in small establishments, the authorization process can take a while and may not succeed at all.

Unfortunately, **travellers' cheques** are not really a viable option. They can almost never be used like cash and fewer and fewer banks seem to accept them. Those places that do accept them charge exorbitant commission and take ages to fill out all the paperwork. If you do take a stock of travellers' cheques (as a precaution in case your credit card goes astray), make sure they're in US dollars and are one of the main brands, such as American Express – their own, not those issued by a bank with the Amex logo – and that your signature is one hundred percent identical to that in your passport, down to the colour of the ink. **Casas de cambio** tend to be the best bet for changing cheques; American Express on Plaza San Martín changes its own cheques.

Opening hours and public holidays

Most shops and services are open Monday to Friday 10am to 7pm, and Saturday 9am to 2pm. Supermarkets seldom close during the day and are generally open much later, often until 8 or even 10pm, and on Saturday afternoons. Large shopping malls don't close before 10pm and their food and drink sections (patios de comida) may stay open as late as midnight. Many of them open on Sundays, too. Banks tend to be open only on weekdays, from 10am to 4pm, but casas de cambio more or less follow shop hours. Post offices' hours vary; most should be open between 9am and 6pm on weekdays, and 9am to 1pm on Saturdays.

The opening hours of attractions are indicated in the text; however, bear in mind that these often change from one season to another. If you are going out of your way to visit something, it is best to check if its opening times have changed. Museums are a law unto themselves, each one having its own timetable, but all commonly close one day a week, usually Monday. Several

Public holidays

On the most important national **public holidays**, such as Christmas Day, or on certain designated events such as election or census days, just about everything closes. On most holidays you will find lots of places stay open. Bear in mind that some of these holidays (marked with an *) are held on the nearest Monday. Many offices close for the whole of Semana Santa (Holy Week), the week leading up to Easter, while the Thursday is optional, as is New Year's Eve. Easter Monday is not a holiday.

January 1	New Year's Day	**June 20**	Day of the Flag
Carnival Monday	Carnival weekend	**July 9**	Independence Day
& Shrove Tuesday		**August 17***	San Martín
(usually February)		**October 12***	Columbus Day
Good Friday	Friday before		(Called Día de la
	Easter (March or		Raza in Latin
	April)		America, or "Day
March 24	Commemoration		of Respect for
	of the 1976 coup		Cultural Diversity")
April 2*	Malvinas Veterans'	**November 20**	Day of National
	Day		Sovereignty
May 1	Labour Day	**December 8**	Immaculate
May 25	Day of the		Conception
	Revolution	**December 25**	Christmas Day

museums are also closed for at least a month in January and February.

Telephones

Argentina operates a GSM 850/1900 mobile phone network, in common with much of Latin America. Most modern mobile phones are tri- or quad-band so should work fine, but if yours is an older model you should check with your phone provider to confirm it will work. Local mobile numbers are prefixed by 011, like fixed lines, and then 15, followed by the number. If you're likely to use your phone a lot, it may be worth getting an Argentine SIM card to keep costs down. These can be obtained before you travel from various providers, or, cheaper still – though you'll need some Spanish here – is to get a pre-paid SIM (*chip*) from a local operator such as Movistar (🕸www.movistar.com.ar) or Personal (🕸www.personal.com.ar).

A cheaper and still pretty convenient alternative to mobile phones are the public call centres known as *locutorios*, widely found throughout the city. You'll be assigned a cabin with a meter, with which you can monitor your expenditure. Make as many calls as you want and then pay at the counter. You can get significant discounts on international calls with pre-paid phonecards, available at the *locutorios*.

Another convenient way of phoning home is via a **telephone charge card** from your phone company back home. Using a PIN, you can make calls from most hotel, public and private phones. Since most major charge cards are free to obtain, it's certainly worth getting one at least for emergencies; enquire first though whether your destination is covered, and bear in mind that rates aren't necessarily cheaper

International phone codes

Note that the initial zero is omitted from the city code when dialling the UK, Ireland, Australia and New Zealand from abroad.
Australia ☏0061 + city code.
New Zealand ☏0064 + city code.
Republic of Ireland ☏00353 + city code.
South Africa ☏0027 + city code.
UK ☏0044 + city code.
US and Canada ☏001 + area code.

To **call Buenos Aires from abroad**, dial your country's International Direct Dialling prefix then:

+ ⊕54 (Argentina's country code)
+ 11 (Buenos Aires local code, without the initial zero) OR +911 for mobile numbers
+ destination phone number. Omit the 15 if dialling a mobile number.

Area codes are provided with all numbers throughout the guide.

than calling from a public phone. Phone boxes on the street take coins or phone-cards, but this is more expensive and less convenient than using the *locutorio* system; in addition, the boxes are often out of order.

Time

Buenos Aires is usually three hours behind GMT.

Tourist information

Buenos Aires has no central tourist office. Instead, the city government runs a number of tourist **kiosks** (see box below); the staff do not generally have much specialist knowledge but they can usually provide maps and a few leaflets. There's also a comprehensive **website** with ideas of where to go and what to do (®www.bue.gov.ar), while the museums directorate runs a superb website (®www.museos.buenos aires.gov.ar) listing the latest news on exhibitions and events at many of the city's museums.

Another excellent source of English-language information is the ever-reliable South American Explorers Club, which has

a **clubhouse** downtown at Callao 341, in San Nicolás (Mon–Fri 9.30am–5pm, Sat 9.30am–1pm; ®www.saexplorers.org). Membership of US$60 a year gets you access to this and all their other clubhouses, where you can store gear, use their computers, consult trip reports, chat with their staff, borrow books, find out about volunteer opportunities, obtain discounts on hostels and other services and generally chill out. The clubhouse also holds events such as movie showings, cookery classes and the odd party, and produces a newsletter.

For sources to consult for information on specific cultural events, clubs, tango shows and the like, see the individual Listings chapters.

Travellers with disabilities

Buenos Aires does not have a particularly sophisticated infrastructure for **travellers with disabilities**, but most locals are extremely willing to help anyone experiencing problems. There have also been some notable, welcome changes of late: a recent innovation has been the introduction of wheelchair ramps to access the city's pavements – though unfortunately the pavements themselves tend to be narrow, are often littered with potholes and, especially in the microcentro, can become almost impassable due to the volume of pedestrians. Public transport is less problematic, with many of the new buses in the city offering low-floor access. Laws demand that all new hotels now provide at least one room that is accessible for those in wheelchairs, but the only sure-fire option for those with severe mobility problems is at the top end of the price range: most five-star hotels have full **wheelchair access**, including wide doorways and

Guided tours

The number of **guided tours** in Buenos Aires has risen in recent years, and there are considerably more options available than simply sitting on a minibus listening to someone without much English pointing out the main sights. The city government organizes free **walking tours** in English and Spanish, usually around a given barrio, but sometimes with themes such as Evita or tango – ask for the current schedule at any tourist kiosk or call ☎011/4114-5791. It also runs hop on-hop off bus tours with audio in a variety of languages, including English, beginning in Roque Sáenz Peña and Suipacha (9am–5.30pm; every 30min; $70; tickets must be bought from the tourist info kiosk on Roque Sáenz Peña and Florida or via ⓦwww.buenosairesbus.com) and stopping at various points of interest between Boca and Palermo. Private outfits offering city tours are listed below.

Buenos Aires Tur Lavalle 1444, Office 10 ☎011/4371-2304, ⓦwww.buenosairestur .com. Conventional city tours as well as visits to tango shows, Tigre and nearby estancias.

Cicerones ☎011/5258-0909, ⓦwww.cicerones.org.ar. NGO that offers two- to three-hour tours of the city. The guides are locals who are passionate about Buenos Aires, rather than professionals. The only cost is any entrance fees etc for your guide, although donations are appreciated.

Español Andando ☎011/3927-8349, ⓦwww.espanol-andando.com. A four-day language course that teaches conversational Spanish on the ground, visiting sights, restaurants and shops.

Graffitimundo ⓦwww.graffitimundo.com. On these brilliant three-hour tours (in English) of the city's fascinating street art, partly on foot and partly in small buses, you find out who and what are behind the vibrant murals that adorn walls and buildings in barrios like Colegiales and Palermo. You might even get to meet one or more of the artists themselves. The tour costing $90 is punctuated with visits to offbeat galleries and restaurants and ends up in a graffiti-soaked bar. Private tours can also be arranged.

Lan & Kramer Bike Tours Florida 868 piso 14 ☎011/4311/5199, ⓦwww.biketours .com.ar. Bilingual guided bike tours around the city. Bike rental also available.

MPTours ⓦwww.mptours.com. A website that offers spoken tours of different neighbourhoods via MP3 download.

Say Hueque Viamonte 749, 6th floor ☎011/5199-2517/20, ⓦwww.sayhueque .com. Highly commendable outfit with English-speaking staff, geared to the independent traveller and offering hotel and tour packages, as well as day-trips to football matches and estancias.

Tangol Florida 971, Office 31 ☎011/4312-7276, ⓦwww.tangol.com. Runs a comprehensive range of tours in and around the city, as well as organizing tickets and transfers for tango shows.

roll-in showers. Those who have some mobility problems, but do not require full wheelchair access, will find most mid-range hotels are adequate, offering spacious accommodation and lifts. In all cases, the only way of finding out if a place meets your particular requirements is to ring the hotel and enquire.

Women travellers

Women planning on travelling alone in Buenos Aires can do so with confidence. Some *machista* attitudes do persist – men usually pay in restaurants, and it is relatively unusual for groups of girls to go out drinking the way they might in Europe or the US – but the next generation seems to be shedding these inhibitions with alacrity and few people will find it strange that you are travelling unaccompanied. You will probably find you are the target of comments in the street and chat-up lines more frequently than you are accustomed to, but those responsible will not persist if you make it clear you're not interested. Such attentions are almost never hostile or physical – Italian-style bottom pinching is very rare here.

The City

The City

1 Monserrat 45

2 San Nicolás 61

3 Puerto Madero 72

4 San Telmo 80

5 Boca 88

6 Retiro 94

7 Recoleta 106

8 Palermo 120

9 The outer barrios 138

Monserrat

The barrio of **Monserrat** is Buenos Aires' historic heart: the longest-settled area of the city, its narrow streets and broad avenues are home to a good number of the capital's oldest, handsomest and most important buildings: churches, museums and national institutions. Bounded by avenidas Rivadavia, Ingeniero Huergo, Independencia and Entre Ríos, the neighbourhood is very accessible on foot, making it an excellent place to begin a tour of the city.

The focal point of the barrio – and indeed, the city – is not a building, however, but the spacious, palm-dotted **Plaza de Mayo**, set in the northeast corner of the neighbourhood. A somewhat mismatched collection of buildings rings this large square: the famous **Casa Rosada**, or government house, from where both Evita and Maradona greeted their adoring fans; the city's **cathedral**; and the colonial-era forerunner to the Casa Rosada, the **Cabildo**. South of the Plaza de Mayo are several close blocks of streets that have changed little since the nineteenth century, and are beguiling to explore. Among them you'll find many great little cafés and old-fashioned bookshops, as well as the **Manzana de las Luces** and the **Manzana Franciscana**, sites which belonged to the Jesuit and Franciscan orders respectively, and two of the city's best small museums, the eclectic **Museo de la Ciudad** and the anthropological **Museo Etnográfico**. Heading west from the plaza, ten-block-long **Avenida de Mayo** is the city's major boulevard, an elegant thoroughfare flanked by an impressive selection of Art Nouveau and Art Deco constructions and a string of *belle époque* hotels and cafés. Highlights along here include the magnificent Dante-inspired **Edificio Barolo**, one of the city's most unusual pieces of architecture, and the renowned **Café Tortoni**, next door to a tango academy and museum. At its western end, the avenue opens into the long, thin **Plaza del Congreso**, named for the enormous Neoclassical **Congreso** building, the seat of the country's two houses of parliament.

While the barrio name, Monserrat (sometimes written Montserrat), appears on official maps it is rarely heard on the ground. It took its name from a chapel founded here in the late eighteenth century by the Catalan Brotherhood of the Virgin of Monserrat, but long since demolished. In referring to this area, most locals tend to use the general term **"el (micro)centro"** – applied to a wider area – and erroneously lump anywhere south of Avenida de Mayo in with San Telmo, technically speaking Monserrat's southerly neighbour (see Chapter 4). The Plaza de Congreso and its immediate environs are commonly described as "Congreso".

Plaza de Mayo and around

The **Plaza de Mayo** – in one corner of the barrio but at the heart of the city – can lay claim to most of the pivotal moments in the history of Buenos Aires.

MONSERRAT

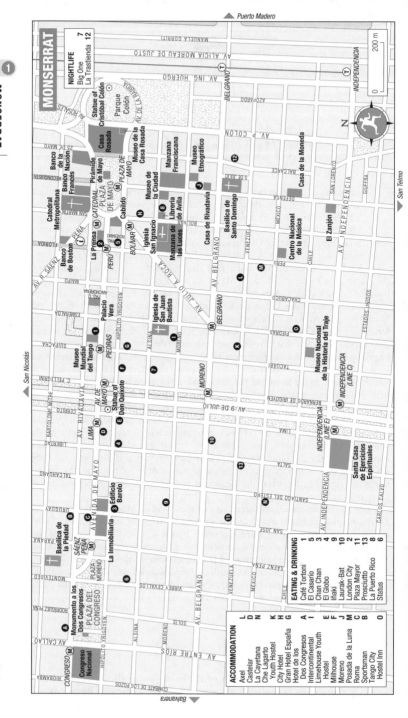

MONSERRAT

NIGHTLIFE
Big One 7
La Trastienda 12

EATING & DRINKING
Café Tortoni 1
El Casario 5
Chan Chan 3
El Globo 9
Iñaki 4
Laurak-Bat 10
London City 2
Plaza Mayor 11
Prosciutto 13
La Puerto Rico 8
Status 6

ACCOMMODATION
Axel L
Castelar .... D
La Cayetana .... N
Che Lagarto
  Youth Hostel .... K
City Hotel .... H
Gran Hotel España .... G
Hotel de los
  Dos Congresos .... A
Intercontinental I
Limenhouse Youth
  Hostel .... E
Milhouse .... F
Moreno .... J
Posada de la Luna C
Roma .... B
Sportsman .... M
Tango City .... O
Hostel Inn .... O

The centre of its civil life since Juan de Garay founded the city in 1580 – he declared the area in front of the Cabildo a public space – the square was originally just half its current size, consisting of two plazas separated by a long, elegant arcade. Its appearance today dates only to the 1880s, when the arcade was demolished.

Throughout the nineteenth and twentieth centuries the plaza was the scene of both celebrations and protests, even taking its name from one of the latter, the **May Revolution** of 1810, which freed the country from Spanish rule – the first provisional junta was announced from the **Cabildo** balcony. In the 1940s the square, and indeed all of Avenida de Mayo, was regularly filled by the *descamisados* (literally "the shirtless ones", or manual workers), who gathered to show support for Juan Domingo Perón and Evita. Later, in 1955, over three hundred people were killed here when the navy bombed a trade-union rally that had been organized to back Perón, who was locked in a conflict with the Catholic Church over the appropriation of religious language for political ends and his campaign to canonize Evita. For many years during, and after, the last dictatorship this was the site of the **Madres de Plaza de Mayo**'s weekly demonstration (see box, p.49). And when then-president Fernando de la Rúa declared a state of emergency after several days of looting in December 2001, it was to the Plaza de Mayo that defiant Porteños headed to chant and protest through the hot summer nights.

More recently, the plaza has been less eventful – although it regularly attracts small, noisy **demonstrations**, it's more often than not sedately filled with office workers lunching and sunbathing, old men gossiping and batting away flocks of squawking pigeons and hawkers selling candied peanuts and Argentine flags. Its

The bicentenary

Argentina observed its **bicentenary** in 2010 (🖥 www.bicentenario.argentina.ar): two hundred years before, on May 25, 1810, locals gathered in Buenos Aires' **Plaza de Mayo** to demand the withdrawal of the viceroy and to form the **Primera Junta** – the first move in throwing off the yoke of Spanish rule and creating an independent nation, though full independence had to wait another six years.

The centenary in 1910 was cause for great celebration: in its first hundred years Argentina had gone from being a fairly small colonial backwater to one of the world's richest countries, still in the throes of an unprecedented immigration and building boom, and bursting with confidence that it was destined to be a great country, perhaps even challenging US hegemony in the Western Hemisphere. Several foreign nations gifted **monuments**, many of which are still standing in Buenos Aires, including the Torre Monumental (Britain; see p.97) and the Monumento de los Españoles (Spain; see p.133).

Now, a century on, Argentina has failed to live up to its original heady promise, but Porteños nonetheless passionately celebrated the country's bicentenary. The new Casa del Bicentenario, at Riobamba 985 (🖥 www.casadelbicentenario.gob.ar), acted as the organizational headquarters and housed temporary exhibitions in 2010, and is set to outlive the bicentenary year as a national space for archives and multimedia documentation.

Highlights of the main festivities included the reopening of the **Teatro Colón** (see p.69), a number of outdoor **concerts** featuring national and international stars, and a triumphal procession along the **Avenida de Mayo**. Other festivities and projects included a **regatta** of navy school boats from around the world; the issue of special one-peso **coins**; the partial **pedestrianization** of the Plaza de Mayo; a new **park**, the Parque del Bicentenario, in Caballito; and joint events with **Chile**, which also celebrated its bicentenary in 2010 (as did Colombia and Mexico).

towering palm trees (shipped down from Rio de Janeiro) give the square a wonderfully tropical feel, particularly when bathed in evening sunlight. The peace is shattered a little by the constant and heavy traffic that circulates around the perimeter, but the plaza was partly **pedestrianized** for the bicentenary celebrations in 2010.

The plaza's most recognizable building is the blushing **Casa Rosada**, at the eastern end, where you can take a guided tour of the splendid interior at weekends. The handsome white **Cabildo** directly opposite also has a small museum, and the columned **Catedral Metropolitana** on the north side is the final resting place of Argentine independence leader General San Martín. Palatial banks (see p.63) and local government buildings line the rest of the northern and western sides of the plaza, while the uglier functional buildings on the south side are government ministries; if you look carefully you can still see scars of the 1955 bombing raid on their outer walls. The central grassy reserve features a monument called the **Pirámide de Mayo**, the headscarves painted around which echo those worn by the Madres de Plaza de Mayo (see box opposite).

Casa Rosada and the Parque Colón

Evita, Maradona, Galtieri and Perón have all addressed crowds from the balcony of the unmissable **Casa de Gobierno**, otherwise known as the **Casa Rosada** (Sat & Sun 10am–6pm; free; take your passport for ID; at busy times you might need to sign up), the pink government palace that occupies the eastern end of the square. The present structure, a typically Argentine blend of French and Italian Renaissance styles, developed in a fairly organic fashion. It stands on the site of the city's original fort, begun in 1594 and finished in 1720 and then in a strategic location overlooking the Río de la Plata – the waters have receded since then. With the creation of the Viceroyalty of the Río de la Plata in 1776, the fort was remodelled as the viceroy's palace, and then in 1862 President Bartolomé Mitre moved the government ministries to the building, refashioning it once again. The final touch, the central arch, was added in 1885, unifying the facade. Today the Casa Rosada continues to be used for official government business, including the usual presidential pomp. The official presidential residence, however, is in the northern suburb of Olivos.

The rather squat building's most distinctive aspect, its **colour**, dates from the 1870s, and Domingo Sarmiento's presidency – but don't listen to guides who propagate the myth that Sarmiento hoped to unify the two warring sides in the country's bloody civil conflict by combining their symbolic colours (red for the Federalists, white for the Unitarists). If that was indeed the case, the palace would be a vibrant purple, as the Unitarists' usual preferred colour was actually blue. In fact, the practice of painting buildings pink was fairly common during the nineteenth century, particularly in the countryside, where you'll still find many similarly coloured estancias. The shade was originally achieved with the use of ox blood, for both decorative and practical reasons – the blood acted as a fixative for the whitewash to which it was added. After being a muted rose for many years, followed by a brief phase in a shocking pink – a legacy of the flamboyant Menem years – the Casa Rosada was restored in 2007 to a deep puce colour, a shade which has been patented as "Casa de Gobierno pink" in a probably fruitless attempt to prevent any future tampering with the tone. Half-hour-long tours inside the Pink House (every 10min) are led by uniformed grenadiers, who parade groups through the impressive official state rooms, including the handsome executive office, but those hoping to step out onto the famous presidential balcony will be disappointed – though you do get a view of the Plaza de Mayo from the lower balcony, where triumphant football teams show off their trophies.

The **Museo de la Casa Rosada**, at Hipólito Yrigoyen 219 (closed for refurbishment until late 2011), on the south side of the building, is devoted to an assortment of objects used by Argentina's past presidents. The collection is mostly rather staid, consisting largely of official photographs and medals, but there are a number of slightly more idiosyncratic exhibits – look for the tango scores composed in honour of politicians, including the rather unmusical-sounding *El Socialista*, written for socialist Alfredo Palacios, who was elected to Congress in 1904, and the inevitable ornate silver cups for drinking *mate* that no self-respecting Argentine president would go without. There is also a stone alleged to have been thrown at President Roca when he was on his way to the state opening of parliament.

Parque Colón

Behind the Casa Rosada, the small, fenced-off **Parque Colón** contains the scant ruins of a nineteenth-century customs house, the Aduana de Taylor, named after the British engineer who designed it in 1855. The park – really a plaza, with heavy traffic zooming past on Ingeniero Huergo – is more famous, however, for its gigantic Argentine flag and Carrara marble statue of **Cristóbal Colón** (Christopher Columbus), looking out to the river and towards the Old World. The sculpture group at the base of the statue represents the European "discovery" of the Americas, and the attributes that it entailed, such as religion and science.

Madres de Plaza de Mayo

Many of those arrested, tortured and executed during the **1976–83 dictatorship** (see Contexts, p.258) were **young dissidents**, who were suddenly bundled into Ford Falcons on street corners before vanishing without trace. Their mothers, frustrated by the authorities' intimidating silence when they tried to find out what had happened to their children, started in 1976 what would become the **Madres** movement.

Comprising at first just a handful of women, the Madres met weekly in the **Plaza de Mayo**, as much to support each other as to embarrass the regime into providing answers to their questions; the wearing of white headscarves emerged as a means of identification. As their numbers grew, so did their defiance – standing their ground and challenging the military to carry out its threat to fire on them in front of foreign journalists, for instance. Some disappeared themselves after the notorious "Angel of Death" Alfredo Astiz infiltrated the group, posing as the brother of a *desaparecido* (disappeared).

In 1982, during the Malvinas/Falklands crisis, the Madres were accused of being anti-patriotic for their stance **against the war**, a conflict that they claimed was an attempt by the regime to divert attention away from its murderous acts. With the return to democracy in 1983, the Madres were disappointed by the new government's reluctance to delve too deeply into what had happened during the "Dirty War", as well as by the later granting of impunity to many of those accused of kidnap, torture and murder. Some of the Madres branched into other areas of social protest: the emblem of the white headscarf was at the forefront of the movement to demand the **non-payment of the country's foreign debt**, among other issues. The respect in which the group is held was key in finally getting the amnesty laws overturned in 2005. The Madres continued to protest about government inaction over the disappeared at the Pirámide de Mayo until early 2006, when, after around 1500 protests, they finally brought their long vigil to an end, citing confidence in President Néstor Kirchner. They continue to gather at the plaza every Thursday, however, to draw attention to other social causes.

Pirámide de Mayo

Looking a little dwarfed by the tall buildings that surround it, the obelisk-like column of the **Pirámide de Mayo** nonetheless stands out from its location on a strip of grass at the centre of the plaza. First erected in 1811 to mark the first anniversary of the May Revolution, the monument has been altered several times, including the addition of the figure of Liberty to its summit in the 1850s. In 1912 it was moved from its original position and placed sixty metres closer to the Cabildo in order to allow for a larger monument to be built around it, although the latter was never completed. Often colourfully decorated in the early years of the Republic in honour of patriotic celebrations, in the twentieth century it became better known as the focal point of protests, most famously those of the Madres de Plaza de Mayo, who marched around it, arm in arm, during their weekly vigils (see box, p.49).

The bronze equestrian statue between the pyramid and the Casa Rosada is of **General Belgrano**, one of the major protagonists in the Independence movement, and the designer of the national flag.

Cabildo

The simple, unadorned lines, green and white shuttered facade and colonnaded front of the **Cabildo**, on the western edge of the Plaza de Mayo, appear in stark contrast with the more ornate buildings around it – the exterior got off relatively lightly during the remodelling craze of the late nineteenth century, with just some light Italianate touches and the loss of three arches. This was Buenos Aires' most important colonial-era civil construction – the centre of government, the jail and the all-purpose seat of authority – from the city's founding until the 1820s. Later, the building was used as law courts. The interior now holds a small **museum** (Wed–Fri 10.30am–5pm, Sat, Sun & hols 11.30am–6pm; $4) of eighteenth- and nineteenth-century memorabilia. The modest collection mostly consists of items relating to the fight for Argentine independence, including colonial standards, a clock belonging to British General Beresford and captured during the 1806 invasion attempt, some delicate watercolours by Enrique Pellegrini and original plans of the city and the fort. The exhibits are really of only minor interest, but the building itself is worth a visit to see the well-preserved interior. Behind the Cabildo, a patio area houses a café and small daytime crafts fair.

You'll notice two impressive-looking buildings flanking the Cabildo: the five-storey French- and Italian-influenced structure to the north is the **Palacio de Gobierno de Buenos Aires**, while to the south the **Legislatura de Buenos Aires** is built in the French academic style, with a distinctive beige clock tower reminiscent of those found on Flemish town halls. They are the headquarters of the city government and parliament, respectively, and neither is open to visitors.

Catedral Metropolitana

The **Catedral Metropolitana** (Mon–Fri 8am–7pm, Sat & Sun 9am–7.30pm; free guided tours of the cathedral Mon–Fri 11.45am, of the art works Mon–Fri 1.15pm and of the crypt Mon–Sat 3.30pm), with its sturdy and rather severe Neoclassical facade, is the city's cathedral but not its most attractive church. Like so many of Buenos Aires' churches, this one, topped with a blue-tiled dome, assumed its final form over a period of many years; built and rebuilt since the 1500s, the present building was completed in the mid-nineteenth century. The twelve columns that front the entrance represent the twelve apostles; above them sits a carved tympanum whose bas-relief depicts the arrival of Jacob and his family in Egypt. Unfortunately, these days the facade is frequently disfigured by graffiti that reappears as quickly as it can be removed, usually slogans directed against the Catholic Church and its stance on issues such as abortion (illegal in Argentina except in extreme circumstances). The interior features Venetian mosaic floors, gilded columns and an eighteenth-century silver-plated altar. However, by far the most significant feature is the solemnly guarded marble **mausoleum** (accessible Mon–Sat 9am–1pm & 3–5pm, Sun 9–11am & 3–7pm) to Independence hero and founding father ("Padre de la Patria") General San Martín; the eternal flame near the cathedral entrance flickers in his honour.

South of Plaza de Mayo

The feel of the city changes as you head south from the plaza – open space quickly turns to narrow streets, and you enter an area that seems to have been frozen in time circa the mid-nineteenth century. Here tradition and religion mix with a certain bohemian tinge, creating an atmosphere not unlike that of San Telmo, adjacent to the south.

One of the best routes for delving into these crowded blocks is along **Calle Defensa**, named in honour of the barrio's residents, who, during the British invasions of 1806 and 1807, impeded the British troops by pouring boiling water and oil on them as they marched down the street (Anglophile Argentines like to carp that they "should have thrown flowers"). Along here you'll find two *manzanas* – complexes taking up entire square blocks – of interest: the **Manzana Franciscana**, dominated by a Franciscan convent, and the more important **Manzana de las Luces**, originally a Jesuit site and home to one of the city's oldest churches. Note that both *manzanas* were undergoing lengthy restoration work at the time of writing. Nearby sits an offbeat museum chronicling life in Buenos Aires, the **Museo de la Ciudad**, and the **Museo Etnográfico**, which concentrates on indigenous culture in Argentina and the rest of South America.

Manzana Franciscana

Walking one block south along Defensa from Plaza de Mayo will bring you to the so-called **Manzana Franciscana**, a block lined by calles Defensa, Alsina, Moreno and Balcarce, and assigned to the Franciscan order since 1580. For visitors, the most accessible part of the complex is the eclectic **Basílica de San Francisco** (erratic opening times), accessed at Alsina 380, on the corner with Defensa. Dating from 1754, this Neo-Baroque church was burnt by angry Peronists in March 1955 in reaction to the navy's bombing of the anti-Church trade-union rally in the Plaza de Mayo. Eventually restored and reconsecrated, the basilica was officially reopened in 1967. The four statues on the small square at its front represent astronomy, industry, geography and navigation, and originally adorned the Pirámide de Mayo in the Plaza de Mayo; they were moved here when the pyramid had its location shifted in 1912. At right angles to the basilica is the **Capilla de San Roque** (usually closed to the public except during the monthly tours; see below for details), a small chapel with a restrained facade.

An oak column from the basilica's original altarpiece, destroyed by the fire, has been preserved in the **Convento de San Francisco**, which holds eighty monks' cells and is the city's biggest monastery, although these days the brothers number in the single figures. After four centuries of seclusion, in 2007 the monks decided to allow the public into the monastery on a monthly guided tour (in theory, 4pm first Sat of the month, but check beforehand; $10; ☎011/4331-0625), which takes in the main cloisters, dining room and the wonderful library – one of the city's oldest, with many valuable volumes – as well as the basilica and chapel. At a small **store** (Mon–Fri 8.30am–7pm) by the basilica the brothers sell bee-derived products, including honey, soap and even anti-wrinkle cream. There's also a **museum**, the **Museo Monseñor Fray José María Bottaro** (Wed–Sun 10am–4pm; $5), opened to help raise funds for the ongoing restoration of the monastery. The collection comprises a variety of religious artefacts dating from colonial times, including the 1650 coffin of Fray Luis de Bolaños – who hailed from Seville and was one of the first Europeans to learn the Guaraní language – paintings, furniture and saints' relics.

Museo de la Ciudad and around

Opposite the basilica, on the first floor of the handsome private residence at Defensa 219, is the quirky **Museo de la Ciudad** (11am–7pm; $1, free Mon & Wed; Ⓦwww.museodelaciudad.buenosaires.gob.ar). Showcased by a tiled entrance hall and tall windows, this museum's permanent collection chronicles children's toys through the ages. The majority of the small space, though, is devoted to regularly changing exhibitions that illustrate everyday aspects of Porteño life, such as holidays or shopping. Witty, tongue-in-cheek descriptions accompany these displays, although sadly they are in Spanish only. Downstairs, a salon open to the street holds larger items, such as rescued doors and a traditional barrow decorated in the *filete* style (see box, p.82), from which *ambulantes* (street peddlers) would have sold their wares. Many of the museum's best exhibits are on permanent display in street-level windows, making visits to the museum proper almost superfluous. The museum staff are active in organizing events around the city, including a small arts fair on Fridays and Sundays (10am–5pm) in front of the Basílica de San Francisco and Sunday's famous Plaza Dorrego antiques market (see p.82).

It's worth glancing into the **Farmacia de la Estrella**, a beautifully preserved old pharmacy just on the corner of Alsina and Defensa. Founded in 1834, it boasts a gorgeously opulent interior of heavy walnut fittings and quirky, old-fashioned medical murals and mirrors, all finished off with a stunning frescoed ceiling.

Manzana de las Luces and around

Taking up the whole block bounded by Alsina, Perú, Moreno and Bolívar – the last one block west of Defensa – is the complex of buildings known as the **Manzana de las Luces** or "block of enlightenment" (guided visits Mon–Fri 3pm, check first, Sat & Sun 3pm, 4.30pm & 6pm from entrance at Perú 272; $7; ☎011/4342-9930, Ⓦwww.manzanadelasluces.gov.ar). Dating from 1662, this block originally housed a Jesuit community, and has been home to numerous official institutions since the order was expelled from the city in 1767. A series of **tunnels** that once connected the city's churches runs underneath the area at about six metres below street level. These were constructed in the eighteenth century as part of a defence mechanism – the churches were used as lookouts for the isolated coastal town, and the tunnels allowed for both quick getaways and communication in the event of an enemy attack. Later, they were also used for smuggling, a common practice in colonial days (see Contexts, p.252).

Tours of the complex (in Spanish, with summary explanations given in English if needed) visit an inner patio, the tunnels, some of the surrounding chambers –

including one that was the scene of a nineteenth-century political assassination – and the reconstructed **Sala de Representantes**, a semi circular chamber where the first provincial legislature sat. The chamber now provides a backdrop for frequent classical and jazz concerts and recitals, while the patios are used for open-air theatre performances (see the website for listings).

In the northwest corner of the block, opposite a statue of General Roca, the **Mercado de las Luces** (Mon–Fri 10am–7.30pm, Sun 2–7pm) has a number of stalls set up in one of the Jesuit corridors, selling antiques, crystals, candles and other artisan products. The block also encompasses the elite **Colegio Nacional**, the high school of choice for aspiring politicians and leaders. Both the exterior and interior of the school building are French-inspired, with a sumptuous events room based on the main salon of the Paris Opera; graduation diplomas are handed out here, traditionally by the Argentine President. It's open to the public on guided visits, but these must be booked at least one week in advance by telephone or email ($5; ☎011/4331-1290, ⓦ www.cnba.uba.ar). Buenos Aires' oldest church, **San Ignacio** (in theory daily 8am–9pm), begun in 1675, is also part of the Manzana de las Luces, on the corner of Bolívar and Alsina. As with many of the city's churches, various later additions have modified San Ignacio's original appearance, the most recent being the tower at the northern end of the church, erected in 1850. Apart from the rather Baroque high altar, the church's interior is fairly simple, an arrangement that makes one of its most notable icons, the beautiful seventeenth-century Nuestra Señora de las Nieves, all the more arresting.

Just as old though a little more secular, the wonderfully old-fashioned **Librería de Avila** (Mon–Fri 8.30am–8pm, Sat 10am–2pm & 3–5pm; ☎011/4331-8989), on Alsina and Bolívar right opposite San Ignacio, has been the site of a bookshop since 1775, and is allegedly where the city's first book was sold. Several owners and remodellings later, it's still a functioning store, selling both fiction and nonfiction (mostly in Spanish), with an emphasis on Argentine history; the stock also includes many rare and antique volumes and first editions. You can enjoy your literature over a coffee or even a Fernet Branca in the downstairs café and bar; the store sometimes puts on readings in the evenings here.

Fans of colonial-era churches should keep an eye out for the **Iglesia de San Juan Bautista**, three blocks west at Alsina and Piedras, with a distinctive facade decorated with horizontal lines and a rose window. The church dates from 1797, and originally belonged to a Capuchin convent; it was also damaged in the 1955 riots.

Museo Etnográfico Juan Bautista Ambrosetti

Part of the Universidad de Buenos Aires, the **Museo Etnográfico Juan Bautista Ambrosetti** lies at Moreno 350 (Feb–Dec Tues–Fri 1–7pm, Sat & Sun 3–7pm; 1hr guided visits in Spanish Sat & Sun 4pm, in English by prior arrangement; $3; ☎011/4331-7788). Housed in this handsome Neoclassical mansion flanked by lofty palms since the 1920s, it was founded in 1904 by philosophy professor Ambrosetti to promote understanding of Argentina's indigenous societies at a time when they were still regarded in many circles as barbaric and inferior. Although the museum has some international anthropological exhibits – including a stunning Shinto altar from Japan accompanied by artefacts from Africa and Oceania in the first room to the right – its real interest lies in its collection of pre-Columbian textiles, ceramics and other objects displayed in permanent and temporary exhibitions on the ground and upper floors.

One of the ground-floor rooms focuses on the **Yámana**, the **Selk'nam** and other peoples of the far southern province of Tierra del Fuego (Fueginos). Neither of the former cultures, which died out in the late twentieth century, used much in the way of adornment, reflected in the simple canoes, harpoons and other everyday items on display here. The upper floor is used for temporary exhibitions, mostly about South America's fascinating pre-Columbian cultures.

South along Defensa

Continuing south along Defensa you'll pass more late colonial-era buildings, including the **Casa de Rivadavia** (not open to the public) at no. 350, where Bernardino Rivadavia, president in the 1820s, was born in 1780. The style is classic eighteenth-century colonial, a white, two-storey construction with upper balconies, though it's in sore need of restoration.

On the next block, at Defensa and Belgrano, the glory of the austere twin-towered **Basílica de Santo Domingo** is somewhat overshadowed by the grand elevated **mausoleum** to General Belgrano that dominates the tiled patio at the front of the church. Dating from the 1780s, the basilica is closer to its original form than many of the surrounding churches, although the altar is modern – the original was another victim of the 1955 arson attacks. The Dominican order had a monastery here from the sixteenth century until the aforementioned Rivadavia expelled them, although the square also belonged very briefly to the British after they took it on June 27, 1806, on which date Catholicism was outlawed; it is rumoured that the left tower retains marks from bullets that flew during the battle. In the corner to the left of the altar as you enter the basilica you can see the flags from British regiments captured by General Liniers and dedicated to the Virgen del Rosario when the city was recaptured two months later.

The final building of note on Defensa before you cross into San Telmo is the former **Casa de la Moneda**, Argentina's original Mint, at Defensa and Mexico. It's a large, white building in the classic Italian style, ringed with palm trees and Argentine flags. It came into use in the 1870s, when the peso was first created as the national currency; coins and bills were produced here until the 1940s. Now, this building and its brick annexe on Balcarce are owned by the army – hence all the flags – and used as its archive and for military historical research.

Centro Nacional de la Música

One block west of the Casa de la Moneda, the **Centro Nacional de la Música**, México 564 (☎011/4361-6238), makes an attractive diversion, if only for its fine classical facade. Although now used as a music archive and rehearsal space, for many years it was the seat of the Biblioteca Nacional, the national library, before it moved to its new, rather less traditional-looking home in Recoleta (see p.117). Jorge Luis Borges (see box, p.129) was its director for eighteen years, and it was here that the Italian scholar and writer Umberto Eco met the man whose writings have clearly influenced his own work – *The Name of the Rose* even has a blind librarian character called Jorge of Burgos. The interior features decorative vaulted ceilings and an exhibition hall with a stained-glass ceiling; it's not normally open to the public, but if you're interested enquire about the music concerts held here occasionally, some of which are free.

Museo Nacional de la Historia del Traje

The **Museo Nacional de la Historia del Traje**, Chile 832 (Tues–Sun 3–7p___, free; ⓦ www.funmuseodeltraje.com.ar), is a small costume museum with Spanish-only labels, displaying mostly women's clothing from the nineteenth and early twentieth centuries. The nineteenth-century townhouse, with its original mosaic doors and attractive patios, is in some ways more interesting than the contents; although many of the clothes were local donations, the styles throughout are all either European copies or imports and there is little Argentine spin on the theme. Of the exhibits, one of the most amusing includes a series of photos documenting the language of the fan – these show how the manner in which a lady held the accessory could indicate a whole range of romantic communication, from "I'm looking for a boyfriend" to "you're ugly" and "my parents are watching". The museum also holds temporary exhibitions on subjects such as the Silk Route or Argentine fashion exports.

Avenida de Mayo

One of the city's grandest thoroughfares, **Avenida de Mayo** stretches ten wide, tree-lined blocks from Plaza de Mayo west to Plaza del Congreso. Part of a project to remodel the city along the lines of Haussmann's Paris in the 1880s, the avenue is renowned for its melange of Art Nouveau and Art Deco constructions; decorative domes, elaborate balustrades and sinuous caryatids adorn many of its buildings, and ornamental street lamps flank the pavements. Be sure to look up, especially as you pass the striking architecture of **La Prensa**, **Edificio Barolo** and **La Inmobiliaria**.

Unimpressed with the city's European pretensions, Borges called Avenida de Mayo one of the saddest areas in Buenos Aires, yet even he couldn't resist the charm of its **confiterías** and traditional restaurants, a handful of which remain open, including the well-known **Café Tortoni**, and the lesser-known but still appealing **36 Billares** and **London City**. The street is also packed with traditional hotels (see p.151 for reviews). A stroll down the avenue is more about imbibing the atmosphere – and perhaps the odd espresso – than visiting specific sights, but there is one small museum of interest here, the **Museo Mundial del Tango**.

La Prensa

Just half a block west of Plaza de Mayo at Avenida de Mayo 567, the magnificent **La Prensa** building, with grand wrought-iron doors, curvaceous lamps and a steep mansard roof, was originally constructed at the end of the nineteenth century as the headquarters of the national newspaper *La Prensa*, which had gone into circulation in 1869. At that time, Avenida de Mayo was Buenos Aires' version of Fleet Street, home to most of the national papers. Squint hard enough (you can get the best view from the parallel street, Hipólito Yrigoyen) and you will see a bronze Pallas Athena figure atop the cupola aspiring to the giddy heights of the journalist's ideal, clutching a written page and a lamp to throw light in dark places. US and Swiss firms were involved in bankrolling the construction, but the French were undoubtedly the biggest influence on the architects, specifically via the extravagant Baroque style of Garnier, the man behind the Paris Opera.

Today the building houses the city's culture secretariat and is sometimes referred to as the **(Espacio) Casa de la Cultura** (Tues–Sun 2–8pm; ☎011/4323-9669, ⓦwww.buenosaires.gov.ar/areas/cultura/casa_cultura). Take a peek at the opulent interior – all ornamental glass and elaborate woodwork – and visit one of the temporary art exhibitions any afternoon (except Mon), or attend one of the cultural events at weekends, all free of charge: open tango classes for beginners in the central patio (Sat 3pm) or tango recitals in the lavish Salón Dorado (Sun 6pm). There are also one-hour guided tours in Spanish and English (Sat 4pm & 5pm, Sun hourly 11am–4pm); for English it might be worth calling ahead to check.

Perú station and around

The splendour of Buenos Aires' golden age is visible underground as well as above in this part of the city – on the corner of Perú and Avenida de Mayo, **Perú station**, the second stop on Line A of the subte, has been refurbished by the Museo de la Ciudad (see p.52) to look as it would have a century ago. Victorian-style lamps swing from the ceiling, posters tastefully implore you to buy long-gone products and even the *kioskos* are made of elegantly decorative iron. This all reflects the history of the line – opened in 1913, it was the city's, and indeed the continent's, first underground train line. You'll need to buy a subte ticket ($1.10) to access the station, but it's worth it both to see the station and take a trip on the wonderful old Line A trains themselves (for more on this, see Getting around, p.24).

Back above ground, the adjoining building on the corner of Perú is an Art Deco gem best known for its *confitería*, **London City**, a typical Buenos Aires café of black and white tiles, smart waiters and wooden tables. Mercifully free of the gaggles of tourists found in the better-known *Tortoni* (see below), it still has a proud history, being for many years a favourite hangout of politicians, poets, writers and journalists. The drinking place dates from 1954, when it opened on the site of what had been a prestigious department store called "A la Ciudad de Londres", which was destroyed by fire in 1910. The staff like to boast about how Julio Cortázar began his 1960 novel *The Winners* with the main protagonists meeting in "el London de Perú y Avenida" – though they make less of the characters' comments on the warm beer and shoddy service.

Palacio Vera, Café Tortoni and the Museo Mundial del Tango

The next showstopper on the avenue is the Art Nouveau masterpiece of the **Palacio Vera**, at no. 767, which was constructed in 1910. The building is of interest at ground level, too, for its antique bookshops, which sell beautiful old rare books and first editions.

Another block west, at Avenida de Mayo 829, you'll find the **Café Tortoni** (☎011/4342-4328, ⓦwww.cafetortoni.com.ar). The café's presence on every tourist's must-visit list – some days you even have to queue to get in – has spoiled the atmosphere a little and hiked the prices a lot, but the *Tortoni*, which has existed in some form for over 150 years, is nonetheless worth stopping by for a *cafecito*. Founded in 1858 by a French immigrant who named it – surprise, surprise – after a Parisian coffeehouse, the *Tortoni* moved to its current site forty years later and is now the city's oldest café still brewing. Like *London City*, it is famous for its literary and artistic connections – notable habitués have included Borges and poets Alfonsina Storni, Rubén Darío and Federico García Lorca. You are also treading in the steps (and possibly sitting in the seats) of Albert Einstein, Carlos Gardel and Juan Manuel Fangio, among many others. The heavy brown columns and Art

Nouveau-mirrored walls create an elegant ambience in the main dining room, while a basement salon hosts tango recitals and radio shows.

Next door, at Avenida de Mayo 833, the fine **Palacio Carlos Gardel** is home to the Academia Nacional del Tango, with year-long courses in elements of tango such as singing or playing the bandoneón, and the rather dusty **Museo Mundial del Tango**, on the first floor (Mon–Fri 2.30–7.30pm; $15; Ⓦ www.anacdeltango.org.ar). Through plenty of memorabilia including old photos and records, the museum traces the history of tango (in Spanish, though an English-speaking guide may be available) with displays such as a glittering dress that belonged to Tita Merello, a hat worn by Carlos Gardel, a typically poetic letter from Aníbal Troilo and a photo of men dancing tango together in 1910 – women were rarely available to dance in those days, except in brothels.

West to Edificio Barolo

A walk of a block and a half further west along Avenida de Mayo takes you to the fringes of the terrifyingly busy **Avenida 9 de Julio** (see p.68) – it's so wide that anyone wanting to cross will find it takes at least two tries. If you get stuck in the central reservation you can admire a stunning black statue of **Don Quixote** on a white base that represents the fictional knight's home of La Mancha; it was unveiled by King Juan Carlos in 1980 to commemorate the 400th anniversary of the city's founding. This mini plaza also contains memorial slabs that recall those who died during the disturbances on December 20, 2001 (see Contexts, p.259). Sparked by the country's chaotic economic downturn, this was the scene of some of the fiercest clashes between protestors and police.

Past 9 de Julio, the **Hotel Castelar**, Av de Mayo 1152, was designed by the same architect as the Edificio Barolo (see opposite), although it's more noteworthy for its past roster of illustrious guests, particularly visitors from Spain – for much of the twentieth century this area was the hub of Buenos Aires' Spanish community, including exiles from the Spanish Civil War. The corner of Avenida de Mayo and Lima is consequently known as the *Esquina de la Hispanidad* ("Hispanic corner") and today you'll find a cluster of Spanish restaurants in the surrounding streets. The *Castelar* is still open to guests – for details on staying here, see p.151.

Two blocks west at no. 1265 there's another famous café, albeit one with a very different atmosphere from the *Tortoni* or *London City*. It was here, at the cavernous and rather spartan **36 Billares**, that the game of billiards was introduced to Argentina in 1882. There's still a popular billiards salon downstairs, as well as a games room at the back of the café, where an almost exclusively male crowd passes the day playing chess, dice, pool and *truco*, Argentina's favourite card game.

The richly detailed **Hotel Chile** building, nearby at no. 1297, is a particularly attractive example of Art Nouveau architecture, with five floors of wedding-cake arched windows and delicate balconies – there's hardly an angle in sight. The *Chile* isn't as grand as it once was, but it's still an interesting place to stay. You probably would not, however, want to spend the night at the former **Hotel Majestic** at no. 1317, which also had an impressive guest-list while it was operational between 1910 and 1925, but is now the central administration for tax collection. Before you get to the Barolo, there's one more Art Deco building to check out – at no. 1333, the federal police offices are housed in what was once the seat of the newspaper *Críitica*.

Edificio Barolo

On the south side of the street, at no. 1370, stands Avenida de Mayo's most fantastic building, the **Edificio Barolo**, named after the extremely wealthy farmer of Italian origin who commissioned it. Designed by Italian architect Mario Palanti and constructed between 1919 and 1923, the unusual top-heavy form is an example of the eclectic, anti-academic style popular at the time – it is a weird but handsome blend of Neo-Romanesque, Neo-Gothic and Indian temple. Created as a monument to Dante's *Divine Comedy* (of which Barolo was a great admirer), it is full of references to the epic poem – its three sections represent Hell, Purgatory and Heaven, its height in metres equals the number of cantos (100) and it has 22 floors, the same as the number of stanzas in each canto. Moreover, in early June, the roof's tip aligns with the Southern Cross constellation – the "entrance to heaven". Rather prosaically, offices take up most of the interior, but on Mondays and Thursdays local guide Miqueas Thärigen gives fascinating 45-minute tours of the building (hourly 4–7pm; $30; ℡011/4381-1885 – call ahead for weekend tours, Ⓦwww.palaciobarolotours.com.ar), explaining its details and complex symbolism, all the way from the imposing lobby to the glass dome and the lighthouse way up at the giddying tip. Every Friday there are evening tours at 8pm – a great way to see the whole city lit up.

La Inmobiliaria

The oddly charming neo-Renaissance **La Inmobiliaria** building takes up the entire last south-side block of Avenida de Mayo, between San José and Luis Peña. Edged with ornate iron balconies hung with washing and flags, and with a certain dilapidated air, the edifice looks as if it could have been plucked straight out of a Naples suburb. Instead, it was built in 1910 for an insurance company, whose name it bears. There's no particular reason to go inside – offices and apartments now occupy the building – but you can admire the exterior and its eclectic architectural touches, including two landmark russet cupolas and some classical statuettes on the eighth-floor level.

Plaza del Congreso and around

Avenida de Mayo comes to an end ten blocks west of Plaza de Mayo, at an oblong wedge of open space dotted with statues, a fountain, swooping pigeons and a number of benches. Although the whole open area, bounded to the north by Avenida Rivadavia and the south by Avenida Hipólito Yrigoyen, is usually referred to as the **Plaza del Congreso**, it's technically made up of three smaller plazas – little Plaza Lorea in the northeast corner, really not more than a traffic island; grassy Plaza Mariano Moreno, the other eastern portion; and the actual, red-gravelled Plaza del Congreso, adjoining Plaza Moreno to the west. Opened in 1910 for the country's centenary celebrations, the plaza is dominated by the country's parliament building, the **Congreso Nacional**, which looms at its western end. The neighbourhood, generally known as "Congreso", also contains a crop of cheap hotels, cafés and shops; it's a bit run-down but has some pockets of faded grandeur.

Congreso Nacional

The Greco-Roman **Congreso Nacional** building (guided visits in English: Mon, Tues, Thurs & Fri 11am & 4pm from the south-side entrance at Hipólito Yrigoyen 1846; free; bring your ID; ℡011/6310-7222) was designed by Vittorio Meano, who was also the architect of the Teatro Colón (see p.69), and inaugurated in

National politics

Argentina's Congress – and politics in general – have been dominated by the party officially known as the **Partido Justicialista (PJ)**, but usually referred to as the **Peronists (Peronistas)**, for the last six decades. As the moniker suggests, this was – and in many ways remains – the party of Perón and Evita; trading on the couple's continuing popularity (which verges on sainthood in some quarters), party members rarely let an opportunity to quote "El General" or his wife pass them by (the late Néstor Kirchner, a former Peronist president, and his wife, Cristina, who succeeded him, were much criticized by other party leaders for not mentioning the Peróns in their addresses). But even in his own time Perón was a contradictory figure, and over the years his legacy has been interpreted by his ideological descendants to allow for the embrace of just about every conceivable strand of political thought.

Nonetheless, there are certain clear trends in Peronism that have been more or less constant since Perón's time, mixing elements of both traditional right-wing and left-wing dogma, and best summarized as a kind of **national socialism**. This includes a tendency on the part of party leaders towards authoritarianism and populism, which at times smacks uncomfortably of fascism, particularly as it is often linked to an avid patriotism that rejects anything perceived as interference, either economic or cultural, from abroad. **Economic policy** has usually been protectionist, although Carlos Menem adopted free-trade policies with a zeal unmatched pretty much anywhere in the 1990s. Néstor Kirchner's administration saw a swing back to government control – for example, it banned beef exports in 2006, a move that bewildered many outside observers but was intended to keep prices down domestically. His successor and wife Cristina Fernández – who is said to model herself to some extent on Evita – attempted to tax farm exports to fund social spending but her Vice-President vetoed the move amid widespread protests. These kinds of action also illustrate two other important elements of Peronism – that its leaders put short-term gain over long-term benefits (not unlike politicians elsewhere, although Peronists take this to extremes), and that they see themselves as the protectors of the poor. This latter aspect, especially, hails back to Perón and his clever understanding that winning the loyalty of the working classes would give his party an unbeatable powerbase. Paired with this is a suspicion of intellectuals and/or entrepreneurs – famously, an early slogan of the movement was *"alpargatas sí, libros no"* – or "yes to espadrilles, no to books".

Not surprisingly, Peronism has never really gained much of a foothold among the urban educated classes (especially in the capital), certain young guerrillas in the 1970s aside (who were, for their trouble, summarily dispatched by Isabel Perón's death squads). But, with the party enjoying the continued backing of both the countryside and the trade unions created by Perón, and with the opposition a severely weakened and fragmented force, the only question at elections in recent times has been which Peronist is going to win.

1906; the granite it is built from gives it a slightly forbidding air. The northern wing is where the Lower Chamber of representatives (*diputados*) sits, while the southern wing is used by the smaller Upper Chamber of senators (*senadores*). The bicameral political system used here is similar to the US model – the President is the executive head of government, voted for in an election, while Congress is made up of representatives from the country's provinces; different parties form voting blocs within the Congress, split between *el oficialismo* (the ruling party or parties) and the opposition. The Vice-President, elected on a joint ticket with the President, acts as Chairman of the Senate and enjoys a casting vote.

The semi circular rooms where debates take place are an interesting mixture of traditional and modern: the seats are a clubbish mix of leather and dark wood and as the politicians take their places a sensor under each chair indicates if the chamber has reached quorum; each member's fingerprint or magnetic card (*senadores*) is read by a computer in the back of each seat before he or she votes. The tours include a visit to the marble Salon Azul (undergoing restoration in 2010–11), right in the centre of the building under the copper cupola; look up to see the giant 2000kg chandelier made from bronze and crystal that features figures representing the Republic and its provinces. Note that guided tours are suspended or restricted during parliamentary sessions (dates vary so call ahead); only school groups and invited guests can watch these.

Monumento a los Dos Congresos

The centrepiece of the Plaza del Congreso is the exuberant **Monumento a los Dos Congresos**, a series of sculptural allegories atop heavy granite steps and crowned by the triumphant figure of the Republic. The monument was erected to commemorate the 1813 Assembly and the 1816 Declaration of Independence, made at the Congress of Tucumán. The figures around the base represent the great rivers of Argentina, including the Río de la Plata. The plaza has traditionally been the final rallying point for many political demonstrations, with the monument often acting as a magnet for graffiti – it was cleaned in 2007 and fenced off, keeping the paint-sprayers largely at bay.

In Plaza Moreno stands a greening bronze statue, a somewhat rain-streaked version of Rodin's *The Thinker*, the only cast of the work in South America. Next to it, a small white rectangular sculpture marks *kilómetro cero* – the point from which all roads that lead from Buenos Aires are measured.

2

San Nicolás

f Monserrat is Buenos Aires' historic heart, then **San Nicolás** is the central nerve of the modern city – a fast-moving, noisy, traffic-filled district packed with offices, banks, bars, hotels and stores. Regardless of whether or not you're staying in the barrio – many travellers do – you're bound to come here frequently during your visit to eat or drink, make travel arrangements or take in the sights, which include some interesting museums, beautiful theatres and varied shopping arcades.

The neighbourhood derives its official name, San Nicolás, from an eighteenth-century church that once stood near the Obelisco (see p.68). The church was torn down to make way for the Avenida 9 de Julio and rebuilt in the 1930s along Avenida Santa Fe. In practice the barrio – bordered by avenidas Rivadavia, Callao, Madero and Córdoba – is more commonly known simply as "el centro" (the centre), with the narrow, busy streets in its eastern half usually referred to specifically as the "**microcentro**". Within this area there are still further divisions: the southeastern quarter, directly north of the Plaza de Mayo, is **La City**, where banks and financial institutions of almost palatial proportions and deliberately British design jostle for space with beautiful churches and a handful of modest museums, while the northeastern corner down by the river, known as "**El Bajo**", is a somewhat gentrified bohemian red-light district. Crowded for many years with late-night bars, El Bajo is now undergoing a renaissance as a trendy area, with increasing numbers of smart restaurants, hotels and funky nightclubs. Cutting right through the microcentro, along the western edge of both La City and El Bajo, is pedestrianized **Calle Florida**, one of the city's liveliest commercial thoroughfares. Along here you'll find a constant stream of human traffic sweeping past elegant *galerías* (arcades; see box, p.66) and stores of every kind, all the while being regaled by a variety of street performers. The busiest intersection, always a scrum of crossing traffic and buskers, is where Florida meets brash **Calle Lavalle**, another partly pedestrianized street filled with mainstream cinemas, cheap souvenir stores and snack bars.

The claustrophobic atmosphere of the microcentro is abruptly curtailed in the west by enormous, multi-lane **Avenida 9 de Julio**, home, at its intersection with Avenida Corrientes, to a 67-metre monument, the postcard-friendly **Obelisco**. Past 9 de Julio, the streets become slightly more tranquil and open. The point of greatest interest in this section of the barrio is **Plaza Lavalle**, a long grassy square surrounded by some imposing buildings, most notably the regal **Teatro Colón**. Meanwhile, **Avenida Corrientes** itself, which runs east–west from the Obelisco, is another busy shopping street, famous in the past as the hub of the city's intellectual, left-leaning café society. There's less plotting going on here today, but it's still a good place to get some culture, as bookstores, music shops, cinemas, theatres and cafés continue to line its pavements.

SAN NICOLÁS

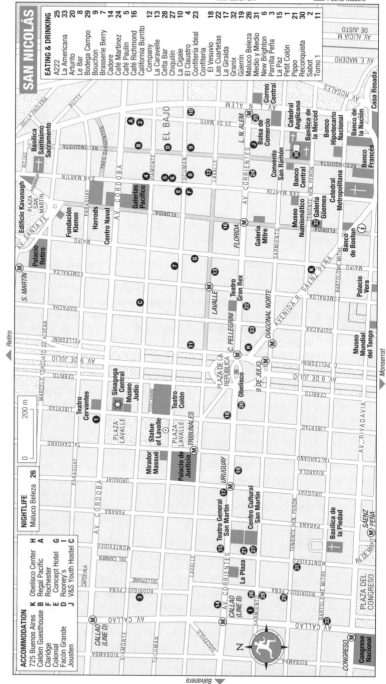

SAN NICOLÁS

EATING & DRINKING

A222	25
La Americana	33
Arturito	20
Le Bar	8
Bodega Campo	29
Bouchon	9
Brasserie Berry	7
Cadore	14
Café Martínez	24
Café Paulin	5
Café Richmond	16
California Burrito Company	12
La Caravelle	13
Celta Bar	28
Chiquilín	27
La Cigale	10
El Claustro	4
Confitería Ideal	23
Confitería	18
El Vesuvio	22
Las Cuartetas	17
La Giralda	32
Granix	19
Güerrín	26
Maluco Beleza	31
Medio y Medio	3
New Brighton	15
Parrilla Peña	1
La Paz	21
Petit Colón	30
Pippo	2
Reconquista	11
Sabot	
Tomo 1	

ACCOMMODATION

725 Buenos Aires	K	Obelisco Center	H
Calden Guesthouse	B	Regal Pacific	A
Claridge	F	Rochester	G
Colonial	E	Concept Hotel	I
Facón Grande	D	Rooney's	
Jousten	J	V&S Youth Hostel	C

NIGHTLIFE

Maluco Beleza	26

La City

Buenos Aires' financial district, known as **La City**, lies immediately north of the Plaza de Mayo, between Calle Florida, Avenida Corrientes and Avenida L.N. Alem. The moniker is rather a wink and a nod towards the City of London, and the British influence on modern Argentina's financial infrastructure. Even the bars and cafés here have names like *Broker*, *City* and *Sterling*. The area remains first and foremost a place of commerce, its atmosphere serving as a barometer of the country's economic ups and downs: during the hyperinflation of the 1980s it saw frantic money-changing, while the short-lived boom years under Menem (1990s) heard the constant ringing of bankers' mobile phones. Following the savings-withdrawal freeze of 2001, this section of the capital was the focus of noisy demonstrations.

The tight confines and endless foot traffic in this area make it difficult to pause and look up, but if you manage to do so (it is especially easy on quiet Sundays) you'll be rewarded with views of an impressive spread of grand facades, most crowned with domes and towers. Down at street level, you'll see that it is these buildings – many of them nineteenth-century mansions – that control and chronicle the country's finances, housing the stock exchange, blocks of offices and the central branches of the nation's biggest **banks** and exchange bureaux. Among the hum of money, though, there are also traces of an older, less materialistic age, including one of the city's finest **churches**, the Basílica de la Merced, with its attached charming **convent**.

The banks

The impact of the British on this part of the city is most visible today in the Victorian (or pseudo-Victorian) style of many of the **bank** buildings clustered between the Plaza de Mayo and Avenida Corrientes – it is said that the Porteño elite thought their houses should be French and their financial strongholds resolutely British in appearance. However, the most impressive of these buildings, the former **Banco de Boston** on the corner of Florida and Avenida Roque Sáenz Peña, happens to be the main exception to this rule – created in a principally Spanish style, it features a gorgeous curved facade with elaborate ornamentation around the main doorway and upper floors and an octagonal tower with a tiled roof. Most of the construction materials are North American, though the door itself is made from bronze imported from England. During the 2001 crisis this became a magnet for angry graffiti, which is still just about visible. Now owned by South Africa's Standard Bank, from the 1920s until 2007 the building housed a branch of the Bank of Boston, a US institution with long-running ties to Latin America – in 1791, as the Massachusetts Bank, it financed the first US ship to visit Argentina – and still retains that familiar name. There are no tours, but it is well worth taking a peek inside during banking hours (Mon–Fri 10am–4pm) to see the magnificent marble entrance hall and neo-Renaissance ceiling, worthy of a palace. The exterior is particularly beautiful when lit up at night.

Heading east along Bartolomé Mitre from the Banco de Boston will take you past a string of more functional-looking, though not unattractive, Victorian-style buildings, to the modern and slightly jarring concrete honeycomb of the **Banco Hipotecario Nacional** at no. 101, constructed in the 1960s on the site of the former Banco de Londres. Argentine architect Clorindo Testa, who also co-designed the equally strange Biblioteca Nacional (see p.117), was responsible for this love-it or hate-it brutalist work. A block south of here, fronting the Plaza de Mayo at Rivadavia 325, is the splendid, monumental **Banco de la Nación**, the central branch of Argentina's largest bank. Built during the inter-war years on the site of the original Teatro Colón (see p.69) by noted Argentine architect Alejandro Bustillo, it has a classical entrance pinned onto a restrained facade. Have a look inside to see the central hall, topped by an immense vaulted ceiling. Across Reconquista, and also fronting the Plaza de Mayo, stands the **Banco Francés**, which dates from the 1920s and is chiefly of note for its ornate doorway. You can complete your tour of the city's banks two blocks north at Reconquista 266, at the **Banco Central**, which has the (at times) unhappy job of preserving the value of the national currency and regulating the country's financial system. Built in the 1870s, it was home to the Supreme Court until the 1940s, and with its classic Corinthian-columned facade and airy entrance hall it certainly looks like a suitable location for the top court in the land (now at the Palacio de Justicia; see p.70).

Bolsa de Comercio

Just east of the Banco Central, the **Bolsa de Comercio**, Buenos Aires' **stock exchange**, curves gracefully around the corner of Sarmiento and 25 de Mayo. The exterior's upper-floor Ionic columns are tastefully backlit at night, while the interior of the early twentieth-century part of the building is suitably palatial, all white marble and delicate and elaborate Louis XVI styling on the black and gold banisters and lifts. **Visits** to take in this splendour and watch the floor in action are possible from the reception at Sarmiento 299 (Mon–Fri noon, 2pm & 4pm; free; take ID; Ⓦ www.bcba.sba.com.ar). Computerization has made proceedings rather staid – no more traders rushing frantically back and forth, shouting and waving their arms. However, there are often interesting art exhibitions to be seen while regular concerts are held free of charge in the building – ask at the reception. The country's main share index, the Merval (from Mercado de Valores, or stock market), has fewer than thirty companies listed; it is small by international standards but counts as a major Latin American index.

Basílica de Nuestra Señora de la Merced and Convento San Ramón

Long the favoured worshipping place of important Argentine political and military figures, the beautiful **Basílica de Nuestra Señora de la Merced** (Mon–Fri 9am–2pm & 3–7pm), is otherwise one of Buenos Aires' least visited churches. The main structure dates from 1783, although by that time it was already the third church on the site, the first being put up in 1603 by the **Mercedarians** (the medieval Order of Our Lady of Mercy). The Mercedarians, and many other religious orders, left Argentina during the ecclesiastical reforms of 1822, and the basilica passed into the hands of the Catholic Church. The sandy-coloured facade was added in 1905, and the exterior tympanum shows General Belgrano after he defeated the Spanish at the Battle of Tucumán in 1812. Meanwhile, every inch of the sombre interior is ornamented with gilt or tiles, creating an air of gloomy sumptuousness. Many of the religious artefacts housed here were destroyed in the anti-Church riots of 1955 (see p.257), but one of the most important icons survived – an eighteenth-century polychrome wood *Cristo* de la Humildad y Paciencia, which is said to have been carved from a tree in nearby Calle Florida by an indigenous craftsman.

Attached to the basilica is another of the city's best-kept secrets, the **Convento San Ramón** (access at Reconquista 269; Mon–Fri 10.30am–6pm; guided visits Thurs 10am & 4pm; free), also known as the Convento de la Merced. Originally a monastery belonging to the Mercedarians, the building has been reconstructed and altered many times since its seventeenth-century founding. After the order departed in the 1820s it was owned by the government, and served, among other purposes, as an orphanage, before finally being handed back to the Mercedarian order in the 1960s. It is now used for cultural events with religious themes, such as Bible readings, prayer meetings and theatre performances. At its heart is a charming courtyard, where you can lunch in the restaurant under the arches, *Reconquista* (see p.169), or just take a break from elbowing your way through the crowds outside.

Catedral Anglicana de San Juan Bautista

There's also an Anglican church in this neighbourhood, the **Catedral Anglicana de San Juan Bautista**, around the corner at 25 de Mayo 276. This house of worship, with its Neoclassical facade adorned with six Doric columns, was built on land donated by General Rosas in 1830, and boasts an altar featuring fine wooden artefacts from the Chaco region in Argentina's north. The building is not generally open to the public, but you are free to attend one of the Sunday services (bilingual English and Spanish Sun 10am); there has been an English-language service here since 1831.

El Bajo

El Bajo, across Avenida Corrientes from La City, takes its name ("The Low Point") from the way the barrio slopes down along this stretch towards the river. Chiefly of interest for its mix of restaurants (see p.169) and bars (see p.179), rather than specific sights, it stretches east–west from Avenida L.N. Alem and north to Córdoba, although similar locales can be found in neighbouring Retiro as far as Plaza San Martín (see p.179). This used to be the city's red-light district, a reputation that still haunts the neighbourhood, but large influxes of classier bars and restaurants frequented by tourists and students have made El Bajo trendy rather than seedy in recent years.

Calle Florida and around

Pedestrianized **Calle Florida** is one of the city's major commercial streets, running between Avenida de Mayo (see p.55) and Plaza San Martín, in Retiro. Named after a successful revolutionary battle against the Spanish in modern-day Peru in 1814 (and not the US state – note the emphasis falls on the "i" and not the "o"), the street's origins actually go back even further to the founding of the city, when it was the first path to lead from the river to the nascent settlement. When the city's wealthy denizens left their homes in yellow-fever-swamped San Telmo for Retiro at the beginning of the twentieth century, Florida became known as one of the city's most elegant shopping streets, and the obligatory route for an evening stroll following tea at Harrods (see p.99). These days it's more democratic, and one of the few places in Buenos Aires where you will see people from every walk of life coming to sell or to spend, each in their own way. It is estimated that over one million people tramp its length every day, and cutting your way through the uninterrupted stream of north–south foot traffic can require considerable determination.

Overwhelming as it can be, this traffic is probably also Florida's most appealing quality; there's always a lively buzz about the place, with music stores blasting out tango and other tunes and a handful of street performers doing their best to charm passers-by out of a few pesos. Its other great asset is its many old-fashioned shopping arcades, or **galerías** (see box below).

Heading north from Avenida de Mayo, Florida's initial blocks are mostly taken up with bookstores, clothes stores and exchange offices. There are also lots of fast-food outlets around here, which get packed with office workers at lunch time. However, at least one vestige of Florida's more sophisticated past remains in the shape of the almost anachronistic **Richmond Café** at no. 468. Famed for its cakes, hot chocolate and large, worn leather armchairs, it also houses a chess and billiards room downstairs. Another classic *confitería*, the **Ideal**, is three blocks west at Suipacha 384 – though it looks a tad shabby on the outside these days, the interior retains plenty of golden-age charm, and regularly hosts excellent *milongas* (tango dances; see p.193 for details) and concerts.

Just north of the *Richmond*, Florida is bisected by **Calle Lavalle**, another busy, partly pedestrianized shopping street. It's a sort of cheap and cheerful, not to say sleazy, version of Florida, known for its cinemas, stores selling trinkets, CDs and fake football tops, and inexpensive eateries.

A few blocks further north is another shopping venue, albeit one in a very different vein – the swanky **Galerías Pacífico**, at no. 753. Perhaps the most famous of Florida's *galerías* (see box, p.66), the building was constructed by Parisian department store Bon Marché at the end of the nineteenth century and revived in 1992 after many years of decline. Inside, if you can tear yourself away from the designer clothing stores and look up at the arcades' ceiling – the best vantage point is on the basement floor by the fountain – you will notice a set of huge and impressive ceiling murals, in the form of four squares linked by four

Florida's galerías

You can still find traces of Florida's old-world glamour in its **galerías** (shopping arcades), some of which sell a bit of everything, some of which specialize in high-end products like computers or leather goods and many of which are of architectural interest in their own right. The most notable of these is the **Galerías Pacífico** shopping centre at Florida 753, which offers a glitzy bit of retailing within a vaulted and attractively frescoed building (see p.66). Another impressive Florida *galería* is **Galería Güemes** (W www.galeriaguemes.com.ar) at no. 165. It was designed by Italian architect Francisco Gianotti, who spent most of his life in Buenos Aires and also did the *Confitería Molino*. Recently restored, the Art Nouveau arcade features a series of beautiful glass cupolas, with walls dotted with ornate marble columns, brass statues and cherubs. Various stores sell everything from children's clothes to cigars, and there are even daily tango dinner shows at the first-floor Piazzola Tango theatre. **Galería Mitre**, at no. 343, has a lovely ornate facade and was previously home to newspaper *La Nación*. In 2005 a branch of the Chilean department store Falabella opened here, selling homewares; a block away, at no. 202, there is a sister branch selling clothing in a huge, four-floor building that was once the famous British-style department store Gath & Chaves. Less noteworthy architecturally but still of interest are **Galería Central**, Florida 378, also recently renovated and selling mostly clothes; **Galería Broadway**, Florida 467, which is a good place for souvenir hunting; and **Galería Jardin**, Florida 537, whose stores deal in computers and PC accessories.

smaller, triangular pieces. Starting with the one above the stairs and going clockwise, the four main works are: *Domestic Life*, by Juan Carlos Castagnino; *Brotherhood*, by Demetrio Urruchúa; *The Dominion of Natural Forces*, by Lino Eneas Spilimbergo; and the particularly noteworthy *Love*, by Antonio Berni. In addition to pricey shops, the Galerías Pacífico building also houses the **Centro Cultural Borges**, a large space displaying a worthwhile selection of temporary photography and painting exhibitions from Argentine and foreign artists, and offering music and dance performances, many of them tango related (see p.194 for venue details).

Past the Galerías Pacífico and Avenida Córdoba, you officially enter the barrio of Retiro, though many take these last two blocks of Florida before Plaza San Martín (see p.95) to be a part of the microcentro. In reality, they act as something of a transition zone between the southern and northern neighbourhoods: the crowds begin to thin, and the goods on sale tend to be furs and tailored suits, art, jewellery and leather designs.

Avenida Corrientes

Running parallel to, and four blocks north of, Avenida de Mayo, **Avenida Corrientes** is another of the city's principal arteries, sweeping all the way down from Chacarita in the heart of the city (see p.142) to the lower grounds of El Bajo, where it ends at the monumental **Correo Central**, Buenos Aires' main post office building and a sturdy example of the capital's favourite French Academic architectural style. A broad avenue today, Corrientes has been a thoroughfare since the seventeenth century, though in those days it was little more than a dirt track leading down to the river. It acquired its modern name in the wake of the 1810 May Revolution, in homage to the northern province of Corrientes, one of the first to join the national independence cause; the name become official in 1822.

Unlike much of the rest of the city centre's avenues, and with the exception of the post office, though, it's not the street's architecture – mostly a mixture of nondescript high-rise blocks interspersed with apartment buildings – that's of note. Rather, it's the potpourri of cafés, bookstores, cinemas, theatres and pizzerias that line both sides of the avenue, particularly in the blocks between avenidas L.N. Alem and Callao. This area has been the centre of Buenos Aires' cultural life for many years, and is even immortalized as such in several tangos, including Carlos Lenzi's famous *A Media Luz* (1925).

Always busy during the day, the avenue takes on still more of a buzz in the evening, when the various plays and shows are on. It's sometimes referred to as **"the street that never sleeps"**, a phrase that originates from the days of the early twentieth century, when Corrientes played a central role in the city's cultural flowering; now it's an epithet that could equally apply to large swathes of Buenos Aires. Theatre-wise, in addition to the grand, well-known places such as **Teatro San Martín**, **Teatro Gran Rex** and **Luna Park**, there is a good smattering of smaller venues on and near the avenue hosting more avant-garde acts, often referred to as "Off Corrientes", as well as a modern café and performance complex called **La Plaza**. See p.187 for more information on the individual theatres and attending shows at them.

As befits a cultural epicentre, Corrientes is also famed for its **bookstores**, many of which stay open till the wee hours. The most basic places are simply one long room open to the street with piles of books slung on tables and huge handwritten price labels, although there are smarter places, too (see p.201 for individual store details). Books in English at these places are few and far between – for those you really need one of the city's specialist bookshops – but they are great to browse, find rare second-hand tomes or buy gifts for Spanish-speaking friends; prices are often more reasonable than in the glitzy chain stores on Santa Fe and Florida. Almost as comprehensive as the bookstores are the street's numerous pavement **kiosks**, proffering a mind-boggling range of newspapers, magazines and books on subjects from psychology to sex to tango.

Avenida 9 de Julio and around

At 140m (and 12 lanes) wide, **Avenida 9 de Julio** is one of the world's broadest avenues, a monster of a road that requires at least two stops at traffic islands to cross. Luckily, there are plenty of both these and pedestrian walkways, so getting from one side to the other takes time but isn't too fraying on the nerves. From south to north the avenue runs for about thirty blocks, connecting with the Autopista 25 de Mayo in Constitución and the Autopista Arturo Illia in Retiro. As it makes its way through the microcentro, it first crosses Avenida de Mayo, where there is a small plaza and a statue of Don Quixote (see p.57), and then forms a larger intersection with Avenida Corrientes, a junction marked by the famous white **Obelisco**. Two blocks further north, 9 de Julio passes in front of the city's majestic opera house, the **Teatro Colón**, worth visiting on a tour, especially if you don't have the chance to catch a recital. The back of the Colón opens onto the **Plaza Lavalle**, a leafy square around which are grouped the country's highest **law courts**, a large **synagogue** and a **Jewish heritage museum**, and another noteworthy theatre, the **Teatro Cervantes**.

Obelisco

The busy intersection of avenidas 9 de Julio and Corrientes is the site of one of Buenos Aires' most iconic monuments, the 67m-tall **Obelisco**. Designed by Alberto Prebisch – who is said to have preferred the more generic name "Monumento" – it was erected in 1936 in just 31 days, to commemorate four key events in the city's history: its first and second foundings (1936 was the 400th anniversary of the former); the first raising of the national flag in 1812, which took place on this spot; and the naming of Buenos Aires as Capital Federal in 1880. Owing to its strategic location – technically the small **Plaza de la República** (a name nobody uses), which until 1931 was home to the barrio's namesake church, San Nicolás de Bari – and grand scale, the Obelisco has always been a natural focal point for such varied events as political demonstrations and the celebrations that follow football victories. Even the government has seized on its advantageous placement: in the 1970s the monument became notorious when, as part of a city clean-up campaign, then-President Isabel Perón had a sign hung on it that read "El silencio es salud" ("Silence is health") – ostensibly a request for drivers to use their horns a little less, this was also seen as a veiled threat from an increasingly repressive government. More recently, the Obelisco has been covered in a giant red condom to commemorate AIDS Awareness Day; in 2007 it was turned the colours of the German and Argentine flags to mark 150 years of bilateral relations between the two countries; and on May 24, 2010, a concert by major artists such as Gilberto Gil, Kevin Johansen, Gustavo Santaolalla and Bajofondo, held around the obelisk, kicked off the bicentenary celebrations (see box, p.47).

Teatro Colón

Two blocks north of the Obelisco, on the western side of Avenida 9 de Julio between Viamonte and Tucumán, sits the handsome **Teatro Colón**, at Cerrito 618 (Ⓦwww .teatrocolon.org.ar), with its grand but restrained French Renaissance exterior. Most famous as an opera house, though it also hosts ballet and classical recitals, the Colón opened in 1908, and has been Argentina's most prestigious cultural institution ever since. Most of the twentieth century's major opera and ballet stars appeared here, from Caruso and Callas to Nijinsky and Nureyev, while classical music performances have been given by the likes of Toscanini and Rubinstein; the acoustics are considered among the best in the world. The interior features an Italian Renaissance-style **central hall**, with a Carrara marble staircase, and the beautiful gilded and mirrored **Salón Dorado** (allegedly inspired by Versailles), which is used for smaller concerts, conferences and temporary theatre-related exhibitions. The stunning **auditorium** itself, which has an audience capacity of around 3500 (including standing room for 1000), is built in five tiers of balconies that culminate in a huge dome decorated with frescoes of ballerinas and musicians by Argentine artist Raúl Soldi and a 7m-wide bronze chandelier with a platform that allows singers literally to sing from on high. Note the boxes on either side of the orchestra pit: known as *palcos de viuda* (widows' boxes), they provided a discreet vantage point for women in mourning who were anxious not to miss out on cultural outings – a grille protected them from the public's gaze. The *palco presidencial*, for the private use of the Argentine president or city governor and guests, has its own entrance, bathrooms and phone line to the Casa Rosada. The Colón also has a huge basement, home to a series of workshops where the sets, props and costumes for the performances are assembled, which extends under Avenida 9 de Julio; these workshops are sometimes visited as part of the theatre tour.

Following extensive and protracted refurbishment it reopened on May 24, 2010 (two years later than originally planned), with a performance of Tchaikovsky's *Swan Lake* and the second act of Puccini's *La Bohème* as part of the gala performance on the eve of the bicentenary. Enquire at the box office (see p.189 for contact details) for guided visits and tickets for performances; it's located in the passageway that cuts north–south through the building, which in the past used to allow horse-drawn carriages access to the theatre.

Plaza Lavalle

A short walk northwest from the Obelisco along Avenida Roque Sáenz Peña takes you past a pretty row of fountains and patio cafés – popular places to take a coffee break or eat lunch – to **Plaza Lavalle**, which also backs onto the Teatro Colón above. Named for Juan Lavalle (a post-Independence political figure commemorated by a statue atop a tall marble column in the middle of the square), it is a pleasant green space notable for its fine collection of native and exotic trees, many of them over a hundred years old. Among the pines, magnolias and jacarandas stands an ancient *ceibo jujeño*, with stunning bright red blossoms in spring, planted by city mayor Torcuato de Alvear in 1870. There is also a fine collection of sculptures, some of politicians but also of musicians and actors, in recognition of the adjoining theatre; these include two ballet dancers performing *Swan Lake*, a homage to members of the Colón's *corps de ballet* who were killed in a plane accident in 1971 just hours after performing the famous ballet.

Although less famous than the Plaza de Mayo, this three-block-long plaza can nonetheless lay claim to its own share of the city's history. It began life as a public park, inaugurated in 1827 by British immigrants, and the following year provided the venue for the city's first funfair. In 1857, the square was the departure point for the first Argentine train journey, made by the locomotive *La Porteña* to Floresta, in the west of the capital. Just over thirty years later, in 1890, it was the scene of confrontations during a revolt against the government, also known as the Revolución del Parque. Over the last half century or so it's become practically synonymous with the city's law courts, which have gradually sprung up around it; the whole area is often referred to as **Tribunales**. The needs of the lawyers working here are catered for by numerous stallholders, who set up tables spread with pamphlets and second-hand books explaining every conceivable aspect of Argentine law.

The southern end of the square is dominated by the eclectic facade of the **Palacio de Justícia**, constructed in 1941 to house the **Supreme Court**, which until then had sat in the building that now holds the Banco Central (see p.64). This, the top court in the land, is appointed by the president of the day, with the Senate's backing, and – as in the US – the appointments are often controversial and are always heavily scrutinized by the media. The panel has traditionally consisted of five members, but was expanded to nine judges in the 1990s by Carlos Menem, who took the opportunity to fill the empty seats with his supporters, thus making the court virtually a rubber stamp for the government. Néstor Kirchner returned the number on the bench to five, made the selection process more transparent and elected judges from previously under-represented sections of society, including two women. The court building itself stands as something of a monument to architectural uncertainty, with a facade decorated in a loose and heavy-handed interpretation of Neoclassicism, adorned with pillars. There are no official tours, but you can normally walk inside during the day to admire the airy halls and white marble Corinthian columns; however, Supreme Court sessions are not open to the general public.

Just across the road from the Palacio de Justicia, at the corner of Talcahuano and Tucumán, look up to see one of the finest, albeit little-known, examples of Buenos Aires Art Nouveau, a pretty corner tower called the **Mirador Massué**. This was originally part of a building dating to 1909 that was demolished to make way for an ugly office block in the 1980s; it's the only part of that building that was preserved.

Sinagoga Central and Museo Judío

At the far northern end of Plaza Lavalle, at Libertad 785, lies the **Sinagoga Central de la Congregación Israelita de la República Argentina**, the non-Orthodox central synagogue of Argentina's Jewish population. Built between 1897 and 1932, the exterior is Byzantine in style. Visits (in English, French, German and Hebrew) are possible (Tues & Thurs 3–5.30pm only; closed on Jewish holi; free; take your passport – security is strict; ☎011/4123-0832) – guides will take you around the synagogue and attached small museum of Jewish culture, the **Museo Judío Dr Salvador Kibrick**, and explain the history of Buenos Aires' sizeable Jewish community (see box opposite). The museum contains religious artefacts, many of which were imported from Europe and donated from the private collection of local resident Dr Kibrick when he passed away in 1981. These include a variety of ritual objects, documents relating to the Diaspora in Argentina, Torahs and paintings.

Teatro Nacional Cervantes

The **Teatro Nacional Cervantes**, just across Avenida Córdoba from the synagogue, at Libertad 815, is rather overshadowed by the proximity of the goliath Teatro Colón, but is an important and attractive theatre in its own right, built in 1921 on

Jewish Buenos Aires

The first **Jewish immigrants** arrived in Buenos Aires from Western Europe around the middle of the nineteenth century; later, refugees fled here in large numbers from pogroms and persecution in Russia and Eastern Europe, and were commonly known as "*rusos*", a term still often used erroneously to refer to all Jews. Perón's government was one of the first to recognize the State of Israel, but he also halted Jewish immigration and infamously allowed Nazi war criminals to settle in Argentina, including Adolf Eichmann, the SS officer who masterminded the systematic massacre of Jews. Eichmann was later abducted from a Buenos Aires suburb by Israeli secret agents and whisked off to stand trial and execution in Jerusalem.

The Jewish community suffered particularly harshly during the 1976–83 dictatorship, when many Jews were among the *desaparecidos*, often because they were artists, intellectuals, left-wing sympathizers or anti-junta militants rather than for overtly religious reasons, although many junta members and torturers were openly anti-Semitic; it is estimated that over one thousand of the disappeared were Jewish. More recently, the Jewish community was the target of two of the country's most murderous **terrorist attacks**: a bomb explosion at the Israeli Embassy in 1992, in which around thirty died, and another at the headquarters of AMIA, the Argentine Jewish association, in 1994, which killed at least 86 people. No one has ever claimed responsibility for the attacks and the perpetrators have yet to be found, with locals who had been accused of complicity, including police, cleared in 2004. In 2006 Argentine prosecutors officially accused the Iranian government and Hezbollah of the crime, a charge Tehran adamantly denies, but nobody has ever been tried. A monument in Plaza Lavalle remembers those who lost their lives.

The Jewish **population** of Buenos Aires is now estimated at around 200,000, around half the size it was during its peak in the mid-twentieth century; economic woes have prompted many to emigrate to Israel and elsewhere. The more well-to-do reside in leafy Belgrano (see p.144), while the lower middle classes are concentrated in Once (see p.139), where you'll find most of the city's kosher restaurants, especially on the streets around Pueyrredón between Córdoba and Corrientes. Approximately eighty synagogues dot the city, along with more than seventy Jewish educational institutions. One of the most dynamic of these is the **Museo de la Shoá** at Montevideo 919 in Recoleta (⚑www.museodelholocausto.org.ar; ☎011/4811-3588; Mon–Thurs 11am–7pm, Fri till 4pm; bring ID; see map on p.107), which hosts excellent exhibitions of Jewish art, mostly relating to the Holocaust, and organizes seminars.

the initiative of two Spanish actors, María Guerrero and Fernando Díaz de Mendoza. As well as maintaining traditionally close ties to Spanish culture – lots of Spanish plays are put on here – its construction and decoration display a strong Spanish influence. The intricate exterior is an example of Plateresque, a richly adorned Spanish architectural style common in the early sixteenth century and named for its supposed similarity to fine silversmith's work. Inside, the theatre, which is also the seat for the national theatre studies institute, has a 1700-seat auditorium featuring Valencia tiles, Madrid textiles, Seville glassware and red Tarragona flagstones; much of this was reconstructed after a fire in 1961. A small museum (Mon–Fri 10am–6pm; free) features models of stage sets, photos of local actors and some rather woebegone costumes. There are no tours at present, but for details on attending performances, see p.188; in addition to plays for adults and children, the theatre also puts on free movie showings (Wed & Thurs 6pm).

Puerto Madero

B uenos Aires' newest and glossiest barrio, **Puerto Madero**, centres on a defunct port that now acts as a luxury yacht marina, nightlife hub and high-flying residential area rolled into one. Four enormous rectangular *diques* (docks) run parallel to the Río de la Plata, connecting the Dársena Sur (Southern Wharf) to the Dársena Norte (Northern Wharf). Lining these docks – numbered from south to north – is a series of beautifully restored brick and iron warehouses, originally used to store grain en route from the Pampas to points around the world, and now converted into a voguish mix of **restaurants** and cafés, luxury apartments and offices, plus a prestigious university. The barrio is ostentatiously prosperous and hasn't yet gained the patina of more historic neighbourhoods, but it's a fun place to stroll around or spend a lazy summer afternoon sitting by the marinas, watching yachts bob on the water and enjoying the gentle breeze off the river.

Opened in 1882, the port was named after **Eduardo Madero**, a local engineer and merchant. By 1898, even before construction was fully finished, though, Puerto Madero could not cope with both the increasing volume of maritime traffic and the growing size of ships. A new, larger port was built to the north (by Retiro, and still operational) leaving Puerto Madero an industrial relic, but in the 1990s private entrepreneurs realized the value of the fine Victorian structures and waterside ambience and began transforming it into a brand new barrio.

The most interesting development is on the western side of the docks, where you can visit two **museum ships** and two **art galleries**, one of which houses the finest private art collection on show in Latin America, the Colección de Arte Amalia Lacroze de Fortabat. Not so long ago much of the **eastern** bank was a derelict no-go area, but then a serious injection of private cash jump-started the creation of **Puerto Madero Este**, the city's newest highly desirable residential locale. Three luxury **hotels** dot the eastern side of the docks and are due to be joined by two or three more of the same ilk by around 2013, including a modern branch of the hyper-traditional *Alvear*. Officially known as the Avenida Costanera Doctor Tristán Achával Rodríguez, **the Costanera Sur**, a wide avenue that still retains traces of its former role as an elegant riverside walk, divides this built-up portion of the barrio from the **Reserva Ecológica Costanera Sur**, a wild nature reserve right at the city's edge. Popular with an eclectic mix of families, joggers, cyclists, bird-watchers and gay men cruising, the reserve allows a nature fix without leaving the confines of the city.

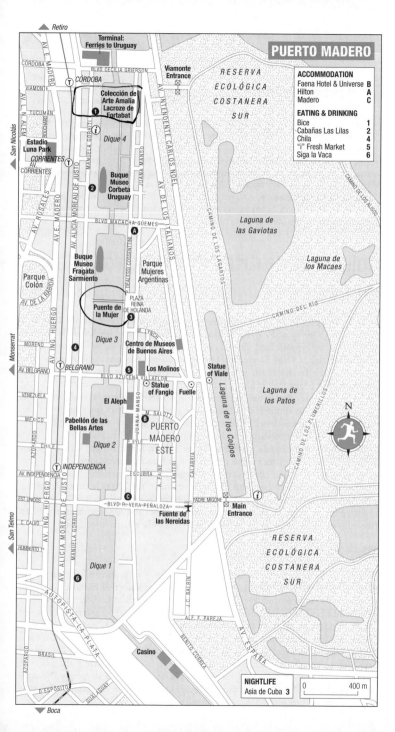

PUERTO MADERO

ACCOMMODATION
Faena Hotel & Universe **B**
Hilton **A**
Madero **C**

EATING & DRINKING
Bice **1**
Cabañas Las Lilas **2**
Chila **4**
"i" Fresh Market **5**
Siga la Vaca **6**

Retiro

Terminal:
Ferries to Uruguay

BLVD CECILIA GRIERSON

Viamonte
Entrance

CÓRDOBA

CÓRDOBA

VIAMONTE

TUCUMAN

Colección de
Arte Amalia
Lacroze de
Fortabat

San Nicolás

Estadio
Luna Park

CORRIENTES

AV.
CORRIENTES

Dique 4

RESERVA
ECOLÓGICA
COSTANERA
SUR

AV. E. MADERO

AV. L. N. ALEM

BOUCHARD

MANUELA GORRITI

AV. ALICIA MOREAU DE JUSTO

AV. INTENDENTE CARLOS NOEL

JUANA MANSO

AV. DE LOS ITALIANOS

Buque
Museo
Corbeta
Uruguay

BLVD MACACHA GÜEMES

AV. ROSALES

Parque
Colón

Buque
Museo
Fragata
Sarmiento

Parque
Mujeres
Argentinas

Laguna de
las Gaviotas

CAMINO DE LOS ALSOS

CAMINO DE LOS LAGARTOS

Laguna de
los Macaes

DEALESSI COSSENTINI

AV. DE LA RÁBIDA

AV. ING. HUERGO

Puente de
la Mujer

PLAZA
REINA
DE HOLANDA

Dique 3

Centro de Museos
de Buenos Aires

CAMINO DEL RÍO

M. LYNCH

MORENO

BELGRANO

Los Molinos

AV. BELGRANO

BLVD AZUCENA VILLAFLOR

Statue
of Fangio

Fuelle

Statue
of Viale

Laguna de
los Patos

VENEZUELA

El Aleph

M. SALOTTI

JUANA MANSO

Monserrat

MÉXICO

AZOPARDO

CHILE

Pabellón de las
Bellas Artes

Dique 2

PUERTO
MADERO
ESTE

P. EYLE

CAMINO DE LOS PLUMERILLOS

N

AV. INDEPENDENCIA

INDEPENDENCIA

AV. ING. HUERGO

AV. ALICIA MOREAU DE JUSTO

MANUELA GORRITI

ESCUBRA

A. PAINE

LANTERI

CALABRIA

Laguna de
los Coipos

EST. UNIDOS

San Telmo

C. CALVO

HUMBERTO 1°

BLVD R. VERA PEÑALOZA

PADRE MIGONE

Main
Entrance

Fuente de
las Nereidas

Dique 1

J. C. BALBIN

RESERVA
ECOLÓGICA
COSTANERA
SUR

AUTOPISTA LA PLATA

AZOPARDO

BRASIL

D'ESPÓSITO

GUAL EGUAY

Casino

ALF. F. PAREJA

BENITO CORREA

AV. ESPAÑA

NIGHTLIFE
Asia de Cuba **3**

0   400 m

Boca

Getting there and around

Puerto Madero seems off on a limb and **public transport** is limited; most residents have cars or chauffeurs. Yet it's easy to **walk** from the city centre – just head east along Belgrano, Juan Domingo Perón or Viamonte – though the train tracks that run its length, sandwiched between Avenida Alicia Moreau de Justo and Avenida Eduardo Madero, can be awkward to cross on foot. From the 1960s to 2007 these tracks were used only by freight trains, but then Celeris began operating the **Tren Liviano del Este** ("eastern light railway"), a shiny, air-conditioned passenger tram that runs silently along them, connecting Avenida Córdoba with Avenida Independencia (approximately every 10min Mon–Sat 8am–11pm, Sun 9am–10pm; $1; buy tickets at machines on platforms). The modern tram was a gift to the city from the French city of Mulhouse, where they were manufactured. With two intermediate stops where it crosses avenidas Corrientes and Belgrano, the tram is an excellent way to get from one end of the barrio's 24 blocks (nearly 3km) to the other. There are plans – sadly on hold – to extend the tramline north to Retiro and south to Boca.

Colección de Arte Amalia Lacroze de Fortabat

Since opening in 2008 the **Colección de Arte Amalia Lacroze de Fortabat** (Tues–Sun noon–9pm; $15; free guided visits in Spanish and English daily at 5pm; audioguide in Spanish and English $25; ☏011/4310-6600, ⓦwww.coleccion fortabat.org.ar) at Olga Cossettini 141, has become the barrio's star attraction. Located at the far northern end of the docks, it is housed in a purpose-built **pavilion** that looks rather like a giant sliding-top bread bin. A state-of-the-art blend of glass and aluminium (the sliding top is a retractable roof with protective panels that open as sunlight diminishes), the pavilion is in fact only the tip of the iceberg: below water level is a breathtakingly huge space showcasing the best private art collection on display in Latin America.

The owner is Ms Lacroze de Fortabat herself, born María Amalia Lacroze de los Reyes Oribe in 1921. After a classical education in Paris she married well, twice – first an Argentine lawyer and later a cement magnate, Alfredo Fortabat, whose immense fortune she inherited in the 1970s, making her one of the 200 richest people on the planet according to Forbes. She sold the Loma Negra cement works in 2005, in order to set up the art museum, while a large fraction of her fortune (estimated at around two billion dollars) is spent on charitable works, mainly education-related.

The collection

The art collection itself, displayed on several tiers, is dominated by Argentine works, mostly from the twentieth century, while a number of European and US artists are also represented. Perhaps the surest sign of Amalia Lacroze de Fortabat's importance both as a personality and art collector is her 1960 **portrait** by Andy Warhol that kicks off the display, alongside two earlier portraits by Catalan painter Vidal-Quadras. Other international stars to look out for include Chagall, Dali and Klimt, while a fine Rodin bronze, *L'Age d'airain*, catches the eye. Jan Brueghel I and Pieter Brueghel II each has a painting in the collection, while the place of honour must go to *Juliet and her Nurse*, a magnificent oil depicting Venice's St Mark's Square by **Turner**, which manages to dominate the main exhibition room, a splendid unadorned space the length of a city block.

Argentina's strong women

Wandering the few streets that line the wharves of Puerto Madero, you may notice something unusual: most of them bear the names of **women**. This innovation dates from a debate on constitutional reform in 1994, in which members of Congress (a high proportion of whom are female) brought up the need for a little redress-in the matter of civic designations – in particular the fact that most Porteño streets are named for politicians (virtually all male), generals, dates and battles. The following year a committee decreed that the streets of the city's newest barrio should honour female achievers from Argentina and other Latin American countries. These include **Juana Manso**, a playwright and pioneer of co-ed schooling in Argentina; **Alicia Moreau de Justo**, who, though born in London, was one of the first Argentine women to enter politics; **Azucena Villaflor**, the founder of the Madres de la Plaza de Mayo movement (see box, p.49), who was disappeared herself in 1977; **Macacha Güemes**, active in the Argentine struggle for independence; **Cecilia Grierson**, born in the 1850s, and the first South American woman to earn a medical degree; **Aimé Paine**, a singer of Mapuche origins; and **Juana Manuela Gorriti**, a nineteenth-century writer and early feminist. Continuing the theme is the **Puente de la Mujer** and a new, if as yet rather bare, green space to the east of the development at Dock Three in Puerto Madero Este, called the **Parque Mujeres Argentinas** ("Argentine Women Park"). It is only fitting that the barrio's major attraction should be a fabulous art gallery housing a collection owned by, Amalia Lacroze de Fortabat, one of the country's wealthiest and most influential businesswomen.

This is where you'll find most of the country's major nineteenth- and twentieth-century artists represented, many of them strongly influenced by European artistic movements such as impressionism (for example, Fernando Fader's *Entre duraznos floridos* – "Among peach trees in blossom", 1915) and symbolism (several works by Xul Solar), while others depict famous sights in European cities such as Venice (see Rómulo Macció's *Puente de los Suspiros* – "Bridge of Sighs", 1998) or London (Nicolás García Uriburu's *Coloration of Trafalgar Square Fountains*, 1974). Several developed their own idiosyncratic styles, though – especially as the twentieth century advanced: a lot of the works by leading artist Antonio Berni (1905–81) are typically *criollo* (native), depicting among other things a rustic lunch or a country girl fondling a pumpkin. Uruguayans Blanes and Figari, often lumped together with Argentine artists, also get a look-in: the former's *La cautiva* ("The captive girl", 1880) is a scene from Argentina's own Wild West while the latter's *En el patio* ("In the patio", undated) is a colonial vignette. Other names to track down are Carlos Alonso, Libero Badii, Raquel Forner, Emilio Pettoruti and Benito Quinquela Martín.

The museum has a **café**, *La Colección*, with a separate entrance next door – the menu is limited but its terrace overlooking the water is a great place to relax and people watch.

The docks

Of the four **docks**, the two northernmost, Four and Three, are where you'll find the main sights, not least the world-class Colección Fortabat (see above), plus most of the best restaurants. Pedestrian **walkways** conveniently flank the length of all four docks: the eastern side is planted with young jacarandas, covered in purple flowers in November.

Dock Four

Enter the western walkway at its northern extreme, where Avenida Córdoba reaches the riverside, and a short stroll south along **Dock Four** brings you to the first of Puerto Madero's museum ships, the well-maintained **Buque Museo Corbeta ARA Uruguay** (daily 10am–7pm; $2), built at the Cammell Laird shipyard in Liverpool in 1874. This was the Argentine navy's first training ship, and is one of its oldest vessels still afloat. The *Uruguay*'s finest hour came in 1903, when it rescued a Swedish scientific expedition stuck in Antarctic ice; photos of this exploit, as well as other moments in the boat's history, are displayed on its deck. Decommissioned in 1929, the boat was used as a powder storehouse until 1945, when, though no longer of practical use, the government decided it should not be allowed to rot. Restoration followed: the boat was granted national monument status in 1963, and it's now immaculately well kept – the brass fittings and wooden deck always gleam.

Dock Three

Puerto Madero's most photographed sight (especially at night when it is lit), a striking white footbridge known as the **Puente de la Mujer** (Women's Bridge), sweeps across **Dock Three** halfway along. Unveiled in 2001, the bridge, designed by Spanish architect Santiago Calatrava, is a fitting symbol for Buenos Aires' renaissance, while its graceful curve, echoing the outstretched leg of a tango dancer, also serves as a reminder of the city's rich heritage. The central suspended section can rotate ninety degrees to allow tall boats to pass. At the eastern end of the bridge a ruined grain silo, another vestige of the harbour's distant past, tragically destined for the wrecking-ball, stands vigil over the decorative Plaza Reina de Holanda – a tribute to the Queen of the Netherlands featuring a fountain and statue are its main features. Beyond, the landscaped **Parque Mujeres Argentinas** (see box, p.75) further reinforces the femininity of the barrio's toponyms.

Dock Three is home to another museum boat, the **Buque Museo Fragata ARA Presidente Sarmiento** (daily 10am–7pm; $2). This clipper, also built in Liverpool, served as a training ship for the Argentine navy between 1899 and 1961. Making 37 journeys around the world, it witnessed many notable historical events, such as the opening of the Panama Canal, and played host to such figures as Germany's Kaiser Wilhelm, Tsar Nicholas II of Russia, US President William Taft and English King Edward VII. After 1939 the boat remained in the waters of the Río de la Plata, making short trips for cadet training, until it was finally fitted as a museum boat in 1964. You can step below deck to admire the huge ships' wheels, steam room (it had a back-up 1800-horsepower steam engine) and cabin quarters, preserved with their original furnishings. There are also some strange, miscellaneous exhibits from the vessel's expeditions around the world, including a chunk from the Great Wall of China and the embalmed body of a dog that was once the ship's mascot.

Docks Two and One

The western side of **Dock Two** belongs to the city's prestigious (and expensive) Catholic university, the Universidad Católica Argentina, which has opened an art gallery here, the **Pabellón de las Bellas Artes** (Tues–Sun 11am–7pm; free; ⓣ011/4338-0801, ⓦwww.uca.edu.ar/esp/sec-pba/index.php). This space shows temporary exhibits of Argentine art lent by private owners, with the carefully selected works often including pieces from artists such as Xul Solar and Rogelio Yrurtia. Classical music recitals also occasionally take place here; enquire at the museum to see if there are any coming up.

Dock One is still in the early stages of development, with a few cafés, restaurants and shops interspersed with building sites where tower blocks are mushrooming. Just beyond it in the Dársena Sur, the wharf that links with Boca, floats the city's **casino** (☎011/4363-3100, ⓦwww.casinopuertomadero.com.ar) on a faux, neon-lit steamship and another vessel for slot machines. Referred to simply as the "*casino flotante*", this is the only casino inside the city limits, and the slot machines and card tables stay open around the clock. Vans take prospective customers to the casino front entrance from the intersection of Córdoba and Alem, (every 15min, 24hr).

Puerto Madero Este

Crossing via Boulevard Azucena Villaflor, between docks Two and Three, or Boulevard R. Vera Peñaloza, between docks One and Two, will take you directly into **Puerto Madero Este**. This sub-barrio is not just a line of converted warehouses – instead, it has a grid of streets that extends east as far as the Costanera Sur (see p.79). From the 1890s to the late 1990s it was an unappealing mix of derelict industrial space, wasteland and shantytowns, but developers have seized on its potential, surrounded as it is by water and nature, yet still so close to the city centre. Puerto Madero Este's streets bristle with elegant apartment blocks and a forest of less elegant but equally expensive high-rise monolith *torres* (towers). Part of Puerto Madero Este's popularity among the local jet set and foreign investors comes from the tight security of all these developments. As a result, it's perhaps not surprising that the area lacks street life, although a few chi-chi restaurants and neighbourhood stores have started to appear, and there's a lot of building work still going on.

The landmark site on this side of the docks is the **Faena Hotel & Universe** (see p.152), an extravagant hotel in a converted grain warehouse. The main entrance is at Marta Salotti 445; you might drop in to admire the surreal stylings of Philippe Starck, have a drink in the *belle époque* bar (*Library Lounge*) or splash out on a gourmet pizza amid the kitsch and antiques in *El Mercado* restaurant.

Boulevard Azucena Villaflor

As mentioned above, **Boulevard Azucena Villaflor**, between docks Two and Three, is one of several ways of reaching Puerto Madero Este and the Costanera Sur (see below). Along it and at its far eastern end are four monuments that add interest to an otherwise slightly bland district of the city. The first, a large beige building called **Los Molinos**, at the corner with Juana Manso, is a converted century-old flour mill, belonging to the Faena group, which when completed will feature an auditorium and art gallery; one of its external walls will be decorated with murals by leading artist Pablo Siquier. The second, nearby on the central pavement at the intersection with Aimé Paine, is a bronze homage to **Juan Manuel Fangio**, Formula One world champion in the 1950s and one of the country's greatest sportsmen (see box, p.213).

Next comes **Fuelle** known popularly as fuelle, a five-metre-tall, two-tonne steel sculpture reminiscent of a bandoneón (literally "bellows"), intended as an abstract monument to tango. Standing at the crossroads of Azucena Villaflor and Avenida de los Italianos, it is the work of artist Estela Treviño and her son Alejandro Coria.

Last but not least, right at the end of the boulevard, at its junction with the Costanera, a semi circular pergola crowns steps leading down to what once was the main *balneario*, now paved over but still enjoyed by picnicking families; there is a statue here of local hero **Luis Viale**, who clutches a life vest – the story goes that sometime around the end of the nineteenth century Viale drowned when a ship sank in nearby waters, having given up his vest to save a pregnant woman.

Costanera Sur

The **Costanera Sur**, originally built as a riverside promenade around 1900, runs diagonally along the eastern edge of the residential portion of Puerto Madero. In its heyday, Porteños would come to this wide avenue to escape the summer heat – to stroll past elegant balustrades by the Río de la Plata, to drink a coffee or beer in one of the many *confiterías*, to be entertained by buskers and to bathe in the designated gender-separated areas, the *balnearios*. The area declined in the 1960s as residents began shifting their attentions towards the Costanera Norte (see p.137), then essentially lost its *raison d'être* in the 1970s, when the government devised a project, based on the Dutch polders, to reclaim land from the river. Dykes were constructed here and the water drawn off, but the project was never completed, leaving the suddenly inaptly named Costanera cut off from the river – the drained land became the Reserva Ecológica (see p.79).

Officially called **Avenida Costanera Doctor Tristán Achával Rodríguez** (which segues into Avenida Intendente Carlos Noel as it moves north), the promenade runs from Padre Mignone (the extension of Boulevard R. Vera Peñaloza) to the private Yacht Club Puerto Madero (by the Buquebus terminal at Dársena Norte). It's been spruced up and, although it no longer boasts the genteel character of yesteryear, it has nonetheless retained many of its original features, making for an interesting stroll if you're in the area – it is lined with countless stands vending cold drinks, ice cream and hotdogs plus the odd *asado* whose meaty aromas fill the air on warm afternoons and evenings.

Set back from the Costanera at Avenida de los Italianos 851, just north of the junction with Boulevard Azucena Villaflor, stands a white Edwardian-style construction which, in its heyday in the 1920s and 1930s, housed the popular *Cervecería Munich*. Now it holds the **Centro de Museos de Buenos Aires** (closed for repairs at time of writing so call ahead; ☎011/4516-0944), the city's museum directorate HQ. In recent years, the centre has been the focal point for the "Noche de los Museos" (see p.223 for details).

Heading south from the Centro de Museos along Avenida Tristán Achával Rodríguez for about half a kilometre will take you to the entrance of the Reserva Ecológica, approximately on a level with the bridge dividing docks One and Two. One of the city's greatest monuments, the flamboyant **Fuente de las Nereidas**, crowns a roundabout at the junction with Boulevard Vera Peñaloza, just outside the entrance to the nature reserve. Protected by glass and railings, this large and elaborate marble fountain was created by the renowned sculptress Lola Mora in 1902. Originally destined for the Plaza de Mayo, it was placed in this out-of-the-way location because its seductive display – a naked Venus perched on the edge of a shell supported by two straining Nereids (sea nymphs), and three Tritons struggling to restrain horses among the waves – was deemed too risqué to be in such proximity to the cathedral.

Reserva Ecológica Costanera Sur

The **Reserva Ecológica Costanera Sur** (Tues–Sun April–Oct 8am–5.45pm; Nov–March till 6.45pm; free; ☎011/4315-4129; ⓦwww.reservacostanera.com .ar) offers an unexpectedly natural environment just minutes from the fury of the city centre. It's easy to imagine this sizeable chunk of wild and watery grassland – about 350 hectares, stretching for 2km alongside the Costanera – to be an oddly neglected remnant of the landscape that greeted Pedro de Mendoza as he sailed into the estuary in the sixteenth century. Its origins, however, are far more recent, and quite accidental. After the polders project of the 1970s and 1980s was abandoned, seeds borne by the wind from other parts of the city took root in the silt left behind here. Before long, the land was covered in vegetation and teeming with wildlife. To the city government's credit, the area was swiftly made into a nature reserve. Nowadays, the Reserva Ecológica is a strange and wonderful place where the juxtaposition of urban and natural is a recurring theme, whether it means glimpsing factory chimneys through fronds of pampas grass or the capital's skyline over a lake populated by ducks and herons. It's an excellent place to take a break from the hustle and bustle of the city streets. Plans are afoot to privatize the reserve, which would probably mean it would no longer be free to enter – but they face strong opposition from locals.

Just inside the reserve's main entrance, at Avenida Costanera Doctor Tristán Achával Rodríguez 1550 and Padre Mignone (the continuation of Boulevard Vera Peñaloza), a **visitors' centre** (same hours as reserve) displays panels explaining the park's development and serves as the starting point for ranger-guided **walks** (Sat & Sun 10.30am & 3.30pm) on some of the park's many trails. It is useful to know that there is a secondary entrance/exit at the northern end of the reserve, on a level with Calle Viamonte. It's worth keeping a lookout for the nocturnal tours occasionally offered at full moons, when, weather permitting, you can spot all manner of creatures, mainly birds, that keep a low daytime profile. If you want to see around the park independently, a walk around its entire perimeter will require the best part of two hours; following the path around the Laguna de los Patos provides a satisfying stroll in around half that time. There is a picnic area in the reserve and plenty of benches.

A surprising diversity of flora and fauna reside in the park, with over two hundred species of **birds** visiting during the year. Aquatic species include ducks, herons, elegant black-necked swans, skittish coots and the common gallinule, similar to the coot but distinguished by the way it propels itself through the water with a jerking back and forth of the head. You may also see the snail hawk, a bird of prey that uses its hooked beak to pluck freshwater snails out of their shells. The park hosts several species of small mammals as well, such as the easily spotted **coypu**, an aquatic rodent, and reptiles such as monitor lizards. The reserve's vegetation includes willows and Argentina's national tree, the **ceibo**, or coral tree – a tall species with a twisted trunk and luxuriant stems of red flowers. The most dominant plant, however, is the *cortadera*, or pampas grass, whose razor-sharp leaves and flossy blooms flourish in the reserve's fertile soil.

San Telmo

t's impossible not to be seduced by the cobbled streets of **San Telmo**, the most attractive of the southern barrios. Described by Borges in his short story *El Sur* as "an older, more solid world" (than the northern barrios, he meant), the streets and buildings here convey an impression of decaying luxury – though sometimes the decay seems to outweigh the luxury. This is the result of a kind of "gentrification in reverse": in the early nineteenth century, San Telmo was the neighbourhood of choice for wealthy landowners, who built grand mansions here, only to abandon them for the fresher air of northern Buenos Aires after a major yellow fever epidemic in 1871. The houses they left behind were put to a new use, as landlords keen to make a quick buck from the waves of immigrants then arriving in the city from Europe converted the buildings into crowded and unhealthy **conventillos** (tenements). Unlike in the northern, central and western sections of the city – which were variously torn down, smartened up or otherwise modernized in the early twentieth century – in San Telmo the effect of this loss of cachet was to preserve many of the barrio's original features: the new inhabitants simply adapted the buildings here to their needs. It remains largely a working-class area today, but its superb architecture also attracts bohemians, students, backpackers and artists. This, together with the arrival of designer clothing and home decor stores among the barrio's traditional **antiques shops**, seems to indicate that San Telmo's status may be on the rise once again – even boutique hotels have opened up for business.

San Telmo is a small square-shaped barrio bounded to the north by Avenida Chile, to the west by Calle Chacabuco, to the east by Avenida Ingeniero Huergo and to the south by Parque Lezama and Avenida Caseros. Just wandering the barrio's streets, admiring its beautiful old houses, traditional bars, markets and antique shops, can easily fill an afternoon. The central square, **Plaza Dorrego**, is the favoured destination for visitors, who come on Sundays for its fascinating and highly popular **antiques fair**. In the streets near the plaza are the barrio's other main stand-alone attractions, among them a lovely parish church, an impressive reconstruction of a *conventillo*, an art museum and the local food market. The neighbourhood also has many marvellous little colourful nooks and crannies, best exemplified by an alleyway known as the **Pasaje San Lorenzo**, a bustling shopping arcade in a converted mansion called the **Pasaje de la Defensa**, and a labyrinth of arts and crafts stores named the **Solar de French**. At the southern end of the barrio, by the border with Boca, tranquil **Parque Lezama** is a good spot for observing local life, and home to the national history museum, as well as a Russian Orthodox church – and more bars. San Telmo is also the area of the city most associated with **tango**, and many of the best-known tango shows and bars lie within its boundaries.

EATING & DRINKING

647 Dinner Club	4
Abuela Pan	3
Amici Miei	10
El Baqueano	1
Bar Británico	14
Café San Juan	13
Del Limonero	8
Gibraltar	6
Naturaleza Sabia	9
Plaza Dorrego Bar	11
La Poesia	2
Pride Café	7
La Vinería de Gualterio Bolívar	5

NIGHTLIFE

Mitos Argentinos	12

ACCOMMODATION

Babel	C
Buenos Ayres Hostel	B
Circus Hostel	D
El Hostal de San Telmo	E
Mansión Dandi Royal	G
Mansión Vitraux	F
Ostinatto Hostel	A
Los Tres Reyes	H

You could simply **walk** to San Telmo from the centre via Calle Defensa, but if you are coming from elsewhere you could also take the **subte** to Independencia or San Juan.

Plaza Dorrego and around

San Telmo's focal point is **Plaza Dorrego**, linked to the Plaza de Mayo by Calle Defensa, the neighbourhood's major north–south artery. Dorrego itself is also by far the best-known attraction in the barrio, thanks to its Sunday **antiques fair**, the **Feria de San Pedro Telmo**, when visitors wend their way past spray-painted artists and buskers to search through stalls of bric-a-brac. Within a few blocks you'll also find two handsome **churches** – traditional Iglesia de San Pedro Telmo and more unusual Iglesia Dinamarquesa; a busy produce **market**, the Mercado Municipal; a restored former mansion called **El Zanjón de Granados**; **tango bars**; crumbling facades along the **Pasaje San Lorenzo**; bric-a-brac at the

Arte de filete, or fileteado

As you wander around San Telmo, look out for examples of **arte de filete**, particularly over doorways and on shop signs. Characterized by ornate lettering, heavy shading and the use of scrolls and flowers entwined with the azure and white ribbons of the national flag, this distinctive art form, also sometimes referred to as **fileteado**, first made its appearance on the city transport system in the early twentieth century. Often associated with tango, its actual origins are likewise a little murky, but it seems to have been introduced by Italian immigrants. Banned from public transport in 1975 – the authorities at the time felt bus destinations and numbers should be clear and unadorned – it moved onto signs above stores and cafés as well as more traditional canvases. Today it is synonymous with Porteño identity, particularly in the south of the city. As well as tango stars, a popular subject for the *filete* artist is the pithy saying, including the classic "*si bebe para olvidar, paga antes de tomar*" ("if you drink to forget, pay first") and the rather more obscure "*si querés la leche fresca, atá la vaca a la sombre*" ("if you want fresh milk, tie the cow up in the shade"). A number of *filete* artists sell their wares at the Sunday antiques market in Plaza Dorrego – one name to look out for is Alfredo Martínez (Ⓦ www.fileteportenio.com).

Pasaje de la Defensa; some quirky arts and crafts shops in the **Solar de French**; and, since late 2010, the city's reborn modern art museum.

Plaza Dorrego

As large as it seems on weekends, when it heaves with people, **Plaza Dorrego**, at the corner of Defensa and Humberto 1°, is really a tiny square. It's also one of the city's oldest plazas, serving for much of the nineteenth century as the location for an open-air food market. Nowadays it's surrounded by elegant mansions, many of which have been converted into bars, antiques shops and restaurants. Most days see the square filled with tables from these establishments, which can be very agreeable places to dine on a summer's evening, when the trees are brilliant with fairy lights and someone with a bandoneón provides some background tango. Some of the bars are renowned sites in their own right, notably the *Plaza Dorrego Bar* (see p.179) on the southeast corner, whose wooden tables are great places to sip a beer and admire life in the slow lane.

On Sunday the tables are cleared away and the Plaza Dorrego becomes the setting for the city's long-running antiques market, the **Feria de San Pedro Telmo** (10am–5pm; Ⓦ www.feriadesantelmo.com), operated by the Museo de la Ciudad (see p.52). Competition for one of the two hundred-odd stalls is fierce: a lottery occurs every three months, to shake up the composition of the market; once a stall is secured, rules that all goods must date from before the 1970s and that the owner must run the stall in person are strictly enforced. The items for sale vary widely, but most tend towards the smaller side – glassware, ceramics, military ephemera, coins, cameras, toys, clothing, books and the like. Highlights include ornate antique *mates*, pieces of *filete* art (see box above), jewel-coloured soda siphons and old-fashioned ticket machines from the city's buses. The whole thing makes for fascinating browsing, but serious shoppers can check the website beforehand (Spanish only) to see the current stalls listed by name and type of item. Be forewarned, though: there are no real bargains to be had – the stall-holders and habitués are far too canny to let a gem slip through their fingers – but among the market's quirky jumble you might just find your own unique souvenir of Buenos Aires. Note that the market's pickpockets are very canny, too, so be careful with your belongings.

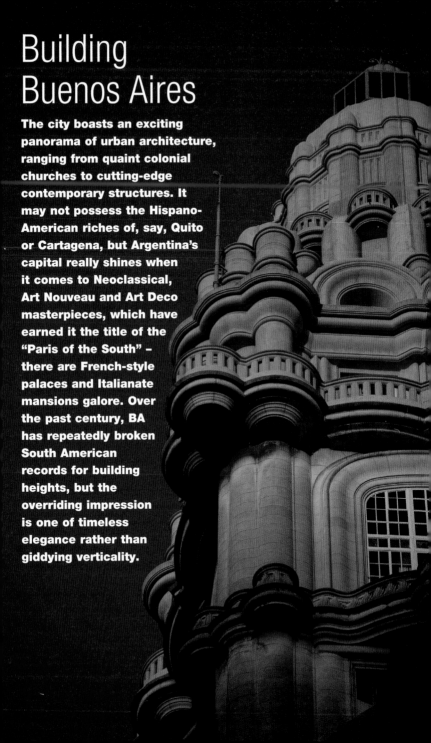

Building Buenos Aires

The city boasts an exciting panorama of urban architecture, ranging from quaint colonial churches to cutting-edge contemporary structures. It may not possess the Hispano-American riches of, say, Quito or Cartagena, but Argentina's capital really shines when it comes to Neoclassical, Art Nouveau and Art Deco masterpieces, which have earned it the title of the "Paris of the South" – there are French-style palaces and Italianate mansions galore. Over the past century, BA has repeatedly broken South American records for building heights, but the overriding impression is one of timeless elegance rather than giddying verticality.

Colonial vestiges

There were no brickworks in Buenos Aires before the 1680s and no nearby quarries, so the earliest buildings put up by the Spanish were made of fragile **adobe** (mud-brick) and lasted only a couple of decades at the most. One of the first edifices to have benefited from the brick-ovens was the city's oldest existing church, **San Ignacio**, part of the historic **Manzana de las Luces**, a complex of Jesuit buildings in Monserrat that now incorporates a market and school. Begun in 1675, it was not completed until the 1720s – and altered around 1850 – hence the hotchpotch of styles, though its facade is overwhelmingly **Baroque**.

Slightly younger – and rather more homogenous in appearance – is the **Basílica de Nuestra Señora del Pilar** (1732), the main vestige of the Franciscan convent (or place for "recollection") that gave its name to the barrio of Recoleta. Look out for the blue glazed tiles from **Calais**, France, decorating the cupola atop the campanile. The interior of the Pilar basilica is certainly sober; for a more sumptuous interior visit the **Basílica de Nuestra Señora de la Merced**, in neighbouring San Nicolás. Contemporary with the Pilar church, La Merced is well worth seeing for its **rococo altar** and fine stained-glass windows, one of which portrays San Martín de Tours, the city's patron saint.

The best example of **secular** colonial architecture still standing is the **Cabildo**. The erstwhile government house, featuring elegant white arches, is the mid-eighteenth-century work of Andrea Bianchi (aka **Andrés Blanqui**), a Jesuit architect from Italy. He worked on all the above-mentioned buildings, making him the most important architect in colonial Buenos Aires.

Basílica de Nuestra Señora del Pilar ▲
Basílica de Nuestra Señora de la Merced ▼

From independence to centenary

Following Argentine **independence** (1810) every field of public life was torn between asserting a national identity and imitating anything **European**. For well over a century, architecture followed the latter route, which explains the plethora of **Neoclassical**, **Art Nouveau** and **Art Deco** buildings that lend the city its smart elegance. Of the last style, the outstanding example is the grandiose **Mercado de Abasto**, now a shopping mall, while Art Nouveau is represented by dozens of buildings dotted around the city. Some of the finest line **Avenida Rivadavia** – look out for the intricate carving at no. 3216.

Like other countries that gained nationhood at the same time, Argentina often looked to **Ancient Greece** and **Rome** for inspiration when creating its new institutions. The **Congreso** building, with its majestic cupola, falls clearly into that category, as does the unmistakeably

▲ The Congreso Nacional

▼ Mercado de Abasto

Iconic BA buildings

▶▶ **Teatro Colón** Not only is Buenos Aires' bombastic opera house an architectural wonder, it also epitomizes the city's Italian roots and Gallic flair. p.69

▶▶ **La Prensa** One of the great Avenida de Mayo landmarks, the former newspaper HQ is a fine example of Bellas Artes architecture, its cupola topped with a bronze figure of Athena. p.55

▶▶ **Palacio de las Aguas Corrientes** Its facade studded with glazed Royal Doulton ceramics, this magnificent former waterworks is one of the city's most unusual buildings. p.141

▶▶ **Casa Rosada** The presidential palace, with its patented pink paint, is one of BA's most famous buildings – but is it thanks to Evita or Madonna? p.48

Neoclassical **Catedral Metropolitana**, with its austere Corinthian columns. The **Beaux Arts** (or "Bellas Artes") movement, whose iconic paragon is the Opéra Garnier in Paris, also came into its own. Firmly rooted in classical tradition, with touches of **Italian Renaissance** and **Mitteleuropa Baroque**, this eclectic school produced landmark buildings, like the **La Prensa** and the **Palacio San Martín**.

Ever higher

When the fourteen-storey **Galería Güemes** (87m) was completed in 1915, it was the tallest building in South America, a record broken successively by the city's **Palacio Barolo** (100m) and the **Edificio Kavanagh** (120m). In recent years, competition has mainly focused on the thrusting new barrio of **Puerto Madero** – though skyscrapers elsewhere on the continent are fierce rivals. As the race continues for the country's tallest building all eyes are on the **Hotel Único**, due to scrape in at 250m if it ever gets finished.

High-rise buildings, Puerto Madero ▲

Edificio Kavanagh ▼

Modern marvels

▸▸ **Edificio Barolo** (1919–23) An eclectic wonder, the Barolo was planned to suit its magnate patron's obsession with Dante. p.57

▸▸ **Edificio Kavanagh** (1935) BA's answer to NYC's Flatiron Building, this elegant tower is still one of the city's top des res addresses. p.97

▸▸ **Biblioteca Nacional** (1992) A 1960s design, the love-it-or-hate-it brutalist national library has been likened to a cuboid toadstool. p.117

▸▸ **MALBA** (2001) This luminous museum of Latin American art is the finest example of contemporary architecture in the city. p.125

Plaza Dorrego is also – weather permitting – the setting for free outdoor **milongas** (see box, p.193), the best of which is held in the southwestern corner of the square on Sunday afternoon, really taking off about the time when many of the stallholders start to pack their wares away (4 or 5pm). The idea is to teach tourists more about the history of the dance and its different steps – and there is a certain amount of audience participation.

The length of Calle Defensa running through the barrio is closed to traffic on Sundays, and the Feria spills all along it, although the goods on sale at the makeshift pavement stalls tend towards **arts and crafts** of varying quality rather than real antiques. Buskers and human statues add to the colour and noise – some of the tango performers are excellent and you can pick up a souvenir CD.

Iglesia de San Pedro Telmo

Just around the corner from Plaza Dorrego, at Humberto 1° 340, stands the **Iglesia de San Pedro Telmo** (Mon–Sat 8am–noon & 4–8pm, Sun 8am–8pm), recognizable for its prettily eclectic facade – a melange of post-colonial, Baroque and Neoclassical influences, crowned with blue- and white-tiled bell towers and adorned with statues and an image of San Pedro Telmo, namesake of the barrio. The church, whose full name is the Iglesia de Nuestra Señora de Belén Parroquia de San Pedro Telmo, was originally constructed by the Jesuits in 1734, making it one of the oldest structures in Buenos Aires, though the octagonal embellishments to the steeples and cupola were added in the late nineteenth century. After the Jesuits were expelled from Spanish America in 1767, the building was occupied by the Bethlehemite order; they used it as a hospital during the English invasions of 1811, tending to both the Argentine and British wounded – the marble table in the sacristy served as an operating table.

Attached to the church is the Jesuit cloister, housing the **Museo San Telmo** (Sat 10.30am–12.30pm, Sun 3.30–6.30pm; guided tour Sun 4pm; free) where you can see a small display of historical items from the building's various incarnations – prominent are some pieces of eighteenth-century Jesuit furniture, original *muslera* tiles (ceramic tiles moulded on a person's upper leg, named for the Spanish *muslo*, or thigh) and a clock donated by British Colonel Dennis Pack, in gratitude for the Bethlehemite brothers' medical attention to his troops.

Solar de French

Named for Colonel Patricio Domingo M. French, an Independence hero who once lived on the site, **Solar de French**, at Defensa 1066, just opposite Plaza Dorrego, has a decidedly Mediterranean feel about it – with its maze of white-washed passages garlanded with bougainvilleas, hibiscus and palms. In contrast to the surrounding antiques and bric-a-brac shops and stores, this enticing arcade specializes in modern arts and crafts, many of them unusual and making original gifts at more accessible prices than most of the wares on offer nearby. The building dates from the early twentieth century.

Mercado Municipal

Heading north along Defensa from Plaza Dorrego will take you past a row of antiques stores and cafés. In the block between Carlos Calvo and Estados Unidos you'll pass the Italianate facade of the **Mercado Municipal** (Mon–Sat 7am–2pm & 4.30–9pm, Sun 7am–2pm). A thriving indoor food market since the 1890s, it's now one of the few of its kind left in the city, still resisting the advance of the supermarkets. Inside, you'll find a great illustration of Argentina's bountiful interior, with rows of stalls piled high with fruit and vegetables, whole fish and racks of salami – this is a great place to pick up picnic supplies. Some of the sea of antiques and jumble sold around the rest of the neighbourhood is encroaching here, too, and you'll see stalls selling various non-comestible items.

Iglesia Dinamarquesa

A reflection of the neighbourhood's melange of European influences, the Lutheran **Iglesia Dinamarquesa** or **Dansk Kirke** (℡011/4362-9154, ⓦwww .iglesiadinamarquesa.com.ar), two blocks away at Carlos Calvo 257, features a stepped Neo-Gothic facade that would look perfectly at home in Copenhagen. Designed in the 1930s by Danish architects, the church is the centre of Buenos Aires' Danish community. In addition to the occasional Mass in Danish, Norwegian and Spanish, it also hosts other Scandinavian-themed cultural activities, such as dances, choir practice, book groups and film showings. Hours of all the above vary from week to week, so check the website or call for times if you're interested in stopping by.

El Zanjón de Granados

El Zanjón de Granados, Defensa 755 (guided visits hourly Mon–Fri 11am–3pm, Sun 1–5pm; $30–50; reservations advisable on ℡011/4361-3002, ⓦwww.elzanjon .com.ar), is a privately financed reconstruction of a site that was first a patrician mansion and later a *conventillo*. Visitors can view this model of the barrio's past on excellent guided tours, which take in the building's sunlit patio, cisterns – used by the tenement dwellers as ovens – and basement; the underground spaces allow you to see where the city's street level sat in 1700, as well as a 120m-long labyrinth of tunnels through which one of the city's rivers once flowed (*zanjón* means ditch). Immaculately rebuilt and tastefully lit, these brick tunnels are the highlight of the visit – they're somewhat reminiscent of a winery cellar in appearance and, indeed, are sometimes used for wine-tastings and private events.

Pasaje San Lorenzo and around

Almost opposite the entrance to El Zanjón, you'll find one of the barrio's most charming streets, the **Pasaje San Lorenzo**. A small alley running for just two blocks east of Defensa, it's lined with typically colourful, crumbling San Telmo houses. You'll pass art workshops, youth hostels and all sorts of cafés along here, as well as a crafts market at weekends. At no. 380 stands the **Casa Mínima**, whose presence on every tourist's must-visit list is out of all proportion to its interest: its most noteworthy feature is that it's the narrowest building in Buenos Aires – its 2.17m front is just wide enough to accommodate a doorway. Legend has it that the house was constructed by liberated slaves on a sliver of land given to them by their former masters in the early nineteenth century, but in truth it's probably just a section of the block that remained standing after successive remodelling work on the surrounding buildings. Said to have been inhabited by a fisherman for decades, later home to a reclusive artist and then left to decay, it was finally given a lick of paint in 2006 and its interior can sometimes be visited as part of the tours run by the same organization responsible for El Zanjón (see p.83 – Mon–Fri 10.30am–4pm).

At the eastern end of Pasaje San Lorenzo you'll find a cluster of **tango bars**, the most famous of which is *El Viejo Almacén*, on the corner of Independencia and Balcarce. Originally the site of a neighbourhood store (hence the name), then a hospital, it was turned into a restaurant in 1900, and finally took on its current incarnation in 1968, when it was founded by Edmundo Rivero, one of Argentina's most revered tango singers, renowned for his gruff style and *lunfardo* classics. For information on attending tango shows here, see p.192.

Pasaje de la Defensa

Heading south from Plaza Dorrego along Defensa, you'll come to the **Pasaje de la Defensa** at no. 1179. This is a typical San Telmo house – originally built in the 1880s by the wealthy Ezeiza clan, it later housed an astonishing 32 families, and then in the 1980s was converted into a genteel shopping arcade. It's kept many of its nineteenth-century details, including an interior of black and white tiles, pastel-coloured walls, internal terraces and a balcony running along the upper floor. As well as a patio café, there are stores here selling antiques and second-hand goods, everything from clothing and tablecloths to artwork, lamps and ashtrays – it's a good place to browse if you find the crowds at Sunday's antiques market impede any actual shopping.

Museo de Arte Moderno (MAMBA)

The old-world appeal of San Telmo's charming centre is interrupted rather abruptly half a block south of the Pasaje de la Defensa by busy Avenida San Juan, where you'll find the renascent **Museo de Arte Moderno de Buenos Aires** (Mon–Fri noon–7pm, Sat, Sun & public hols 11am–8pm; $1, free on Tues; ☎011/4342-3001, ⓦwww.museodeartemoderno.buenosaires.gob.ar/mam2.htm) at no. 350. Housed in the late nineteenth-century Nobleza Picardo tobacco factory, with a distinctive brick facade adorned with elegant arches, it showcases a permanent collection of mostly Argentine art from the 1920s to the present day, featuring big names such as Enio Iommi, Emilio Pettoruti, Guillermo Kuitca and Xul Solar. After years of closure for renovation, it reopened in December 2010, with a small exhibition in each of the two bright rooms ready so far: one dedicated to promising young local artists including Sebastián Gordín and Dino Bruzzone, the other showing off national and international treasures by the likes of Paul Klee, Julio Le Parc, Henri Matisse and Juan del Prete. The rest of the museum, including a modern extension at the corner with Defensa, should open to the public by 2012, and will also feature a sculpture patio, bookshop, café and auditorium.

Parque Lezama and around

A walk of four blocks south along Defensa from Plaza Dorrego will bring you to **Parque Lezama**, a pleasing green expanse sandwiched between San Telmo and Boca, and the hub of the southern portion of the barrio. The park is bordered on its northern edge by some classic bars and *parrillas*, and houses a museum of Argentine history, the **Museo Histórico Nacional**.

Parque Lezama

On a bluff overlooking Paseo Colón, **Parque Lezama** is generally regarded as being the site where Pedro de Mendoza founded Buenos Aires in 1536. An imposing statue of the conquistador looms above visitors as they enter the park from the corner of Defensa and Brasil; in the foreground, a bronze of the conquistador thrusts his sword into the ground, while behind him a marble bas-relief of an indigenous man, in something of the style of an Inca carving, throws up his hands in surrender. The land that makes up the park was bought by one José Gregorio Lezama in the nineteenth century, who built the mansion that now houses the Museo Histórico Nacional (see below) as his home and used the rest of the grounds as his personal garden. His widow sold the lot to the city government at a bargain price in the 1890s, with the provision it should be used as a public park carrying her husband's name.

Parque Lezama is best visited in early evening, when the sun filters through its palms and *tipa* trees, children run along its paths and groups of old men play cards or chess at stone tables. This is also a good time to grab a beer or sandwich at **Bar Británico**, on the corner of Defensa and Brasil just outside the park, one of the neighbourhood's best-loved, longest-running café/bars. Its origins are a little misty, but most people agree there's been a bar here since at least the 1920s, when British veterans of World War I and railway company directors who lived in the nearby streets used to gather here to drink. It hasn't changed much in appearance since. Journalists, poets, artists and night-owls of various stripes have flocked to its door for decades – it's open 24 hours – and it was rescued from closure in 2006 after a sustained and vociferous neighbourhood campaign.

Within the park, attractions include a multicoloured **amphitheatre** at the eastern side, used for all kinds of impromptu open-air shows in the summer. Nearby is a bust of Ulrich Schmidl, a German mercenary soldier who accompanied Mendoza on his founding expedition. Schmidl's chronicles of the trip, published as *Log of a Journey to Spain and the Indies* (1567), recount how the would-be settlers had to resort to eating rats, snakes, shoe leather and, in a few extreme cases, the corpses of hanged men. On the southeast edge of the park the grimy and rather tattered **Monumento a la Cordialidad Internacional** was a 1936 gift from the Río de la Plata region's sister capital, Montevideo, on the four hundredth anniversary of Buenos Aires' founding; the engravings on the column reflect the celestial constellations on the founding day itself. If you come via the park on your way to Boca, look out for the large **mural** opposite the southeast side of the park on the corner between Avenida Paseo Colón and Avenida Almirante Brown. Made with recycled materials from a nearby *conventillo* in 1991, the mural is an artistic depiction of the local poor but colourful slums and a preface to Boca's Caminito to the south (see p.89).

Museo Histórico Nacional

Within the park, though entered via Defensa 1600, the rather disappointing **Museo Histórico Nacional** (Tues–Sun 11am–6pm; $5 voluntary contribution) has had its home in José Gregorio Lezama's magnificent Neocolonial mansion since 1897. The facade (arguably the museum's best feature) is startling, painted a deep red and covered with elaborate white mouldings that look very much like piped icing. Inside, the small collection takes a chronological tour through Argentina's history, concentrating mainly on the tumultuous nineteenth century.

Inside you'll find portraits and busts of all the big names from the formative years of Argentina, with emphasis on Independence heroes like Moreno and Rivadavia. Special place is given, as you'd expect, to national liberator José de San Martín – the whole exhibit kicks off with an appealing reproduction of his study in the house in Boulogne-sur-Mer, northern France, where he spent most of his time in exile. A number of important paintings of historical, rather than specifically artistic, interest, line the walls as well, including a huge one by Uruguayan master Juan Manuel Blanes that occupies an entire wall and shows a pensive General Roca leading his troops during the Conquest of the Desert. Several paintings, including a beautiful oil by Figari, show the daily life of Buenos Aires' **Afro-Argentine** community, which formed around a third of the city's population in the early nineteenth century, but about which little is known (see box, p.253).

Though the paintings are interesting, the highlight of the museum's collection is the absolutely stunning **Tarja de Potosí** (undergoing lengthy restoration and therefore not on display at time of writing), an elaborate silver and gold shield given to General Belgrano in 1813 by the women of Potosí (a silver-mining town in Alto Peru, now Bolivia) in recognition of his role in the struggle for independence from Spain. Over a metre tall, it's a delicately worked and intricate piece complete with tiny figures symbolizing the discovery of America.

Iglesia Ortodoxa Rusa

Looking rather out of place among all the French- and Italian-influenced architecture of the barrio, the exotic **Iglesia Ortodoxa Rusa** (open for visits Sat 6pm and Sun 10am; free; women must wear long skirts; ℡011/4361-4274) lies opposite the northern end of the park, at Brasil 313. A collection of bright blue curvaceous domes, it was the first Russian Orthodox Church in Latin America; there are an estimated half a million or so members of the church in Argentina, most of them concentrated in the capital. Built in 1899, the church contains many valuable icons donated by Tsar Nicholas II and brought from Russia as that empire was falling into decline. Outside the visiting times, you can admire the Venetian mosaic of the Holy Trinity, made in St Petersburg, on the front of the building. Call ahead for Mass times, usually held at the weekend (in Spanish and Ukrainian).

Boca

More than any other Buenos Aires barrio, **Boca** (or "La Boca"), in the city's southeast corner, flaunts its idiosyncrasies – resisting gentrification, the riverside neighbourhood hangs on to its distinctive blue-collar aesthetic. Much of this is a legacy of the poor Italian (mainly Genoese) immigrants who settled here in the nineteenth century, bringing with them a sense of fun, a love of art, a strong community spirit and culinary delights such as pesto and chick-pea dough. The barrio's best-known characteristics are its brightly coloured corrugated-iron houses and an obsessive identification with the local football team, **Boca Juniors**. Indeed in 1882 a group of local youths raised the Genoese flag, declaring the secession of the "República de la Boca", a term used to this day. Today's inhabitants, proudly working class, are often referred to as "Xeneizes" (as the Genoese call themselves in their own Ligurian dialect), a name also used by and for Boca Junior fans.

The barrio is named after the **boca** (mouth) of the Río Riachuelo, which snakes along its southeast edge. Bounded by Avenida Patricios and the barrio of Barracas to the west, Calle Brasil and San Telmo to the north and the city limits to the south, Boca's irregularly shaped, rather longer than it is wide. The main thoroughfare, Avenida Almirante Brown, cuts through the neighbourhood from the southeast corner of Parque Lezama, in San Telmo, to the towering iron **Puente Transbordador** ("Transporter Bridge") straddling the Riachuelo. Apart from some excellent pizzerias, though, there's little to detain you along the avenue: by far the most visited area huddles around the **Vuelta de Rocha**, an acute bulge in the river's course, which includes the barrio's most famous street, the **Caminito**. Lined with the most pristine examples of Boca's coloured houses, it's highly photogenic but not very lived-in – an outdoor museum that has undeniably become a tourist trap. Alongside the river, Avenida Pedro de Mendoza is home to two of the city's best **art museums**. A few blocks north of Caminito, the barrio's other renowned sight is the **Bombonera**, Boca Juniors' stadium, which has its own museum and offers tours that are a must for football fans.

Boca is within walking distance from Parque Lezama (San Telmo) but you are better off taking a taxi or buses #64 and #86 from Plaza de Mayo or #53 from Constitución. Daily afternoon **tours** of the neighbourhood are run by Oyst Argentina, aboard a 1970s Leyland bus, from Pedro de Mendoza and Palos (℡011/4302-7234, Ⓦwww.oystargentina.com.ar; call ahead to check times and prices, and to reserve). Boca has gained an appalling reputation for being unsafe, with muggings fairly common. There's no need for paranoia, but take the advice of the police who patrol the area, do not stray, be extremely careful (especially after dark) and keep all valuables out of sight.

Caminito and around

The most visited area of Boca – and arguably the most famous sight in all of Buenos Aires – is the **Caminito**, which has the greatest concentration of the barrio's vibrantly painted houses. The volume of tourists – most of whom snap photos and buy a souvenir or two before being whisked off to the next destination – hereabouts can be off-putting. Yet, time spent exploring the nooks and crannies around here is well rewarded (as long as you don't stray too far): you will find some beguiling art galleries, led by the splendid **Fundación Proa**, tucked away nearby, and the unmissable **Museo de Bellas Artes de La Boca**, which celebrates the work of local artist Quinquela Martín. The best time of day to visit this district is around 10am, before the tour buses arrive and when the light best captures its bright hues.

Caminito

A former railway siding transformed into a short pedestrian street and open-air art museum, the **Caminito**, which runs diagonally between the riverfront and Calle Olavarría, was "invented" by the barrio's most famous artist, **Benito Quinquela Martín**, who painted epic and expressive scenes of daily life in the neighbourhood. Quinquela Martín rescued the disused siding from oblivion after the railway tracks were removed in 1954. He encouraged painting the houses in bright colours – a tradition derived from a Genoese custom of using up the paint left over from boats – and took the name for the street from a famous, typically melancholy 1926 tango by Gabino Coria Peñaloza and Juan de Dios Filiberto. There's something of the pastiche about the Caminito these days: locals refer to it as the best (or worst) example of "Buenos Aires for export". Nonetheless, the bold blocks of rainbow-coloured walls, set off with contrasting window frames and iron-railed balconies, are still an arresting sight. All along the street, there's a daytime open-air **arts and crafts fair** dominated by garish paintings of the surrounding area – Mondays are quieter as the local museums are closed. Tango dancers frequently perform along the street, too, accompanied by the sound of cameras clicking – tourists love to pose with the dancers for a souvenir photo.

At the western end of the Caminito, the charmingly ramshackle **Calle Garibaldi** has some less polished examples of the area's coloured buildings, though it has gradually been renovated by the city government. Garibaldi is a favoured locale for artists' workshops and one block along it to the south of the Caminito, you will cross **Calle Magallanes**, another colourful street lined with art galleries and shops with slightly less tacky goods, such as the **Centro Cultural de los Artistas** at no. 861, which showcases local art for sale in a typical former *conventillo*, or tenement. A colourful mural of Boca life, complete with comical *papier-mâché* figures peering out of the "windows", decorates the exterior, while inside there is an attractive patio and a viewpoint. More gaudy facades and souvenir shops spill into **Calle del Valle Iberlucea**, at right angles to Calle Magallanes.

The eastern (riverside) end of the Caminito joins Avenida Pedro de Mendoza, where the Riachuelo bulges dramatically to create a kind of inlet known as the **Vuelta de Rocha**. A wide pedestrian walkway stretches alongside the water in an ambitious attempt to tempt passers-by closer to the notoriously polluted and foul-smelling river. Some of this contamination is caused by the fact that approximately 3.5 million people live close to the river, though the vast majority is caused by the hundreds of factories that empty their waste directly into it. Political promises to clean up the Riachuelo have been repeatedly made and broken over the years, a source of some frustration for locals. Mention Boca to any Porteño outside the barrio – particularly River Plate fans – and they'll hold their nose. If the smell in this part of the barrio doesn't get to you (and it's not always bad), the area does have a number of pleasant outdoor cafés, where you can soak up a bit of local colour over a beer.

The view across the Vuelta is of a jumbled but majestic mass of picturesque boats and rusty warehouses, disused factories and soaring bridges: directly south, across the river, extends the Gran Buenos Aires suburb of Avellaneda (a working-class area that was the setting for one of Argentina's best movies of recent years, *Luna de Avellaneda*), while to your left there's one of Boca's major landmarks, the massive iron **Puente Transbordador**, built in the early years of the twentieth century and now out of use. Next to the transport bridge is **Puente Nicolás Avellaneda** – a very similar construction built in 1939. This functioning road bridge is one of the major causeways in and out of the city. Far below it, small rowing boats still ferry passengers to and from the suburb.

Fundación Proa

On the Vuelta, at Pedro de Mendoza 1929, you'll find one of Buenos Aires' best art galleries, the innovative, non-profit **Fundación Proa** (Tues–Sun 11am–7pm; $10; frequent 1hr guided visits in Spanish and English, call ahead; ☎011/4104-1000, ⓦwww.proa.org). Housed in a converted mansion – all traditional Italianate elegance outside and bright modern angular galleries within – Proa has no permanent collection but hosts some fascinating and diverse exhibitions, usually with a Latin American theme, ranging from traditional ponchos to modern Argentine art, photography and video. Beautifully restored in 2008, the gallery also hosts events such as mini-film festivals and DJ nights.

On the top floor there is an excellent if expensive **café** with a terrace, offering snacks and light meals (the menu gives a calorie count for each dish) – the panoramic views of the Vuelta are fabulous. This and the outstanding **bookshop**, which sells art books but also a good selection of literature, are both accessible independently of the museum, so you don't have to pay the entrance fee to make use of them.

Museo de Bellas Artes de la Boca

Further east along Pedro de Mendoza at no. 1835 there's the long-established **Museo de Bellas Artes de la Boca** (Tues–Fri 10.30am–5.30pm, Sat & Sun 11am–5.30pm; $5; guided visits Sat noon, 1, 3 & 4pm in Spanish, 1 & 3pm in English; ☎011/4301-1497, Ⓦwww.museoquinquela.gob.ar), a neighbourhood fine arts museum dominated by paintings by the museum's founder, **Benito Quinquela Martín** (1890–1977); it was created in 1938 on the site of his studio (now also a school). One of Argentina's most popular artists, Quinquela Martín is also the painter most associated with Boca – he succeeded more than any other artist in conveying the industrial grandeur of the barrio. Indeed, he was so linked with the city's least salubrious neighbourhood that, like the tango, he only garnered respect at home once he had become famous abroad in the 1920s, though one of his biggest supporters for many years was President Marcelo T. de Alvear (see box, p.110). There is a larger-than-lifesize **statue** of the artist on the quayside opposite the museum.

You'll find examples of Quinquela Martín's work scattered around the city's museums, but the Boca museum is the best place for seeing the bulk of his oeuvre. It's also the perfect setting, since you can actually see much of his subject matter, or what remains of it, simply by peering out of the windows of the gallery or climbing up to the viewpoint on the roof. His oil scenes of everyday life in the busy but impoverished port area are perhaps somewhat in the spirit of his contemporary L.S. Lowry's depictions of the industrial northwest of England, albeit in a much more exuberant and uplifting style – see particularly *Día de Sol* ("Sunny Day") or *Lluvia Espiritual* ("Spiritual Rain").

The museum also has a collection of ornate figureheads from the prows of ships, as well as works by other important contemporary Argentine artists, including Antonio Berni, Raquel Forner and Lino Spilimbergo. Classical music **concerts** are held in the museum every Saturday (3pm; free).

La Bombonera

La Bombonera, home to **Boca Juniors**, Argentina's most popular football club, is really Boca's beating heart, sitting just three blocks north of Caminito at Brandsen 805. The club was founded in 1905 by five Genoese immigrants and, in keeping with its location, its support has traditionally been solidly working class, though its nationwide popularity brings in some serious pesos via ticket sales and merchandising; the club thus provides much of the neighbourhood's income, as well as its decorating scheme. Around the stadium, a huddle of stalls and shops sell Boca souvenirs, from footballs and key rings to huge blue and yellow flags and replica shirts, while on the pavement stars with the names of Boca players past and present, some featuring their footprints, were laid as part of the club's centenary celebrations in 2005. Some of the neighbouring houses have taken up the blue and yellow theme, too, with facades painted like giant football shirts.

Originally built in 1940, the stadium itself was remodelled in the 1990s by the club's millionaire president, **Mauricio Macri**, who was elected mayor of Buenos Aires in 2007 – proving that sport and politics do mix, at least in Argentina. The

Diego Armando Maradona is widely considered the best footballer in history, his only serious rival to the crown being Brazil's Pele. His story is a rags-to-riches classic: one of eight children, Maradona was born in 1960 in the poor neighbourhood of Villa Fiorito in Lomas de Zamora, in southeastern Gran Buenos Aires. He claims in his autobiography *Yo Soy El Diego* ("I am The Diego") that he became obsessed with football almost as soon as he could walk. His talent was noted when he was still very young; he debuted for **Argentinos Juniors** club at the tender age of 15, and just three months later he was selected for the national side in an international friendly. Maradona remained with Argentinos until 1981, making occasional appearances for the national squad in this time, though he was left out of the 1978 World Cup campaign (which Argentina went on to win), a decision about which he has remained bitter. As with most Argentine players of skill, he soon found himself choosing between **Boca Juniors** and River Plate – River offered him more money, but his heart, and his affections, were with Boca, and he went on to play with them from 1981 to 1982. Then came a spell in **Europe**: after a fractious season at Barcelona, he moved to Napoli, whose status as Italy's poorer, southern underdog suited him better – Napoli went on to win its first championship in sixty years.

It is not this win that he is most known for, though, but for the **1986 World Cup** quarter-final, in which he played for Argentina against England – a highly charged match, owing to the recent Malvinas/Falklands conflict in the South Atlantic. Maradona scored two goals, including the infamous **"Hand of God"** goal, in which he tapped the ball in with his hand (very much against the rules – but it made him a hero in Scotland and elsewhere), and a second, legitimate goal considered to be one of the finest ever scored and the subject of a "Monumento al gol" in Garibaldi's "Barrio Bonito" (see p.90), with ceramic figures recreating the goal that left the English "standing like statues". Argentina went on to win the 1986 World Cup, and this turned out to be the high point of Maradona's career: in the years after he was dogged by **drug problems and poor fitness**, and was repeatedly suspended for failing doping tests. He returned to play again for Boca in 1995 but never regained his best form, and retired in 1997.

Following retirement as a player Maradona divided his time between Buenos Aires, where he even hosted a TV talk show and had a spell on Boca's management team, and Havana, where he is friends with Fidel Castro. He was plagued by ill health linked to obesity, alcohol and drug abuse, suffering a heart attack in 2004 and hospitalization for hepatitis in 2007. Throughout his ups and downs, though, he has always remained a Boca fan – when he played his testimonial at the Bombonera (see p.91) in 2001 he tearfully told an emotional crowd that they were the best fans in the world, and the Bombonera the best stadium. That didn't stop him coaching Racing for a while in 2005, though.

As Argentina national coach for the 2010 South Africa World Cup he lapped up the limelight (though his verbal fights with journalists often got him into hot water) but the team, especially Barcelona star and championship hopeful Lionel Messi, apparently reacted badly to the media pressure. Maradona was heavily criticized for chopping and changing the line-up during the qualifying rounds that nearly saw Argentina eliminated (they lost 6-1 to Bolivia in one match) – and was sacked after Argentina lost to Germany in the quarter-finals by a humiliating 4-0.

Award-winning Serbian film director Emir Kusturica finally got round to making a film about his hero in 2008. Premiered at Cannes that year it deals with the many facets of this larger-than-life sportsman, including the fact that he is worshipped as a deity by the 100,000 estimated adepts of the Maradonian Church, one of whose ten commandments is "Love football over all things".

stadium's name, literally "the chocolate box", refers to its tightly tiered structure, aimed at fitting in as many fans as possible. Despite this design, though, and the fact that Boca probably has more fans than any other Argentine team, the stadium's capacity is only 44,000, significantly less than several of its city rivals. But that doesn't mean it's quiet: the truly fanatical *hinchada* (fans) make such a noise with their chanting and singing that, as with Liverpool FC's famous Anfield stadium, visiting teams are said to be intimidated before they've even jogged onto the pitch – hence the nickname of "twelfth player" given to the supporters. This is where to come to see many of the country's best young players cut their teeth before heading to Europe on lucrative deals – the Bombonera's most famous veteran is **Diego Maradona** (see box opposite), who retains a VIP seat at the stadium; other notable former Boca players include Carlos Tévez, Martín Palermo, Juan Riquelme, Gabriel Batistuta and Alfredo "El Tanque" Rojas. Seeing a game here is an incredible experience, even if you are not a fan, and it's worth arranging your itinerary around one (see p.211 for match practicalities).

If you don't get the opportunity to watch a match, you could still pay a visit to the **Museo de la Pasión Boquense** and go on its **stadium tour** (daily 10am–6pm; $28 for museum visit only or tour only, $40 for both; Ⓦwww.museoboquense .com). The museum is a modern audio visual experience, where the highlights are a 360-degree film that puts you in the boots of a Boca Juniors player and a charming model of how Boca would have looked and sounded in the 1930s. The tour not only includes the stands, pitch and press conference room, but also the players' dressing room, complete with statues of the Virgin Mary. Just inside the stadium entrance you'll see a large painting by Benito Quinquela Martín (see p.91) entitled *Orígen de la Bandera de Boca* ("The Origin of Boca's Flag"), which illustrates one of the club's most famous anecdotes. Though the exact date and circumstances of the event are disputed, all agree that Boca chose its colours from the flag of the next ship to pass through its then busy port. The boat was Swedish, and thus the distinctive blue and yellow strip was born.

Eastern Boca

Follow Avenida Pedro de Mendoza east from the Vuelta de Rocha and you'll quickly leave the tourists behind; the streets east of Avenida Almirante Brown are unreconstructed working class, where the influence of the port and Italy are still strongly felt. Around here you'll find many less pristine examples of Boca's colourful architecture, as well as authentic (and cheap) Italian restaurants (see p.171 for reviews). Remember, though, that this is an extremely poor neighbourhood – if San Telmo is described as crumbling then this part of Boca can be said to be falling apart – so don't wander by yourself, stick to the main streets and keep valuables firmly out of sight.

Running parallel to Almirante Brown and one block east, **Calle Necochea** was known for many years as the "street of **cantinas**", fantastically gaudy and rowdy late-night restaurants. Their heyday was in the 1970s and there is now only one left – *Il Piccolo Vapore*, at no. 1190 (see p.171).

The main plaza in eastern Boca is **Plaza Solís**, a tree-fringed square that is best known for being the site where Boca Juniors was founded, an event commemorated with a small plaque. Finally, at Almirante Brown 400, a short walk from Parque Lezama, there's an unusual sight in this part of town – a stately mansion, the **Casa Amarilla**, painted, as the name would suggest, in a bright mustard yellow. The house is a replica of that where Admiral William Brown (see p.109) lived, on the same site, when he retired. Today it is the seat of the Instituto Browniano (Ⓣ011/4362-1225; open to members or invited guests only), which promotes Argentine naval interests and has a library for the study of maritime history.

6

Retiro

Given the small area covered by **Retiro** – squeezed between Recoleta to the west, Avenida Córdoba and the microcentro to the south, and inhospitable docklands to the north and east – this central barrio is unexpectedly varied in character. Nowhere is Buenos Aires' favourite nickname – the "Paris of the South" – more apparent than in the neighbourhood's smart streets or its magnificent French-style **palaces** built in the early twentieth century. At the same time, few areas of the capital demonstrate so clearly the divide between haves and have-nots: the northeast fringes of the barrio, along the water, are taken up mainly by urban wasteland and one of the city's most notorious **slums**.

For visitors, Retiro tends to have two focal points, around which the majority of its sights can be found: **Plaza San Martín**, an enticing green space surrounded by some of the city's most exclusive addresses, and **Estación Retiro**, a venerable British-style train station northwest of the plaza that, together with the intercity bus terminus, forms Buenos Aires' largest public transport hub. The streets southwest of Plaza San Martín, especially the northern end of **Calle Florida**, have a strong commercial feel and are great places for hunting down a coffee-table book, a pair of shoes or a painting. The southeast corner of the barrio bulges with cafés and pubs popular with office workers at lunch time and a more questionable portside clientele at night. To the northwest of the plaza, the streets are more elegant and refined – here you'll find pricey art galleries, a remarkable collection of Spanish-American art, and palaces converted to ministries and embassies, clubs and hotels.

On the eastern side of the plaza and the station, Avenida Antártida Argentina effectively marks the edge of the barrio for visitors. If you venture at all into the section of the barrio beyond it – an isolated no-man's land that was reclaimed from the Río de la Plata – it will probably be either to seek out ferries to Uruguay (see p.245) or to visit Migraciones, the immigration headquarters. This area is also home to the **Gran Hotel de los Inmigrantes**, the hotel where many immigrants had their first taste of the New World in the nineteenth century. For many years an immigration museum (☎011/4317-0285), the site is closed for renovation work for the foreseeable future.

Retiro is an easy walk from downtown or Recoleta. Additionally, many of the city's **buses** terminate in front of Estación Retiro, while **subte** Line C links the station with Buenos Aires' other major rail terminus, Constitución, stopping at San Martín station on the plaza.

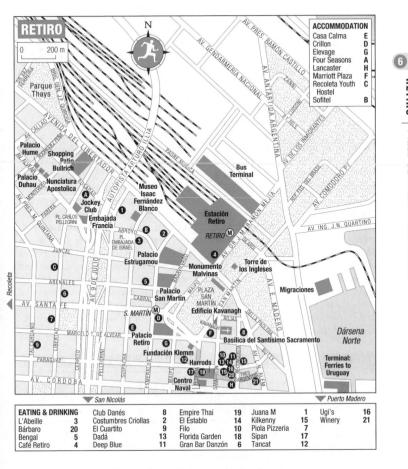

RETIRO				

ACCOMMODATION

Casa Calma	E
Crillon	D
Elevage	G
Four Seasons	A
Lancaster	H
Marriott Plaza	F
Recoleta Youth Hostel	C
Sofitel	B

EATING & DRINKING		Club Danés	8	Empire Thai	19	Juana M	1	Ugi's	16
L'Abeille	3	Costumbres Criollas	2	El Establo	14	Kilkenny	15	Winery	21
Bárbaro	20	El Cuartito	9	Filo	10	Piola Pizzeria	7		
Bengal	5	Dadá	13	Florida Garden	18	Sipan	17		
Café Retiro	4	Deep Blue	11	Gran Bar Danzón	6	Tancat	12		

Plaza San Martín and around

Leafy **Plaza San Martín** makes a perfect place to take a break from a tour of the barrio or if you've just walked up from Monserrat or San Nicolás. It's flanked all around by interesting or extravagant buildings: to the south, in the last three blocks of Calle Florida, you can see a former branch of **Harrods**, a Beaux Arts **naval officers' club** and a significant collection of **contemporary art** – the Fundación Federico Jorge Klemm; and to the east and west there's a clutch of the city's most palatial twentieth-century residences, with varying degrees of accessibility to the public – including lofty **Edificio Kavanagh**, grandiose **Palacio Estrugamou**, ostentatious **Palacio San Martín** and Louvre-inspired **Palacio Retiro** – plus a gorgeous church. The more open, northern half of the plaza, facing Estación Retiro and containing two important city **monuments**, slopes down to Avenida del Libertador, a major artery that runs through northern Buenos Aires all the way to Tigre, outside the city limits.

Plaza San Martín

Plaza San Martín plays many roles – green lung, romantic meeting place, military parade ground, picnic area for office workers, children's playground. It was designed by Argentina's most important landscape architect, Frenchman **Charles Thays** (see box below), and created especially for a monument to founding father **General San Martín**, placed in the plaza's southwestern corner for the country's centenary in 1910. Aligned with busy Avenida Santa Fe, the imposing bronze equestrian statue – cast in 1862, it was the first of its kind in Argentina – stands proudly on a high marble pedestal decorated with scenes representing national liberation. It was designed by French sculptor Louis Joseph Daumas and is one of an identical pair – the other was inaugurated in Chile a year later. The statue of the Libertador points west across the Andes, a tradition followed nationwide.

Lush lawns carpet most of the plaza, making good sunbathing spots in the warmer months. There are also benches dotted throughout, beneath luxuriant palms, spiky-trunked *palos borrachos*, *ceibos* (coral trees), monkey puzzles, lime trees and acacias – you'll see people cooling down on these when it gets too hot to sunbathe any more. The biggest shade of all is cast at the far southern end of the plaza by a mammoth *gomero* (rubber tree), whose gnarled boughs, stretched out like a giant hand, are so heavy they need props; as one of the biggest specimens in the city, it's worth a look, especially its surreal trunk – stringy and sinewy, it looks like an overzealous weight lifter's torso. In October and November, the park's spectacular jacarandas blush mauve with trumpet-shaped blossoms.

Charles Thays: Buenos Aires' landscape artist

In the 1880s, French botanist and landscape architect **Charles Thays** (1849–1934) travelled to South America to study its rich flora, particularly the continent's hundreds of endemic tree species. He settled in Argentina, where his services were in great demand as municipal authorities across the country sought to smarten their cities up. They, like their European and North American counterparts, were spurred by the realization that the country's fast-growing urban sprawls needed parks and gardens to provide vital breathing spaces and recreational areas.

In 1890, Thays was appointed director of parks and gardens in Buenos Aires, in no small part due to his indefatigable adeptness at transforming open plazas formerly used for military parades, or *plazas secas*, into shady *plazas verdes*, or green squares, such as **Plaza San Martín**. He also designed the capital's zoo – which he planted with dozens of *tipas* (rosewood trees) – as well as Palermo's **Parque 3 de Febrero** and Belgrano's **Barrancas**. Thays received countless private commissions, too, including the garden of Palacio Hume, on Avenida Alvear in Recoleta, and the layout of the exclusive residential estate known as Barrio Parque, in Palermo Chico.

Despite his French origins, he preferred the informal English style of landscaping, and also experimented with combinations of native plants such as jacarandas, *tipas* and *palos borrachos*, with Canary Island palms, planes and lime trees. Oddly enough, given the high regard in which he was held and his contributions to the greening of Buenos Aires, the lone plaza named in his honour, **Plaza Carlos Thays**, in Palermo, is disappointingly barren, and definitely not the best example of landscaping the city has to offer. That is more than compensated for, though, by the fact that his name was added to the city's marvellous **botanical gardens** (see p.133), which he also designed. For more on the city's trees, see p.124.

Monumento a los Héroes de la Guerra de las Malvinas

The **Monumento a los Héroes de la Guerra de las Malvinas** stands on the brow of the northern slope of the Plaza San Martín, a sombre cenotaph comprising 25 black marble plaques inscribed with the names of the 649 Argentine servicemen who fell during the Malvinas/Falklands conflict. Its eternal flame partly symbolizes the immortality of the human spirit, but also Argentina's persistent claim over the South Atlantic islands. A rotation of army, navy and air force servicemen permanently guard the monument, which is the scene of both remembrance ceremonies and demonstrations on April 2 each year, the day on which Argentina began its brief occupation of the islands in 1982.

Torre de los Ingleses

The Malvinas monument was deliberately placed opposite the former Plaza Británica, officially renamed the Plaza Fuerza Aérea Argentina in 1982. There are echoes of London's Big Ben in the 76m-high **Torre de los Ingleses** clock tower (Mon–Fri 10am–5pm, Sat & Sun 10am–6.30pm; free), the Anglo-Argentine community's contribution to the 1910 centenary, which stands at the centre of the plaza. Its inauguration was delayed for several years owing to the death of Edward VII – Britain was in mourning in 1910 and no official representatives attended Argentina's centenary celebrations. During and after the 1982 conflict there was talk of demolishing the tower, and it was officially renamed **Torre Monumental**, but everyone still calls it Torre de los Ingleses. The lift that used to carry visitors to the top for great views has been out of operation for years, but it is still worth going inside to see the collections of interesting old photos of Retiro or to chat to the tower's caretaker – a fount of knowledge on local history and museums throughout the city.

Estación Retiro

A massive complex of rail terminals looming at the northern end of the Plaza San Martín, **Estación Retiro** is in fact a trio of train stations: General San Martín, General Belgrano and General Mitre. The third of these (the one nearest Avenida del Libertador) is by far the most impressive, a massive stone and metal structure completed in 1915 by Charles John Dudley, a British constructor based in Liverpool. Decorated with Royal Doulton porcelain tiles, it is a majestic, airy edifice with an iron roof that, at the time, was the largest of its kind in the world. Recently restored to its former glory, it's worth a visit for its splendid café, *Café Retiro* (see review, p.160). From here, too, suburban rail lines lead out into the northern suburbs and onwards to Tigre (see p.232). Nearby, stretching beyond the railway lines into neighbouring Recoleta, is one of the city's most unfortunate areas, Villa 31 (see box, p.98).

Edificio Kavanagh

The sleek thirty-storey block of private apartments known as **Edificio Kavanagh**, on the east side of Plaza San Martín at the junction of San Martín and Florida, sums up pretty well the social and architectural trends of early twentieth-century Buenos Aires, which were largely about upstaging your neighbour and, if possible, leading the world. It's believed that the building's commissioner, **Corina Kavanagh**, a socialite of Irish origins, had to sell most of her property in the country to finance the project. There's also a rumour that Señora Kavanagh deliberately built the tower in front of Mercedes Castellanos de Anchorena's Basílica del Santísimo Sacramento (see p.98) as an act of revenge following the cancellation of

Villas miseria – the shantytowns of Buenos Aires

Every major city in Latin America has its **shantytowns**, the most famous being the *favelas* of Rio, which have become a rather strange tourist attraction. Sadly, Buenos Aires is no exception, and locally these makeshift settlements are known as **villas miseria**, or *villas de emergencia*, or just *villas*. They first appeared around the harbour area in the north of **Retiro** at the beginning of the twentieth century, when the city's housing could not keep up with the huge influx of immigrants from Europe and internal migrants from poorer provinces like Santiago del Estero. Their number increased drastically during the 1930s, a notorious period of working-class hardship in the city; indeed, the term "villa miseria" was coined by local writer Bernardo Verbitsky, whose 1957 work *Villa Miseria también es América* described the horrors of living in these shantytowns at that time. By the middle of the century there were over two hundred such settlements scattered around the city fringes, and they were given **numbers** rather than names, as if to emphasize their inhuman, anonymous nature. Massive home construction schemes have since reduced the number of *villas* but several still exist, mostly inhabited by poor Bolivian and Paraguayan immigrants.

The most famous – or infamous – of Buenos Aires' shantytowns is **Villa 31**, sometimes ironically known as Villa Esperanza ("Hopeville"). Its makeshift huts of breezeblock, corrugated iron and plastic, with no proper sanitation and illegal (and hazardous) cable links to the electricity grid, stretch north beyond Retiro's train and bus terminals, with some buildings teetering up to five storeys high. The current city government has announced plans to put in proper streets, sewers and a school after several previous administrations tried unsuccessfully to eliminate the villa. Indeed, during the Dirty War and its lead-up to it anyone seen to be helping its inhabitants was a prime target for torture and disappearance, starting with the priest Carlos Mugica, assassinated by the neo-fascist Triple A militia in 1974 – Mugica is now a hero for the residents of Villa 31.

The best that can be said about Buenos Aires' *villas* is that they are not quite as wretched or violent as the ones around other Latin American cities, such as Rio, Lima or Caracas. Nonetheless, casual visitors to the city should resist any temptation to see what "*villa* life" is like and keep dangerous places like Villa 31 strictly off itineraries.

an engagement between one of her daughters and an Anchorena because his family refused to let him marry a "commoner". At 120m, it was the tallest building in South America for several years after its completion in 1935, and quite adequately blocked the basilica from view.

Whatever the tittle-tattle, the emblematic Kavanagh building – often likened for its bold beauty to New York's Chrysler building, though it is far more minimalist in style – was the world's largest at the time to be built of reinforced concrete. Hailed as a brilliant example of Rationalist architecture, with the two facades of its distinctive flatiron shape built in a wedge formed by San Martín and Florida, it was inhabited in the early years by many of the city's rich and famous. Still impressive, the building nonetheless long ago lost its title as the city's tallest.

Basílica del Santísimo Sacramento

The **Basílica del Santísimo Sacramento**, at San Martín 1035, lurks east of the Plaza San Martín at the end of narrow Pasaje Corina Kavanagh. Built at a dog-leg angle, the tiny side street conceals the church's facade until you are right upon it – another part of Señora Kavanagh's alleged revenge (see p.97) on her rival, basilica-financer **Mercedes Castellanos de Anchorena**. A matriarchal figure, Señora Anchorena had married into one of Argentina's wealthiest and most influential landowning clans (hence the Argentine expression "as rich as an Anchorena"). She spared no expense on the interior of the basilica: red onyx from Morocco, marble from Verona and Carrara, red sandstone from the Vosges, glazed mosaic tiles from Venice and bronze from France were imported to decorate her monument to devotion, while the Byzantine-styled altarpiece is the work of an Italian artist and the wooden confessionals, pulpit and doors are that of Flemish craftsmen. Like so much of the city, it was the work of French architects, and its white marble dome and five slender turrets were designed to resemble Paris's Sacré-Coeur. Consecrated in 1916, the basilica is still regarded in some circles as the smartest place to get married in Buenos Aires; its handsome roof and facade were scrubbed clean and painstakingly restored in 2007.

Down in the crypt (ask the staff to be allowed down) and behind a protective grille is Mercedes Castellanos de Anchorena's **mausoleum**, an ostentatious yet doleful concoction of marble angels guarded by a demure Virgin Mary. The basilica also has a world-class organ, shown off to good effect at occasional classical concerts advertised in the church itself.

Harrods and the Centro Naval

The three northernmost blocks of pedestrianized **Calle Florida** between Avenida Córdoba and Plaza San Martín fall within Retiro's boundaries, and tend to attract thinner crowds and fatter wallets than the rest of the street (see p.65). Every other shop seems to sell smart clothing – everything from tailored suits to capybara jackets – or art or leather goods. At no. 877, between Avenida Córdoba and Paraguay, you'll see that there was even once a **Harrods**; until the 1960s, this huge edifice operated as the South American branch of the world-famous department store, with visitors flocking to marvel at its full-size London bus and live Indian elephant. Despite occasional rumblings that it is to reopen and its intermittent use as an exposition hall and arts venue, it has been sadly shuttered for years, and is no longer linked to the London store.

On the same block, also look out for the decorative facade and door – embellished with shields and tridents, fishes and ropes – of the **Centro Naval** (Naval Officers' Club; ☎011/4311-1011), on the corner of Florida and Avenida Córdoba. Designed by Swiss architect Jacques Dunant and opened in 1914, this building is one of Buenos Aires' finest models of Beaux Arts architecture. Open to members only, the interior boasts a barbershop, a sauna and a tailor, as well as the magnificent Salón Almirante Brown, a Neoclassical dining room of lavish proportions. Enquire at the door for news of occasional concerts, a means for nonmembers to see the club's impressive interior; you could also call ahead for a guided visit (free; in Spanish only). Otherwise, make do with admiring the majestic cupola, the finely decorated stonework that shows elements of Italian rococo, and the bronze torso of a sea god in a Spanish galleon perched above the intricate wrought-iron doorway.

Fundación Federico Jorge Klemm

Wedged between the leather shops and busy cafés on the southern side of the Plaza San Martín, the **Fundación Federico Jorge Klemm**, Marcelo T. de Alvear 626 (Mon–Fri 11am–8pm; free; ☎011/4312-4443, ⊛www.fundacion fjklemm.org), houses a major **contemporary art collection** in the basement of an arcade. Klemm (1942–2002) was born in what was Czechoslovakia, and came to Buenos Aires in 1948. Here he tried his hand at singing, acting and painting; a kind of self-styled Porteño Andy Warhol, straight down to the Peter Pan looks and dyed blond hair, he produced bizarre portraits of modern-day Argentine celebrities in mythical, often homoerotic, poses. Klemm came to the attention of the bemused Argentine public in the 1990s, when he had his own television show, *El banquete telemático*, described by the local press as "a philosophical and academic reflection upon classical and modern art, all presented with unprecedented histrionics".

Throughout his life, Klemm was a serious patron and collector of modern art, building an impressive collection that includes works by Picasso, Dalí, Fontana and, of course, Warhol, together with leading lights of the late twentieth-century Argentine art scene, such as **Antonio Berni** (*La Familia del Peón*) and **Guillermo Kuitca** (a self-portrait and *El Ejército del Ebro*). Photography is a major component at the foundation – you'll see everything from a Man Ray, via a couple of Mapplethorpe nudes, to a piece by Marcos López entitled *Flavio* (2000), depicting a statuesque bald youth garlanded with a necklace of *morcillas* (blood sausages). Some of Klemm's own horrifically bad oeuvre can usually be contemplated, too, as a grand finale. In addition to the permanent display, interesting temporary exhibits are staged from time to time.

Palacio Retiro

Press baron José Paz, founder of daily newspaper *La Prensa* and related by marriage to the Anchorenas, wanted his Buenos Aires home to look like the Louvre, so he commissioned the **Palacio Retiro** (visits with a guide only, minimum 4 people: in English Wed & Thurs 3.30pm, in Spanish Tues–Fri 11am & 3pm, Sat 11am; $35; ☎011/4311-1071) – previously known as the **Palacio Paz** – to be built by a French architect between 1902 and 1914, but he died in 1912, without ever seeing the finished product. The palace runs along the southwest side of Plaza San Martín, and access is via magnificent wrought-iron gates at Avenida Santa Fe 750. It remains the largest single house ever built in Argentina, and its main facade is an uncanny replica of the Sully wing of the Parisian palace, with steeply stacked slate roofs in the shape of truncated pyramids, a double row of tiny windows and a colonnaded ground floor.

Inside, the eighteen rooms open to the public and visited on the tour – less than one-sixth of the whole building – are decorated in an eclectic range of French styles, from Gothic to Empire, including a scaled-down copy of the Hall of Mirrors in Versailles, but the *pièce de résistance* is the great Hall of Honour, a cavernous, circular room lined with several types of European marble and crowned with a stained-glass dome from the centre of which the Sun King beams down. Artur Rubinstein entertained guests in the little music room and the Prince of Wales dined here during his visit to the city in 1925. Sadly, the Paz family, like so many others, fell on hard times in the late 1930s and nearly all of the original furniture was sold off. Most of the building became the Círculo Militar, an officers' club, and the Museo de Armas de la Nación (see below).

Museo de Armas de la Nación

A surprisingly voluminous corner of the Palacio Retiro is occupied by the **Museo de Armas de la Nación** (enter at Av Santa Fe and Maipú; Tues–Fri 1–7pm; $10), a large and impressive exhibition of Argentine armour, weapons and military uniforms, some dating back to the Wars of Independence. These are complemented by an incredibly eclectic and comprehensive collection of military items from around the world, including a marvellous set of Japanese armour, guns from all over Europe and the US, Persian swords and an English coat of mail from the twelfth century. Every kind of weaponry, from tiny pistols to giant cannons, is on display, while much of the country's military-dominated history is recounted by means of uniforms and toy soldiers. Rosas' horseback conquest of Patagonia, for example, is depicted through a magnificent set of large glazed ceramic figures. The section on the Malvinas/Falklands conflict is much smaller than you might expect, but curiously there is a jar of soil brought back by one combatant as a souvenir from the islands.

Palacio San Martín

Opposite the Palacio Retiro, at Arenales and Esmeralda, the **Palacio San Martín** (open to the public for guided visits only; in English and Spanish Mon & Wed 2.30pm; free, no need to reserve; ☎011/4819-8092) is a particularly extravagant example of the showy palaces commissioned by the city's elite in the early twentieth century. Built in 1905, the enormous building is actually divided up into three subtly different palaces, all sharing a huge Neoclassical entrance and ceremonial courtyard. Its overall structure is based on a nineteenth-century Parisian banker's mansion, with slate mansard roofs, colonnades and domed attics, while the Neo-Baroque interior is inspired by the eighteenth-century Hôtel de Condé, also in Paris. Fashionable Art Nouveau details, such as ornate stained-glass windows and the flowing lines of wrought-iron staircases, were also incorporated. Commissioned for the **Anchorena** family, it was originally known as the Palacio Anchorena. Mercedes Castellanos de Anchorena (see p.99) lived here with her family for twenty years, until the Great Depression left them penniless.

After the palace and its accumulated treasures were hurriedly sold off in 1927, the government turned it into the Ministry of Foreign Affairs, and renamed it Palacio San Martín. Since the 1980s, when most of the ministry moved into the larger plate-glass building across Calle Esmeralda, the palace has been largely reserved for state ceremonies. Some of the original furniture and paintings are on display, though they are not the main attractions – the guided visits offer, above all, a rare opportunity to see the opulent interior of a Retiro palace. The enormous gilt mirrors, marble fireplaces, gleaming tropical wood furniture, giant chandeliers, collections of French porcelain and imposing family portraits are on a grandiose scale, yet they still look lost in the cavernous reception rooms and dining halls, with their polished parquet floors, inlaid wooden panelling and frescoed ceilings.

Palacio Estrugamou

If you want to see another one of the reasons "Retiro" looks good on a visiting card, continue one block north along Esmeralda to the **Palacio Estrugamou**, also known as "Edificios Estrugamou", a huge Parisian-style block of apartments. The best vantage point for taking in the full extent of the giant residential complex, built in the 1930s, is at the corner of Esmeralda and Juncal; the rounded angle of the block is flanked by two elegant facades of sober stonework, set off with fine wrought-iron balconies and mansard roofs. This building of private apartments, some of which were sold for astronomical sums in 2007, is famous for housing an exact replica, though in bronze, of the Louvre's *Victory of Samothrace* in one of its many inner courtyards. Generally, it drips with opulence – the archetypal Porteño *palacio*, if ever there was one.

Museo de Arte Hispanoamericano Isaac Fernández Blanco and around

A short way northwest of Plaza San Martín, just before you reach Avenida 9 de Julio, is one of the city's undisputed cultural highlights, a museum of **Latin American art**. The museum building, a fabulous Neocolonial mansion, had to be restored at the end of the twentieth century, having been damaged in a terrorist bombing that destroyed the nearby Israeli embassy. One of the worst atrocities ever committed on Argentine soil, the event is marked by a **monument** on the location of the former embassy.

The museum

The outstanding **Museo de Arte Hispanoamericano Isaac Fernández Blanco** (Tues–Sun 2–7pm; $1; guided visits on Wed & Fri at 3.30pm, $10, reserve ahead ☎011/4327-0228), at Suipacha 1422, takes its name from a patrician Porteño engineer who, in his 30s, inherited a fortune and began collecting books and works of art from all over Latin America. He turned his house into a public museum, directing it himself from 1922 until his death in 1928. In his will, he left the works he had assembled to the city authorities, who combined it with several other private holdings to form the current contents of the Museo de Arte Hispanoamericano.

This large and varied collection occupies the **Palacio Noel**, a stunning house built in 1920 in the Neocolonial style by architect Martín Noel for himself and his brother Carlos, mayor of the city; the two jointly donated it to the municipality in 1936, along with their own impressive collection of colonial art, some of which appears here. The building's style imitates eighteenth-century Lima Baroque, a deliberate backlash against the slavish imitation of Parisian palaces fashionable at the time. With its plain white walls, lace-like window-grilles, dark wooden bow windows and wrought-iron balconies, it's the perfect residence for the superb collection of Spanish-American art exhibited inside. Occasionally, excellent classical music concerts are staged at the museum, too – look out for posters.

Most of the **artefacts** on display were produced in the seventeenth and early eighteenth centuries, in Peru and Alto Perú (present-day Bolivia). There is also an important collection of objects from nineteenth-century Argentina, mostly in the basement. The whole collection is fabulously presented – perfect lighting, informative panels and legends (mostly in Spanish only), and atmospheric sound effects – over three floors.

Ground floor

The ground floor takes as its theme the people who made up South America in colonial times, with the focus on three racial groups – Europeans, Native Americans and Africans – and three cultures – the Southern Cone (*surandina*), the jungle-based mix of Jesuit and Guaraní, and the port of Buenos Aires. Two of the most striking pieces in the museum sit just inside the entrance: a fantastic eighteenth-century silver **sacrarium**, embellished with a portrait of Christ on a copper plaque, and a matching "**arco**" (metal arch); both were made in La Paz, Alto Perú, around 1735. Behind a panel opposite the entrance are a couple of paintings illustrating the terminology used for the offspring of different racial groups. Created as a way of trying to ensure a Spanish/white hierarchy, it became increasingly complicated as the years went by and the possible permutations rose. In a small room to the left, a set of fine Jesuit/Guaraní statues, all carved from wood, adorn the walls, along with other objects from the northeast of Argentina. Decorating the long vaulted room to the right, where the concerts take place, is an extensive display of anonymous paintings from the **Cusqueña school** – one of the most prodigious in colonial South America. Its masters, based in the Peruvian city of Cusco and especially active in the eighteenth century, were gifted with an ability to produce subtle oil paintings, mostly of religious, devotional subjects, that combined sombre understatement with a startling vitality and mixed traditional Catholic imagery with indigenous motifs.

Upper floor

With the binding theme of *criollo* (Spanish-American) culture, a series of rooms on the upper floor recreate the exotic and prosperous atmosphere of **colonial South America**, with varied themes such as the cult of the Virgin Mary; the masters of Potosí, Alto Perú, who were famous for their silverwork; or the artisans of Quito, Ecuador. Mexican art is also represented, along with a set of ivory figures and a number of objects revealing the Oriental influence on Latin American fashion, taste and artwork. A large exhibit illustrates visually how Buenos Aires became a cultural capital for the whole region under colonial rule: handsome furniture, exquisite painting and elegant fashions made it a serious rival to Lima in the eighteenth century.

Basement and garden

This theme of cultural dominance continues in the basement, where the time frame switches to early Independence. The main exhibition room focuses on the symbolic power of **silver**, featuring wrought-silver *mate* vessels and fine ornaments in the shape of rheas (native ostriches). Don't miss the reconstructed **kitchen**, whose walls are lined with handsome *azulejos* (glazed tiles) from Spain – one of the main reasons that Argentina fought for its independence was that Spain maintained a strict monopoly on products within its empire: nearly everything had to be imported, even kitchen tiles.

One of the larger basement rooms is used to hold **temporary exhibitions** – they vary from black-and-white photographs to pre-Columbian artefacts. This space can be directly accessed from the splendid garden, which with its palms and shrubs is an oasis of greenery in this heavily built-up part of the city. Across from the main entrance is a small bookshop with a limited but high-quality selection of art publications, including museum catalogues.

Plaza Embajada de Israel

Though now fully restored, the Palacio Noel was badly damaged in 1992 by a terrorist **bomb** that tore apart the Israeli embassy that stood just opposite the museum (see box, p.71), killing 29 people and injuring more than 240, many of whom were children in a nearby school. On one side of the empty site at the corner of Suipacha and Arroyo (the Israeli embassy is now in another part of the city), called **Plaza Embajada de Israel**, is a scarred, bare white wall, to which a few fragments of the embassy building still cling. At the foot of the wall is an unadorned plaque bearing the names of those who lost their lives, while two rows of commemorative trees, representing the immortality of the human soul, form a simple, living monument to the atrocity.

Plaza Carlos Pellegrini and around

Bordered by calles Arroyo and Libertad and Avenida Alvear, the elegant triangle of **Plaza Carlos Pellegrini** is the hub of Retiro's well-heeled residential streets west of Avenida 9 de Julio. On or near it you'll find a variety of spectacular buildings that share a common theme: a meticulous French style. If Retiro in general has a Parisian feel, then here it is taken to extremes. Most of the buildings around the plaza are closed to the general public, but you can admire their opulent exteriors and then browse or have a coffee in one of the city's finest shopping malls.

Plaza Carlos Pellegrini

The plaza is named for **Carlos Pellegrini** (1846–1906), president of Argentina in the 1890s, whose feats include founding the Banco de la Nación and Argentina's influential **Jockey Club**. In the middle of the plaza sits an imposing Carrara marble **statue** of Pellegrini, flanked by bronze allegories of Justice and Progress. French sculptor Félix Coutan depicted the former president seated on the prow of a ship, grasping the Argentine flag in his left hand, while standing over him is another bronze figure, La República, who protects him with her shield and holds a tied bundle, or *fasces*, the Roman symbol of unity.

Around the plaza

The Jockey Club's national headquarters occupy the massive honey-coloured stone hulk of the **Palacio Unzué de Casares**, on the north side of the plaza at Avenida Alvear 1345. Built in the severely unadorned *style académique*, it's alleviated only by its delicate wrought-iron balconies.

Opposite the Jockey Club, on the south side of the plaza, stands the magnificent **Palacio Celedonio Pereda**, named after a member of the Argentine oligarchy who wanted a carbon copy of the Palais Jacquemart-André in Paris. This Porteño palace, now home to the Brazilian embassy, is a uniformly successful replica, classical columns and all, crowned by a huge slate-tiled cupola.

Directly east of the plaza, at the corner of Calle Cerrito, **Casa Atucha** presides, a soberly stylish Second Empire mansion by René Sergent, a French architect who never set foot in Argentina but designed dozens of aristocratic houses here. Curiously, the mansion's rear facade is a blind wall, painted with *trompe-l'oeil* windows and mansard roofs, the work of Catalan artist Josep Niebal. It dominates the rather barren Plaza Cataluña, an oblong of gravel and a few benches, which affords sweeping views across 9 de Julio to the **Edificio Chrysler**, a smooth, white cylinder of a tower that looks absolutely nothing like its Manhattan namesake.

Mansión Alzaga Unzué and Palacio Ortiz Basualdo

Half a block north of the Casa Atucha, at Cerrito 1455, the **Mansión Alzaga Unzué** is a faultless duplicate of a Loire chateau, built in attractive red brick and cream limestone and topped with a shiny slate mansard roof. It now forms a luxurious annexe of the *Four Seasons* hotel (see p.153 for review).

Dominating the whole area immediately to the east of the Brazilian embassy, at Cerrito 1399, the Louis XIV-style **Palacio Ortiz Basualdo** has been the location of the French embassy since 1925. This grandiose palace with slightly incongruous detailing, including Art Nouveau balconies, monumental Ionic pilasters and bulging Second Empire corner turrets, mercifully escaped the fate of many similar buildings that were demolished in the 1950s when Avenida 9 de Julio was widened, though it did have to be altered considerably to accommodate the highway.

Shopping Patio Bullrich

A stone's throw to the north, **Shopping Patio Bullrich**, tucked up in the far corner of Retiro, at Avenida del Libertador 750, is one of the city's oldest shopping malls (inaugurated in 1988) and is definitely the most refined, with marble floors, smart cafés and boutiques selling the latest Argentine and international fashions. Built in 1867, the fabulous building was originally a *tattersall*, or livestock auction-house, as symbolized by the stone bulls' and horses' heads that adorn the balconies.

7

Recoleta

For the last century, **Recoleta** has clung resolutely to the title of Buenos Aires' grandest barrio. Even today, although it no longer possesses the city's most expensive real estate – that honour falls to glossy Puerto Madero – it continues to exude timeless wealth: classical elegance and the latest fashions are flaunted in its streets, which are lined with European-style mansions, ornate Neoclassical facades and a plethora of lofty cupolas, noble statuary and fancy ironwork. For Porteños and visitors alike the barrio is intrinsically tied to the patrician **Cementerio de la Recoleta**, but there's certainly more to see here than the famous graveyard. Most of Recoleta's major sights – including the cemetery and its adjoining basilica, one of the capital's best-preserved colonial buildings – are squeezed into the streets northeast of **Avenida Las Heras**, a busy two-way thoroughfare that links verdant Plaza Vicente López, on the border with Retiro, with Plaza Italia in Palermo. Among these attractions are the country's richest assemblage of nineteenth- and twentieth-century **fine art**, a series of landscaped **plazas** dotted with significant **monuments** (including a statue of Evita), the controversial **national library** and the startling **Floralis Genérica**, a giant metallic flower that opens and shuts. Also here is **Avenida Alvear**: to the southeast of the cemetery and only a few blocks long, it's nonetheless the city's swankiest street, lined with swish art galleries, fashion boutiques and a prestigious hotel.

And even if Recoleta's cultural sights don't appeal, you'll undoubtedly find yourself coming to the barrio for its more consumable offerings at least once during your trip to Buenos Aires. Another smart corner of Recoleta, the ill-defined **Barrio Norte** – generally considered to be the irregular chunk of land bounded by avenidas Las Heras, Pueyrredón, Santa Fe and Coronel Díaz – is an especially fruitful hunting ground for places to eat and drink. As well as hosting numerous **restaurants** and **bars**, Recoleta is home to the city's **design centre** – a showcase of Argentine creativity, it's a great place to track down quality gifts – while myriad stalls of the barrio's Sunday craft fair offer everything from scented candles to jewellery via leather wallets and all manner of *mate* paraphernalia.

The barrio is a pleasant half-hour walk from the microcentro. **Subte** Line D runs through the western fringes of Recoleta, far away from most of its sights, and a dense network of **buses** covers the rest of the barrio – see each attraction for transport details.

Some history

This part of the city has not always been as inviting as it now appears. Indeed, until the end of the seventeenth century the main residents were brigands, who hid out in the area's plentiful groves of Barbary figs. In 1716, drawn by the peace and quiet – it

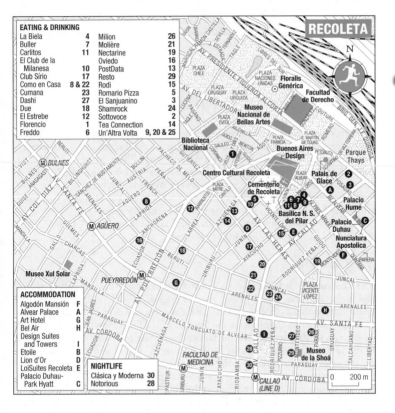

RECOLETA

N

EATING & DRINKING

La Biela	4	Milion	26
Buller	7	Molière	21
Carlitos	11	Nectarine	19
El Club de la		Oviedo	16
Milanesa	10	PostData	13
Club Sírio	17	Resto	29
Como en Casa	8 & 22	Rodi	15
Cumana	23	Romario Pizza	5
Dashi	27	El Sanjuanino	3
Due	18	Shamrock	24
El Estrebe	12	Sottovoce	2
Florencio	1	Tea Connection	14
Freddo	6	Un'Altra Volta	9, 20 & 25

ACCOMMODATION

Algodón Mansión	F
Alvear Palace	A
Art Hotel	G
Bel Air	H
Design Suites and Towers	I
Etoile	B
Lion d'Or	D
LoiSuites Recoleta	E
Palacio Duhau-Park Hyatt	C

NIGHTLIFE

Clásica y Moderna	30
Notorious	28

0   200 m

was known as "El Pago de Monte Grande" ("Land of the Great Woodlands") – **Franciscan monks** set up a monastery here, deeming it perfect for meditation, or "recollection" (hence the barrio's name). They put up buildings in the grounds of a small farm known as La Quinta de los Ombúes, for the grove of ombú trees that thrived there. A century later the city governor ejected the monks from their monastery to make way for a burial ground, now the renowned Cementerio de la Recoleta. The sole surviving vestiges of the religious settlement today are the Basílica del Pilar and the building that houses the Centro Cultural Recoleta.

Modern Recoleta began to take shape only in the 1860s and 1870s, when cholera and yellow fever epidemics chased the city's wealthy north from hitherto fashionable San Telmo. These newcomers built elegant **townhouses** and mansions, each one more elaborate than the last. The barrio soon became the city's most sought-after residential locale, for both the living and the dead, as the repute of the cemetery increased. It took another century, though – and the admittance of Evita's remains into La Recoleta – for the area to turn into the tourist attraction it is now.

The past few years have seen the demolition of some of Recoleta's extravagant nineteenth-century apartment blocks to make way for more modern, less appealing edifices, along with another mass migration of residents – this time from the barrio to the suburbs further north. Even so, the neighbourhood continues to be much as it was in the late nineteenth and early twentieth centuries: prosperous and self-assured. Certainly, just as La Recoleta cemetery has become the city's most desirable resting place for the deceased, Barrio Norte remains a highly attractive address for the living.

Cementerio de la Recoleta and around

Recoleta's star is its grandiose namesake cemetery, the **Cementerio de la Recoleta**. Very near to the graveyard are also a number of the barrio's other attractions, including the beautiful **Basílica Nuestra Señora del Pilar**; one of the city's best cultural centres, the **Centro Cultural Recoleta**; an **exhibition hall**; *La Biela*, a classic *confitería* (see p.160); a **craft market**; **Avenida Alvear**, the city's most fashionable street; and a number of ancient rubber trees. You could easily spend a whole day here without venturing far from the cemetery gates.

There are no subte stations close to La Recoleta, but **buses** #10, #17, #60, #67, #92 and #110 all stop within walking distance.

The cemetery

The **Cementerio de la Recoleta**, also known as La Recoleta, at Avenida Quintana and Junín (daily 7am–5pm; guided tours in English Tues & Thurs 11am; free), is really a city within a city – it's just that all the residents are dead. Opened as a public burial ground in 1822, following the removal of the Franciscan monks from their monastery, La Recoleta became the fashionable resting place for the city's wealthy in the 1870s and 1880s, when the barrio became the stylish address for the living. By the early twentieth century, the upper classes were falling over each other to build elaborate and stylish tombs or, better still, mausoleums, within its gates, and the authorities presiding over the space had begun treating it more like a gentleman's club than a mere graveyard – a practice that continues even now. Today there's an ever-lengthening waiting list for a plot, and money and status in life count less than a great-grandfather's surname in determining who is buried where.

Thanks, in large part, to this elitist admissions policy, La Recoleta presents an exhilarating mixture of architectural whimsy and a panorama of Argentine history. Undoubtedly awe-inspiring, the place tends to exert a magnetic attraction on anyone passing by: it's great for an aimless wander, exploring narrow streets and wide avenues of yews and cypress trees, where dozens of feral cats prowl among the graves. The giant vaults, stacked along avenues inside the high walls, resemble a fanciful Utopian town, and the necropolis gives a visual lesson in architectural styles and fashions, with bits of Argentina's past immortalized in monuments of dark granite, white marble and gleaming bronze, all decorated with countless stone angels and statues of the Virgin Mary.

Over the years the cemetery – the resting place of **Evita**, among a whole host of other national celebrities – has proved a favourite subject of Argentine writers. In his 1923 poem *La Recoleta*, Borges eulogized the graveyard and its beautiful markers covered with Latin inscriptions and fateful dates, its mixture of marble and flowers and its little plazas. Another Argentine writer, Martín Cáparros, was even more melancholy: for him, the burial ground was a magnificent tribute to many great civilizations of the past – from Babylonian and Egyptian, to Roman and Byzantine – and its flamboyant architecture embodied the grandiose hopes of Argentina's heroes and historians that their country would become just as great. But in the end, he concluded, the only fatherland they managed to build was the cemetery itself.

We highlight some of the best sections of La Recoleta below, but to find out more about the cemetery's history and the individual tombs, and find your way around, check out Robert Wright's comprehensive blog/guide at ⓦwww .recoletacemetery.com.

Evita's grave

Without a doubt, La Recoleta's most famous resident is **Evita**, or Eva Perón, second wife of President Juan Perón, and one of Argentina's most enduring figures (see box, p.256). For years after her 1952 death, Porteño high society tried to prevent Evita, champion of the people, from being buried here – hardly surprising, given the snobbishness surrounding the cemetery – but her family, with Perón's support, finally overcame this stiff resistance during his second presidency. Evita has been allowed to rest in her family's tomb – a plain, polished black granite vault pithily marked "**Familia Duarte**" – since the 1970s. It's rumoured that her remains will eventually move to San Vicente, where Perón himself is buried, but for now you can locate the mausoleum by following the signs to President Sarmiento's, over to the left when you come in, then counting five alleyways further away from the entrance, and looking out for the pile of bouquets by the vault. Inside here, Evita's coffin is said to be set in cement to prevent it from disappearing. Some poignant quotes from her speeches are inscribed on several bronze plaques around the tomb, including a tribute from the union of taxi drivers.

Other graves and monuments

The only thing that most of the **graves** here really have in common is the patrician nature of their occupants. The tombs themselves range from simple headstones to bombastic masterpieces built in a variety of styles, including Art Nouveau, Art Deco, Secessionist, Neoclassical, Neo-Byzantine and even Neo-Babylonian. The oldest monumental grave, dating from 1836, is that of **Juan Facundo Quiroga**, a much-feared *caudillo* (provincial chief) from the northwestern province of La Rioja and henchman to General Rosas, an autocratic leader of Argentina in the 1840s and 1850s. The tomb stands straight ahead of the main entrance, along with the recently restored marble statue of the *Virgen Dolorosa*, said to be a likeness of his widow. Next to it, inscribed with a Borges poem, stands the solemn granite mausoleum occupied by several generations of the eminent **Alvear family** (see box, p.110), including **Torcuato de Alvear**, who, as the city's first mayor, had the ceremonial portico of Doric columns added to the cemetery's entrance in the 1880s.

Most of the great artists, scientists, financiers and politicians buried here would not have been granted a space without a resoundingly noble surname like San Martín or Dorrego, Anchorena or Pueyrredón, Mitre or Hernández. The main exceptions to this rule are the military men, many of them Irish or British seafarers, who played a key part in Argentina's struggle for independence, such as **Admiral William Brown**, an Argentine hero of Irish origins, who at the beginning of the nineteenth century decimated the Spanish fleet near Isla Martín García. An unusual monument decorated with a beautiful miniature of his frigate, the *Hercules*, is a highlight of the cemetery's central plaza, and a bronze urn made from melting down the cannons of one of his ships holds his ashes.

In addition to individual tombs and family vaults, La Recoleta contains a number of monuments, such as the magnificent **Panteón de los Guerreros del Paraguay**. Up against the far western corner of the cemetery, this is the mass grave of Argentines who fell in the War of the Triple Alliance fought against Paraguay in the 1860s – it's guarded by two bronze infantrymen. Over by the northwest wall, due west of the central plaza, is the **Monumento a los Caídos en la Revolución de 1890**, a

Though Argentina has always been a republic in principle, much of its past reads like an oligarchy, with a few aristocratic families dominating the political scene. The **Alvears** were one such family, and you can spot their influence all around Buenos Aires. **Carlos María de Alvear** (1789–1852) founded the line, ensuring his place in the history books by playing a leading role in the fight for independence in both Argentina and Uruguay. A majestic statue of the general by French sculptor Bourdelle dominates the busy avenues next to the Palais de Glace, not far from the Cementerio de la Recoleta, while both Avenida Alvear and the luxury hotel there are named after him. His son **Torcuato** (1822–90) served as the first mayor of the city in the 1880s, and is mainly remembered for modernizing the infrastructure, especially paving the streets and improving the water supply. Torcuato's own, unashamedly aristocratic, son, **Máximo Marcelo Torcuato de Alvear Pacheco** (1868–1942), better known as Marcelo T., was also a prominent politician. Elected Radical president of Argentina in the 1920s, he oversaw the country's rise to the rank of one of the world's five wealthiest nations. Married to leading opera singer Regina Pacini, he also took a strong interest in Argentina's cultural activities. Like his grandfather, Marcelo T. is honoured with a street name: Calle Marcelo T. de Alvear runs through Retiro and much of Recoleta, parallel to Avenida Santa Fe. All three men are buried in a conspicuous mausoleum in Recoleta Cemetery.

huge granite slab smothered in commemorative bronze plaques, beneath a centenarian cypress tree. This tomb holds the remains of several Radical Party leaders, including founding father Leandro Alem and two-time president Hipólito Yrigoyen.

Three aisles to the south, a statue of a boxer, complete with gown and boots, looks almost out of place. The statue marks the final resting place of **Luis Ángel Firpo**, the so-called "Raging Bull of the Pampas", who fought Jack Dempsey for the world heavyweight title in 1923 – and lost despite throwing Dempsey out of the ring, something which Argentines remain bitter about to this day.

Basílica Nuestra Señora del Pilar

Just north of the cemetery gates is the stark white silhouette of the **Basílica Nuestra Señora del Pilar** (Mon–Sat 10.30am–6.15pm, Sun 2.30–6.15pm; monthly guided visits in Spanish Sun at 3pm; free; ⊛www.basilicadelpilar.org .ar). Built by Jesuits in the early eighteenth century, it's the second oldest church in Buenos Aires, inaugurated in 1732. Despite its beauty and strategic location, it was allowed to decline from around the 1820s, when the monastic community was expelled from its home, until 1936, when Pope Pius XII named it a basilica and it became, effectively, the parish church for the Recoleta elite. Using eighteenth-century watercolours as a guide, the sky-blue Pas-de-Calais ceramic tiles atop its single slender turret were then painstakingly restored, along with the plain facade. The interior was also remodelled, and the monks' cells turned into side chapels, each decorated with a gilded reredos and polychrome wooden saints. These include a statue of San Pedro de Alcántara, the Virgen de la Merced and the Casa de Ejercicios, all attributed to a native artist known simply as "José". The magnificent Baroque silver altarpiece, embellished with an Inca sun and other pre-Hispanic details, was made by craftsmen from Alto Perú. Equally admirable is the fine altar crucifix allegedly donated to the city by King Charles III of Spain. It is possible to visit the **cloisters** above the church (same hours) via the staircase on the left-hand side, next to the third altar from the entrance. These restored rooms, once home to Franciscan monks (refugees from the demolished monastery), now hold a collection of religious paintings and artefacts, including some impressive colonial and *criollo* silverware. From the windows you get a good view over the cemetery.

Centro Cultural Recoleta

Immediately north of the basilica, the **Centro Cultural Recoleta**, or **CCR** (Tues–Fri 2–9pm, Sat & Sun 10am–9pm; free; Ⓦwww.centroculturalrecoleta.org), Junín 1930, is one of the city's leading arts centres, a good deal bigger and more impressive inside than its modest front suggests. The main two-storey building, which dates from the 1730s, is one of Buenos Aires' oldest and originally housed Franciscan monks and the beggars who came seeking food and shelter from them. It was extensively, but tastefully, remodelled in the 1980s and retains its former cloisters. These cool, white, arched hallways and simple rooms on the upper level make an excellent setting for the changing art, photography and audio visual exhibitions that the centre hosts (some are free, others charge a small entrance fee). These are mostly of works by contemporary Argentine or other South American artists and tend to be avant-garde, often with a political flavour.

Accessed by the same entrance, and part of the CCR, a series of cobbled patios runs alongside the cloisters, sometimes hosting temporary outdoor exhibitions. To the right of the first patio, the **Museo Participativo de Ciencias** (Mon–Fri 10am–5pm, Sat & Sun 3.30–7.30pm; $16) is a small but colourful hands-on interactive science museum; it's quite popular with local children, but the Spanish-only explanations may make it less so with those who don't speak the language. The next patio hosts "**El Aleph**" auditorium, a converted chapel, painted garish pink. Jazz, rock and tango concerts are regularly on the programme here, along with poetry readings and literary recitals. Further along, the roof terrace – just crying out for a roof café – affords views of the surrounding plazas.

Finally, the **Sala Villa Villa**, at the far end, puts on contemporary theatre and dance recitals; it's the occasional home of the internationally renowned anarchic theatre troupe De La Guarda/Fuerza Bruta, who swing on trapezes above the audience, among other performance techniques.

Buenos Aires Design

Adjoining the cultural centre at the corner of Avenida Pueyrredón and Azcuénaga, **Buenos Aires Design** is a shopping mall specializing in design for the home. Alongside the latest classy furniture from Europe and the US, you can find high-quality Argentine products ranging from blown-glass vases and leather table mats to native-wood desks and alpaca carpets. Over five dozen outlets compete for custom on two floors, while a host of bland bars and places to eat lurk under its Neoclassical arches.

Plaza San Martín de Tours and La Biela

Opposite the Centro Cultural, the grassy slope of **Plaza San Martín de Tours**, dedicated to the city's male patron saint, lies at the northern end of Avenida Alvear. It is shaded by three of the biggest *gomeros*, or **rubber trees**, in the city – these are impressive sights with their huge buttress-roots, contorted like arthritic limbs.

Another hundred-year-old rubber tree, the famous Gran Gomero, shelters the terrace of nearby **La Biela**, on the corner of Avenida Quintana, 100m west. One of the city's most traditional *confiterías*, it gets its name, which means "connecting-rod", from being the haunt of racing drivers, including Juan Manuel Fangio (see box, p.213) in the 1940s and 1950s; it was also a favourite target of Trotskyist guerrillas in the 1970s, owing to its conspicuously wealthy patrons. Nowadays, though, the only disturbance you're likely to experience comes from the odd busker, or the pigeons and parrots that roost in the branches of the Gran Gomero.

⑦ Plaza Francia

Not far from Plaza San Martín de Tours, on the parkland sloping down north-wards from the cemetery, street performers often entertain crowds during the **Feria Plaza Francia**, also known as the **Feria Hippy** because of its flower-power ambience (Sat & Sun 9am–7pm; free). In the market, artisans sell hand-crafted wares, including *mate* gourds and ceramics of mostly good quality, at stalls arranged along the park's wide paths. You'll also often find pieces of unusual jewellery on sale, some of it made of pink and red rhodochrosite (see box, p.208), an extremely rare semiprecious stone that is mined only in a remote mountain location in northwest Argentina.

Across Avenida Pueyrredón, a rhomboid piece of lawn bounded by Avenida del Libertador and calles Doctor Ricardo Levene and Doctor Luis Agote is **Plaza Francia** proper – its highlight is a splendid Neo-Baroque monument to Liberty, created for Argentina's centenary in 1910. A gift from the French government (its official name is "Francia a la Argentina"), it is the work of French sculptor Emile Peynot, and depicts two female figures, representing both countries, an angel of prosperity ("Gloria") and four smaller figures: Science, Industry, Agriculture and the Arts. Bronze bas-reliefs around the base relate significant moments in each nation's history, including the storming of the Bastille and the crossing of the Andes by San Martín.

Along Avenida Alvear

Only five blocks in length, stretching from Plaza San Martín de Tours to Plaza Carlos Pellegrini (in Retiro; see p.104), **Avenida Alvear**, named after Independence hero General Alvear, is one of the city's shortest but most exclusive avenues, lined with expensive **art galleries** – selling mostly conventional portraits and landscapes but also some avant-garde pieces – and international designer **fashion boutiques** like Ralph Lauren, Louis Vuitton and Emporio Armani. At its corner with Ayacucho, and also taking its name from the general, stands the city's most famous and traditional luxury hotel, the French Art Deco **Alvear Palace**, built in 1932 and restored in the first years of the twenty-first century. Over the decades its guests have included the world's royalty, opera divas, pop icons and Hollywood stars. If you're not on a budget, consider a stay here – see p.153 for details. Two blocks south, opposite elegant apartment buildings between Montevideo and Rodriguez Peña, are three palaces that were home to some of Argentina's wealthiest families at the beginning of the twentieth century. Although none is open to the public, the exteriors are worth a peek for their splendid architecture. The northernmost, behind a Charles Thays-designed garden, is the **Palacio Hume**. This perfectly symmetrical Art Nouveau creation, embellished with intricate wrought-iron work, now looks a little the worse for wear. It was originally built for British rail-engineer Alexander Hume, but was sold to the Duhau family in the 1920s, who staged the city's first-ever art exhibition inside. The Duhau family also built the middle palace, the **Palacio Duhau**. This austere imitation of an eighteenth-century French Neoclassical *palais*, with plain columns and an unadorned triangular tympanum, has been converted into a Park Hyatt hotel (see p.154). The third palace, the severely Neoclassical **Nunciatura Apostólica**, on the corner of Montevideo, was designed by a French architect for a member of the Anchorena family (see p.101). Nowadays it's the seat of the Vatican's Argentina representative, and was used by Pope John Paul II during his visits to the country.

Palais de Glace and around

The **Palais de Glace** (Tues–Fri noon–8pm, Sat & Sun 10am–8pm; guided visits in Spanish, free, Sat & Sun 4 & 5.30pm; Ⓦ www.palaisdeglace.gob.ar), a distinctive circular *belle époque* building, sits directly northeast of the Centro Cultural Recoleta at Posadas 1725. Also known as the Palacio Nacional de las Artes, and used for a variety of art exhibitions and trade shows, including popular wine tastings, the building boasts a long and interesting history. It opened in 1910 as an ice-skating rink (the original name, "Palais de Glace", translates as "Ice Palace" in French), but just five years later the ice was replaced with oak flooring and the building converted to a ballroom. As this new incarnation, the venue became famous for being the "home of tango" – or at least the place where tango crossed over from being considered a sordid feature of brothels to a fashionable society dance – when Porteño trendsetter Barón de Marchi staged tango soirées here in the 1920s. There is even a popular tango entitled *Palais de Glace*. In 1931 renowned architect Alejandro Bustillo was given the job of transforming the building once again, this time into an art gallery. The exhibitions (some free, some with a charge levied) put on these days often have a political tinge, such as themes relating to the military dictatorship and the disappeared.

Immediately north of the Palais de Glace an **equestrian statue** of General Carlos M. de Alvear (see box, p.110) surveys the traffic – the bronze figure stands 5m high, atop a reddish granite pedestal nearly 13m tall, surrounded by allegorical figures representing Freedom, Victory, Strength and Eloquence. An acutely elegant creation by **Émile-Antoine Bourdelle**, a pupil of Rodin, it's considered both one of the city's, and the artist's, finest sculptures – it took him over a decade to produce, part of which was spent studying Argentine horses at the Longchamp racecourse. At the time of its inauguration in 1926, however, many were shocked by the fact that the general is depicted without a hat.

Museo Nacional de Bellas Artes and around

Between Avenida del Libertador and the railway lines that snake out from Retiro station in the south, an area of greenery – a foretaste of the huge parklands just over the barrio border with Palermo – forms Recoleta's northern fringe. Dotted among the regularly mown lawns here are Argentina's principal art museum, the **Museo Nacional de Bellas Artes**; the pompous-looking Law Faculty building; and one of the city's newest and most unusual landmarks, a giant metallic flower called the **Floralis Genérica**.

Buses #59, #60, #93 and #102 all have stops near the museum.

The museum

The **Museo Nacional de Bellas Artes**, or **MNBA** (Tues–Fri 12.30–8.30pm, Sat & Sun 9.30am–8.30pm; free; Ⓦ www.mnba.org.ar), at Avenida del Libertador 1473, a few minutes' walk due north of Recoleta Cemetery, was founded in 1896 at the instigation of President Uriburu. Initially housed in part of the glamorous

Au Bon Marché department store on Calle Florida (now the Galerías Pacífico; see p.66), since 1932 the museum has made its home in a disused 1870s pumping station. This unassuming, slightly gloomy, brick-red Neoclassical building was converted for museum use by leading Argentine architect **Alejandro Bustillo**, whose many designs in Buenos Aires include the headquarters of the Banco de la Nación, in the microcentro (see p.64). Inside, in addition to over thirty exhibition rooms, there is an **auditorium** where films are screened and good classical concerts are held, and a **bookshop**.

Today the museum's art collection is one of the largest (over 11,000 pieces) and most comprehensive in Latin America – only São Paulo's MASP is a serious rival – but less than a tenth of it is ever on display at one time. The whole of the **ground floor** is given over to mostly minor works by European masters, while the **first floor** is dominated by Argentine art, much of which clearly shows the influence of the Old World. Apart from the pieces by the rare Argentine artists who managed to break free of those shackles (to see more of their works, visit the

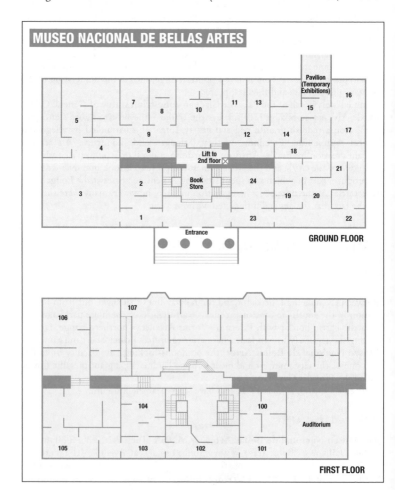

Rodin and Buenos Aires

Of all international artists, the great French sculptor **Auguste Rodin** (1840–1917) has had perhaps the greatest hold on Buenos Aires. The city boasts the only public monument in the Americas – the monument to President Sarmiento in Parque 3 de Febrero, Palermo – to have been commissioned from the artist. Other works of his are also on prominent display at various locations around the city, including the Museo de Arte Decorativo in Palermo (see p.121) and the MNBA. The latter boasts an impressive collection that includes *Jeune mère dans la grotte* ("Young Woman in the Cave", a bronze that is part of the Santamarina collection. Taking pride of place in **Room 10A** is *La Terre et La Lune* ("The Earth and The Moon"), an 1899 marble composition purchased by director Eduardo Schiaffino in 1906. At the same time, Schiaffino also bought an original copy of the sculptor's famous *Thinker* (now in the Plaza del Congreso; see p.60), and Rodin made him a gift of *Le Baiser* ("The Kiss"), also currently displayed in Room 10A of the MNBA. Another small work belonging to the Santamarina collection and valued at US$10,000, *Estudio de Manos Para El Secreto* ("Study of Hands for The Secret"), mysteriously disappeared from the MNBA in May 2003, only to be found four months later by a *cartonero* (unofficial scrap recycler), who sold it to an antiques store for $50. The antiques dealer then returned the piece to the very grateful museum. In addition to these pieces by Rodin, you can also see his undeniable influence in designs by such Argentine sculptors as **Rogelio Yrurtia** (see p.145) and **Pedro Zonza Birano**, whose works are also widely displayed throughout the city.

MALBA, in Palermo; see p.125), the main exception to this rule lies in the small collection of pre-Columbian treasures, also on the first floor. On the less visited **second floor** (accessible by a small lift near the main entrance) are a smaller set of rooms used exclusively for temporary exhibitions, often of photographs, plus two outdoor sculpture terraces featuring works by Argentine artists such as Pedro Zonza Birano, whose inspiration came from Rodin (see box above). Further **temporary exhibits** – often of Argentine art, and including pieces from the permanent collection not otherwise on display – are held in rooms 16 and 17 on the ground floor and in the purpose-built pavilion behind the main building.

You can rent a recorded **audioguide** ($35), which will take you on a ninety-minute tour of the museum, but in view of its technical flaws, professorial tone and the poor translation into English, you're better off without it.

Ground floor

Rooms 1 to 9, which begin to the sharp left as you enter the museum, contain European painting and sculpture from the tenth to eighteenth centuries. The highlight here is the small but wide-ranging **Hirsch bequest (Room 3)**, which was left to the nation by wealthy Belgrano landowner and art-collector Alfredo Hirsch and includes some fabulous art objects from all over Europe, including a retable from Spain, a French tapestry and a 1634 portrait Rembrandt painted of his sister. Look out also for the series of Goya works acquired in the 1880s by Argentine writer Miguel Cané (Room 8).

Room 10 contains a number of works produced by **Rodin** (see box above). **Room 11** is given over to works by the **Macchiaioli group** of Italian artists, active in the 1850s, whose use of rapid strokes to create vibrant works presaged the Impressionists – check out Carcano's *The Believers*. Manet's *La nymphe surprise* ("The Nymph Caught by Surprise"; 1861) overshadows the other pre-Impressionist works in **rooms 12 and 13**, while Gauguin's *Femme de la Mer* ("Woman of the Sea";

1892) stands out from among paintings by Monet, Toulouse-Lautrec and Degas in the **Impressionist rooms (14A and B)**.

Private collections form a vital part of the museum's displays and rooms 18 and 19 are taken up by the collection of Mercedes Santamarina (her aristocratic family, of Spanish origins, owned a huge estancia in the province of Buenos Aires), who donated furniture, sculptures and paintings, including a pastel of ballerinas by Degas and a bronze by Rodin, to the museum before her death in 1972, with the proviso that they should all be on display together.

In **Room 20**, devoted to the work of Rodin's pupil, French sculptor Émile-Antoine Bourdelle, you can see the copies of two heads of the allegorical figures surrounding the equestrian statue of General Alvear (see p.113), which stands close to the museum at the junction of Avenida del Libertador and Posadas. **Rooms 21 to 24** house an array of twentieth-century European art by the likes of Klee, Pollock and Rothko, with Picasso's *Mujer acostada* ("Reclining Woman"; 1931) a highlight.

First floor

The **first-floor galleries** are an excellent introduction to **Argentine art**, containing a selection of works by most of the country's major artists. At the top of the staircase, you can see a bronze torso by Rogelio Yrurtia, one of the few Argentine artists to have a museum of his own (see p.145), while Antonio Berni's *Juanito Laguna aprende a leer* ("Juanito Laguna learns to read"; 1961) and Antonio Seguí's *Autorretrato de las vocaciones frustradas* ("Self-portrait of Frustrated Vocations") are two important contemporary works. For a historical overview of Argentine art and sculpture illustrated by the galleries on the first floor, see Contexts, p.262.

Dimly lit **Room 100** displays a small but fabulous collection of pre-Columbian art, with terracotta, textiles and other objects from northwest Argentina and Peru – a highlight is the bronze disc incised with a geometric face and double-headed serpents. The antechamber, **Room 101**, contains an unusual set of wooden panels, produced in Mexico at the beginning of the eighteenth century, which are inlaid with mother-of-pearl and depict scenes from the Spanish Conquest.

Room 102 chronicles the infancy of art in Argentina – the first four or five decades after the country's independence in 1810 – which was still dominated by foreign artists such as Scotsman Richard Adams (*Port of Buenos Aires*; 1834) and

Uruguayan artists at the MNBA

One of the MNBA's gems is its collection of **Uruguayan art** in **Room 104**. In 1995, just before her death, the great Argentine film director **María Luisa Bemberg** (whose films include Oscar-nominated classic *Camila*) donated a collection of 27 art objects to the museum, including pictures by three major painters from across the Río de la Plata. The short distance between the two countries' capitals means that mutual influences were inevitable, but the works of **Pedro Figari** (1861–1938), **Rafael Barradas** (1890–1929) and **Joaquín Torres García** (1874–1949) are idiosyncratically Uruguayan and highly regarded. Figari is known for his colourful oils depicting scenes of urban and rural everyday life; in the case of *Candombé*, one of the highlights here, the subject is one of the region's African-influenced carnivals. Barradas, a fellow Montevideño, was more interested in the sophistication of the city, and was inspired by French Cubism – see his *Impresión de caffe* ("Impression of Italian Café"), produced in 1913. Torres García's *Catedral constructiva* ("Constructive Cathedral"; 1931), meanwhile, is typical of the artist's abstract phase, and, though painted in Paris, it was inspired by Incan stonework. Torres García has his own museum in Montevideo, but you can also see more of his paintings in Buenos Aires, at the MALBA (see p.125).

Brazilian-born Frenchman Jean-Léon Pallière (*Idylle créole*, or "Creole idyll") and are as much of interest for their historical/sociological depictions of life on the Pampas as they are for any artistic merit. An 1851 portrait of Manuelita Rosas by Prilidiano Pueyrredón is one of the first likenesses of a non-military Argentine figure done by an Argentine painter – though the bright red dress sported by señorita Rosas is a clearly political reference to the Federalist red of her dictator father (see Contexts, p.254). More works of Pueyrredón's are in **Room 103**, along with pictorial records of the 1860s' War of the Triple Alliance against Paraguay by Cándido López, who learned to paint with his left hand after losing his right arm in battle. The fabulous Bemberg Collection in **Room 104** (see box opposite) is a small but exquisite selection of works by Río de la Plata masters.

Rooms 105 and 106 trace the progress of Argentine artists such as Ernesto de la Cárcova and Cesáreo Bernaldo de Quirós as they tried to break away from European influences, with paintings that depict such subjects as the city of Buenos Aires or the rural culture of the gaucho. The beautiful oils of Bordeaux-born Fernando Fader (1882–1935), such as *La Mazamorra* ("Blackberry Pie"; 1927) stand out, as does *Riachuelo*, a 1949 work by Boca artist Benito Quinquela Martín depicting life on the eponymous river that runs through the barrio (see p.91).

Down some steps you arrive at the sixteen sections that make up the vast **Room 107**, which covers the evolution of Argentine art from 1920 to the present. Names to look for here include Xul Solar (who has his own museum in Recoleta – see p.118), Lino Enea Spilimbergo, Raquel Forner, Libero Badii and Guillermo Kuitca. Nicolás García Uriburu's 1993 work *Utopía del Sur* ("Utopia of the South"), on display near the entrance, Fermín Eguía's *Pintura* ("Painting"), depicting a hen with a woman's head and a fork in its back, perched on a table laid for a surreal lunch, and Raúl Soldi's peaceful oil *La hamaca* ("The Rocking Chair"), with a young woman relaxing as horses gallop across the Pampas in the background, are particular highlights of this section.

Floralis Genérica

While in this part of the city you might like to take a look at the 25m-tall aluminium and stainless-steel bloom of the **Floralis Genérica**. It stands in the grassy Plaza de las Naciones next to the massive Doric columns of the University's **Facultad de Derecho** (Law Faculty), behind the Museo Nacional de Bellas Artes. One of the city's newest sculptures, it was donated in April 2002 by Argentine architect Eduardo Catalano as a tribute to all the world's flowers and, in his words, a symbol of "hope for the country's new spring" – a reference to the 2001 crisis. A system of light sensors and hydraulics closes the six petals at sunset and opens them again at 8am (the sculptor was afraid people would miss it if it opened at daybreak), but they stay open 24 hours on May 25, September 21 (the beginning of spring), Christmas Eve and New Year's Eve. A large pool of water at the base both enhances its beauty and protects it from vandals.

Biblioteca Nacional and around

Argentina's copyright library, the futuristic concrete **Biblioteca Nacional** (Mon–Fri 9am–8pm, Sat & Sun noon–7pm; guided visits in English Mon, Tues & Thurs 3pm; free; ☎011/4808-6026), stands back from Avenida del Libertador at Agüero 2502, about half a kilometre west of the MNBA. Six floors high, it's built on the

RECOLETA | Biblioteca Nacional and around

site of **Quinta Unzué**, the elegant palace where the Peróns lived when they were in power and where Evita died – a happening marked by a bronze plaque inside the library. After the so-called Revolución Libertadora, which overthrew Perón in 1955, Argentina's new leaders were petrified that the residence would become a shrine to Evita, and so had it razed to the ground. The government eventually decided to build a library on the site, but political upheavals, financial scandals and disagreements over the design held up construction for over three decades; the library was finally inaugurated only in 1992. The design is definitely a result of the 1960s, though – it's a kind of giant cuboid mushroom, complete with ribbed gills, perched on four hefty stalks. For the Argentine architects Clorindo Testa, Alicia D. Cazzanica and Francisco Bullrich, much influenced by Le Corbusier, it represented a table, and their aim was to create a transparent structure, with shafts allowing indirect daylight into the public reading rooms.

Inside, what you see is but a small sampling of the library's extensive **collection**: most of the five million tomes and documents housed here – including a first edition of *Don Quixote*, a 1455 Gutenberg Bible and the personal collection of General Belgrano, plus 21 valuable incunabula – are tucked away and can only be seen if you have special authorization. The guided visits offer a detailed explanation of the library's history and function and often include access to the top floor – in addition to the retro reading desks and lamps rescued from the old library on Avenida Moreno (now the national music school), you can admire a breathtaking view of the library's surroundings.

On the library's land, attractively landscaped gardens, the **Plaza del Lector**, a café – *Café del Lector* – and a terrace stretch out towards Avenida Las Heras from the Biblioteca Nacional's southwest corner, while on the other side, along Avenida del Libertador, the lush park adjoining the library has been symbolically renamed **Plaza Evita**. A statue of Eva Perón, unveiled by President Menem a week before his term in office ended in 1999, overlooks the square; it's the only full-size statue of a woman in the entire city. Peronists saw the placement of this monument as a way of avenging Evita's ill-treatment at the hands of the oligarchy even after her death. Surveying her is a statue of Pope John Paul II, funded by Buenos Aires' Polish community.

A block to the southeast along Avenida del Libertador, **Plaza Mitre** is dominated by an enormous monument to **Bartolomé Mitre**, a nineteenth-century president who founded the influential broadsheet *La Nación* in 1870. Behind the square, next to the British embassy, is a very green bronze statue of **George Canning**. Lord Canning was British Foreign Secretary in the 1820s and instrumental in getting the South American nations' independence from Spain recognized by the rest of Europe. Previously next to the Torre de los Ingleses in Retiro (see p.97), the tonne of bronze was chucked into the Río de la Plata at the height of the South Atlantic conflict (hence the colour), then fished out several years later and moved to this less conspicuous position.

To reach the library and its surroundings, take **bus** #59, #60, #93, #102 or #130 – most of these run along Avenida Las Heras or Avenida del Libertador.

Museo Xul Solar

Over in the southwest corner of Recoleta, far from most of the barrio's other sights at Laprida 1212, near the corner of Mansilla, the **Museo Xul Solar** (Tues–Fri noon–8pm, Sat noon–7pm; closed Jan; $10; W www.xulsolar.org.ar) presents the life and work of eccentric Porteño artist Xul Solar (1887–1963). The museum, run by the **Fundación Pan Klub** (a non-profit organization set up by his widow and other admirers in 1986 to promote Solar's work and his universalist ideas), is housed in the early twentieth-century townhouse where Solar lived for the last twenty years of his life. The building was remodelled in the 1990s and its award-winning design is as exciting as the display of the artist's works. The space, which makes use of several different levels built of timber and glass, contains pieces spanning nearly five decades – each level is dedicated to a period in Solar's career.

Solar's preferred media were watercolour and tempera, though in addition to his very Klee-like paintings, you can also see several more curious objects of his design, including a set of **"Pan Altars"**, multicoloured mini-retables intended for what he liked to call his "universal religions" – sets of universalist beliefs that combined monotheistic doctrine with the animist credence of indigenous peoples. Solar once told his friend Borges that he had "founded twelve new religions since lunch". Unfortunately, these "religions" apparently never gained more than one follower – Solar himself. In some of the later works you can detect the artist's passion for linguistics, best summed up in his plans for universal understanding based on his versions of Esperanto. His "Neocreole" – mixing Spanish, Portuguese, Guaraní and English – was to be a common language for all Americans, while "Panlengua" was a set of monosyllables based on arithmetic and astrology, Solar's "ideal universal language". Texts written in these languages are the inspirations behind some of the more child-like paintings on view. Another of the more interesting pieces to look for here is a piano whose keyboard he replaced with three rows of painted keys with textured surfaces, created both for blind pianists and to implement his notion of the correspondence of colour and music.

The museum is equidistant from the Pueyrredón and Agüero stops on **subte** Line D.

Palermo

P alermo is Buenos Aires' largest and leafiest barrio, stretching all the way from Recoleta to Colegiales and Belgrano (a distance of over 4km from south to north), and from the river to Avenida Córdoba. As you might expect of such a vast area, its character is by no means homogenous – indeed, Palermo really encompasses several distinct sub-neighbourhoods, each with a different feel. Despite these internal subdivisions, the whole of Palermo does have one common feature: it is a prosperous, vibrantly verdant and appealingly well-kempt neighbourhood. Many of its wide avenues are lined with leafy *tipas* (native trees with distinctive zigzagging branches), while plane trees, palms and jacarandas shade the older, cobbled streets. Three of Palermo's areas will be of most interest to visitors: **Palermo Chico**, a haven of tranquillity that boasts some of the city's most exclusive residences, including a number of embassies, and three important arts museums; **Bosques de Palermo** ("Palermo Woods"), a series of beautifully landscaped **parks and gardens** that come alive with locals practising in-line skating, playing football or walking their dogs, all while parrots squawk overhead and hummingbirds sip at hibiscus blossoms; and mostly low-rise **Palermo Viejo**, which itself is divided still further into boho-chic **Palermo Soho** and media-linked **Palermo Hollywood**. You may well find yourself staying in the relative calm of Palermo Viejo, the setting of some of the city's most appealing boutique hotels and best-value hostels. Its streets are also home to some chic shopping outlets – with an emphasis on Argentine fashion, furniture and art – and a variety of excellent restaurants and lively bars. Meanwhile, the northern fringes of the barrio comprise some eclectic smaller neighbourhoods, including a trendy zone of crowded bars and restaurants near the country's main polo ground and hippodrome called **Las Cañitas**; and the **Costanera Norte**, which is home to the city's domestic airport and a couple of hot nightspots.

Palermo's main transport arteries are avenidas del Libertador and Sarmiento – which intersect at a roundabout dominated by one of the city's most striking landmarks, the dazzling **Monumento de los Españoles** – and shop-lined Avenida Santa Fe, whose intersection with Avenida Sarmiento forms the semicircular **Plaza Italia**, a major hub. Subte Line D runs underneath Santa Fe the full length of the barrio, with five evenly spaced stations (including Plaza Italia) that can be useful for reaching some sights. Otherwise, getting around the neighbourhood requires tackling the bus system or hailing a cab.

Some history

Palermo takes its name not from the Sicilian city but from an Italian farmer, **Giovanni Domenico Palermo**, who bought the flood plains to the north of Buenos Aires at the end of the sixteenth century, drained them and turned them into vineyards and orchards, which soon became known as the "campos de Palermo" ("Palermo fields"). In the 1830s, tyrannical President Juan Manuel de Rosas bought up the farmland and later built a mansion here, La Quinta, where he lived with his family and a domesticated tiger until his 1852 overthrow here. The barrio began to take on its present-day appearance in the 1890s, when its large parks and gardens were laid out, many of them by French landscape artist **Charles Thays** (see box, p.96). It was considered rather insalubrious at the time, due to its tendency to flood, but it gradually became gentrified throughout the twentieth century, and is now regarded as a distinctly classy place to live, even though parts are still prone to flooding.

Palermo Chico

The section of Palermo known as **Palermo Chico**, or Little Palermo, takes up the barrio's southeast corner, hemmed between Avenida del Libertador and the train tracks running north from Retiro. Around its periphery you'll find two of Buenos Aires' top museums – the **Museo de Arte Decorativo**, a fabulous assemblage of European paintings and artefacts, and the **Museo de Arte Latinamericano de Buenos Aires (MALBA)**, an outstanding collection of Latin American modern art. The blocks due north of tree-filled Plaza Chile, at the sub-barrio's core, are occupied by an exclusive residential district called **Barrio Parque**. Another museum – the **Museo de Arte Popular José Hernández**, which houses traditional arts and crafts – is an added attraction if you have time on your hands.

Museo de Arte Decorativo

There's no finer example of the opulent decor money could buy in early twentieth-century Buenos Aires than the remarkable collection of art and furniture on display in the **Museo de Arte Decorativo**, Av del Libertador 1902 (Tues–Sun 2–7pm; $5, free on Tues; guided visits in English Tues–Sat 2.30pm, $15; Ⓦwww.mnad.org.ar). The museum is housed in the **Palacio Errázuriz**, one of the city's most original private mansions, albeit of typically French design. The palace was built in 1911 for Chilean diplomat Matías Errázuriz and his patrician Argentine wife, Josefina de Alvear, who lived here until 1937, when it was turned into a public museum. Designed by René Sergent, a French architect and proponent of the Academic style, it has three contrasting facades. The western one, on Sanchez de Bustamante, is inspired by the Petit Trianon at Versailles; the long northern side of the building with Corinthian pillars, on Avenida del Libertador, is based on the palaces on Paris's Place de la Concorde; and the eastern end, near the entrance, is dominated by an enormous semicircular stone porch, supported by four Tuscan columns. The coach house, now a restaurant and tearoom with outdoor tables, *Croque Madame* (Mon–Fri 8am–midnight, Sat & Sun 10am–midnight), sits just beyond the monumental, Louis XVI-style wrought-iron and bronze gates.

The interior is as Gallic as the exterior, especially the Regency ballroom, lined with gilded Rococo panels and huge mirrors, all stripped from a Parisian house. The whole building is on an incredible scale, not least the French Renaissance **Grand Hall**, where some of the museum's prize artworks are displayed. The Errázuriz and Alvear family arms feature in the hall's magnificent stone fireplace, while next to it is a bronze model of a Rodin sculpture they desired, but even they

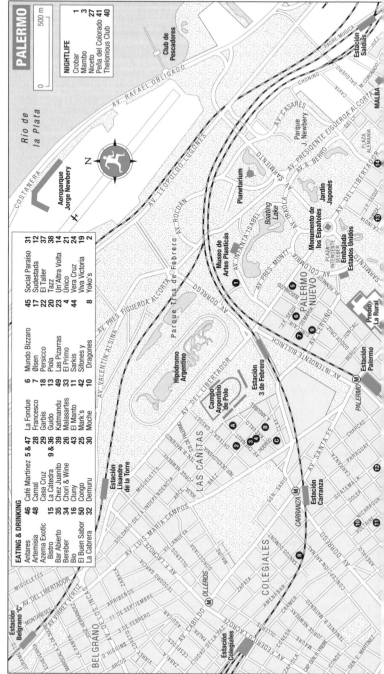

▲ Recoleta

ACCOMMODATION	
1551 Palermo	U
Boutique Hotel	O
Bed and Baires Hostel	J
Bo Bo	C
Casa Las Cañitas	C
Craft	K
Eco Pampa Hostel	B
Finisterra	P
Five Cool Rooms	D
Home	E
Krista	L
Legado Mítico	R
Magnolia	Q
Malabia 1555	M
Nuss	S
La Otra Orilla	T
Posada Palermo	I
Rendezvous	G
So Hostel	A
Tailor Made Hotel	H
Vain	F
Vitrum	

PALERMO CHICO

Biblioteca Nacional

Museo de Arte Decorativo

BARRIO NORTE

Museo de Arte Popular

Parque Las Heras

ALTO PALERMO

Shopping Alto Palermo

Museo Evita

Jardín Zoológico

Jardín Botánico

PLAZA ITALIA

Borges' House

VILLA FREUD

BALVANERA

ALMAGRO

MEDRANO

PALERMO VIEJO

PALERMO SOHO

PALERMO HOLLYWOOD

VILLA CRESPO

MALABIA

▶ Caballito

Thanks to its subtropical climate, Buenos Aires is the perfect habitat for a variety of native and imported **trees**. There are nearly **half a million** deciduous and evergreen trees dotted around the Capital Federal, along with an estimated 1500 or so palms. While some are quite young, others are well over a hundred years old, and a few even enjoy the status of national monument. Serving the practical purpose of providing the city with welcome shade, these trees are also an aesthetic boon, bringing touches of colour to the metropolis – depending on when you visit, you may see shades of red, pink, yellow and, in the case of the jacaranda (a native tree that flowers twice yearly, in March and Oct–Nov), a bluish mauve.

Over half the trees in Buenos Aires are imported. **Ashes** from the US are the most numerous of these. Cheap to plant and fast growing, these can also have some disastrous effects on their surroundings – mainly that their roots push up paving stones and ruin pavements. Another ten percent are **planes** (*plátanos* in Spanish), also imports, whose handsome foliage and distinctive flaky trunks line avenues all around the city, notably Avenida de Mayo and those in Palermo Viejo. Many people are allergic to their pollen, which explains all the sniffs and sneezes you'll hear if in the city in October or November, when they're flowering. A further ten percent is accounted for, surprisingly, by the **chinaberry**, or Persian lilac (*paraíso*), a native of the Himalayas that produces lilac-like blooms in the early summer. Another import from Asia, the glossy **privet** (*ligustro*), is well described by its English common name and often used for hedging; it is most abundant in Parque Chacabuco, Plaza Vicente López in Recoleta and in the streets of Monserrat. Other imports include a huge **magnolia** near the entrance to the Jardín Japonés – one of many transported from the US in the 1870s – which was declared a national monument in 1946, and still thrives, and the eight tall **Canary Island palms** embellishing the Plaza de Mayo, which are rightly regarded as city landmarks. A tree that features prominently on the city's postcards is the **gomero** – the evergreen rubber tree – a native of tropical Asia, which forms huge parasols with its plastic-like leaves, while its comically gnarled trunks look like the blood vessels of an over-enthusiastic weight lifter. The best of these shade the Plaza San Martín, the Plaza San Martín de Tours and, most famously, the front of *La Biela confitería* in Recoleta.

Of the native trees, one of the most widespread and unusual is the **tipa**, whose dusky, disjointed boughs and feathery lime-green foliage form ethereal tunnels along many of the city's avenues and provide much of the shade in the Plaza San Martín. Look out, too, for the swollen, spiky trunks of the **palo borracho**, which boasts handsome pink flowers and huge pod-shaped fruits that open to reveal powder-puffs of cotton wool. It's related to the **ceibo**, or coral tree, Argentina's national tree, which owes its English name to its fleshy scarlet florescence; there's a particularly attractive *ceibo* at the corner of 9 de Julio and Carlos Calvo. The **lapachos** – trees native to northern Argentina – found all around the parks and leafy streets of Palermo are simply fabulous: their huge deep pink trumpet blooms cover the trees entirely every September.

Last but not least, the **ombú** (*Phytolacca dioica*), technically a shrub, is the archetypal plant of the Pampas (where, legend has it, houses built in its shade will bring bad luck on their dwellers). Gauchos, they say, would mix its leaves – effective laxatives – with *mate* to get rid of people they didn't like. Whatever the *criollo* lore, the ombú is a noble plant, with dense vegetation (which is said to repel mosquitoes and flies), delicate white blossoms and strange greenish fruit that resembles crinkly tomatoes. The best ombúes are at the Plaza Chile, the Barrancas de Belgrano and in the Plaza Roma.

couldn't afford. This was the location of the city's first private charity ball, which fittingly had the theme of seventeenth- and eighteenth-century French fashion. High society was frequently entertained here in the Errázuriz days; García Lorca and Blasco Ibáñez gave readings, Artur Rubinstein played and Anna Pavlova danced *Swan Lake* in the massive halls. Concerts and classical classes are still held here – see the website for what's on.

The couple's extravagant taste in **art** is obvious – Flemish furniture and French clocks, Sèvres porcelain, bronzes by Bourdelle, tapestries from Brussels, Gallé glassware, and paintings ranging from El Greco (*Christ Bearing the Cross*) to Manet (*The Sacrifice of the Rose*) are all on display. On the upper floor, the room that served as Matías Errázuriz's boudoir features scenes of the *Divine Comedy* painted in 1919 by Catalan artist José Maria Sert, who also decorated the Rockefeller Center in New York. In the basement resides a Gothic chapel, transferred from the Château de Champagnette in France and decorated with a French polychrome wooden chancel, an early sixteenth-century Spanish alabaster effigy of a knight and seventeenth-century Swiss stained-glass windows. Temporary exhibitions of ancient and contemporary art are also held down here, or in the garden in the summer.

To get to the museum, catch **bus** #10, #59, #60, #67 or #130.

Barrio Parque

Further east of Plaza Chile is anomalous **Barrio Parque** (a name confusingly used by some locals to describe the whole of Palermo Chico), a maze of winding, curving streets that contrasts sharply with the strict rectilinear grid formed by most of the rest of the city. This largely residential neighbourhood was laid out in 1912 by the ubiquitous Charles Thays (see box, p.96), whose natural landscaping techniques are clearly evident. There's no central plaza here; instead, Oval Calle Ombú serves as the area's hub, with several streets radiating out from it like spokes. If you're in the area it's worth taking a leisurely stroll around to admire the variety of architectural styles – Art Deco, Neocolonial, Tudor, Secessionist, Flemish and Italian Renaissance among them – of the lavish houses lining the neighbourhood's arteries. Each has its own landscaped garden, planted with subtropical trees and shrubs; two of the finest houses are the manor at Ombú 2994 and the curious circular building at no. 3088.

Museo de Arte Latinoamericano de Buenos Aires (MALBA)

The **Museo de Arte Latinoamericano de Buenos Aires**, or **MALBA** (Mon & Thurs–Sun noon–8pm, Wed till 9pm; $20, or $8 on Wed; Ⓦwww.malba.org.ar), on the northern fringe of Barrio Parque at Avenida Figueroa Alcorta 3415, easily qualifies as one of the city's top museums. It is also one of the few museums in Buenos Aires to have been purpose-built – nearly all others are housed in structures originally intended for other uses. The modern, glass-fronted building, designed by a trio of young architects from Córdoba, Argentina – Gastón Atelman, Martín Fourcade and Alfredo Tapia – is an attraction in its own right, with airy, spacious galleries that contrast with the dark nooks and crannies of most of the city's more traditional venues. Financed entirely by private money, the museum nearly fell foul of the 2001 recession, opening in the thick of it, but the project went ahead and the MALBA is now firmly established as part of the city's booming art scene.

The museum's displays are fresh and exciting: the **permanent collection** (the **Costantini Collection**, see below) concentrates solely on Latin American art, with an important set of twentieth-century works from the length and breadth of the continent, while the impressive temporary exhibitions showcase pieces by prominent modern artists – mostly from Latin America, and often Argentine.

Every art form is present – in addition to painting, there are works of fashion and design, video and sculpture, performance and photography. Moreover, you are often treated to an avant-garde creation even before you enter the museum – large eye-catching pieces are regularly displayed, on a temporary basis, outside the main doors, though they usually have nothing to do with any of the temporary shows inside. The MALBA also has an excellent art house **cinema** (see website for programme), a fun **gift shop** and a serious **bookstore** with a great selection of art and architecture publications, including the museum's own outstanding catalogues. The very decent museum **café** – partly outside, and open for longer hours than the galleries themselves (Sun–Wed 9am–9pm, Thurs–Sat till midnight) – serves a range of salads, sandwiches and other light dishes, plus coffees, teas and desserts.

Buses #67, #102 and #130 stop outside the museum.

The Costantini Collection

The permanent collection is called the **Colección Costantini**, for Eduardo Costantini, the multi-millionaire real estate magnate who financed the museum's construction. It is arranged chronologically, beginning around 1910, when the modernist movement in Latin America heralded a real sense of regional identity. Highlights of the collection are listed below, though the not-infrequent rotation of displays can mean that not everything is on view at one time.

A series of works by Argentine master **Xul Solar** (see p.118), including his 1923 *Hipnotismo* ("Hypnotism"), a Frida Kahlo self-portrait with monkey and parrot (1942), and a Cubist portrait of Mexican intellectual Ramón Gómez de la Serna (1915) by Kahlo's husband, Diego Rivera, help lead things off. Other **Mexican artists** are also prominent: Miguel Covarrubias, with his 1929 oil *George Gershwin, un americano en París* ("George Gershwin, an American in Paris"), and a 1931 pencil-and-ink sketch called *Accidente de la mina* ("Accident in the Mine"), by revolutionary muralist David Alfaro Siqueiros. A Mexican influence is even present in works by Brazilian modernist Tarsila Do Amaral, such as her 1928 masterpiece *Abaporu* ("The man that eats", in the Tupi-Guaraní language), with its wonderful stylized cactus.

Dark **political undercurrents** run through the works dating from the 1930s to the 1950s – you can see them best in pieces by Argentine Antonio Berni (*Manifestación*; "Demonstration"; 1934), Catalan-born Juan Batlle Planas (*Radiografía paranoica*; "Paranoid X-Ray"; 1936), Chilean Roberto Matta (*La decadencia de misticismo*; "The Decadence of Mysticism"; 1942) and Brazilian Maria Martins (*O Impossível*; "The Impossible"; 1945). The same period also saw the emergence of **Surrealism**, and abstract art produced far more playful works, such as Remedios Varo's 1945 votive box *Ícono* ("Icon"), which gives Catholic tradition an amusing twist. A number of rival groups, with members from Argentina and Uruguay, tried to give Surrealism a specific Río de la Plata flavour in the post-war years: check out Enio Iommi's *Construcción* ("Construction"; 1946), Rhod Rothfuss's *Tres círculos rojos* ("Three Red Circles"; 1948) and Lidy Prati's *Composición serial* ("Serial Composition"; 1948) to see if they succeeded. Bringing the period to a close, Venezuelan Alejandro Otero (better known for his later kinetic works) is represented with a stark 1951 canvas, *Líneas coloreadas sobre fondo blanco V* ("Coloured Lines on a White Background V").

Things get more **conceptual** in the part of the collection from the 1960s, with the kinetic installations of Julio Le Parc – see *Six cercles en contorsion* ("Six Contorted Circles"; 1967) – and the "end of art" collages by the "Nueva Figuración" movement. Argentine Jorge de la Vega was one of the movement's leaders and his *Rompecabezas* ("Puzzle"; 1969) is a good example of his psychedelic oeuvre. Equally controversial is veteran Porteño artist León Ferrari, whose 1964 work

Manos ("Hands") is part of a painstaking series entitled "Writings and Wires". Another important contemporary Argentine artist, Guillermo Kuitca, takes pride of place with his acrylic *Siete últimas canciones* ("Seven Last Songs"; 1986). Equally prominent is *Exclusión* ("Exclusion"), a three-dimensional composition by local iconoclast Pablo Suárez – it graphically shows a young man wearing jeans and trainers clinging for dear life to the outside of a moving train. Nicolás García Uriburu, a major name in modern Argentine art, is represented by *Hidrocromía intercontinental* ("Intercontinental Hydrochromy"; 1970). Finally, no museum of modern Latin American art would be complete without a work by Colombian Fernando Botero: his painting *Los viudos* ("The Widowers"; 1968) is a fine example of his wry, moving compositions of comically rotund figures.

Museo de Arte Popular José Hernández

The small but interesting **Museo de Arte Popular José Hernández**, also known as the Museo de Motivos Argentinos ("Argentine designs"), sits nearby at the northern tip of Palermo Chico, half a dozen blocks northwest of the Museo de Arte Decorativo on the other side of the road, at Avenida del Libertador 2373 (Wed–Fri 1–7pm, Sat & Sun 10am–8pm; $1; guided tours in English on request; ☏011/4803-2384, ⓦwww.museohernandez.org.ar). José Hernández, after whom the museum is named, wrote the great gaucho classic *Martín Fierro* (1872), a revolutionary epic poem that made *campo* (peasant) culture respectable, and in this vein the museum's ongoing purpose is to highlight the value of **popular crafts**; a visit here after a trip to the Museo de Arte Decorativo offers a good lesson in the contrast between the traditional *criollo* culture of provincial Argentina and the European-influenced "civilization" preferred by the urban upper classes.

The building itself, a Neo-Italianate mansion that dates from the 1890s, was occupied by dilettante and arts patron **Félix Bunge**, scion of an extremely wealthy family of *estancieros*, until his untimely death in 1935. A controversial figure – he was murdered by an employee – Bunge dabbled in reactionary politics, supported popular traditions such as gauchos and tango, collected Argentine art and crafts and campaigned for the legalization of boxing in the country. In the 1920s and 1930s, the house's stables were used as the headquarters of the national boxing association, and for many years Bunge was personal coach to the most famous boxer in Argentine history, Luis Ángel Firpo, who is buried in Recoleta cemetery (see p.110). In his will Bunge left the house to the city, provided it became a museum.

The museum's **exhibits** begin in the house's main room – once host to Bunge's social gatherings – where an array of traditional Argentine **textiles**, including a number of beautiful Mapuche hand-woven ponchos, lie alongside some similar factory-made examples. One of these industrial ponchos was made in Birmingham, England, in the late nineteenth century, when gaucho fashion was briefly all the rage there. Downstairs, the old library and kitchen hold an impressive but unimaginatively presented display of mostly nineteenth-century rural **silverware**; the seemingly endless arrays of spurs, stirrups, saddles, knives and gaucho weaponry stand side by side with a large collection of fine silver *mate* vessels.

You can see more Argentine folk heritage in the mansion's former stables (and later the garage and a boxing ring), across a patio shaded by an ancient *ceibo* and a tall *tipa*. Here you will find a small but handsome collection that takes you on an arts and crafts tour of all of South America: *fileteado* (see box, p.82) from Buenos Aires, reed baskets from Tierra del Fuego, Peruvian textiles and Brazilian ceramics, plus objects made from copper, wood and silver are all on display. There is also a garish set of glittery Carnaval costumes and feathery headdresses from the city of Corrientes.

You can take **bus** #10, #59, #60, #67 or #130 to the museum.

Palermo Viejo

Bounded by avenidas Santa Fe, Córdoba, Dorrego and Raúl Scalabrini Ortiz, **Palermo Viejo** ("Old Palermo") is the only part of the barrio that still has a truly old-fashioned Porteño feel to it, although it's also become one of the swankiest places in the city to live, shop or have an evening out. An obstructive train track divides the area even further into two equal-sized but subtly different parts. The first is **Palermo Soho**, where you'll find the barrio's official epicentre, Plaza Palermo Viejo, a park-like square dominated by a children's playground and some huge lime trees, as well as its unofficial epicentre, the far more colourful **Plaza Serrano** (aka Plaza Cortázar), the district's commercial, gastronomic and artistic hub. The second is **Palermo Hollywood**, a media mecca that borders the next barrio north, Colegiales.

Sizable communities of Polish, Ukrainian, Lebanese and Armenian **immigrants** have lived in this part of Palermo since the early twentieth century, alongside a larger Italian contingent and some old Spanish families. All these groups have their own shops, bars, churches and clubs, adding a great deal of variety and colour to the area. There's also a dazzling blend of outstanding **restaurants**, serving dishes from an equally large variety of cuisines (see p.173 for reviews). There are no sights here, as such: a visit to relaxed Palermo Viejo is more about lapping up the ambience and doing a little shopping and eating rather than racing around sightseeing.

Palermo Soho

Part run-down and part gentrified, old-fashioned in places and increasingly trendy in others, the compact rectangle of Palermo formed by avenidas Scalabrini Ortiz and Juan B. Justo has been popularly dubbed **Palermo Soho** for its similarities to the Soho neighbourhoods of London and New York. This is the area of the city most closely linked to **Borges**, who lived and began writing poetry here in the 1920s; its physical appearance, alluded to in some of his works, has changed little since then. Most of its streets are still cobbled and lined with brightly painted one- or two-storey Neocolonial villas and townhouses. Many have been restored in recent years, and now accommodate independent designer boutiques selling pricey jewellery, furnishings and bohemian clothes (see p.202), or artists' studios, while others remain dilapidated, hidden behind luxuriant gardens, and still others have been converted into places to stay (p.154)

This city that I believed was my past,
is my future, my present;
the years I have spent in Europe are an illusion,
I always was (and will be) in Buenos Aires.

Jorge Luis Borges, "Arrabal", from *Fervor de Buenos Aires* (1921)

8

PALERMO

While there's no shortage of literary works inspired by Argentina's capital city, few writers have chronicled it so passionately as **Jorge Luis Borges**. Born in 1898, his early childhood was spent in Palermo, now one of the more exclusive neighbourhoods, but a somewhat marginal barrio at the start of the twentieth century. Borges' middle-class family inhabited one of the few two-storey houses on Calle Serrano, and, although his excursions were strictly controlled, from behind the garden wall Borges observed the colourful street life that was kept tantalizingly out of his reach – such were the beginnings of his fascination with the city's humbler areas. In particular, his attention was caught by the men who gathered to drink and play cards in the local *almacén* (a sort of shop-cum-bar) at his street corner. With their tales of knife fights and air of lawlessness, these men appeared time and again in Borges' early short stories and, later, in *Doctor Brodie's Report*, a collection published in 1970.

Borges' writing talent surfaced at a precocious age: at 6 he wrote his first short story together with a piece in English on Greek mythology and, in 1910, when he was 11, the newspaper *El País* published his translation of Oscar Wilde's *The Happy Prince*. However, it was not until he returned from Europe in 1921, where he had been stranded with his family during World War I, that Borges published his first book, **Fervor de Buenos Aires**, a collection of poems that attempted to capture the essence of the city. Enthused by his re-encounter with Buenos Aires at an age when he was free to go wherever he wanted, Borges set out to explore the marginal corners of the city, which, during his seven-year absence, had grown considerably. His wanderings took him to the city's outlying barrios, where streets lined with simple one-storey buildings blended with the surrounding pampas, or to the poorer areas of the city centre with their tenement buildings and bars frequented by prostitutes. With the notable exception of Boca, which he appears to have regarded as too idiosyncratic – and, perhaps, too obviously picturesque – Borges felt the greatest affection for the south of Buenos Aires: **El Sur**. His exploration of the area that he regarded as representing the heart of the city took in not only the traditional houses of San Telmo and Monserrat, with their patios and decorative facades, but also the humbler streets of Barracas, a largely industrial working-class neighbourhood, and Constitución, where, in a gloomy basement in Avenida Juan de Garay, he set one of his most famous short stories, *El Aleph*.

For a writer as sensitive to visual subtlety as Borges – many of his early poems focus on the city's atmospheric evening light – it seems particularly tragic that he should have gone virtually blind in his 50s. Nonetheless, from 1955 to 1973, Borges was **Director of the National Library**, then located in Monserrat (see p.54), where his pleasure at being surrounded by books – even if he could no longer read them – was heightened by the fact that his daily journey to work took him through one of his favourite parts of the city, from his apartment in Calle Maipú, near Plaza San Martín, along Calle Florida. As Borges' fame grew, he spent considerable periods of time away from Argentina, travelling to Europe, the US and other Latin American countries – though he claimed always to return to Buenos Aires in his dreams. Borges died in 1986 in Geneva, where he is buried in the Plainpalais cemetery.

and eat (p.173). At the same time, traditional local life goes on: brightly painted kindergartens and grimy car garages, cheap canteens with formica tables, and corner stalls selling fresh produce still abound, giving the district an authentic air despite all the fancy newcomers.

The nearest **subte** stop for the whole of Palermo Soho is Plaza Italia on Line D.

Plaza Serrano and around

Palermo Soho's cultural and social centre is **Plaza Serrano**. It is officially called Plaza Cortázar (a designation used on maps but unknown by most taxi drivers), after Argentine novelist Julio Cortázar, who frequented this part of the city on visits to Buenos Aires in the 1960s and set his Surrealist novel *Hopscotch* here. The space is surrounded by trattorias, cafés and bars, some of them doubling as hip arts centres and avant-garde galleries, and at weekends the circular plaza hosts an art fair (10am–8pm).

The stretch of Calle Serrano leading due east from Plaza Serrano to Avenida Santa Fe has been officially renamed **Calle J.L. Borges**, although many signs still read Serrano. The world-famous writer (see box, p.129) spent part of his childhood at **no. 2135**, in a two-storey villa with its own mill (now demolished), while a few blocks away, at the corner with El Salvador, a commemorative **plaque** is inscribed with a stanza from *Mythical Foundation of Buenos Aires*, a poem where the colonial beginnings of Buenos Aires are narrated with a typical Borgesian twist: in it the city is founded not in San Telmo, its historical starting point, but here smack in the middle of Palermo.

Palermo Hollywood

North of the rail track, and centred on calles Honduras and Fitzroy, **Palermo Hollywood** is currently the city's "in" evening destination, home to an ever-changing pantheon of restaurants, bars and clubs, which range in character from lively and fun to painfully trendy. Formerly known as "Pacífico", the area was given its cinematic moniker by the media at the start of the millennium, when many of Argentina's active film and TV industries set up their studios here. Boutique hotels and smart B&Bs have also mushroomed in this sub-barrio in recent years – see Chapter 10 for suggested places to stay. During the day, however, the district is relatively quiet, and there are no sights to visit.

Bosques de Palermo

A substantial section of Palermo is dominated by greenery, and known as the **Bosques de Palermo** ("Palermo Woods") – though it's landscaped parkland rather than forests you'll find here. Porteños from all walks of life head here in good weather to make the most of the huge amount of open space it offers – some come to relax, others to kick a ball around between sips of *mate*, to fly a kite, to picnic or even just to feed the birds. Their most common destination is enormous **Parque Tres de Febrero**, which, though crisscrossed by avenidas Sarmiento, Iraola and Montt, is a haven of grass and trees and encompasses a boating lake, a beautiful **rose garden**, a **pergola**, an **art museum** and the city's **planetarium**. One southern corner is home to a quiet **Japanese garden**, while to the southeast, past the **Monumento de los Españoles** – one of the most impressive monuments in the entire city – are a separate rhomboid and triangle of green that are a **zoo** and a **botanical garden**, respectively.

The **Predio La Rural** is a major exhibition centre bordering the zoo and Plaza Italia, dominated – like so many of the plazas in this part of the city – by a monument, in this case to Italian statesman Garibaldi. When northern Buenos Aires was being landscaped at the beginning of the twentieth century, the fashion was for great open squares to be presided over by the statue of a famous man – Borges once complained that "there wasn't a single square left in the city that hadn't been ruined by a dirty great bronze statue of someone or other". A short walk from the botanical garden you'll find a museum dedicated to the country's most famous woman – **Eva Perón**.

Three **subte** stops on Line D (Plaza Italia, Palermo and Ministro Carranza) will get you to the vicinity from the city centre; otherwise, a taxi is probably the best way to reach specific destinations.

Parque Tres de Febrero

Yet another Buenos Aires fixture designed by Charles Thays, **Parque Tres de Febrero** (Ⓦ www.parquetresdefebrero.gov.ar) is one of the biggest parks in the city – officially it covers some three square kilometres and extends all the way to Palermo's border with Belgrano, taking in the national racecourse and a number of sports clubs, including the polo field (see p.136) along the way. However, the name "Tres de Febrero" is usually applied only to the small, vaguely fan-shaped chunk of land hemmed in by avenidas del Libertador and Casares and a main railway line. It's sliced into more manageable segments – known officially as Plaza Sicilia, Parque Jorge Newbery, Plaza Almirante R. Fernández and Plaza Holanda – by avenidas Sarmiento, Figueroa Alcorta and Iraola.

Parque Tres de Febrero was originally envisioned by **Domingo Sarmiento** (see p.255), who believed that green spaces were a civilizing influence. There are two **statues** of the statesman in the park: one, an Art Nouveau design, is located near a vine-garlanded **pergola** next to the boating lake and was a gift from the people of Chile, and the second, a Rodin work in marble and bronze, stands at the corner of Plaza Sicilia, supposedly on the exact location of the mansion of Sarmiento's arch-enemy General Rosas. Ultimately, the park was named in honour of the date in 1852 when Rosas was defeated by progressive forces. You can see a dramatic equestrian statue of **Juan Manuel de Rosas** himself in Plaza Seeber – a segment of grass and trees across Avenida del Libertador.

The park's most interesting – and best-tended – features are in its northernmost sector, which focuses on the **boating lake**; here you can rent wooden rowing-boats and pedalos from the boathouses on the lake's western banks (about $40 per half-hour). The quiet **Jardín de los Poetas**, entered from Avenida Montt, is dotted with stone and bronze busts of major Argentine and international poets, including Borges, Federico García Lorca and Shakespeare. Not far to the east is the **Patio Andaluz**, an Andalucían garden decorated with vibrant ceramic tiles donated by the city of Seville. As you head north you'll find an immaculate rose garden, the **Rosedal**, which showcases dozens of new and colourful varieties of the flower – the place is a blaze of colour in early summer, with November being the best time to visit. At the northernmost end, meanwhile, an Edwardian-style bridge, topped with a trellis dripping with vines, delicately arches over the boating lake. Throughout the summer free outdoor music recitals – mostly tango and Latin – are held in this sector, usually on Sunday afternoons.

Even if you're not interested in smelling roses or pedalling boats, with beautiful trees, lawns and patios, Tres de Febrero makes a wonderful place to stroll, and offers a great opportunity to see Porteños at play. While you'll pass the typical scenes of families drinking *mate* under the shade of palms or rubber trees, you may also come across less expected sights, such as tai chi classes, or transvestite volleyball games. At weekends you shouldn't expect total peace and quiet – the wide pathways running along the banks of the boating lake become particularly crowded with joggers, cyclists and in-line skaters. The whole area is rather more serene on weekdays, though also less characterful.

Museo de Artes Plásticas Eduardo Sívori

You'll find a fine arts museum, the **Museo de Artes Plásticas Eduardo Sívori** (Tues–Fri noon–8pm, Sat & Sun 10am–8pm; $1; ☎011/4778-3899, ⓦwww .museosivori.org.ar), on the other side of the bridge from the Rosedal, at Avenida Infanta Isabel 555. Named for Argentine painter Sívori (1847–1918), who helped found the National Academy of Fine Art, the museum owns a collection of some five thousand paintings and sculptures. However, only a handful of these are usually on display at one time – the majority of the floor space is used for temporary exhibitions of home-grown artists, plus short theatrical works of a high quality (free). You can see a small selection of pieces from the permanent collection in a series of rooms on the ground floor. Most of these date from the first six decades or so of the twentieth century, though a major exception to this chronology kicks off the collection: Prilidiano Pueyrredón's *Dama porteña* ("Buenos Aires Lady"), which is from the mid-nineteenth century. The first room includes a discreet work by the museum's namesake artist – his oil *Pampa* (1902) is so delicate it looks more like a watercolour. Most of Argentina's major artists are represented in the following few rooms, along with the odd Uruguayan: Figari's 1930 *Colonial*, for example, shows Montevideo men in top hats and ladies in lace veils. The Boca School of painting is here in force, not least its leader, Benito Quinquela Martín, whose *Reflejos* ("Reflections"; 1965) glows with the colours of the neighbourhood's boats and painted houses. You cannot miss the vibrant yet static and mural-like *Chacareros* ("Farmhands"; 1935) by Berni, another highlight. Sculptures are less numerous than paintings, but the quality is high. Italo-Argentine Lucio Fontana's 1943 bronze entitled *Hombre del Delta* ("Man of the Delta") is interestingly juxtaposed with Rogelio Yrurtia's 1914 work, a model of his monumental *Canto al Trabajo* ("Hymn to Work"), which is located in Paseo Colón, San Telmo.

After viewing all this art, you may want a rest and refreshment – the museum's very agreeable **café** (the building was originally built as a restaurant) is open the same hours as the exhibits.

Planetario Galileo Galilei

The far eastern tip of the park, at Avenida Sarmiento, serves as the lakeside setting for the UFO-shaped **Planetario Galileo Galilei** (☎011/4771-9393, ⓦwww .planetario.gov.ar), inaugurated in 1966. Outside the entrance you can see a huge metal meteorite, weighing over 1500kg, discovered in the Chaco – the northern region of Argentina bordering on Paraguay – in the 1960s. Alarmingly, it is minute in comparison with its sibling, "El Chaco", which is still in the Campo del Cielo, the area where it fell some four millennia ago. The planetarium's *raison d'être* is to teach the public about the solar system and beyond, via shows ($10), some of which are particularly suitable for children, while others are aimed more at grown-ups; there is usually one daily at around 4.30pm, plus several more at the weekends; the website has the schedule.

Additionally, every Saturday and Sunday at 7.30pm (weather permitting) local astronomy enthusiasts gather here to peer at the cosmos. For such a big city, Buenos Aires has surprisingly clear skies, and both planets and constellations are easily visible from the park (the planetarium website provides a monthly star chart – look for *cielo del mes*). Don't linger here late at night, though – transvestite prostitutes and their clients are the main nocturnal inhabitants of this section of the Bosques.

Jardín Japonés and around

Taking up a large chunk of Plaza Sicilia, on the other side of Avenida Sarmiento from the boating lake, the beautiful **Jardín Japonés**, or Japanese garden, has its entrance on Plaza de la República Islámica de Irán (daily 10am–6pm; $8; ⓦwww .jardinjapones.org.ar) guarded by a lovely magnolia. Despite the purr of traffic on all sides, the garden manages to be a relatively peaceful place. The landscaping includes a bonsai section and standing stones, and some handsome black pines, ginkgos, almond trees and azaleas, the last at their loveliest in the spring. Great shoals of huge coy carp, in lakes crossed by typical red-lacquer bridges and zigzagging stepping-stones, kiss the air with pouting mouths. Donated to the city by Buenos Aires' Japanese community in 1979, the space is also home to a temple-like **café** and a Japanese cultural centre.

The area around the Jardín Japonés is home to a couple of the city's more curious monuments, both of which involve cattle. Due south of the garden, in a small square of neatly mown grass known as **Plaza Alemania**, is *Riqueza Agropecuaria Argentina* ("Argentina's Farming Wealth"; 1910), a gleaming fountain-statue that juxtaposes an effete white-marble youth standing coyly next to a sturdy ox with three embarrassed-looking youths posing by a plough. A centenary gift to Argentina from the city's German community, it is the work of sculptor Adolfo Bredow. The bovine motif continues at Plaza de la República Islámica de Irán, northeast of the Japanese garden, with the **Columna del Templo Persa**. A gift to Argentina from the Shah of Iran, this 19m stone pillar, topped with a figure of two two-headed oxen, is a replica of a detail of the Apadana of Persepolis.

Monumento de los Españoles

The busy rotunda at the junction of Avenida del Libertador and Avenida Sarmiento, at the western edge of Parque Tres de Febrero, is taken up by (arguably) the most glorious monument in the city, the **Monumento de los Españoles**, an Art Nouveau wedding cake that towers 25m above the traffic. Erroneously referred to by many locals as the "Monumento a los Españoles" (monument *to* the Spanish), it was in fact a 1910 centenary gift *from* the city's Spanish community to their new motherland. Fine bronze sculptures at the tower's base symbolize four regions of Argentina: the Andes (with the obligatory condor), the Chaco, the Pampas and the Río de la Plata, while a number of buxom nymphs, also in bronze, frolic in the fountains there. Representing the **Magna Carta** (the 1853 constitution), the central structure's allegorical figures, including the dainty angel at the top, are sculpted from Carrara marble. Manufactured in Spain, the bronzes were designed by Catalan sculptor Agustín Querol i Subirats, but the monument was not inaugurated until 1927 owing to various mishaps, including the untimely deaths of Querol and his successor, and the sinking of the original bronzes in the ocean liner *Príncipe de Asturias*, off the coast of Brazil.

Jardín Botánico Carlos Thays

Buenos Aires' charming **botanical garden** (Mon–Fri 8am–7pm, Sat & Sun 9.30am–7pm, winter closes at 6pm; free) is its best homage to the man responsible for the majority of the city's public spaces, **Charles Thays** (see box, p.96). Recently restored to its early glory, the garden was originally established at the end of the nineteenth century by Schubeck, the gardener to the royal courts of Bavaria, who died before getting very far. Upon his death, the layout was handed over to Thays, who completed the work in 1899. Intending the garden to be didactic as well as aesthetic, he divided it into distinct areas representing different plant families, various regions of Argentina and the five continents – in all, there are over 8000 species, including gingkos, eucalyptus and oaks. The space was officially named after Thays when he died in 1934; he is also honoured with a bronze bust inside the garden – it sits alongside the red-brick bulk of the city's Headquarters of Parks and Gardens, which comes into view as soon as you enter the gardens. Known as the **Casona Carlos Thays** (the "Big House"), this building's mock battlements give it the look of an English folly. Poke your head inside to see the beautiful plan of the garden drawn by Thays in 1898; art exhibitions, often related to botany, are regularly held inside, too. Behind the Casona stands a large **glasshouse** brought back from the 1900 Universal Exhibition in Paris, where it was part of Argentina's pavilion. The ethereal Art Nouveau construction of engraved crystal and wrought-iron shelters delicate botanical specimens, such as orchids and cacti.

Entering the garden via Plaza Italia, you'll be greeted by a lush water-lily pool around an elegant stone statue by Lía Correa Morales (see p.145), *Ondina de Plata* – a river-nymph from a legend about the Río de la Plata, she has a decidedly coquettish look about her. This section of the garden – the **Italianate section** – is dotted with a number of sculptures, including a white marble Venus copied from a Roman statue in the Louvre; a bronze of a she-wolf suckling Romulus and Remus (a centenary gift to the city from its Italian community); and *Saturnalia*, an enormous and riotous ensemble of a Roman orgy, apparently intended to warn city folk against debauchery. Cypress and laurel trees are some of the main plantings here, representing "Roman flora". Further away from the entrance, the **French garden** is typically formal, with regular lines and more statuary, while the different **regions of Argentina** are represented botanically over to the left of the lily-pond, towards Avenida Las Heras. The so-called **Universal section**, with some species from Australasia and Asia, is in the corner of the triangle furthest from the entrance, and sadly is the least tended part.

Above all, the garden is a shady haven of peace from the noisy avenues around it; the brighter grassy spots are popular with sunbathers. Musical and other entertainments, often aimed at children, take place here at weekends.

Jardín Zoológico

Another Charles Thays design, the city's **Jardín Zoológico** (Tues–Sun 10am–6pm; \$15, or \$22 for the "pasaporte", entitling you to certain added attractions, children under 12 free) sits next door to the botanical garden. Fauna from throughout the world, ranging from apes to zebras, is represented. Borges fondly wrote that the Jardín Zoológico "smelled of toffee and tiger", a description that still holds true. For overseas visitors, the zoo probably functions best as a place to see South American species close up – the four native camelids (guanacos, llamas, vicuñas and alpacas) are all here, as are condors, capybaras and coatis, while maras (or "Patagonian hares", actually a type of rodent) wander freely around. Architecture buffs will find the monumental pavilions and cages of interest – built around 1905, they include a fabulous replica of the temple to the goddess Lakshmi in Mumbai, a Chinese temple, a Byzantine portico and a Japanese pagoda. If you skip the added "pasaporte" attractions, such as the poorly maintained "jungle house" and seal show, you won't miss much.

Outside the zoo, traditional **mateos** (horse and carriages), decorated with the ribbons and swirls of *filete* art (see box, p.82), cart off the romantically minded on trips around Palermo's parks (\$40–60, depending on trip length).

Predio La Rural

Argentina's principal exhibition hall, the **Predio La Rural** (official entrance at Av Santa Fe 4363; ☎011/4324-4700, ⓦwww.la-rural.com.ar), occupies a mammoth chunk of land immediately north of Plaza Italia. The building takes its name from the Sociedad Rural Argentina, an association that unites farmers and landowners in the struggle to maintain *criollo* traditions. It was put up at the beginning of the twentieth century and inaugurated at the time of the 1910 centenary celebrations. Part of the original complex, abutting Avenida Santa Fe, is a majestic structure known as Pabellón Frers, which features a huge wrought-iron and glass entrance, and mock Neoclassical pilasters – the sole ornament on the beige facade. Behind it stretches a series of far larger constructions, most of which are more functional than aesthetic, though the magnificent grandstands, or Pabellones Equinos, are fine exceptions to the rule. These buildings host all manner of national and international exhibitions with themes ranging from tourism and wine to medicine and farming equipment. The annual high point comes in mid-winter, when the fortnight-long **Exposición de Ganadería, Agricultura e Industria**, known as La Rural (see p.221), brings the country to the city with gauchos galore, plus all manner of livestock on parade. Throughout the year, the space also accommodates **Opera Pampa** (Thurs–Sat 8pm; ⓦwww.operapampa.com.ar; $120 or $300 with dinner), an extravaganza of dance, music and horse-riding skills tracing the history of gaucho culture.

Museo Evita

A block east of the botanical garden and Avenida Las Heras at Lafinur 2988, the **Museo Evita** (Tues–Sun 11am–7pm; $15; call ahead for guided visits in English, $25 including entrance; ☎011/4807-0306) is a long-delayed temple to the memory of Argentina's world-renowned heroine, Eva Perón. The handsome two-storey townhouse, built around 1902 and remodelled in the 1920s to include Spanish Renaissance elements, was purchased in 1948 by Eva Perón's **Social Aid Foundation**, for use as an emergency temporary residence for homeless families and single mothers. The years of the anti-Peronist governments saw the building abandoned, and only in 2003 was it finally restored and turned into a museum, at the initiative of city authorities and under the watchful eye of María Cristina Álvarez Rodríguez, Evita's great-niece and a Peronist politician. The museum chronicles the life and passions of the controversial former First Lady, along with the daily existence of the families who were once given shelter here. Overall, the presentation is mostly uncritical, glossing over the less salubrious facts of Evita's life, including her Nazi sympathies, although it does include a small cabinet of pro- and contra-Evita books. The displays are all well laid out, and helpful info sheets in English appear in each room.

The **museum circuit** starts with a mirrored room, presided over by a copy of Evita's death mask, where a video loop projects images of the extraordinary scenes in the city after she died onto a huge screen, with the haunting beat of a *tango nuevo* soundtrack adding to the drama. In the following rooms are magazines that featured articles about her when she was still Eva Duarte the radio star, and excerpts from the films she appeared in, including *La Pródiga*, the only movie in which she played the lead. Made in 1945, it wasn't shown until the 1980s, as Perón had ordered the destruction of all the negatives – this one reel survived. Upstairs, photos and other memorabilia trace her transformation into Eva Perón, the First

Lady, and Evita, the political activist in her own right. You can also see the suits and gowns designed by Argentine couturier Luis Agostino that she wore during her triumphant state visit to Europe. More dramatic film footage shows her making the famous speech from the balcony of the Casa Rosada in which, her body racked with cancer, Evita renounced her Vice Presidential candidacy (later immortalized in the song *Don't Cry for Me, Argentina!*). Throughout the museum, the walls are adorned with quotes from Evita's speeches and her autobiography *La Razón de mi Vida* ("My Mission in Life").

A small space on the ground floor is given over to minor **temporary exhibitions** related to Evita, while next door, with a separate entrance at Gutiérrez 3926, is an excellent **café**, open all day for coffee, tea, cakes and full-blown dinners.

Subte station Plaza Italia, on Line D, is within easy walking distance of the museum.

Northern Palermo

North of the parks lie another three or four sub-barrios of Palermo. Up here there are fewer specific sights, per se, but a couple of minor attractions make these far-flung parts worth visiting if you have time. The residential enclave bounded by avenidas Santa Fe, Bullrich and del Libertador is known as **Palermo Nuevo**, owing to its yuppie population, shiny skyscraper apartment blocks and voguish restaurants. Immediately north of here sit two traditional Argentine institutions, the national **racecourse** and **polo ground**. The habitués of these venues also frequent the trendy *parrillas* and bars of **Las Cañitas**, another tiny sub-barrio that has become synonymous with fashion and glamour. The far northeastern fringe of the barrio, past Avenida Leopoldo Lugones towards the Río de la Plata, is known as **Costanera Norte**, and is popular with anglers.

Campo Argentino de Polo

A perfect piece of turf sits at the corner of avenidas del Libertador and Dorrego – the **Campo Argentino de Polo**, inaugurated in 1928. Known as the "Cathedral of Polo" – its stands have a capacity of 30,000 – the pitch is home to the national **polo** tournaments, which take place every year from March to May and September to December (see p.213 for details of attending a match). During the rest of the year, the field is used for pato and for hockey, and also large-scale concerts and recitals. **Bus** #36 stops nearby.

Hipódromo Argentino

You can admire more horses on the other side of Avenida del Libertador at the **Hipódromo Argentino**, the country's major **racecourse** (☎011/4778-2800, ⓦwww.palermo.com.ar), inaugurated in 1876. To the right as you enter, there are the stables where you can get a close-up view of the horses stamping and snorting prior to the race, while to the left are the stands – both simple benches and the elegant main grandstand, or **Tribuna Official**, which was built in 1908 by French architect Faure Dujarric. Races generally take place in the late afternoon and evening (see p.212 for details of attending one). **Buses** #64 and #160 stop outside the track.

Costanera Norte

The far northeastern edge of Palermo, beyond the highway known as Avenida Leopoldo Lugones, is mostly taken up by the city's busy domestic airport, **Aeroparque Jorge Newbery**. The low wall running along the riverfront here, or Avenida Costanera Rafael Obligado – known popularly as the **Costanera Norte** – has long been a popular haunt for fishermen. Near the beginning of a 500m-long jetty, one of the most distinctive buildings in the whole city pays homage to the anglers: the **Club de Pescadores**, or Fishermen's Club, a cross between a mock-Tudor cottage and a fairy-tale castle. In summer, the Costanera comes alive during the nocturnal hours with a whole string of lively **nightclubs** (see p.183), some of which only last the season and some of which reappear the next year. **Buses** #33 and #45 run out here.

9

The outer barrios

S hould you exhaust the huge array of things to do in the city centre, or if you want to explore a rawer side of Buenos Aires, or just feel the need to escape the hustle and bustle of downtown without venturing too far afield, a whole network of **outer barrios** awaits you. A vast, roughly fan-shaped expanse of avenues and parks, homes and offices, shops and restaurants, factories and warehouses, these barrios sprawl south, west and north of central Buenos Aires towards the city limits. Since the main thing they have in common is a relative lack of tourists, these outer reaches present a prize glimpse of the daily lives of ordinary Porteños. Indeed, the further you travel in each direction, the more you will be struck by each barrio's very distinct character, somehow instilled with a more intense essence of the respective inner city neighbourhoods beyond which they extend. **South** of San Telmo and Boca, for example, lie dyed-in-the-wool working-class neighbourhoods that are home to some of the city's most authentic tango venues. **West** of Monserrat and San Nicolás, meanwhile, you move into the capital's steadfastly lower-middle-class heartland, where good consumer deals are found far more easily than in the city-centre boutiques. And **north** of Palermo, affluent Porteños have settled in a long string of leafy riverside districts replete with great restaurants and the odd boutique hotel.

The south

The **south** of Buenos Aires – "**El Sur**" – can be described as the most down-to-earth section of the city, and has fascinated everyone from Borges to tango lyricists. Mainly home to working-class Porteños, it's functional rather than pretty, and it's not geared towards visitors. This said, there are a few places worth checking out. Up-and-coming **Barracas**, immediately west of Boca, is the most alluring of all the southern barrios. Increasingly popular with artists, it features some promising cultural spots, such as the Centro Cultural del Sur (see p.186) and some major tango venues (see Chapter 15). Neighbouring Barracas and best known for its homonymous rail terminus, rather grimy **Constitución**, which also borders San Telmo, has some interesting places to stay and eat for those who like to escape the gringo trail. **Nueva Pompeya** hosts a colourful weekend **bird market** (Sun 8am–2pm), at the corner of avenidas Perito Moreno and Sáenz – a couple of dozen stalls sell decorative companion birds. Finally, **Boedo** is a fertile hunting ground for good-value bars, restaurants and tango shows.

Because the southern barrios are relatively **poor**, foreign tourists tend to stick out in them like trekking boots at a milonga. Though crime rates are lower here than in more visited areas, don't take any risks, especially at night. Daytime wandering can be rewarding and is generally safe as long as you keep your head about you; at night, however, get a taxi to and from your destination. When leaving a place you should call for a car, as cabs tend to prowl the streets far less here than in wealthier or busier parts of the city.

Constitución is the southern terminus of **subte** Line C, which starts at Retiro, while Line E serves Boedo. Otherwise, the **bus** network serves the whole area.

The west

The swathe of mostly residential barrios that stretches out west from the city centre does not feature prominently in tango lyrics or great works of literature. However, this is not to say that these solidly "middle Buenos Aires" neighbourhoods lack their own strong character, or are places not worth your time. **Balvanera** is where Porteños with a more modest income come to do their shopping, either at an enormous mall or in the noisy streets. This is also where you'll find a surprising architectural masterpiece, and a museum dedicated to the godfather of tango. Large **Caballito**, gradually gentrifying where it almost bumps up against Palermo, has an intriguing natural science museum, stacked with the bones and fossils of long-dead critters from the South American continent. **Chacarita** is chiefly of interest for the cemetery at its heart, more idiosyncratic and less visited than Recoleta's famous burial ground. Way out west, and a day trip in itself, **Mataderos** gives you the chance to get a taste of pampas culture at its weekend gaucho fair, especially good if you don't have time to see the real deal.

Balvanera

Balvanera, just west of the city centre, is a highly commercial, somewhat downmarket barrio, home to many of the city's immigrants from other countries in South America. As with many official barrio titles, the name Balvanera is seldom used by Porteños themselves. Instead, people tend to use the names of the barrio's twin hubs: **Once**, a busy wholesale and retail area wrapped around a major train station, and **Abasto**, focused on a shopping mall.

Once

The bustling **Once** quarter, with its sizeable Bolivian, Peruvian and Paraguayan communities, is the closest Buenos Aires gets to feeling like a stereotypical Latin American city – the soundtrack is *cumbia*, the faces Andean and the *panchos* (hot dogs) a couple of pesos. For decades it has also been home to the city's lower-middle-class Jewish community, many of whose members are involved in the district's lively wholesale (*venta mayor*) business.

The sub-barrio's name derives from the unremarkable-looking Once **train station** (built 1882) that stands at the corner of Avenida Pueyrredón and Mitre. The station fronts Once's major plaza, the **Plaza Miserere**, where a bizarre monument by Rogelio Yrurtia (see p.145) guards the ashes of **Bernardino Rivadavia**, Argentina's first president. There are two bronzes of him – one in Roman garb, the other naked except for a cloth draped suggestively over his leg.

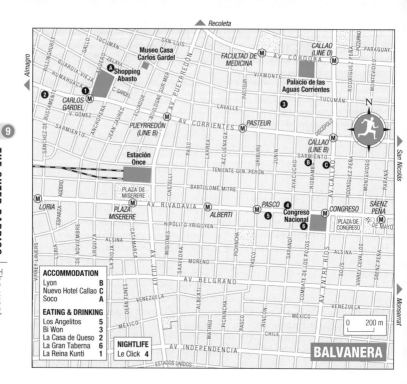

The blocks surrounding the plaza are a good place to head if you want to pick up a **bargain** football shirt or *rock nacional* T-shirt, a *chamamé* CD or some carnival gear. You can simply wander the streets here, which are all lined with stores and stalls, or head down Pueyrredón, which after ten blocks or so leads into Recoleta.

Abasto and the Museo de los Niños

Looming at the corner of Avenida Corrientes and Calle Anchorena, the monolithic **Shopping Abasto** mall utterly dominates the surrounding district, also known popularly as "Abasto". Mercifully, the venue is not just a modern air-conditioned hulk, but an attractive 1890s building with an Art Deco facade, added when it was remodelled in the 1930s. For nearly a century this was the home of one of the biggest fruit and vegetable markets on the continent (*abasto* translates as provision, or supply). Now it's one of the city's largest shopping complexes, managing to fit over 200 stores, a multi-screen cinema, a food hall, an arcade and fairground rides – including a small Ferris wheel, a pirate ship and a monorail – inside its vast interior.

If you're travelling with children, you may want to visit the **Museo de los Niños** (Tues–Sun 1–8pm; adults $12, children $24; ⓦwww.museoabasto.org.ar), also a part of Shopping Abasto. Kids can explore diminutive recreations of banks, factories, supermarkets and other commercial establishments, along with a number of hands-on scientific and technological exhibits. Some parents may object to the advertising by all manner of government institutions and private enterprises, but the kids lap up the fun and games.

Museo Casa Carlos Gardel

The **Museo Casa Carlos Gardel**, about three blocks away from Shopping Abasto at Jean Jaurès 735 (Mon & Wed–Fri 11am–6pm, Sat & Sun 10am–7pm; $1; ⓣ011/4964-2015), is dedicated to the life of Argentina's most popular tango singer. Known as the *Zorzal Criollo* ("Criollo Songbird"), Gardel (1887–1935) popularized **tango** abroad in the early twentieth century, making films in Hollywood and inspiring devotion for his distinctive voice and charismatic personality. The museum is housed in his former home, which has been lovingly restored to capture his life here, down to the two caged canaries in the courtyard. Although the collection is a bit limited and out of the way for general interest, tango aficionados will enjoy the old photos and tango scores and the temporary exhibits on themes relating to Gardel, such as his passion for racehorses. At one point it gets quite postmodern, with a collection of photos of pictures of Gardel from around Buenos Aires – photographer Luis Martin points out: "wherever you go in the city, he is always watching you". As if to confirm this, some of the houses in the immediate area, painted in a variety of cheerful colours, have murals of a grinning Gardel on the sides.

The nearest **subte** station, suitably, is Carlos Gardel on Line B – after exiting the station, head north up Corrientes two blocks to reach Jean Jaurès.

Palacio de las Aguas Corrientes

The stunning **Palacio de las Aguas Corrientes**, at Córdoba and Riobamba, is every bit as palatial as its name suggests and boasts an exterior that has been described quite accurately as a cross between London's Victoria and Albert Museum and the Uffizi in Florence, with a bit of Babylon thrown in for good measure. Somewhat incongruously, it shelters the twelve giant water tanks that supplied Buenos Aires with water from 1894 until 1978 – its name means "Palace of Running Water". Also referred to as **Aguas Argentinas**, the glorious shell was intended to serve as a monument to the importance of public health – Buenos Aires was the first city in Latin America to have a network of clean drinking water. Note the glazed coloured ceramics of flowers and shields that dot the facade: these were all manufactured by Royal Doulton of London and shipped over to be painted in situ, following the original designs like a jigsaw puzzle. The building's function as a supplier of water was overtaken by a larger out-of-town replacement in 1978, but the *palacio* still houses the head office of Argentina's water board. There is a small **museum** (Mon–Fri 9am–1pm; free; ⓣ011/6319-1104) inside – enter via Riobamba – displaying blueprints and panels recounting the story of the building's construction, as well as all sorts of water-related paraphernalia, including valves, taps and an extraordinary collection of toilet bowls.

Callao station on Line D of the **subte** is just a hop away.

Caballito

Moving west from Balvanera will take you through the unassuming, mostly lower-middle-class barrios of Almagro, Villa Crespo and **Caballito**. The main attraction hereabouts is the **Museo Argentino de Ciencias Naturales**, at Ángel Gallardo 490 (daily 2–7pm; $3; Ⓦwww.macn.secyt.gov.ar), in the circular **Parque del Centenario**, in the northeastern corner of Caballito. The museum houses an impressive **paleontological** collection, with many specimens from Argentina – such as a spiky-necked amargasaurus from Neuquén, which lived during the Cretaceous period, about 130 million years ago. From the later Cenozoic period – which extends from around 65 million years ago to the present

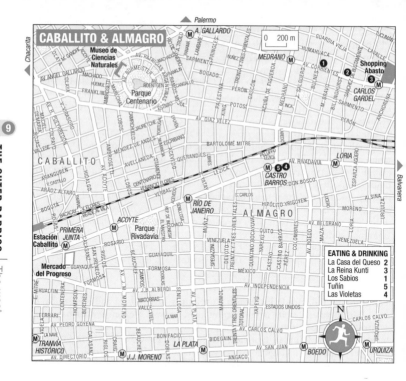

Palermo

Chacarita

0   200 m

Museo de
Ciencias
Naturales

Parque
Centenario

A. GALLARDO

MEDRANO

Shopping
Abasto

CARLOS
GARDEL

CABALLITO

LORIA

CASTRO
BARROS

RÍO DE
JANEIRO

ALMAGRO

ACOYTE

Parque
Rivadavia

Estación
Caballito

PRIMERA
JUNTA

Mercado
del Progreso

EATING & DRINKING
La Casa del Queso   2
La Reina Kunti   3
Los Sabios   1
Tuñín   5
Las Violetas   4

TRANVÍA
HISTÓRICO

LA PLATA

J.J. MORENO

BOEDO

URQUIZA

N

Balvanera

day – there are the remains of a host of **megafauna**, giant herbivores that evolved in South America when the region was separated from the other continents – such as the glyptodont, forerunner of today's armadillo. Many of these were wiped out around three million years ago, after South America reconnected with North America and more successful fauna, such as the sabre-toothed tiger (also found in the museum) and, later, humans, arrived.

Ángel Gallardo **subte** station (Line B) is a manageable six blocks away, east along the avenue of the same name. **Buses** #55 and #105 stop closer by.

Chacarita

Crisscrossed by railway lines, **Chacarita**, to the west of Palermo, takes its name from the days when the barrio was home to a small farm (*chacra*) run by Jesuits. Nowadays, the neighbourhood is synonymous with the enormous **Cementerio de la Chacarita** (daily 7am–6pm; free) laid out here. Less aristocratic than the graveyard in Recoleta (see p.108), but impressive nonetheless, it lies at the northern end of Avenida Corrientes, with a monumental main entrance at Avenida Guzmán 780. Designed as a grid of streets and diagonals, the paths are flanked by marble and polished granite tombs, often with decorative glass fronts.

By far the best sight in the cemetery is **Carlos Gardel**'s tomb, on the corner of streets 6 and 33, a brisk five-minute walk to the left of the entrance and a little towards the middle. It is topped by a life-sized statue of the singer in typical rakish pose: hand in pocket, hair slicked back and characteristic wide grin. Every inch of the surrounding stonework is plastered with plaques and flowers placed there by the singer's devotees, for whom he has become a kind of saint. Many visitors light a cigarette and place it between the statue's fingers; you will often see a dog-end still dangling.

Not far from Gardel's grave, slightly nearer the entrance, is one of the most majestic mausoleums in the whole cemetery, that of aviation pioneer **Jorge Newbery**, after whom Buenos Aires' domestic airport is named. He died near Mendoza while preparing for the first flight across the Andes and is honoured with a tomb that somehow manages to be magnificent, sinister and camp all at once: four hungry-looking condors overlook a supine nude male form – presumably the athletic Newbery himself – who is outstretched in a melodramatic pose like some latter-day Prometheus. At the centre of the graveyard, the **Recinto de Personalidades** is a collection of rather kitsch statues adorning the graves of some of Argentina's most popular cultural figures, including tango composer and bandoneón player Aníbal Troilo, pianist Osvaldo Pugliese, poet Alfonsina Storni and painter Quinquela Martín.

The most convenient public transport for the cemetery is **subte** Line B to station Federico Lacroze.

Mataderos

Lying just inside the boundary of Capital Federal, around 6km southwest of Chacarita, the remote barrio of **Mataderos** has a gory past – the very name means "abattoirs". In the late nineteenth and early twentieth centuries, its streets were home to the city's slaughterhouses, earning it its alternative name, Nuevo Chicago (a reference to the US city's own abattoir tradition). Though the slaughterhouses have long gone, Mataderos is still home to the **Mercado Nacional de Hacienda Liniers**, or livestock market. Set back from the intersection of Lisandro de la Torre and Avenida de los Corrales, its faded pink walls and arcades provide the backdrop for one of Buenos Aires' most fabulous events: the Sunday **Feria de Mataderos** (11am–sunset; ☏ 011/4687-5602 on Sun, 4374-9664 Mon–Fri, ⓦ www.feriademataderos.com.ar).

A celebration of Argentina's rural traditions, this busy street fair attracts thousands of locals and tourists for its blend of folk music, traditional crafts and regional food. You can also try your hand at regional dances such as *chamamé* and *chacarera*. The undoubted high point, however, is the display of **gaucho skills**, which usually gets going around 3pm. Gaucho-garbed riders participate in events such as the impossible-sounding *sortija*, in which, galloping at breakneck speed and standing rigid in their stirrups, they attempt to spear a small ring strung on a ribbon. Take plenty of cash – the artisan wares here, including woollen ponchos and leather purses, are good quality and considerably cheaper than in the central stores, but the stallholders do not take credit cards – and make sure the fair is actually on before setting out, as in the summer (approximately Dec–Feb) it sometimes closes or moves to Saturday evenings.

Buses #55, #80, #92 and #126 leave for Mataderos from Plaza Italia, Barrancas de Belgrano or Plaza San Martín. If in doubt, however, take a **taxi** and ask for the intersection of Lisandro de la Torre and Avenida de los Corrales. This is a desperately poor neighbourhood, and aimless wandering in the surrounding streets, especially after dark, is definitely not to be recommended.

The north

The northern barrios of Buenos Aires act as a buffer between Palermo and the suburbs of Zona Norte (see p.227). Quieter and more unassuming, they are not without places to visit. The barrio most people head for (and where you can even stay; see Chapter 10) is **Belgrano**, a largely residential neighbourhood with several interesting museums, plus the city's Chinatown. Right on the border with Belgrano and its slightly less prosperous northern neighbour **Núñez** rise the stands of River Plate's football stadium, the **Monumental**, now with its own museum and stadium tour. Núñez was also home to the infamous ESMA (Escuela de Mecánica de la Armada), a naval school used as a concentration camp during the 1976–82 dictatorship; the facility is now a human rights centre.

Belgrano

The mainly residential barrio of **Belgrano** lies immediately north of Palermo, and is similarly green and prosperous. It was named after **Manuel Belgrano**, the "inventor" of the national flag, whose surprisingly diminutive statue stands in central Plaza Belgrano. Although there are some lively shopping streets on either side of the barrio's main artery, Avenida Cabildo, much of the neighbourhood has a decidedly suburban feel, especially western **Belgrano "R"**, whose quiet cobbled blocks are lined with huge trees, mock-Tudor villas and Neocolonial mansions. **Belgrano "C"**, whose nucleus lies at the junction of avenidas Cabildo and Justamento, is the central and most interesting section of the barrio. In addition to shops, cafés and galleries, this is where you'll find the neighbourhood's first-rate museums. Nearby is **Barrio Chino**, Buenos Aires' tiny Chinatown, which since the 1990s has been the destination of immigrants from Taiwan. East towards the river, the outstanding restaurants of **Belgrano Chico**'s seven-by-seven-block square of streets cater to residents and visitors alike.

Juramento station, one stop before the end of **subte** Line D, is close to the museums, as is the Belgrano "C" **train** station on the Retiro–Tigre line (see p.234). Plenty of **buses** also run along Avenida Cabildo, including #41, #57, #59 and #60.

Museo de Arte Español

The **Museo de Arte Español** (Mon–Fri 2–8pm, Sat & Sun 10am–8pm; $1) – a fantastic, priceless assemblage of **Spanish art** in a well-restored, whitewashed colonial building – sits on the northern side of central Plaza Belgrano at Juramento 2291. Amassed by an aristocratic Uruguayan exile, **Enrique Larreta**, the collection comprises pieces from the Renaissance to the early twentieth century. From around 1900 to 1916, the dandyish Larreta – married to Josefina Anchorena, the daughter of Mercedes Castellanos de Anchorena (see p.99) – spent many of his days in Spain. During that time he visited churches and monasteries, buying up pieces of art for his Belgrano home – statues and paintings of saints, but also furniture, porcelain, silverware and tapestries, all of which are displayed in this house, which he bequeathed to the city when he died in 1961.

Greeting visitors to Larreta's former home – through the iron-grilled window by the entrance – is a Munch-like portrait of the novelist, painted in 1912 by Spanish artist Ignacio de Zuloaga. The five rooms of the single-storey building, arranged around the original Roman-style atrium, contain several masterpieces. The atrium itself is dominated by an imposing fireplace, decorated with fine Baroque ceramics depicting the **Sagrada Familia** – a work dated around 1600. Another notable item is the **Retablo del Maestro de Sinivas**, a Gothic altarpiece dedicated to St Anne, dating from 1503 and painted for a church near Burgos, Spain. In a similar vein, an immaculate early sixteenth-century retable, *La Infancia de Cristo* ("The Infancy of Christ"), delicately painted and decorated with gold leaf, is thought to have once belonged to William Randolph Hearst.

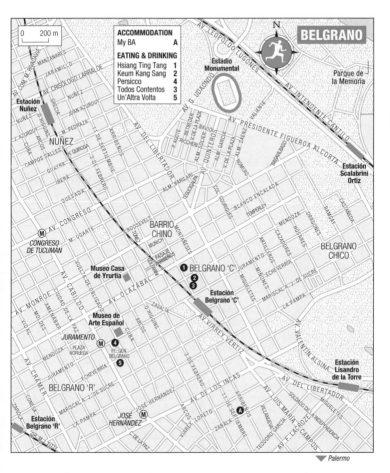

▼ Palermo

Noteworthy temporary exhibitions, usually of works by leading exponents of Argentine painting or drawing, are displayed in a set of rooms at the back of the house. Behind the house, with a separate entrance around the corner at Vuelta de Obligado 2155, a serene Andalucían **garden**, dominated by a huge ombú tree and surrounded by a profusion of magnolias, hydrangeas and agapanthus, makes for a lovely respite before heading back out to explore the rest of the barrio.

Museo Casa de Yrurtia

Three blocks north and two east, at O'Higgins 2390, the **Museo Casa de Yrurtia** (Tues–Fri 1–7pm, Sun 3–7pm; guided visits Tues–Fri 3pm, Sun 4pm; free; Ⓦwww.casadeyrurtia.gov.ar) is a beautiful single-storey Spanish-style house remodelled in 1923 by leading Argentine sculptor **Rogelio Yrurtia** (1879–1950). The artist lived here for over twenty years with his second wife, **Lía Correa Morales**, herself an important painter and sculptor. Their work is now displayed in the house, along with that of other artists, as well as the couple's collection of furniture and decorations from around the world, including a pianola, Kashmiri shawls, Chinese vases and Spanish cabinets. A courtyard behind the house, luxuriant with grapevines, plane trees and a tall Canary Island palm, serves as the setting for a large Yrurtia bronze of two naked men boxing.

The house's eleven rooms contain a large number of pieces by Yrurtia and several of Correa Morales' still lifes, landscapes and portraits, including many of her husband. The ceilings are just high enough to take the full-sized trial moulds of his monumental sculptures, some of which are city landmarks. These include the strangely homoerotic *Mausoleo Rivadavia* on Plaza Miserere, Once (see p.139), *La Justicia* in the Palacio de Justicia, and the statue of Federalist leader Manuel Dorrego on Plazoleta Suipacha, at the corner of Viamonte and Suipacha.

Barrio Chino (Chinatown)

Across the rail tracks, just east of the Belgrano "C" train station, is the tiny **Barrio Chino**, Buenos Aires' Chinatown. Covering only a handful of blocks, the neighbourhood stretches along Arribeños and Montañeses between Juramento and Olazábal. In addition to busy Chinese supermarkets and low-cost clothes shops, a small Oriental art gallery and the Tzong Kuan Buddhist **temple** at Montañeses 2175, this is also where you'll find the most authentic Far Eastern food in the city (see p.175). It's fairly quiet most of the year, but really comes alive during the Lunar New Year celebrations (Jan or Feb), when there are street stalls, parades and fireworks.

Estadio Monumental

The huge concrete stands of the **Estadio Monumental** (☎011/4323-7600) rise up at Avenida Pte Figueroa Alcorta 7597, in the far northeast corner of Belgrano, right up against the border with Núñez. Known simply as "El Monumental", and home to River Plate football club, it can seat 70,000, making it the country's largest stadium. The original structure dates from 1938, but it was remodelled and expanded for the 1978 World Cup, held at the height of the Dirty War; victims of state torture being kept nearby at the ESMA (see p.257) reported years later that one of the few sounds they heard from the outside world was the roar of the Monumental crowd. Matches at the Monumental are a glorious riot of red and white shirts, banners and streamers – see p.211 for details of attending. The stadium also hosts **concerts** by major Argentine and international artists.

In 2009 a new **museum** (daily 10am–7pm, tours 11am–5pm, closes early on match days; $45 museum and tour, $35 museum only) was opened, an audiovisual experience that makes every effort to be bigger and better than the Boca museum in the Bombonera (see p.93), although it's less tourist-friendly – both the tour and museum are in Spanish only. Highlights are a "time machine" that takes you with whizzes and bangs through a tunnel that relates the history of the club in the twentieth century, with plenty of fascinating historical and cultural context, and era-appropriate TVs that show you River's greatest goals. On site there is also a comprehensive souvenir shop, and a café that's surprisingly swanky for a football stadium.

Bus #130 from Boca via Paseo Colón and Avenida del Libertador stops right by the stadium.

Listings

Listings

⑩ Accommodation 149

⑪ Cafés 158

⑫ Restaurants 164

⑬ Bars, live music and clubs 177

⑭ The arts and entertainment 185

⑮ Tango 191

⑯ Gay and lesbian Buenos Aires 195

⑰ Shopping 198

⑱ Sports and outdoor activities 209

⑲ Kids' Buenos Aires 216

⑳ Festivals and events 219

Accommodation

Buenos Aires' rapid rise in popularity with international visitors in recent years has meant great things for its hospitality industry: not only is the number of places to stay steadily increasing, but also the quality of the establishments on offer has noticeably improved. Nonetheless, this same popularity has had two negative effects: prices, especially at the higher end, have rocketed, in some cases nearing European and North American rates, while much of the city's best **accommodation** – in all categories – is frequently full. While you should always be able to find somewhere to stay, you are advised to **book** as far in advance as possible, especially if you are fussy about where you lay your head. It is usually most straightforward to contact establishments directly for reservations: many of them offer user-friendly internet booking and online payment. Where possible, we've also included details of central booking agencies for the city's different types of accommodation. The well-known international booking websites can, of course, be a good bet for finding the best deals, too. As you look for a place to spend the night, keep in mind that a fan or **air-conditioning** is really a requirement in summer (Dec–March) – there may be a surcharge for the latter in budget places – and **heating** is a big plus in the depths of winter (July & Aug).

As in many large cities, the biggest challenge in Buenos Aires is finding a **middle-range hotel**: those that do exist – especially those in the city centre – can be bland or even grim. Travellers on a budget may be better off staying at one of the city's **hostels** or **B&Bs**. The former are generally clean and comfortable, with facilities such as free internet and laundry the norm; the latter, mostly located in quiet residential areas, offer rather more privacy and comfort for a slightly higher price. There are plenty of higher-end options, including a wide array of **boutique hotels** – smaller, more personalized places catering to international visitors with generally high levels of service and charming or cutting-edge decor. The city's traditional **luxury hotels** – many of them housed in *palacios* where royalty and heads of state have long been welcomed – have also been joined by a range of slick newcomers at the top end, some of which present the very latest in Argentine or international design, making them favourites with visiting celebrities. Trusty **international chains** are also present – a few of these are even superior to those found in Europe or North America. While the city is home to a handful of lodgings specifically for **gay and lesbian** travellers, discrimination is illegal in the city, and many hostels and hotels overtly advertise themselves as gay-friendly. For advice on **long-term accommodation**, see "Living and working in Buenos Aires", p.36.

To help you choose a place to stay, the **listings** in this chapter have been divided by area, using the same barrio designations as used in the Guide. You can find them plotted on the corresponding **chapter maps**.

Hotels

A wide variety of **hotel** accommodation is available in all of the barrios frequented by travellers. The majority of the traditional **budget** to **mid-range hotels** are found in the city centre, particularly on and around Avenida de Mayo and Congreso. In many of these you face a choice between internal, windowless rooms, or street-facing rooms where it can be hard to escape the noise of traffic; many of these places are historic sites of interest in their own right, however, and their great locations, together with details such as stained-glass windows and antique elevators, can often make up for these shortcomings. En-suite bathrooms are the norm, though the cheapest rooms sometimes have shared bathrooms; facilities such as cable TV or internet access are rarely found in budget joints. Breakfast is usually either a rather basic *medialuna* and coffee or nothing at all. With the exception of some rather unsavoury places near the train stations, most budget hotels in Buenos Aires are quite safe, though note that an "*albergue transitorio*" is a short-stay hotel where rooms are rented by the hour by couples; these places are usually pretty obvious by their choice of name and lobby design.

Buenos Aires' top-flight **luxury hotels** tend to be clustered around Retiro and Recoleta, including a handful in the blocks around Calle Florida, plus a trio in Puerto Madero (likely to increase over the next couple of years). The best are housed in the city's French-influenced mansions, where you'll be made to feel like royalty; classy restaurants and facilities such as pools, spas and more-than-you-can-eat American-style buffet breakfasts are usually part of the package. If you prefer a more modern, designer-magazine approach to your lodgings, the city's fabulous, if expensive, **boutique hotels** may be more your style. As with the luxury hotels, you'll get all mod cons and excellent service. Such places are sprinkled all over the city, but most are concentrated in green and trendy Palermo

Accommodation prices

Prices quoted in this chapter refer to the **least expensive double in high season** (usually Christmas and Easter) and are given in either **US dollars (US$)** or **Argentine pesos ($)**, depending on the type of establishment. Generally speaking, higher end lodgings will give a dollar rate (often not including the 21 percent IVA, or VAT) while places like hostels and B&Bs will usually post a peso rate (normally with VAT factored in). In all cases you will be able to pay in pesos or dollars, or even another hard currency such as euros (most places also accept credit cards). Note that the inflation rate in Argentina is high by international standards and hits accommodation prices especially hard (by as much as 30 percent a year) so prices can vary a lot annually.

In general, **rates** for lower-end accommodation in Buenos Aires are reasonable compared with European capitals and most North American and Australasian cities: you can count on paying US$6–13/$25–50 per night for a dorm bed in a hostel. When it comes to the mid- to upper-range, double rooms aren't always much, if at all, less expensive than their equivalent elsewhere: expect to pay US$28–50/$110–200 in a hostel or a budget hotel; US$50–88/$200–350 in a mid-range hotel; US$75–200/$300–800 in a B&B; US$100–350/$400–1400 in a boutique hotel; and US$400–600/$1600–2400 or more (expect 4-digit dollar rates for special suites) in one of the city's top-flight hotels.

Discounts can sometimes be negotiated, particularly if you book online, are staying for more than a few days or are travelling outside normal holiday times, but the city is popular with visitors year-round, so don't expect major low-season deals. Also note that credit cards may entail a surcharge, while conversely paying cash might win you a lower rate. For more on costs, and the practice of dual pricing, see p.31.

and Belgrano. In the event that all the ones we've listed here are full, you might consult ⓦ www.destinationargentina.com and www.innsofargentina.com for further suggestions.

Monserrat

Axel Venezuela 649 ☎ 011/4136-9393, ⓦ www.axelhotels.com. The first gay hotel in Latin America, *Axel* is also hetero-friendly. It's all built and decorated in a markedly contemporary style – the grey and white bedrooms are minimalist and hi-tech, while the top-floor deck features a glass-bottom pool, a sauna, a hammam and jacuzzis. There's another outdoor pool with a deck-bar, and a restaurant that is open to the public for all three meals. US$250.

Castelar Av de Mayo 1152 ☎ 011/4383-5000, ⓦ www.castelarhotel.com.ar. A Buenos Aires institution (see p.57), this old-fashioned hotel offers attractive and soundproof rooms with big comfortable beds. There's also a glamorous bar downstairs, as well as a sauna/spa. $320.

🎿 **La Cayetana** México 1330 ☎ 011/4383-2230, ⓦ www.lacayetanahotel.com.ar. Beautifully renovated nineteenth-century townhouse, with a huge sun-lit central patio and much of the original furniture worked harmoniously into the rooms, each of which is individually decorated. The only drawback is the location – several blocks away from anywhere of interest – but taxis are always available. Reservations essential. US$120.

City Hotel Bolívar 160 ☎ 011/4121-6464, ⓦ www.nh-hotels.com. The comfortable beds, attentive service, rooftop swimming pool and central location – just half a block from the Plaza de Mayo – make this a good option in its price range. US$155.

Gran Hotel España Tacuari 80 ☎ 011/4343-5541. Good budget option in central yet quiet location, with clean, basic rooms, helpful staff and a lovely antique, manually operated elevator. It's worth paying a few pesos more for the front rooms with little balconies. $150.

Hotel de los Dos Congresos Rivadavia 1777 ☎ 011/4371-0072, ⓦ www.hoteldoscongresos .com. Well-maintained hotel in a late nineteenth-century building. Modern rooms feature a/c, TV and mini-bar; the interior ones can be on the stuffy side, while the best rooms at the front overlook the Congreso building and have a spiral staircase and mezzanine within them. US$80.

Intercontinental Moreno 809 ☎ 011/4340-7100, ⓦ www.ichotelsgroup.com. Part of the inter national chain, the *Intercontinental* manages to have its own style and personality – lots of marble, leather and wood in the public areas, and toned-down bedrooms that exude understated luxury. US$210.

Moreno Moreno 376 ☎ 011/6091-2000, ⓦ www.morenobuenosaires.com. Following the *Moreno's* stunning Art Deco facade and sumptuous tiled entrance, the 40 spacious but rather minimalist rooms come as rather a disappointment. There is a deck terrace, offering amazing views, but no restaurant for the time being and few facilities; even so it is one of the best options in this part of the city. US$110.

Roma Av de Mayo 1413 ☎ 011/4381-4921. A good deal, given its pleasant and central location, the *Roma* has some nice, if slightly noisy, rooms with balconies looking onto Avenida de Mayo, and a fabulous antique elevator. $110.

Sportsman Rivadavia 1425 ☎ 011/4381-8021, ⓦ www.hotelsportsman.com.ar. Popular budget hotel in a rambling old building with lots of character, though the interior is beginning to show its age. There's a variety of rooms available, all with fans and some with shared bathrooms; the nicest ones are the en-suite doubles at the front, which have balconies. $95 with shared bath, $140 en suite.

San Nicolás

🎿 **725 Buenos Aires** Roque Sáenz Peña 725 ⓦ www.725buenosaireshotel.com. A swish bar, trendy restaurant, spa and swimming pool are just some of the attrac- tions at this fabulous hotel, in an equally remarkable 1920s building; the decor combines dark wood with vibrant colour schemes, with gorgeous results. US$220.

Claridge Tucumán 535 ☎ 011/4314-2020, ⓦ www.claridge.com.ar. Fronted by white Doric columns and uniformed door staff, the *Claridge* announces itself as a traditional luxury hotel. Originally dating from 1946, the hotel has been tastefully modernized to include smart rooms with black marble bathrooms; a restaurant that serves five o'clock tea (as well as breakfast and dinner) on starched white tablecloths; and a heated outdoor pool with coloured lighting and a sundeck. US$205.

Facón Grande Reconquista 645 ☏ 011/4312-6360, ⓦ www.hotelfacongrande.com. Named after a gaucho hero, "Big Knife", this medium-sized hotel has pleasant a/c rooms. The decor is plain but appealing, enlivened by some suitably gaucho-style artwork. $270.

Jousten Av Corrientes 280 ☏ 011/4321-6750, ⓦ www.nh-hotels.com. High-end accommodation in a beautiful early twentieth-century building popular with business travellers but with appeal for all; also has an excellent restaurant serving modern Spanish cuisine. US$230.

Obelisco Center Roque Sáenz Peña 991 ☏ 011/4326-0909, ⓦ www.obeliscohotel.com.ar. Large, comfortable rooms in a hotel overlooking the Obelisco monument – you won't have any trouble finding your way back after a late night. Apartments with kitchenettes also available. US$125.

Regal Pacific 25 de Mayo 764 ☏ 011/4310-7000, ⓦ www.regal-pacific.com. Another five-star chain hotel. Rooms are luxurious and discreet, and the service excellent. The hotel has a small gym and swimming pool. US$135.

Rochester Concept Hotel Maipú 572 ☏ 011/4326-6076, ⓦ www.hotel-rochester concept.com. Bright rooms combine a trendy minimalist style with comfort and functionality. Lots of dark wood and lime green create a soothing ambience. US$170.

Puerto Madero

Faena Hotel & Universe Marta Salotti 445, Puerto Madero Este ☏ 011/4010-9000, ⓦ www.faenahotelanduniverse.com. Buenos Aires' hotel for the in-crowd, this former grain-storage building has been given a serious Philippe Starck makeover and now has a *belle époque* jazz bar, a café stuffed with kitsch antiques, a floor-to-ceiling white restaurant with unicorn heads on the walls, an oriental spa and, of course, swish rooms. There is also a decent-sized outdoor pool. It's the kind of place that's too cool for a reception – you get an "experience manager" – and where the movie producers and celebrities that stay here certainly don't talk about anything as crude as money; count on US$520 and up for a room.

Hilton Av Macacha Güemes 351 ☏ 011/4891-0000, ⓦ www.hilton.com. It may belong to a ubiquitous chain, but the *Buenos Aires*

Hilton is hard to beat for its dockside location, fabulous outdoor swimming pool and sheer scale, from the glasshouse lobby to the giant suites. US$410 and up.

🏃 **Madero** Rosario Vera Peñaloza 360 ☏ 011/5776-7777, ⓦ www.hotelmadero .com. Colour is obviously a big deal at this sumptuously stylish hotel, formerly a Sofitel: the *Red* restaurant is done out in wood, in the *White* bar only the barstools are white, and *Blue*, the hotel's "sky bar", is only blue when the sky is (thankfully often). The spacious rooms, the indoor pool (with an open roof in the summer), the restaurant and all services, including a spa, are absolutely tip-top. US$240–500.

San Telmo

Mansión Vitraux Carlos Calvo 369 ☏ 011/4300-6886, ⓦ www.mansionvitraux.com. Boutique hotels are a rarity in San Telmo, but this one offers top-rate comfort and design, with a roof deck and plunge pool, plus an appealing breakfast room that doubles up for wine tastings. US$175–235.

Los Tres Reyes Brasil 425 ☏ 011/4300-9456. Just half a block from Parque Lezama, the simple but comfortable rooms and spotless private bathrooms here are excellent value for money. Breakfast included. $120.

Retiro

🏃 **Casa Calma** Suipacha 1015 ☏ 011/5199-2800, ⓦ www.casacalma.com.ar. About the only boutique hotel in Retiro, *Casa Calma* lives up to its name of "Quiet House", and takes a decidedly ecological approach, with hanging gardens and environment-friendly toiletries – many bathrooms have jacuzzis, while you can ask for massages in your room. There is also an honesty bar. US$230–280.

Crillon Av Santa Fe 796 ☏ 011/4310-2000, ⓦ www.nh-hotels.com. In a handsome 1950s building, the *Crillon* has become a classic Porteño hotel, and was recently refurbished to join the growing number of NH chain hotels in the city. The usual high Spanish standards apply, but it does feel a little impersonal. US$260.

Elevage Maipú 960 ☏ 011/4891-8018, ⓦ www .elevage.com.ar. Although this well-run hotel is aimed more at the business traveller, its prime location and comfortable rooms, plus an outdoor pool, make it a good choice for this barrio. The restaurant is surprisingly good and breakfasts are excellent. US$170–230.

Four Seasons Posadas 1086 ☏ 011/4321-1200, ⓦ www.fourseasons.com/buenosaires. Part of the international chain, this fantastically luxurious hotel is divided between a modern tower-block and the *belle époque* Alazaga Unzué mansion (see p.104), which looks like a French chateau inside and out. Sunday brunch, open to the public, is served in the latter. Around US$500 and up.

Lancaster Av Córdoba 405 ☏ 011/4131-6464, ⓦ www.nh-hotels.com. Like its sibling the *Crillon*, this establishment has been going strong for years and is an emblematic city hotel – the NH chain look has brightened it up, though some of the original charm has been lost. That said, it is extremely comfortable, with all the latest technology including TV, internet and the like. US$260.

Marriott Plaza Hotel Florida 1005 ☏ 011/4318-3000, ⓦ www.marriottplaza.com.ar. Long-established luxury hotel now run by the Marriott chain, who've given it a slightly corporate feel. Rooms are plush but rather bland; the nicest ones have a stunning view over Plaza San Martín. Elegant 1930s-style bar and good restaurant. US$225 and up.

Sofitel Arroyo 841 ☏ 011/4131-0000, ⓦ www.sofitelbuenosaires.com.ar. Housed in a restored Art Deco monument of a building, this swish Gallic chain member is solid and classy, though the rooms could be bigger. The hotel restaurant, *Le Sud*, is regarded as one of the best of its ilk in the city for French-influenced cuisine. There is a gym and a bistro-style café popular with locals. US$400 and up.

Recoleta

Algodón Mansión Montevideo 1647 ☏ 011/3530-7777, ⓦ www.algodon mansion.com. When this sumptuous Recoleta mansion was converted into a hotel and restaurant so much could have gone wrong in terms of design and layout, but nothing did. The rooms and especially the bathrooms are enormous and handsomely appointed, the decor is stunning and the service is utterly professional, from reception to the bar, where delicious cocktails are shaken to taste. There is a roof deck with plunge pool and spa, while the groundfloor restaurant is already winning awards for its haute cuisine. US$400 and up.

Alvear Palace Hotel Av Alvear 1891 ☏ 011/4804-7777, ⓦ www.alvearpalace .com. Once the choice of wealthy landowners and now the favourite of politicians, royalty, musicians and film stars, this is the most stylish but traditional of all Buenos Aires' luxury hotels. It offers fabulously refurbished rooms in a hyper-Gallic Louis XV style and all the extras you would expect, including a personal butler (who will pack and unpack for you). There is a spa and an indoor pool, both of which are quite underwhelming. US$800 and up.

Art Hotel Azcuénaga 1268 ☏ 011/4821-4744, ⓦ www.arthotel.com.ar. Four-poster beds and lots of flounce add to the romantic ambience of this quiet hotel, with its own art gallery. Rooms vary from "small and cosy" (read: pokey) to spacious (the "king" has its own balcony). US$100–155.

Bel Air Arenales 1462 ☏ 011/4021-4070, ⓦ www .hotelbelair.com.ar. An elegant 1920s building with a pristine white facade and 80 equally immaculate rooms and suites, each with parquet floors and peach bedspreads. $500.

Design Suites and Towers Marcelo T. de Alvear 1683 ☏ 011/4814-8700, ⓦ www.designsuites .com. One of the first modern design hotels to open in the city, it has maintained sky-high standards, with enormous apartment-like rooms and some even more gigantic suites (US$255), plus a designer-goods shop and art gallery. US$180.

Etoile Pres. Ortiz 1835 ☏ 011/4805-2626, ⓦ www.etoile.com.ar. Modern, glitzy hotel with very large rooms and its own health club. The slightly more expensive front rooms have fantastic bird's-eye views of Recoleta Cemetery. US$145.

Lion d'Or Hotel Pacheco de Melo 2019 ☏ 011/4803-8992, ⓦ www.hotel-liondor.com.ar. Homely, friendly place, with a mix of appealing rooms that vary considerably in size, style and price, ranging from $120 for an internal single with shared bath to $350 for a lovely, spacious triple with a fireplace and balcony. $200.

LoiSuites Recoleta Vicente López 1955 ☏ 011/5777-8950, ⓦ www.loisuites.com.ar. This large hotel with luxurious suites, done out in white and pastel shades, with lots of native wood, is very well located, near Recoleta Cemetery. If it's full there are a couple of others across 9 de Julio in Retiro belonging to the same local chain and offering the same high level of service. US$280.

Palacio Duhau-Park Hyatt Av Alvear 1661 ℡011/5171-1234, Ⓦbuenosaires.park.hyatt .com/hyatt. The Duhau family home on the city's most desirable street (see p.112) is now a luxury hotel, with medium to large rooms decorated with soothing woods and marble baths; the top-floor "Duhau" suite has a wrap-around terrace, among its many enticing features. The indoor swimming pool and spa, restaurant, *vinoteca* and *Oak Bar* mean you never need to leave the building. Even so, the service is sometimes below par. US$600 and up.

Palermo

1551 Palermo Boutique Hotel Acuña de Figueroa 1551 ℡011/4867-3292, Ⓦwww.1551palermo.com. Truly charming boutique hotel with a variety of rooms – the less expensive ones do have slightly kitsch decor, though. The staff can fix you up at the city's best tango venues. US$120.

Bo Bo Guatemala 4882 ℡011/4774-0505, Ⓦwww.bobohotel.com. In addition to a refined restaurant, this stylish but friendly boutique hotel offers rooms done out in different styles from classical to pop – which basically means lots of yellow. The soundproofing leaves a lot to be desired, though. US$200–280.

Casa Las Cañitas Huergo 283 ℡011/4771-3878, Ⓦwww.casalascanitas.com. Nine extremely well-appointed rooms ranging from relatively basic to deluxe in a beautifully designed house with a wine bar, terrace and garden. The top-notch linens come in natural hues complemented by striking purple and orange walls. US$130–200.

🏃 **Craft** Nicaragua 4583 ℡011/4833-0060, Ⓦwww.crafthotel.com. Overlooking the beautiful Plaza Armenia at the heart of Palermo Viejo, this trendy little hotel revels in its minimalistic decor, which includes functional shower cubicles divided from the bedroom by a curtain. The cheapest room, "Song", includes a vinyl record player (choose from a collection at reception). An excellent self-service breakfast is served on the top floor, where a sunny roof-terrace includes four-poster beds. US$150.

Finisterra Báez 248 ℡011/4773-0901, Ⓦwww.248finisterra.com. A garden, terrace and outdoor jacuzzi are some of the extras justifying the high prices at this converted Las Cañitas townhouse, furnished with early twentieth-century antiques. US$170–240.

Five Cool Rooms Honduras 4742 ℡011/5235-5555, Ⓦwww.fivehotelbuenosaires.com. The name says it all, really – you just have to pick a size: small, medium, large, large with jacuzzi or extra-large. Everything is of state-of-the-art design, from the bathrooms to the terrace with BBQ facilities. US$125–240.

🏃 **Home** Honduras 5860 ℡011/4778-1008, Ⓦwww.homebuenosaires.com. Owned and run by a British record producer and his Irish-Argentine wife, this masterpiece of modern architecture and hotel design is simply incredible: from the wallpaper in each room to the swimming pool and deck, the attention to detail is breathtaking. Every Fri night a DJ adds further coolness to the restaurant/bar, while weekend brunch is a local attraction. The gorgeous garden comes into its own in spring and summer. For the outstanding "Garden" suite you'll have to fork out US$395 plus tax. US$160–350.

Krista Bonpland 1665 ℡011/4771-4697, Ⓦwww.kristahotel.com.ar. This elegant mansion in Palermo Hollywood functions as a fine boutique hotel, where the rooms each have their own character thanks to details such as wood panelling, stained-glass windows and mouldings. US$180–260.

🏃 **Legado Mítico** Gurruchaga 1848 ℡011/4833-1300, Ⓦwww.legadomitico .com. This fine boutique hotel goes in for themed rooms. You can choose from Argentine heroes like San Martín and Evita or arty types like Borges and Tita Merello. Most (but not all) are spacious and stylishly decorated and furnished, with all manner of memorabilia recalling each historical figure. The breakfast room resembles the library of a gentleman's club. US$250–320.

🏃 **Magnolia** Julián Álvarez 1746 ℡011/4867-4900, Ⓦwww.magnoliahotel .com.ar. At this gorgeous Art Nouveau townhouse with period furnishings, nothing is too much trouble – from the welcome glass of wine on arrival to help with all you need during your stay. Breakfast is excellent and copious. US$180–240.

Malabia 1555 Malabia 1555 ℡011/4833-2410, Ⓦwww.malabiahouse.com.ar. This converted convent led the way when it came to Palermo boutique hotels and it maintains its charm. Pluses include high ceilings and late breakfasts but the bathrooms are quite cramped and some of the rooms are a little gloomy. US$140–190.

Nuss El Salvador 4916 ☎011/4833-6222, ⓦwww.nusshotel.com. This utterly classy boutique hotel in a converted convent at the corner of Serrano houses 22 beautiful rooms, ranging from spacious superior category to sizeable suites. The convent's inner courtyard has been preserved, adding to the sense of space and airiness, while the top-floor deck with its plunge pool, and a small gym and spa is refreshed by the majestic plane trees in the neighbouring street. US$250.

Rendezvous Bonpland 1484 ☎011/3964-5222, ⓦwww.rendezvoushotel.com.ar. This French-owned boutique hotel in trendy Hollywood combines style with charm while the whole place has been done out according to the rules of feng shui. Avoid any room overlooking the street though – it can get noisy late at night during the weekend. US$110–155.

Tailor Made Hotel Arce 385 ☎011/4774-9620, ⓦwww.tailormadehotels.com. Located in the trendy Las Cañitas sub-barrio, the five exquisite suites here are organized by the concept encapsulated in the hotel's name – every personal whim is catered for, from an iPod lease to the wines in your cooler. US$180–320.

Vain Thames 2226 ☎011/4776-8246, ⓦwww.vainuniverse.com. A complimentary drink and massage let you know what you have to look forward to at one of the most pleasurable boutique hotels in the city: gorgeous decor, designer furniture, a beguiling interior patio and a wine bar all lurk behind a fabulous Neoclassical facade. US$170–270.

Vitrum Gorriti 5641 ☎011/4776-5030, ⓦwww.vitrumhotel.com. In the heart of Hollywood, this hotel is slick and voguish from its *Sushi Club* to its spa and roof deck; glass (as the Latin name hints) and aluminium dominate. The rooms are minimalist, with a small kitchenette in some, while the breakfast is delicious. US$250–315.

Bed and breakfasts

Driven by the increase in visitor numbers, **B&Bs** are now opening regularly in Buenos Aires. In general, they're chic, converted townhouses with exclusive but cosy atmospheres, and make excellent and more economic alternatives to boutique hotels and similarly priced mid-range hotels. So far focused mostly on **Palermo**, but also increasingly scattered around the central and southern barrios, B&Bs here tend to go for funky, fresh decor – with nary a candlewick bedspread in sight – attractive, individual rooms that vary in size and price, and a friendly welcome. Breakfasts are usually elegant; some places also serve lunch and dinner, but only a very few.

Monserrat

Posada de la Luna Perú 565 ☎011/4343-0911, ⓦwww.posadaluna.com. A beautiful gem of a guesthouse at the edge of San Telmo, with a spa, solarium and patio. The rooms, all with moon-related names, have gorgeous wood floors and are done out mostly in white and bright colours. US$120.

San Nicolás

Calden Guesthouse Reconquista 755 ☎011/4893-1060, ⓦwww.caldenargentina.com. Five beautiful en-suite rooms on the first floor of a handsome townhouse, each named after a famous Argentine personage: "Borges" is classy, while "El Che" is a bit more racy. Lots of retro furniture and ornaments. US$80–140.

Rooney's Sarmiento 1775 3rd floor ☎011/5252-5060, ⓦwww.rooneysboutiquehotel.com. The owner – Mr Rooney himself, from Belfast – has put his heart and soul into restoring this handsome historic townhouse to its former glory. From retro bathrooms to glittering chandeliers, the place looks and feels like a small palace, while breakfasts come complete with freshly prepared eggs. If you stay at least two nights, they offer a free airport pickup. US$125–160.

San Telmo

Babel Balcarce 946 ☎011/4300-8300. Charmingly run place in one of the quieter, less grungy parts of the barrio. The rooms are spruce, the bathrooms have lovely tiled walk-in showers, while the copious breakfast includes pancakes and waffles made to order. US$110.

Mansión Dandi Royal Piedras 922 ☎011/4361-3537, ⓦ www.dandiroyal.com.ar. Another late nineteenth-century mansion transformed into a guesthouse, but with quirkier design – the place's *raison d'être* is to demonstrate and teach tango, with shows laid on every weekday evening. US$160.

Palermo

Bed and Baires Hostel Malabia 1935 ☎011/4832-4420, ⓦ www.bedandbaires .com.ar. Ultra-friendly place in the heart of Palermo Viejo, with an alluring green patio and an unusual brick-walled living space, plus a handful of bright rooms, most with small balconies. US$70.

La Otra Orilla Julián Álvarez 1779 ☎011/4867-4070, ⓦ www.otraorilla.com.ar. Lovely, quiet little B&B in Palermo Viejo, with seven rooms of varying sizes; all are comfortable, bright and tastefully decorated, and some have balconies. Prices, including buffet breakfast and free internet, range from US$50 for the smallest single with shared bath to US$170 for the suite with a/c and TV. US$95.

Posada Palermo Salguero 1655 ☎011/4826-8792, ⓦ www.posadapalermo.com. Wonderful B&B in a more residential corner of Palermo, not far from Soho. A typical *casa chorizo* (kind of elongated townhouse found in most Argentine cities), it offers smart rooms, a homely atmosphere and a great breakfast, including home-made preserves. US$125.

The outer barrios

1890 Salta 1074, Constitución ☎011/4304-8798, ⓦ www.buenosaires1890byb.com.ar. The numerical name refers to the date the building went up, but each of this guesthouse's six plush suites is modern and stylish. US$120–240.

Posada Histórica Gotan Sánchez de Loria 1618, Boedo ☎011/4912-3807, ⓦ www.posadagotan .com. This late nineteenth-century house has been done up by a descendant of the Italian couple who built it, and the host's attachment to the place shines through – the rooms, kitchen and patio are all delightful. The only drawback is the distance from any public transport. US$80.

Soco Lavalle 3119, Balvanera ☎011/4864-2032. Friendly, relaxed B&B right behind the Abasto shopping centre in Gardel-land. The rooms are large and pleasantly picturesque, with a slightly rustic feel, and there is a huge roof terrace where barbecues are held, weather permitting. US$100.

Hostels

Buenos Aires' **hostels** are for the most part concentrated in the southern part of the city, especially **San Telmo** and **Monserrat**, where cheap accommodation, cobbled streets, prettily crumbling buildings and a student/bohemian nightlife act as a backpacker magnet, although there are also well-appointed hostels in the more tranquil streets north of the centre. You'll find Porteño hostels pretty liberal – all-night parties, on-site *parrilladas* (BBQs) and outings to dance clubs and tango shows are the rule here, not curfews. As a result, they're not always the quietest places to stay, but most have private en-suite rooms available; note, however, that these rooms tend to be booked well in advance. Most hostels are independent, but some are affiliated with Hostelling International (HI) and give discounts to members. These are noted in the listings; see ⓦ www.hostels.org.ar for a complete list of affiliates. The website ⓦ www.ba-h.com.ar also carries an updated list of all the city's hostels.

Monserrat

Che Lagarto Youth Hostel Venezuela 857 ☎011/4304-7618, ⓦ www.chelagarto.com. Long-running, laid-back hostel popular with a younger (and sometimes rather noisy) crowd. $32 per person for a dorm bed, or $220 for a double with private bath.

Limehouse Youth Hostel Lima 11 ☎011/4383-4561, ⓦ www.limehouse.com.ar. This attractive nineteenth-century house faces Avenida de Mayo; inside, lime green is the colour scheme. The dormitories are cheap (from $35 per person), if nothing to write postcards home about, but there are impressively huge common areas, including one with a pool table, as well as friendly staff and a spacious terrace that is sometimes used as a bar and sleeping area in summer. $160 for an en-suite double.

Milhouse Hipólito Yrigoyen 959 ⓣ011/4345-9604, ⓦwww.milhousehostel.com. Large, popular hostel in a three-storey nineteenth-century house a block from Avenida de Mayo. As well as providing a big communal area, this HI affiliated hostel regularly arranges in-house events such as tango lessons as well as trips to football matches and nightclubs. Dorms $50, doubles with private bath $200.

Tango City Hostel Inn Piedras 680 ⓣ0800/666-4678 or 011/4300-5764, ⓦwww.hostel-inn.com. Wildly popular with young backpackers – expect significant alcohol consumption, if less than snappy service – this hostel is now something of an institution. Beds start at $50, which includes internet access and extras such as Spanish and tango lessons. Its smaller, slightly quieter sister establishment, the *Hostel Inn*, is nearby at Humberto Primo 820. Advance reservation essential Dec–March. Both HI affiliated.

San Nicolás

Colonial Tucumán 509 ⓣ011/4312-6412, ⓦwww.hostelcolonial.com.ar. The brightly coloured rooms at the *Colonial* are on the small side, but the hostel is well located if you want the convenience of being in the microcentro. PCs with internet are available at no extra charge. $39 for a dorm bed, or $200 for a double with private bath.

V&S Youth Hostel Viamonte 887 ⓣ011/4322-0994, ⓦwww.hostelclub.com. One of the most luxurious hostels in Buenos Aires, the *V&S* is centrally located in a 1910 French-style mansion. A bar and giant TV top the list of amenities, as well as all kinds of interesting organized excursions to keep you occupied. In addition to dormitory accommodation ($52 per person) there are three great-value double rooms ($264) with private bathrooms and balconies.

San Telmo

Buenos Ayres Hostel Pasaje San Lorenzo 320 ⓣ011/4361-0694, ⓦwww.buenosayreshostel .com.ar. Sleeping between two and four, the rooms at this hostel are smart, and some have a balcony looking out onto San Telmo's characterful Pasaje San Lorenzo. A bed for the night is $40, but many guests are

long-term – ask about their monthly rates, breakfast and laundry included.

Circus Hostel Chacabuco 1020, San Telmo ⓣ011/4878-7786, ⓦwww .hostelcircus.com. *Circus* successfully bridges the gap between hostel and hotel, offering the ambience and friendliness of the former with the comforts of the latter – the beds have decent mattresses, each room has its own bathroom and there is even a smart decked pool. The street has other hostels, so it's a good place to try your luck if you haven't got anything booked. Double rooms go for $200, while a dorm bed costs $48.

El Hostal de San Telmo Carlos Calvo 614 ⓣ011/4300-6899, ⓦwww.elhostaldesantelmo .com. In one of the prettiest parts of San Telmo, this small hostel is friendly and well kept, with laundry facilities, a terrace and a barbecue area. Rooms have two, four or eight beds costing $40–52 per bed.

Ostinatto Hostel Chile 680 ⓣ011/4362-9639, ⓦwww.ostinatto.com. A recycled building with minimalist decor, new beds and lots of light – breakfast is included in the rate ($44) for a dorm, and they hold art exhibitions and run guided tours.

Retiro

Recoleta Youth Hostel Libertad 1216 ⓣ011/4812-4419, ⓦwww.trhostel.com.ar. Smart hostel in an attractively modernized and spacious old mansion just inside Retiro, even though it's called Recoleta. Accommodation is in a mixture of dormitories ($40 per person) and double rooms ($156–180), and there is a large terrace area and good facilities including TV and internet access. HI affiliated.

Palermo

Eco Pampa Hostel Guatemala 4778 ⓣ011/4831-2435, ⓦwww.hostelpampa .com. Dubbing itself the city's first green hostel – the vibrant lime-hued facade sets the tone – *Eco Pampa* is comfortable as well as eco-friendly, with its leafy terrace and low-energy computers. Dormitories $60 and $240 for a double room.

So Hostel Charcas 4416 ⓣ011/4779-2949, ⓦwww.sohostel.com.ar. Excellent Palermo Soho hostel with accommodation ranging from dorms at $40 per person to double rooms with private bath and TV ($185); all rooms have a/c and there is a decent café serving breakfast.

11

Cafés

B
uenos Aires' **cafés** play an integral part in the city's social life – like their Southern European cousins, Porteños are much more likely to meet a friend for an espresso in a café than for a beer in a bar – and the quantity and quality of places reflect these traditions. Since the 1920s, the city's cafés have hosted a grand cross-section of society – everyone from artists, revolutionaries, novelists and tango singers to office workers grabbing a quick croissant (*medialuna*) in the morning, ladies of leisure taking afternoon tea (*merienda*) and students gossiping over a juice or beer in the evenings. Some places are destinations in their own right, with opulent *belle époque* interiors of marble columns and stained glass, while others are more modern and simpler in design; almost all have table service, though, where white-jacketed waiters take your order. Contemporary US-style coffeehouses, with squishy sofas and counter ordering, have started to appear as well, but are for now few and far between.

Though the main reason to visit a café in Buenos Aires is to drink an unhurried – and almost always excellent – **espresso** (taking breaks, perhaps, to read, write or indulge in a little discreet people-watching), many cafés and *confiterías* (tearooms) do **food**, too. This ranges from light snacks to complete meals; in the latter case the food is almost always Porteño standards such as pasta or *milanesas* (breaded cutlets). You can find more snacks, including the Argentine version of fast food – empanadas and other delicious *criollo* specialities – at hole-in-the-wall **snack bars** all over the city. And in the warmer months you can stave off hunger during the long afternoon wait for dinner by doing as the locals do: have an ice cream. With dozens of delicious flavours, dominated by *dulce de leche*, the **heladerías** (ice cream parlours) of Buenos Aires count among the world's best.

The **hours** of cafés vary, but most open for breakfast at around 7am, stay open throughout the day – they're often particularly busy at tea time (4–5pm) – and close at around 8pm. Many *confiterías* serving full meals stay open throughout the evening, though. Expect to pay around $8 for a coffee (more in famous or swish joints), $15–25 for a sandwich and $25–35 for a cooked meal. The rule for tipping is the same as for restaurants – if service is not included, you should add around ten percent.

The **listings** in this chapter have been divided by area, using the same barrio designations as used in the Guide. You can find them plotted on the corresponding chapter **maps**.

Cafés and confiterías

You will find neighbourhood **cafés** throughout the city, but the most notable ones, with rich histories and elegant surroundings, tend to be concentrated in the centre. However, there are a couple of excellent and authentic places in the outer barrios that are worth the journey, too. Some of the more old-fashioned **cafés** describe themselves as **confiterías**. Traditionally these were a kind of tearoom (also known as *salones de té* or *casas de té*) specializing in sandwiches, biscuits, cakes and pastries to accompany your tea and coffee, but the line between these and other cafés is quite subtle and increasingly blurred. **High tea** – one of many outward signs of the city's rampant Anglophilia – is often best at the top hotels, such as the *Alvear* (see p.153) or *Claridge* (see p.151). It's worth remembering, too, that many of the city's **museums** – notably the MALBA (see p.125), the Museo de Arte Decorativo (see p.121), the Museo de Artes Plásticas Eduardo Sívori (see p.132) and the Museo Evita (see p.135) – have their own cafés/restaurants, allowing you to take a break from all the culture and enjoy a drink, an intake of caffeine or even a full-blown meal.

Monserrat

Café Tortoni Av de Mayo 825 ☎011/4342-4328. Buenos Aires' most famous café (see p.56) exudes pure elegance, but it is in grave danger of turning into a tourist trap – something already reflected in the prices, which are higher than elsewhere in the city. Some evenings it hosts live jazz or tango in *La Bodega* downstairs, but there are many far more authentic music venues around. Mon–Sat 8am–3.30am, Sun 8am–1am.

London City Av de Mayo 599 ☎011/4342-9057. One of Avenida de Mayo's long-established cafés with literary associations (see p.56), *London City* serves main meals as well as the usual coffee and cakes, and puts on musical performances (often tango) on Sat evenings. Closed Sun.

La Puerto Rico Alsina 420 ☎011/4331-2215. Simple and elegant, one of the city's timeless *confiterías*, famous for its outstanding espressos. Meals are served, too. Mon–Fri 7am–8pm, Sat 8am–midnight, Sun noon–7pm.

San Nicolás

A222 Corrientes 222, 19th floor ☎011/5199-0222. Near the top of one of the most sumptuous Rationalist towers in the city, the 1932 CoMeGa building, *A222* offers breathtaking views of Puerto Madero and its surroundings with your tea or coffee; stay for a glass of wine and watch the same scene turn into a sea of lights as dusk turns to night. Pass on dinner, though: it is overpriced and the service is poor. Mon–Fri 8.30am–1am, Sat 4pm–1am.

Café Martínez Av Corrientes 450 (San Nicolás), Talcahuano 948 (Recoleta), Bulnes 1790 (Palermo), Libertador 3598 (Palermo) and many others, ⓦ www.cafemartinez.com.ar. Decades-old, faux-traditional café chain. The quality is good and their speciality drinks enticing. Try the "Cappuccino Martínez", a rich mix of chocolate, honey, steamed milk, cream, cinnamon – and a little coffee. Hours and days vary from branch to branch, but most are open at least Mon–Fri.

Café Paulin Sarmiento 649 ☎011/4325-2280. With the same owners as the *New Brighton* two doors down (see p.160), this Porteño institution is frequented mostly by gossiping old men; its range of sandwiches and baguettes is considered to be among the best in the city. Mon–Sat 6am–9pm.

Café Richmond Florida 468 ☎011/4322-1341. Something of a legend – it was the meeting-place of Borges and his entourage – the *Richmond* (see p.66) and its nostalgia-inducing interior aren't exactly exciting, but are steeped in history (as are many of the clients and waiters) and the coffee is still good. Mon–Sat 7am–10pm.

Le Caravelle Lavalle 726. Authentic Italian-style café, stand-up only, dishing out espressos all day, plus fresh sandwiches and the house speciality, Neapolitan *sfogliatelle* (flaky pastries).

Confitería Ideal Suipacha 384 ☎011/5625-8069. It's not quite as famous as the *Tortoni*, and therefore less frequented, though it is just as beautiful, if a little worn at the edges. The main reason to go here is to see a milonga in the upstairs tango salon (see p.194). Do not be put off by the dusty, smelly entrance. Tues–Sun 8am–4am.

Confitería El Vesuvio Av Corrientes 1181. Originally opened as a *heladería* in 1902 (they claim it was the country's first), *El Vesuvio* is now best known for its *chocolate con churros* (lauded in a Ferrer/Piazzolla tango) and its period stained-glass windows.

La Giralda Corrientes & Uruguay ☏011/4371-3846. A brightly lit and austerely decorated Corrientes café that is a perennial hangout for students and intellectuals and a good place to experience the Porteño passion for conversation. Its *chocolate con churros* makes for a calorific but very enjoyable breakfast.

New Brighton Sarmiento 645 ☏011/4322-1515. The Anglo–Porteño *New Brighton*, which first opened in 1908, has been recently renovated, but retains many of its original features, including a long wooden bar. Wood panelling and stained glass help recreate a *belle époque* atmosphere, with a café area at the front and expensive but quality restaurant at the back – its speciality is a beef Wellington served with potatoes au gratin. Mon–Sat from 8am.

La Paz Av Corrientes 1599 ☏011/4373-3647. The classic Corrientes (and Porteño) café; it's less sumptuous than the *Tortoni*, but also has fewer tourists. In the pre-Proceso 1970s *La Paz* was the chosen hangout of left-wing intellectuals and writers, and it's still a good place to meet a friend or read a book over a coffee, especially when it's raining outside and the windows steam up.

Petit Colón Libertad 505. A favourite with patrons of the nearby Teatro Colón, it also gets busy with business folk during the day – expect a brisk trade in coffees and glasses of bubbly. Daily 7am–11pm.

Puerto Madero

"¡" Fresh Market Azucena Villaflor & Olga Cossenttini, Puerto Madero Este ☏011/5775-0330, ⓦ www.ifreshmarket.com.ar. By Dique 3, this is the pick of the chic new places in Puerto Madero Este. It's a great place for lunch or *merienda*, with a selection of inventive sandwiches, salads and bruschettas, accompanied a range of yummy *licuados* (fruit shakes) and herbal teas by; full meals such as pasta and steak are also available. Daily 8am–midnight.

Siga La Vaca Av Alicia M. de Justo 1714 ☏011/4315-6801. You can eat till you drop at this posh version of a *tenedor libre* for around $80; the fixed rate includes a carafe of wine, a dazzling choice of salads and, of course, a mountain of meat. As with all *tenedor libres*, go for quantity, variety and speed, rather than quality. Daily noon till late.

San Telmo

Del Limonero Balcarce 873 ☏011/4307-3109. This store/café is themed around lemons, with the scent of citrus wafting from the jams, liqueurs, candles and other goods for sale. The café itself does a range of light meals and herbal teas, as well as an excellent-value *merienda:* a generous serving of cakes accompanied by tea or *mate* – flavoured with lemon, if you like. Mon–Fri & Sun 10am–8pm.

La Poesía Bolivar & Chile, San Telmo ☏011/4300-7340. Self-consciously traditional San Telmo café bar with wooden tables and a mind-boggling choice of sandwiches and *picadas* (platters of salami, cheese etc). Tango is the usual backdrop. Mon–Thurs 8am–2am, Fri & Sat till 4am, Sun till 2am.

Retiro

Café Retiro Estación Retiro. Beautifully restored, along with the rest of the Tigre-bound section of the magnificent train station, this café is worth visiting for its breathtaking interior, with dark wood panelling, opulent columns, stained-glass cupola and a handsome chandelier. Apart from coffee and drinks, you can have lunch, which is nothing extraordinary but good value.

Florida Garden Florida 899 ☏011/4312-7902. From the decor to the waiters, this Retiro classic seems to be caught in a 1960s time warp. Known for delicious turkey and tomato sandwiches, it's also an excellent spot for breakfast, serving some of the best *medialunas* in the barrio. Mon–Fri 6am–midnight, Sat 6am–11pm, Sun 8am–11pm.

Recoleta

La Biela Quintana 600 ☏011/4804-0449. Institutional *confitería* famed for its *lomitos*, draught beer and coffee, served in the elegant (if slightly dowdy) bistro interior or, with a surcharge, in the shade of a gigantic gum tree on the terrace (*vereda*). It's not cheap and the service can be slow, but it is an essential component of any visit to the city.

Como en Casa Riobamba 1239 ☏011/4813-4828. This chain's main teahouse (there are also branches at Laprida 1782 in Recoleta, and Céspedes 2647 in Belgrano) is in a sumptuous building adjoining the former Vatican HQ in

BA. *Como en Casa*'s slogan promises cakes and much more – namely delicious teas, tarts and coffees. Daily from 8am.

PostData Azcuénaga 1739 ☎011/4803-0496. Unusual and delightful café employing the theme of an old-fashioned post office and serving up snacks from around the world, from Mexican wraps and Italian grilled vegetable panini to British high tea, with stacks of cakes and finger sandwiches. Mon–Sat 9am–8pm.

Tea Connection Uriburu 1597 ☎011/4805-0616. Main branch of a chain of modern tearooms serving the real brew, made with loose leaves, together with delicious quiches, tarts, sandwiches and cakes. Mon–Sat 8am–midnight, Sun 9am–midnight.

The outer barrios

Los Angelitos Av Rivadavia & Rincón, Balvanera ☎011/4952-2320. A tango written in its honour refers to *Los Angelitos* as "that old corner where old friendships come back".

Reopened in 2007, it serves excellent classic *confitería* fare – sandwiches, *milanesas*, pastas and *flan con dulce de leche* – in a beautifully appointed building with marble-top tables and stained glass. Occasional live music during the day and showy tango dinners in the evening; the all-female tango orchestras are unique. Daily 10am–10pm.

Las Violetas Av Rivadavia 3899, Almagro ☎011/4958-7387. Rescued from closure by popular demand, this *confitería*/restaurant is a monument to the Porteño heyday of the 1920s, with its fine wood panelling, gorgeous stained glass, Carrara marble table-tops and impressive columns; it was a favourite hangout of writers such as Roberto Arlt. The *confitería* is justly famed for its breads, cakes and pastries, while the restaurant combines attentive service with copious and refined cuisine – try the delicious *agnelottis* (pasta) filled with ricotta, ham and walnuts. Closed Sat.

Snack bars and fast food

The places listed here are ones where you would predominantly go for a **quick meal**, rather than the coffee and atmosphere (though some have these, too). The food varies from typical empanadas and other Argentine specialities (see box below) to slices of pizza and more recent imports, such as burritos.

Snack break

If you start to feel peckish during a long day of sightseeing, never fear: you'll find the city has plenty of traditional *criollo* **minutas**, or snacks, to offer. **Lomitos** are sandwiches filled with juicy slices of steak, often made with delicious *pan árabe* (pita bread), while the **chivito** (another type of sandwich, originally from Uruguay) is made with a less tender cut. Other street food includes the **choripán**, South America's version of the hot dog, but made here with natural meaty sausages (*chorizos*), and at cafés a popular snack is the **tostado**, a toasted ham-and-cheese sandwich, usually daintily thin and sometimes called a *carlitos*. **Barrolucas** are beef-and-cheese sandwiches, a local variant on the cheeseburger, named after a former Chilean president. **Milanesas**, breaded veal escalopes, can be served either as a snack in a sandwich, hamburger-style, or as a main course with a garnish. **Picadas** are a sort of Argentine hors d'oeuvres – a selection of salamis, cheese and pickles served with bread. The Porteño snack par excellence, though, is the **empanada**. Found throughout South America, with regional variations, in Argentina this is rather like a small version of the English pasty – a pastry turnover filled with assorted combinations of meat, corn, vegetables and cheese, and then either baked (Salta-style) or fried (Tucumán- or Catamarca-style); it's hard to beat the classic *empanada de carne*, made with chopped beef. Less conventional fillings, meanwhile, can include tuna, Roquefort cheese and pineapple.

San Nicolás

La Americana Callao 83–99 ☎011/4371-0202. A Callao landmark, serving up juicy empanadas – some say they're the city's best – to be consumed standing up at metal counters. Daily 11.30am–12.30am.

Le Bar Tucumán 422 ☎011/5219-0858. Come here for light meals and snacks – salads, sandwiches and burgers – in a beautiful lounge-like interior, which is done in cool pinks, purples and oranges. Don't miss the cold chocolate soup with *ras-al-khanout* (Moroccan spices), or the excellent coffee. Mon–Fri lunch and dinner, Sat dinner only.

California Burrito Company Lavalle 441 ☎011/4328-3057. Taking its place among Calle Lavalle's more traditional fast-food joints, this Tex-Mex café lets you choose the filling for your burrito or tacos from a selection of meats, beans, salad, guacamole and jalapeños. Fast, yummy and messy. Mon–Fri 8am–11pm.

Medio y Medio Montevideo & Perón ☎011/4371-6212. Named after Montevideo market's famous wine drink, the Uruguayan-themed *Medio y Medio* serves *chivitos* and, of course, *mate*, from behind its ornate facade. Closed Sun.

San Telmo

Abuela Pan Bolívar 707 ☎011/4361-4936. Homely vegetarian café and wholefood store offering a daily menu with options such as tofu burgers, stuffed aubergines and vegetarian sushi. Mon–Fri 8am–7pm.

Pride Café Balcarca 869 & Pasaje Giuffra ☎011/4300-6435. Delicious sandwiches, pies, cookies and coffee in a bright, modern locale that doubles up as an art gallery. As the name indicates, it is gay-friendly. Closed Sat morning & Sun eve.

Retiro

Costumbres Criollas Esmeralda 1392, at Av Libertador ☎011/4393-3202. A small restaurant specializing in excellent *empanadas tucumanas* and other regional dishes such as *locro* and tamales. Worth seeking out for a snack if you have an hour or two to kill in the vicinity of Estación Retiro. Daily 11am–4pm & 7pm–midnight.

Ugi's Paraguay & San Martín, plus numerous other branches throughout the city. The ubiquitous *Ugi's* offers a quarter of a fast and very

reasonable cheese and tomato pizza, either to take away or eat at the counter with a soda, for a few coins.

Recoleta

Carlitos Guido 1962 ☎011/4801-1112. BA branch of a famous pancake café in beach resort Villa Gesell. Choose from over 100 different generous savoury and sweet fillings for their signature pancakes, from the expected (mozzarella, tomato and basil) to the less so (sauteed apple and ham).

El Club de la Milanesa Las Heras & Uriburu ☎011/4809-3548. Just around the corner from Recoleta cemetery, and packed with locals at lunch time, this wood-panelled café offers a menu for under $30 that includes a comprehensive *milanesa* choice – veal, chicken, fish, soya and pumpkin are all on offer. Daily lunch and dinner.

Cumaná Rodriguez Peña 1149 ☎011/4813-9207. Popular with students and office workers, this is a good place to try *mate*, served from 4 to 7.30pm with a basket of crackers. There's also a selection of provincial food, such as empanadas and *cazuelas* (casseroles), on the menu. Daily from noon.

Florencio Francisco de Vittoria 2363 ☎011/4807-6477. Salads, soups, patés and the like in a bijou tearoom. In the evening the menu broadens to include risottos and other hot dishes. The *rogels*, cakes with *dulce de leche*, are famous in the city. Closed Sun.

Molière Juncal 1293 ☎011/4811-1822. Open day and night, this Parisian-style bistro serves food and cocktails; the evenings see a younger crowd nursing drinks and chatting away for what seems like hours on end. Daily from 8am.

Palermo

Farinelli Bulnes 2707 ☎011/4802-2014. Refreshingly informal, bright café where you order from a delicious range of salads, *milanesas*, tarts, gazpacho and other dishes at the counter. Big hit with local residents of all ages. Mon–Sat 8am–8pm.

Mark's El Salvador 4701 ☎011/4832-6244. A good example of what Porteños like to think of as an authentic US-style coffeehouse, with frothy coffees, armchairs for newspaper browsing, a mind-boggling array of sandwiches, the scrummiest brownies, and baristas with low-slung jeans. Mon–Sat 8.30am–9.30pm, Sun 10.30am–9pm.

Viva Victoria República Árabe Siria 2982 ☎011/4804-4980. One of a cluster of nice, if slightly twee, cafés in the vicinity of the botanical garden, *Viva Victoria* serves home made tarts, salads and cakes, washed down with juices and excellent coffee. Mon–Fri 8am–10pm, Sat & Sun 9am–8pm.

The outer barrios

La Casa del Queso Corrientes 3587, Almagro ☎011/4862-4794. Along with its sister establishment *La Tasca*, next door, large, airy *Casa del Queso*, its ceiling hung with hams, operates both as a Spanish-style deli, with a huge range of cheeses and cold meats on offer, and a café that does great *picadas* and tapas, with microbrewed beer from around Argentina to wash it down. Live music in the evenings and weekend lunch times. Mon–Fri 10am–midnight, Sat & Sun till 2am.

Heladerías

If there is one institution in Buenos Aires that serves as a constant reminder of Argentina's strong Italian inheritance, it is the **heladería**, or **ice cream parlour**. Ubiquitous, varied and extremely popular, these minefields of temptation serve millions of cones and cups daily. There are dozens of flavours available, including all kinds of rich chocolate and fruity sorbet varieties, Italian-style *sambayón* (zabaglione) and, best of all, *dulce de leche* (see box below) and its variants, including *dulce de leche* with almonds, with chunks of brownie or with chocolate chips. Prices for a cup start at around $12, for which you usually get to pick two flavours. The hours of *heladerías* vary according to location, but they generally open around 11am and close quite late – about midnight.

Cadore Corrientes 1695, San Nicolás. One of the best old-fashioned, non-chain *heladerías*, *Cadore* offers a wide range of home-made wonders, but its *dulce de leche* flavour has the biggest following.

Freddo Guido & Junín, Recoleta, plus many other branches, ⊛www.freddo.com.ar One of the longest established ice cream chains – *dulce de leche* aficionados will be in heaven and few will fail to be seduced by the banana split or *sambayón*.

Persicco Salguero 2591, Palermo, plus other branches, ⊛www.persicco.com. This small, family-run chain of stylish parlours – part modern, part retro – dishes out fabulous ice creams and sorbets, with an emphasis on chocolate flavours; they also serve excellent cakes, croissants, coffees and ice cream gateaux, while the toast and jam served for breakfast are delicious.

Un'Altra Volta Av del Libertador 3060 (Palermo), Echeverría 2302 (Belgrano), Santa Fe 1826 (Recoleta), Callao & Melo (Recoleta), Ayacucho & Quintana (Recoleta). Fighting it out with *Freddo* and *Persicco* to be the city's number-one ice cream chain, *Volta*, as it is usually known, produces delicious desserts rivalling those in Italy, clearly the inspiration for its gourmet *gelato*; fabulous cakes, pastries and coffee, too. The branches are all bright and comfortable – the one on Libertador has a large terrace.

Dulce de leche

Dulce de leche, a sticky, sweet goo made by laboriously boiling large quantities of vanilla-flavoured milk and sugar until they almost disappear, is claimed by Argentines as a national invention. The country's annual production of the stuff could probably fill a large lake. Most people buy it ready-made, in jars: the divisions between those who favour the Havanna brand and those who would only buy Chimbote run deep, and foreigners are advised to maintain a diplomatic neutrality on the issue.

12

Restaurants

Buenos Aires has firmly established itself as South America's **gastronomic capital** – São Paulo may rival it for variety, Santiago might have better seafood and Lima is undoubtedly more exotic, but nowhere else on the continent can touch it for quality. While the crowning glory of most menus are the beautiful cuts of world-famous **beef** delivered daily from the city's hinterland, Buenos Aires has an evolving *bon vivant* ("*buen vivir*") culture, which in recent years has seen palates grow finer, customers become more demanding and chefs make greater use of fish, herbs and fresh produce. In fact, *cocina de autor* (haute cuisine) is now a well-established part of the city's culinary landscape. Additionally, Argentina's ever-improving **wines** (see box opposite) – especially the full-bodied reds – make an excellent accompaniment to the outstanding food. All these tip-top ingredients now combine to make eating out a highlight of any visit. The general rule of thumb in Buenos Aires is that the central and southern barrios tend to offer more traditional foods, such as **parrillas** (*criollo* barbecues), **pizzas** and **pastas** – the last two a legacy of the city's long-established Italian immigrant community – while in the northern barrios dishes are often more innovative and cosmopolitan.

Across the board, **prices** tend to be lower than in large North American and European cities, and even higher-end places will offer a reasonable **menú ejecutivo** (set lunch, usually only available on weekdays), which usually includes a glass of wine or another drink. You can find places where a good meal will cost under $50 a head – most pizzerias come into this category – but a main course in a good restaurant will generally cost between $50 and $80. At the top end of the places we have listed, or in the restaurants of five-star hotels, you will easily fork out $300 per person for a three-course meal, without drinks or coffee. For **wine pricing**, see the box opposite. Note that many places add a **cover charge** (*cubierto* or *servicio de mesa*) to the bill, often $10 to $15; it will sometimes be pointed out that the **tip** (*propina*) is not included, and the custom here is around ten percent, though a little less in pricier restaurants. On the plus side, quite a lot of *parrillas* throw in a free empanada, while a glass of limoncello or other home-made liqueur is frequently on the house.

Almost no restaurants open in the morning for **breakfast** – that's the preserve of cafés and *confiterías* (see Chapter 11). A couple of the restaurants listed here do serve **brunch** on Sundays. **Lunch** time is from noon till 3 or even 4pm; Porteños like to linger over their midday meal, especially at weekends. Restaurants reopen in the **evening** around 8pm, but locals don't usually go out to eat until a couple of hours later. Kitchens tend to close around midnight on weekdays; at weekends many keep serving till the small hours. You shouldn't have any trouble satisfying your appetite at any time, though – the same cafés and *confiterías* that open early for breakfast also serve snacks and light meals throughout the day. Many places **close** one day a week (usually Sun or Mon), or for Saturday lunch and Sunday dinner, but in the busier tourist areas restaurants serve food seven days a week. In the less residential city centre, many restaurants are closed at weekends and even in the evening, as most of their customers are office workers. Smoking is banned in restaurants and **strict dress codes** are virtually non-existent, although customers dress up for smarter places.

The places listed here are but a small sampling of the city's seemingly infinite number of places to eat. If you want to do some restaurant hunting yourself, there is a very useful **online guide** at Ⓦwww.guiaoleo.com.ar, which arranges hundreds of establishments by category and district, and lets diners have their say (in Spanish only). We've divided the restaurants according to the barrio designations used in the Guide; you can find them plotted on the **maps** in each of the corresponding chapters. Where possible, we've included phone numbers, should you want to try to **reserve** a table in advance (strongly recommended, especially Thurs–Sun).

Wining and dining in Buenos Aires

Argentina is currently the world's fifth largest **wine** producer and consumer of wine per capita. Although not so long ago oenologists used to think first of Chile when contemplating **South American** wines, many feel that the quality of Argentina's vintages has now begun to outstrip those of its western neighbour. One of the main reasons for this improvement is that the country's domestic market has become much more discerning of late – unlike Chile, where most of the best wine is exported, Argentina holds back a lot of its premium vintages for itself. However, wine bars – and cocktail bars, too – are very few and far between in Buenos Aires (Porteños always eat when they drink), and most of the wine consumed here is drunk in **restaurants**. Like food in the city, the quality and variety of wines in restaurants has improved markedly in recent years – the city's top restaurants have dozens upon dozens of bottles on their **cartas de vino** (wine lists), and trip over each other to find innovative ways of displaying their cellars.

If you're in doubt about what to order with your meal, ask your sommelier for suggestions (most smarter places have one), but some good **bodega** (vineyard) names to look for include Chandon, Graffigna, Navarro Correas, Carlos Pulenta, Catena Zapata, Escorihuela Gascón, Salentein, Finca Flichmann and Weinert. So far, most of these vintners have concentrated on making **varietal wines**, the main grapes being riesling, chenin blanc and chardonnay for whites, and pinot noir, cabernet sauvignon and malbec for reds – the reds tend to be better than whites. **Malbec** is often regarded as the Argentine grape par excellence, giving rich fruity wines, with overtones of blackcurrant and prune that partner perfectly with a juicy steak. The latest trend, however, is a **combination** ("blend" or "*corte*") of two or more grapes: for example, mixing malbec for its fruitiness and cabernet for its body. Growers have also been experimenting with previously less popular varieties such as tempranillo, san gervase, gewurztraminer, syrah and merlot. **Torrontés**, another white grape, produces highly perfumed whites that go very well with trout and salmon. Convincing **sparkling wines** are being made locally by the *méthode champenoise*, including some produced by Chandon and Mumm. These are often made into deliciously refreshing cocktails.

In terms of **prices**, a nice bottle at an average restaurant will cost about $50–80, while the house wine (which can be pretty poor plonk, though some is drinkable) will be $20–30. For something special, you are talking about the $150 mark, while you shouldn't be surprised to see rare vintages and imported quality wines and champagnes with price tags of several hundred pesos. An increasing number of eateries offer wine by the **glass** – expect to pay between $15 and $25 for this privilege. The concept of **BYOB** (bring-your-own-bottle) is practically unheard of in Buenos Aires – producing a bottle and asking for it to be uncorked would produce quite a shock at most establishments.

Cuisines

Traditional Argentine, or **criollo**, cooking is simple, hearty and delicious – and dominated by red meat. The mainstay of Porteño cuisine is the **parrilla** – a barbecue served at special restaurants also known as *parrillas* – which when prepared at home is known by its alternative name, *asado* (from *asar*, to roast). *Parrillas* vary enormously in style and price, but the meat itself is always fabulous (for a guide to what you're chewing, see the box opposite). Other typical *criollo* dishes include: **locro**, a warming, substantial stew based on maize, with onions, beans, meat, chicken or sausage thrown in; sweet or savoury **humitas**, made of steamed creamed sweetcorn and usually served in neat parcels made of corn husks and sometimes containing cheese; and **tamales**, maize-flour balls stuffed with minced beef and onion, wrapped in maize leaves and simmered. Although Argentines tend not to like anything too spicy, Andean cuisine is the exception – these dishes are often served with *salsa picante*, a fresh tomato sauce containing a good kick of *ají*, or hot chilli pepper.

Italian influences on Buenos Aires' cuisine are very strong, and authentic Italian cooking, usually with a marked Genoese flavour, is available all over the city. The abundance of **fresh home-made pasta** (*pasta casera*) and **pizza** is an example of this – good in Italian restaurants, the pasta dishes in particular can be rather bland in other establishments, though. **Ñoquis** (gnocchi) are a great, cheap staple – they even have a day dedicated to them (the 29th of each month), when you'll find them served all over the city. You'll recognize most pizza toppings, though one ingredient may be unfamiliar: the palm-heart (*palmito*), a sweet, crunchy vegetable resembling something between asparagus and celery. Argentine pizzas are nearly always of the thick-crusted variety, wood-oven baked and meant to be divided between a number of diners. Herbs and chilli oil are not used much, although you occasionally see people squirting ketchup, mayonnaise or Argentina's national condiment, **salsa golf**, a mixture of the two, onto blander pizzas to liven them up.

If you're looking for a complete change from pizza, pasta and *parrillas*, tap into the cuisines of other communities that have migrated to the city over the centuries. **Spanish** restaurants serve tapas and familiar Iberian dishes such as paella, while specifically **Basque** restaurants are also commonplace, especially in the central barrios – these are often the places to head for if you're in search of fish or seafood. **Chinese** and, increasingly, **Korean** restaurants are all over the city, but they rarely serve anything remotely like authentic Asian food, specializing instead in cheap but low quality *tenedor libre* (all-you-can-eat) buffet diners, where one or two token dishes might be slightly more exotic. **Indian**, **Thai** and **Japanese** foods have become fashionable (sushi is a real craze), and **Arab** and **Middle Eastern** food, including specialities such as kebabs and *keppe crudo*, seasoned ground raw meat, are quite popular as well. A huge variety of other regional cuisines, from **Armenian** to **Vietnamese** via **Mexican** and **Danish**, are also on offer. **Vegetarians** may have better luck at international restaurants than at traditional Argentine places – see the box on p.168 for ideas on how to get around all the meat.

Monserrat

Central **Monserrat** is home to a crop of solid, if not spectacular, places to eat, including a concentration of old-fashioned Basque and Galician restaurants serving fish and seafood favourites. There are also a number of typical neighbourhood establishments popular with families (especially for Sun lunch); the best of

Parrilla basics

Parrillas, or barbecues, are an integral part of life in Buenos Aires, so it's good to know your way around the vocabulary of beef-eating, especially as meat here isn't cut in the same way as in the rest of the world – cuts are sliced through bone and muscle rather than across them.

Porteños like their meat **well done** (*cocido*), and indeed, some cuts are better cooked through. If you prefer your meat medium, ask for *a punto*, and for rare – which really requires some insistence – *jugoso*. If you order a **parrillada**, or "full works barbecue", before you get to the steaks you'll be offered a range of **achuras**, or offal (sweetbreads, kidneys and intestines being the most common), and different types of sausage: **chorizos** are excellent beef sausages, while **morcilla**, blood sausage, is an acquired taste. Sometimes **provoletta**, provolone cheese grilled till crispy on the edges, will be on the menu.

After these "appetizers" – which you can always skip – you move on to the **asado** (brisket) cut, followed by the **tira de asado** (ribs; aka *costillar* or *asado a secas*). There's not much flesh on them, but they explode with a meaty taste. Next is the muscly but delicious **vacío** (flank). But save some room for the prime cuts: **bife ancho** is entrecôte; **bife angosto** or **lomito** is the sirloin (referred to as **medallones** when cut into slices); **cuadril** is a lump of rumpsteak; **lomo**, one of the luxury cuts, is fillet steak; and **bife de chorizo** (not to be confused with *chorizo* sausage) is what the French call a *pavé*, a slab of meat, cut from either the sirloin or entrecôte. People either love or hate the **entraña**, a sinewy cut. The **peceto** (eye round steak) is a tender lump of flesh, often braised (*estufado*) and served on top of pasta, roasted with potatoes (*peceto al horno con papas*) or sliced cold for *vittel tonne* – a classic Argentine starter made with tuna and mayonnaise.

The traditional accompaniment to all this meat is pretty simple – chips/fries (*papas fritas*), a basic mixed salad (*ensalada mixta*), bread (*pan*) and of course lots of red wine, though you can sometimes get more interesting veggies. Sides are served separately from the meat and come in huge portions, meant for sharing. **Mustard** (*mostaza*) may be available, but the lightly salted meat is usually best served with nothing on it but the traditional **chimichurri** – olive oil shaken in a bottle with salt, garlic, chilli pepper, vinegar and bayleaf – and **salsa criolla**, similar but with onion and tomato as well.

these are in the western section of the barrio, away from the more touristy areas east of Avenida 9 de Julio. Towards Congreso you'll find a number of Peruvian places catering to immigrants from that country, Porteños and tourists alike.

El Caserío Hipólito Yrigoyen 575 ☎011/4331-1336. The food here is Porteño through and through – locals come back day after day for its low-cost *sorrentinos a la crema de camarones* (shrimp ravioli in cream sauce), but the *matambrito* (rolled pork fillet) and roast kid are also good. Mon–Fri, lunch only.

Chan Chan Hipólito Yrigoyen 1390 ☎011/4382-8492. One of the best Peruvian restaurants in the city – the decor is bright and fresh, the *picante de mariscos* (a kind of seafood stew) delicious and the prices very reasonable. Closed Mon.

El Globo Hipólito Yrigoyen 1199 ☎011/4381-3926. One of several Spanish restaurants in the area, *El Globo* has a gorgeous old-fashioned

interior and serves classic dishes such as *gambas al ajillo* (spicy prawns) and *puchero* (a filling meat and vegetable stew, around $50) that are perfectly acceptable, if a little lacking in Mediterranean flair.

Iñaki Moreno 1341 ☎011/4382-8486, ⓦwww.iñakirestaurante.com.ar. This institutional Basque *taverna* has a plain decor, but excellent, honest home cooking – its specialities include all manner of fish in a fine tomato sauce plus a juicy paella, and there's a top-notch wine list. Around $100 for two courses. Closed Sun.

Laurak-Bat Belgrano 1144 ☎011/4381-0682, ⓦwww.restolaurakbat.com.ar. A moderately priced Basque restaurant within the *Club*

Vegetarian options in Buenos Aires

Being a **vegetarian** in Buenos Aires isn't always easy, what with the amount of meat on the menu. While there are a few dedicated vegetarian restaurants, or **restaurantes naturistas**, in the city, and meat-less offerings are on the rise elsewhere, you'll have to be a bit inventive at most eating places: always check the ingredients of a dish before ordering, as the addition of meat, especially *jamón* (ham), is not always included on menus. Fortunately, locals have become somewhat accustomed to dealing with foreigners and their strange aversion to a beef-only diet – though don't be surprised if your *"no como carne"* (I don't eat meat) is dismissed with a glib *"no tiene mucha"* (It doesn't contain much).

In general, when you can get them, locally grown vegetables, fruits and herbs are delicious. Stuffed pasta dishes, pies and empanadas are often filled with vegetarian-safe options, such as ricotta cheese, **spinach** (*espinaca*) and **Swiss chard** (*acelga*). **Milanesas** (breaded fillets) are often found made with soy or aubergine instead of veal. The city's Chinese-ish **tenedor libres** usually feature a good smattering of veggies, if you're looking for produce without the accompanying carbohydrates. Another possibility is to **self-cater** – supermarkets are usually fairly well stocked with vegetables and soya products, and health-food shops are plentiful (see p.204 for details of markets).

Vasco (the city's Basque association HQ), *Laurak-Bat* boasts timeless dishes such as *bacalao al pil-pil* (salt cod in an olive-oil and garlic sauce). Mon–Sat 9.30pm till late.
Plaza Mayor Venezuela 1399 ☎011/4383-3802, ⓦwww.plaza-mayor.com.ar. Many people visit here just for the *pan dulce* (fruit bread), but the menu covers just about every Hispanic delicacy, from tripe to tortilla (Spanish omelette). The walls are decorated with a collection of Castilian fans, to remind you of the chef's inspiration.
Prosciutto Venezuela 1212 ☎011/4383-8058. This converted *conventillo* (tenement block) somehow manages to combine an old

bicycle, an ancient pizza oven and hanging hams (a house speciality, as the name indicates) to create a fun atmosphere, in which plates brim over with budget, no-nonsense pasta and a pianist plays requests on a slightly out-of-tune upright. Freebies include a glass of sherry to start and a slice of home-made *pan dulce* with your coffee.
Status Virrey Cevallos 178 ☎011/4382-8531. Simple Peruvian restaurant frequented by Peruvians, so it must be authentic. Very good-value dishes, many of which are big enough to share; try the ceviche – fish marinated with chilli and lime.

San Nicolás

San Nicolás, encompassing the city's main financial and commercial districts, is the place to go for tried and true down-to-earth cooking (including a good many traditional *parrillas*), although the large number of expense-account patrons and office workers in the area means that menus are often conventional, prices somewhat inflated and opening times revolve around business hours – many places are closed at weekends and even weekday evenings. Among all the *parrillas* are also some of the city's finest gourmet locales, plus a number of very convincing French-style brasseries. One special pleasure here is eating in an interior patio – two beautiful sets of convent cloisters in the barrio provide shady oases that are perfect for a relaxing alfresco lunch.

Arturito Av Corrientes 1124 ☎011/4382-0227. An old-fashioned haven reigned over by courteous white-jacketed waiters, *Arturito* is a Corrientes landmark, and its *bife de*

chorizo con papas (rump steak and chips) is an unquestionably good deal.
Bodega Campo Rodríguez Peña 264 ☎011/4371-0225. Friendly, inexpensive little

place specializing in food from Argentina's northwest – empanadas, *locro* and the like – with the added attraction of live tango music and song on Thurs eve. Mon–Sat, eve only.

Brasserie Berry Tucumán 775 ☎ **011/4394-5255,** ⊛ **www.brasserieberry.com.ar.** A bit less stuffy (and less expensive) than most of BA's French restaurants, with a very good-value daily menu and à la carte dishes, such as "grandmother's style chicken", with mushroom sauce and chips. Mon–Thurs 8am–7pm, Fri & Sat till 1am.

Chiquilín Sarmiento 1599 ☎ **011/4373-5163.** A long-running, very typical Porteño restaurant serving traditional dishes at moderate prices in a friendly atmosphere. The *pollo al verdeo* (chicken with spring onions) is good, but it's the revered *bife* (steak) that brings most people in.

El Claustro San Martín 705 ☎ **011/4312-0235.** The vaulted dining room here was originally part of a convent, and it continues to be a haven of peace and quiet amid the frantic financial district. Considering the inventiveness of the cuisine – including a tajine-like lamb dish and pears with lemongrass – the two-course lunch is quite moderately priced. Mon–Fri 8.30am–7.30pm.

Las Cuartetas Av Corrientes 838 ☎ **011/4326-0171.** A pared-down pizza and empanada joint where you can grab a slice at the counter or while away a few hours after the cinema over a cold Quilmes. Closed Sun lunch.

🏃 **Granix Florida 165, Galería Güemes, Entrada Mitre, 1st floor** ☎ **011/4343-4020.** You pay a small fixed charge on entry at this large, airy, self-service vegetarian restaurant located in one of Florida's magnificent shopping arcades, and then eat as much as you want. Salads are straight-from-the-market fresh and the variety of soft drinks, warm dishes and delicious desserts, including some unusual options, is overwhelming. Mon–Fri 11.30am–3.30pm.

Güerrín Av Corrientes 1368 ☎ **011/4371-8141.** A quintessential Porteño pizza experience, the traditional order here is a portion of *muzzarella* and *fainá* (chickpea bread) eaten at the counter and accompanied by a glass of sweet moscato. Some locals hold that

the pizzas served in the proper dining area are a notch above the counter versions; however, all are inexpensive.

🏃 **Parrilla Peña Rodríguez Peña 682** ☎ **011/4371-5643.** Knowledgeable liveried waiters serve up some of the juiciest meat in town (*bife de chorizo* for around $30), as well as fine wines and mouth watering salads at this great-value, no-nonsense *parrilla*. Closed Sun eve.

Pippo Montevideo 341 ☎ **011/4374-0762.** Running for some decades now, the budget *Pippo* is a Porteño institution. Most people come to eat the thick *vermicelli mixto*, with Bolognese sauce and pesto, and chat with friends in an informal setting. You may be blinded by its bright lights, but it's worth a visit just to catch a glimpse of Porteño dining in all its noisy, gesticulating glory.

Reconquista Reconquista 269. Generously portioned, well-cooked and inexpensive food with daily specials such as *pollo al horno con puré de batata* (roast chicken with sweet potato puree). The real attraction, however, is the stunning location – the patio of an old convent where, among palm trees and birdsong, you might even forget that you're at the heart of Buenos Aires' financial district. Mon–Fri, lunch only.

Sabot 25 de Mayo 756 ☎ **011/4313-6587.** Catering to a faithful collar-and-tie clientele, this fairly expensive restaurant serves up succulent fish dishes, such as crab pancakes, plus plenty of meat and great desserts. Wooden panelling, black-and-white photos and white-coated waiters accentuate the retro feel. Mon–Fri, lunch only.

🏃 **Tomo 1 Carlos Pellegrini 525, in same building as Hotel Panamericano** ☎ **011/4326-6695,** ⊛ **www.tomo1.com.ar.** Considered by many to be Buenos Aires' best *haute cuisine* restaurant, this is an elegant but refreshingly unpretentious place where the emphasis is squarely placed on the exquisitely cooked food, such as chilled melon soup and quail with pistachios. Not cheap, but good value, particularly if you go for the set menus, available both at lunch times and evenings, and including wine.

Puerto Madero

Puerto Madero is knee-deep in big, glitzy themed restaurants, though these are hardly the barrio's most exciting eating options, let alone the city's. The places we've listed below – including one of Buenos Aires' most famous *parrillas* – are exceptions to the rule, but wherever you eat out in this area will leave a large hole in your wallet. Most of the district's luxury hotels have very decent restaurants of their own, options if you're staying there and don't feel like going out.

Bice Av Alicia M. de Justo 192 ☏ 011/4315-6216, ⓦ www.bicebuenosaires.com.ar. Style often trumps content in Puerto Madero, but the excellent pasta and gnocchi at this highly regarded, if expensive, Italian restaurant will not disappoint.

Cabaña Las Lilas Av Alicia M. de Justo 516 ☏ 011/4313-1336, ⓦ www.laslilas.com. The place to head if you want to splurge on just about the finest steak around; an *ojo de bife*, best savoured from a shaded veranda on the waterfront, will set you back what it would cost to eat for a week in a standard *parrilla*. Very popular with tourists; reservations advisable.

🏃 **Chila** Av Alicia M. de Justo 1160 ☏ 011/4343-6067, ⓦ www.chilaweb .com.ar. A truly sophisticated restaurant with refined decor (there's even a private dining room for twenty guests) and prices to match. The menu includes several fish dishes, such as black rice and sole stuffed with mushrooms and langoustines in a lime and coconut sauce, as well as duck, venison or lacquered suckling-pig for those who prefer meat.

San Telmo

The current gentrification of **San Telmo** means that expensive and fashionable restaurants are starting to appear here among the older, humbler places dishing up heaps of pasta and chunks of meat. There are several restaurants gathered around Plaza Dorrego, at the centre of the barrio, but for the most part these are tourist traps – you're better off looking elsewhere in the neighbourhood.

Amici Miei Defensa 1072 ☏ 011/4362-5562, ⓦ www.amicimiei.com.ar. This simple, brick-walled Italian restaurant overlooking Plaza Dorrego is discreetly located on the upper floor, and is less tourist-oriented than most of the places around it. The delicious pasta is prepared before your eyes, and the tiramisu is memorable. Around $100 for two courses. Closed Mon.

El Baqueano Bolívar & Chile ☏ 011/4342-0802, ⓦ www.restoelbaqueano.com. Unusual, highly regarded restaurant with a seven-course *degustación* menu ($135) that uses local ingredients, particularly meat from indigenous animals, to create gourmet dishes such as provençal cayman tails and ñandú (rhea) stuffed with liquor-soaked fruit. Tues–Sun 7pm–late; reservations recommended.

🏃 **Café San Juan** Av San Juan 450 ☏ 011/4300-1112. A small, family-run joint whose reasonably priced huge portions and fresh-from-the-market meals mean it's always full. Try the "hunter's-style" rabbit. Closed Mon.

Naturaleza Sabia Balcarce 958 ☏ 011/4300-6454, ⓦ www.naturalezasabia .com.ar. Friendly and appealing, this bright new vegetarian health food restaurant marries delicious quiches and pastas, plus salads and sandwiches, with organic wines and microbrewery beers. They deliver within a reasonable radius, too. Closed Mon.

La Vinería de Gualterio Bolívar Bolívar 865 ☏ 011/4361-4709, ⓦ www.lavineriade gualteriobolivar.com. If your budget is not too tight, you have an adventurous palate and three hours to spare, make sure you go to *La Vinería*, the city's most experimental restaurant. The chef studied with Catalan food wizard Adriá, and applies techniques like ultra-freezing and deconstruction to superb Argentine produce like lamb, octopus and *alfajores* (cookie sandwiches). The wine cellar is full of surprises, too. Tasting menu around $230. Tues–Sun 12.30–4pm & 9pm–midnight; reservations recommended.

Boca

Boca remains resolutely faithful to its working-class Italian origins, with a sprinkling of traditional *cantinas*, inexpensive pizzerias and pasta restaurants.

Banchero Almirante Brown 1200 ☎011/4301-1406, **plus branches around the city.** One of the city's first pizzerias, opened by a Don Banchero, who arrived from Genoa in the 1890s. Many famous Argentines, including Fangio and Evita, have dined here. The inexpensive food is traditional stone-baked pizzas with the usual range of toppings, as well as some *fugazettas* (without tomato).

Il Matterello Martín Rodríguez 517 ☎011/4307-0529. Traditional, reasonably priced Italian food in a lovely red, green and yellow painted house in Boca. The profiteroles are excellent. Closed Sun eve.

El Obrero Caffarena 64 ☎011/4362-9912, ⊛www.bodegonelobrero.com.ar. With Boca Juniors souvenirs decorating the walls and tango musicians sauntering from table to table at weekends, the atmosphere at the hugely popular and moderately priced *El Obrero* is as much a part of its appeal as the simple home-cooked food, including great *milanesas*. Closed Sun.

Il Piccolo Vapore Necochea 1190 ☎011/4301-4455. The last of the famous, colourfully painted *cantinas* that once lined this street. The food – seafood and pasta – is less important than the wine and shows that accompany it. Thurs–Sun, dinner only.

Retiro

In many ways **Retiro** is a transitional zone between the city's modest south and chic north – and its dining options perfectly reflect this character. There's a bit of everything here, from retro *parrillas* and brash pizzerias to classy places where you can savour cuisines as varied as Danish, Indian, Peruvian and Catalan. As in Monserrat and San Nicolás, business folk pack many places at weekday lunch times, but some of the trendier restaurants are so busy in the evenings that reservations are a must. Weather permitting, you could also to make like the locals and grab a sandwich – Plaza San Martín is as attractive a picnic spot as anywhere in the city.

Bengal Arenales 837 ☎011/4314-2926. Although, as the name suggests, this smart restaurant offers Indian specialities, including a perfectly passable *rogan josh*, it oddly excels in its Mediterranean Italian dishes too, with a strong focus on fish. The decor and ambience are decidedly posh but the highly attentive service is not snobbish, and the wine and food, albeit not budget-priced, are impeccable, down to all the nibbly bits they serve before and after. Closed Sat lunch & Sun.

Club Danés Av Alem 1074, 12th floor ☎011/4312-9266. This Danish restaurant serves a mean *smörrebrod* – lots of herring, anchovies and blue cheese – and other regional specialities in a suitably airy dining room with great river views. Brown ale brewed in Buenos Aires Province is available. The set menu goes for under $50. Mon–Fri, lunch only.

El Cuartito Talcahuano 937 ☎011/4816-1758, ⊛www.galeriaelcuartito.com.ar. This is regarded as a classic budget BA

pizzeria, down to the noise, unflattering lighting and uncomfortable chairs – all of which are worth dealing with for the delicious dough and toppings. Be prepared to queue for a table – you can indulge in some great people-watching while you wait.

Empire Thai Tres Sargentos 427 ☎011/4312-5706, ⊛www.empirethai.net. Unbeatable cocktails and a trendy ambience (very gay-friendly) make up for the slight lack of authenticity in the cuisine – the red and green curries (around $40) are not quite right, but are nonetheless very palatable. Closed Sat lunch & Sun.

El Establo Paraguay 489 ☎011/4311-1639. Timeless old-fashioned *parrilla*, popular with both locals and tourists; the beef is good quality, the service professional. Traditional *puchero* stew is also served here. About $75 for two courses.

Filo San Martín 975 ☎011/4311-0312, ⊛www.filo-ristorante.com. Some of the centre's best salads, featuring less common ingredients such as rocket, radishes and sultanas soaked in wine, in addition to imaginative pizzas, pastas and other reasonably priced, Italian-inspired fusion dishes, like Venetian mussel soup with Patagonian clams. Daily from noon.

Juana M Carlos Pellegrini 1535 ☎011/4326-0462. The art galleries nearby seem to have spilled over into this cavernous restaurant, with its model-like staff and fashionable clients. The moderately priced food is much more straightforward than the ambience, mainly steaks and pastas, with an unlimited salad bar.

🏃 **Piola Pizzería** Libertad 1078 ☎011/4812-0690, ⓦ www.piola.it. You'll find dozens of toppings to choose from at this huge, hip, gay-friendly pizza joint, where thin crusts meet the city's upper crust. It is so popular they have opened another branch in Palermo Hollywood (Gorriti 5751 ☎011/4777-3698). Closed Sat & Sun lunch.

🏃 **Sipan** Paraguay 624 ☎011/4315-0763, ⓦ www.sipan.com.ar. Stylish, though not cheap, Peruvian-Japanese fusion cooking, offering ultra-fresh ceviche and sushi, as well as a number of delicious takes on the classic Peruvian sautéed beef dish *lomo saltado*: try the one with calamari. Closed Sun.

🏃 **Tancat** Paraguay 645 ☎011/4312-5442. A beautifully decorated and lit Spanish-Catalan *tasca*, where the *cañas* (small glasses of draught beer), varied tapas and other mainstays, like grilled baby squid, are totally genuine; the service is brisk, it gets very busy at lunch times (bookings recommended) and can be noisy, but that only adds to the authenticity. Moderately priced (unless you opt for seafood, which will push the bill through the ceiling). Closed Sun.

Winery Av Alem 880 ☎011/4314-2639, ⓦ www.winery.com.ar. As well as a store that holds regular tastings of all the best Argentine wines, *Winery* has a restaurant serving cheeses, gourmet sandwiches and unusual specialities such as braised goat. Mon–Sat 9am–11pm.

Recoleta

As you would expect of the city's classiest barrio, **Recoleta** has plenty of high-end eating spots, often with a French flavour. That said, there is nothing like the choice you can find in Palermo, to the north, and not all places are expensive. Steer clear of the tourist traps along Ortíz, by Recoleta Cemetery – there are much better places only a short walk away.

Club Sírio Ayacucho 1496 ☎011/4806-5764. Every major Argentine city has a Syrian club/restaurant, and this palatial place is one of the best, with an excellent, varied and relatively inexpensive menu of meze. Evenings only.

Dashi Montevideo 1059 ☎011/5811-3353, ⓦ www.dashi.com.ar. Very good, fresh sushi, eaten either from a small seating area or a bar, where you can watch it being rolled. The lunch-time set menu – popular with local business folk – is good value at under $60. Closed Sat & Sun lunch.

Due Juncal 2391 ☎011/4829-9400. You could easily walk past the unremarkable front of this restaurant in a residential part of Recoleta – but you won't be sorry if you make the effort to seek it out. *Due* serves beautifully prepared pasta and fish dishes – try the grilled catch of the day with quinoa – and most dishes cost less than $40. Mon & Tues lunch only, Wed–Sat lunch and dinner, closed Sun.

🏃 **El Estrebe** Peña 2475 ☎011/4803-0282, ⓦ www.elestrebe.com.ar. What eating out in Buenos Aires is all about really – white tablecloths, pictures by gaucho cartoonist Molino Campos on the walls, enormous *copas* of velvety red malbec, and thick, tender steaks at very reasonable prices.

🏃 **Nectarine** Vicente López 1661 ☎011/4813-6993. A classical dining room painted in a suitable peachy hue is the setting for what some locals say is the city's best *cordon bleu* food: pheasant and duck grace the menu, with expensive wines to accompany them. Closed Sat lunch & Sun.

🏃 **Oviedo** Beruti 2602 ☎011/4822-5415, ⓦ www.oviedoresto.com.ar. Fairly expensive but a classic – Spanish-style seafood and fish, not forgetting the fabulous paella, are the true specialities of the house, with the odd tropical touch here and there, and the cellar is full of the best wines pesos can buy. Make sure to try the passion fruit ice cream at the end of your meal. Closed Sun.

Restó Montevideo 938 ☎011/4816-6711. Set back from the street in the building housing the Sociedad Central de Arquitectos, this elegant but good-value little French restaurant serves just four or five starters, main courses and desserts, with wine by the glass. Quail, duck and other less common ingredients grace the menu, while puddings include the likes of candied kumquat tartlets with peanut frangipane and muscovado sugar ice cream. Mon–Wed lunch only, Thurs & Fri lunch and dinner, closed Sat & Sun.

Rodi Vicente López 1900 ☎011/4801-5230. This traditional and inexpensive Porteño *bodegón* (bistro) has all the trappings of its genre: bright lighting, Galician dishes (such as rabbit in white wine) and white-coated waiters, and serves a loyal Barrio Norte clientele. Closed Sun.

Romario Pizza Vicente López 2102 ☎011/4511-4444, ⒲www.romario.com.ar. Famous for their rollerblading delivery boys and girls, the *Romario* chain does a good selection of pizzas that will feed two for less than $50; this branch has a small outdoor seating area.

El Sanjuanino Posadas 1515 ☎011/4805-2683. The place to try empanadas, this inexpensive restaurant also has other regional fare such as *locro* and *humitas*, as well as more exotic dishes like pickled vizcacha. Closed Mon.

Sottovoce Av del Libertador 1908 ☎011/4807-6691. Customers – mainly businesspeople for lunch and well-heeled locals for dinner – flock here for the absolutely delicious though relatively pricey pasta; beautiful wood panelling and a low-key, mellow atmosphere are bonuses. Try the tagliatelle, the house speciality.

Palermo

The streets of **Palermo** are home to some of the best places to eat in all of Buenos Aires. In recent years the part of the barrio known as **Palermo Soho**, especially, has seen a huge increase in the number and variety of restaurants – in addition to establishments run by the district's Armenian community, you can taste Mexican, Turkish, Mediterranean cuisines and more. Prices here range from low – there are plenty of basic places – to very high by local standards, such that one or two of the restaurants are frequented almost exclusively by expats and foreign visitors, and require reservations. Neighbouring **Palermo Hollywood**, catching up in terms of quantity and quality of options, hosts an assortment of Peruvian, Scandinavian and Southeast Asian places. **Las Cañitas**, around Báez and Chenaut, also accommodates a good many places to eat, but these tend to be voguish rather than reliable. A couple of truly outstanding restaurants are located in **Palermo Nuevo**, and it's also worth checking out the area around **Parque Las Heras**, which has some great neighbourhood establishments.

Artemisia Cabrera 3877 ☎011/4863-4242, ⒲www.artemisiaresto.com.ar. Possibly BA's best non-meat restaurant, the reasonably priced vegetarian and fish dishes here make no sacrifices flavour-wise. Even die-hard carnivores will enjoy *Artemisia's* twist on polenta lasagne or lime and coriander (cilantro) spiked *abadejo* (pollock). The food is freshly cooked, so it's not the place to go if you're in a hurry – but it's worth the wait. Mon–Sat, dinner only.

Azema Exotic Bistro Angel Carranza 1875 ☎011/4774-4191. The name really says it all: Azema is the owner/chef, the "exotic" refers to the food specials – *nems* (Vietnamese spring rolls), tajines, green curry with chicken

– and "bistro" applies for its certain French feeling of nonchalance. About $100 for two courses. Mon–Sat, dinner only.

Bereber Armenia 1880 ☎011/4833-5662. Really genuine and moderately priced Moroccan food, including fluffy couscous and spicy tajines, in a pleasant North African ambience. Mon–Fri dinner only, Sat & Sun lunch and dinner.

Bio Humboldt 2199 ☎011/4774-3880, ⒲www.biorestaurant.com.ar. Stylish vegetarian restaurant, wholesome like most but more inventive (and more expensive), with dishes that incorporate ingredients such as quinoa, tofu and, of course, lots of vegetables. Organic wine and beer are also served. Daily from noon.

La Cabrera Cabrera 5099 & 5127
☎011/4831-7002. This fabulous, good-
value and down-to-earth *parrilla* serves
hard-to-beat *bifes de chorizo* (the half
portion can feed two) with an array of
delicious *tapa* garnishes; it's so popular the
owners had to open a second restaurant
just up the road. Reservations aren't
accepted, so go early and grit your teeth
until a table is free. Mon, Sat & Sun lunch
and dinner, Tues–Fri dinner only.

Casa Cruz Uriarte 1658 ☎011/4833-1112,
ⓦwww.casacruz-restaurant.com. Book ahead
to experience this mind-bogglingly trendy
place. The red mahogany panelling makes
you feel as if you are dining inside a Chinese
lacquered box, while the food is eclectic,
sumptuously presented and absolutely
delicious: warm oysters are served with
tapioca caviar and a pear salad; grilled
octopus comes with passion fruit sauce and
chorizo juice. Faultless service and subdued
lighting, but the bill is steep by local
standards. Mon–Sat, dinner only.

La Cátedra Cerviño 4699 ☎011/4777-4601.
Traditional Argentine restaurant in a beautiful
Neocolonial house, with a fairly standard
menu of *puchero* (stew), pasta and dishes
such as *tira de asado* (ribs) with potatoes in
a creamy sauce. Popular with the polo crowd
and relatively dear, despite its simplicity.

Chez Juanito Cabrera 5083 ☎011/4833-2610.
Small pizzeria producing an excellent variety
of delicious, cheap stone-baked pizzas.
Closed Sun lunch.

Chori & Wine Costa Rica 5198 ☎011/4773-
0954, ⓦwww.choriandwine.com.ar.
Serving a superb *ojo de bife* (rib eye steak),
this intimate yet informal *parrilla* has attentive
service and delicious wine and desserts – its
chocolate mousse is renowned. Good value
for money. Tues–Sat, evenings only.

Cluny El Salvador 4618 ☎011/4831-7176.
Smart, moderate to expensive modern
locale, with tables outside in a patio. The
food is French with Mediterranean touches
– try the lamb or frogs' legs. Closed Sun.

Demuru Honduras 5296 ☎011/4831-5812,
ⓦwww.demuru.com.ar. Named for one of the
country's meteoric chefs, this unpretentious
and inexpensive restaurant dishes up
refined French-influenced cuisine, with
some Italian and Asian touches thrown in.
Closed Sun dinner.

La Fondue J.F. Segui 4674 ☎011/4778-0110,
ⓦwww.la-fondue.com.ar. A small, friendly

side-street bistro and deli that makes
unbeatable pasta and fondue. About $120
for two courses.

Francesco Sinclair 3096 ☎011/4878-4496,
ⓦwww.francesco.com.pe. Classy, fairly pricey
Peruvian cuisine with an emphasis on fish,
including several different ceviches and
parihuela – a wonderful soup filled with all
kinds of seafood. Mon–Fri noon–1.30pm &
8pm–midnight, Sat 8pm–midnight.

Garbis Scalabrini Ortiz 3190 ☎011/4511-6600.
A stand-out diner in the local Armenian
community, *Garbis* prepares a delicious and
very different *picada* (cold platter), as well as
a range of kebabs, with change from $100
for a meal with drinks.

Guido Cerviño 3948 ☎011/4802-1262. Deservedly popular, this authentic Italian trattoria,
replete with red-checked tablecloths, serves
pasta cooked properly *al dente* (about $60 a
dish) and stone-baked pizza, followed by
desserts that include a fine tiramisu, winding
up with a menu of Italian liqueurs. Tues–Sat
7pm–late, Sun 1–5pm.

El Manto Costa Rica 5801 ☎011/4774-
2409, ⓦwww.elmanto.com. Lamb,
yogurt and mint dominate the menu at this
authentic and good-value Armenian restaurant, where a Carrara marble statue of the
Virgin presides over dinner. Mon–Fri dinner
only, Sat & Sun lunch and dinner.

Moche Nicaragua 5901 ☎011/4772-4160,
ⓦwww.mocherestaurante.com.ar. The
Peruvian chef here used to work for his
country's embassy, so he knows how to
make ceviche and other national dishes,
plus inventive concoctions such as pisco
sour mousse. Moderate prices. Dinner only.

Ølsen Gorriti 5870 ☎011/4776-7677.
This large, modern restaurant serves
exciting cuisine with a Scandinavian touch,
such as salmon pizza or goat's-cheese
ravioli. There are around forty different kinds
of vodka and all manner of cocktails to kick
things off, as well as an admirable wine
cellar. Weather permitting, there are tables in
the shady, secluded garden, which would
look more like a tiny patch of Swedish forest
if it weren't for the exuberant bamboo.
About $100 for two courses. Tues–Sat
noon–late, Sun 10.30am–late.

Las Pizarras Thames 2296 ☎011/4775-0625.
Informal restaurant that's all about the
fabulous (and reasonably priced) food. Run
by a chef who has worked in top London
restaurants, the menu varies according

to what is available and is written up on blackboards (*pizarras*), so it's a bit of a lottery – but that's all part of the fun. Tues–Sun, dinner only.

El Primo Báez 302 ☎011/4775-0150, ⓦwww .parrillaelprimo.com.ar. This popular *parrilla* in Las Cañitas offers traditional Porteño dishes with a bit of flair; the steak is especially savoury and it's not too pricey for such a fashionable neighbourhood. Closed Mon lunch.

Sarkis Thames 1101 ☎011/4772-4911. Spartan decor, but excellent tabbouleh, *keppe crudo* (raw meat with onion – much better than it sounds) and falafel at this popular and cheap restaurant serving a fusion of Armenian, Arab and Turkish cuisine.

Social Paraíso Honduras 5182 ☎011/4831-4556. *Social Paraíso* goes for reasonably priced quality rather than quantity – the menu is just

a selection of dishes such as a trio of salmon, roast lamb and caramelized apple with passion-fruit mousse and Szechuan pepper sorbet. Closed Sun dinner & Mon.

Sudestada Guatemala & Fitzroy ☎011/4776-3777, ⓦwww.sudestadabuenosaires.com. Smart noodle bar with a Vietnamese chef who prepares tasty curries and other Southeast Asian food at reasonable prices, all in modern, minimalist surroundings. Closed Sun.

Vera Cruz Godoy Cruz 1819 ☎011/4833-6958, ⓦwww.restauranteveracruz.com.ar. Yummy Mexican fare, about $60 a dish, with attentive customer service, brightly coloured Aztec decor and plenty of outdoor tables. Tues–Thurs dinner only, Fri–Sun lunch and dinner.

Yoko's Baez 121 ☎011/4899-2368, ⓦwww.yokos .com.ar. Well-presented, quality sushi in Las Cañitas, as well as other Asian and seafood dishes – try the salmon ceviche. Dinner only.

The outer barrios

An exploration of some of the city's farther-flung barrios can pay off handsomely – this is an excellent hunting ground for more authentic, local joints, and even the odd gourmet venue, and the prices are often lower. **Balvanera**'s eating options are not unlike those of Monserrat to the east – a mix of Peruvian, Basque and traditional *parrillas* that reflects the barrio's social makeup. **Belgrano** is home to Buenos Aires' Chinatown, and though that district's food is mostly Taiwanese, adapted for local tastes, there are other excellent Asian options, as well as a generous sprinkling of really good, gourmet restaurants. Where there is a convenient **subte** stop, we have given it, but remember the underground system grinds to a halt at dinner time; it's best to take a cab.

Les Anciens Combattants Santiago del Estero 1435, Constitución ☎011/4305-1701; **Constitución subte.** People don't come to this tiny dive for the service, the decor or the location – it's the French onion soup and game dishes that draw in the crowds. Fairly pricey, but worth it. Tues–Sat, dinner only.

Bi Won Junin 548, Balvanera ☎011/4372-1146; **Facultad de Medicina subte.** Ignore the drab surroundings – *Bi Won* serves excellent, authentic and inexpensive Korean food, brought sizzling to your table. Catering well for both meat-eaters and vegetarians, the food is preceded by a dazzling array of spicy nibbles that are practically a meal on their own. Closed Sat lunch & Sun.

El Buen Sabor Camargo 216, Villa Crespo ☎011/4854-8800, ⓦwww.elbuensaborafricano .com.ar; **Malabia subte.** With a chef hailing from Cameroon, this small Villa Crespo diner offers tasty and reasonably priced African

cuisine, mainly fish and chicken dishes served with sides like mandioc or plantain. Tues–Fri dinner only, Sat & Sun noon–late.

Café Margot Av Boedo 857, Boedo ☎011/4957-0001; **Boedo subte.** This historic corner brasserie (founded 1904) has always doubled up as an arts centre – the walls are often hung with paintings – and a down-to-earth eatery, specializing in turkey sandwiches and home-made pasta. Try the *picadas* of cold cuts and the home-brewed wheat beer. Daily 7pm–late.

La Gran Taberna Combate de los Pozos 95, Balvanera ☎011/4951-7586. A bustling unpretentious restaurant just a block from Congreso; its vast, mid-priced menu offers a mixture of classic Spanish dishes, including a good selection of seafood, and Porteño classics. Daily 11am–4pm & 7pm–late.

Hsiang Ting Tang Arribeños 2245, Belgrano ☎011/4788-0371; **Juramento subte.** A smart though not very expensive Barrio Chino restaurant offering a wide range of Taiwanese dishes, including a scrumptious pork sautéed in ginger, in soothing surroundings. Closed Mon lunch.

Katmandu Av Córdoba 3547, Almagro ☏011/4963-1122, Ⓦwww.katmandu .restaurant.com.ar; Medrano subte. Indian cuisine is not the city's strongest culinary point, but *Katmandu* prepares a respectable sampling, including a very reasonable *rogan josh*, amid Indian antiques. Two courses will set you back less than $100. Closed lunch times and Sun.

Keum Kang Sang Mendoza 1650, 1st floor, Belgrano; Juramento subte. Genuine, fairly expensive Korean fare with some Japanese dishes thrown in, served as a choice of four set menus, ranging from "classic" to "deluxe". Dinner only, closed Tues.

🏃 **Masamadre es con M** Olleros 3891, Chacarita ☏011/4554-4555; Federico Lacroze subte. In an unpretentious, slightly bohemian environment – simple wooden tables with paper tablecloths – you can try chicken tajine with cheese, spinach and mint, or even a tasty sandwich, such as a pumpkin and coriander chapatti with apple chutney. Wine by the glass, unbeatable-value set lunches and efficient service are welcome bonuses. Mon–Sat 9am–midnight, Sun dinner only.

Miramar Sarandí 1190, San Cristóbal; Entre Ríos subte. Describing itself as a *rotisería*, *Miramar* is also an *almacén* – a store selling fine wines and delicacies such as dried figs. The handsome restaurant part, with its wooden panelling and white tablecloths, also has an outstanding wine list to accompany Spanish-style specials such as serrano ham and octopus. Live tango music on Sun eves. Closed Mon.

El Patio de Aldo Av Entre Ríos 1965 ☏011/4306-3970. On the border between Barracas and Constitución, this is one of the best restaurants in an otherwise under-served area, with classic Porteño cooking such as *milanesas*, *sorrentinos* (circular ravioli) and *matambre* (a thin slice of meat rolled up with egg and vegetables) served efficiently at a bargain price in a lovely patio filled with palm fronds. Closed Sun & Mon eve.

🏃 **El Pobre Luis** Arribeños 2393, Belgrano ☏011/4780-5847; Juramento subte. A classic Uruguayan *parrilla* in Bajo Belgrano, famed for its suckling pig; dinner is about $100 per person. Dinner only, closed Sun.

La Reina Kunti Humahuaca 3461, Almagro ☏011/4863-3071; Carlos Gardel subte. Hare Krishna-style vegetarian restaurant that serves veggie versions of Argentine classics and Indian food at low prices, close to Abasto shopping centre. Tues–Sat 10am–midnight.

Los Sabios Av Corrientes 3733, Almagro ☏011/4865-9585; Medrano subte. This extremely inexpensive vegetarian Chinese *tenedor libre* is well worth the journey out to Almagro for non-meat eaters: all the fake duck and assorted takes on tofu noodles you can eat for about $30. Closed Sun.

🏃 **Sifones y Dragones** Ciudad de la Paz 174, Belgrano ☏15/4413-9871 (mobile); Ministro Carranza subte, see map p.122. The beef *daube* in syrah wine and the pink salmon *tian* with *furikake* (a dried Japanese condiment) – about $60 each – are specialities at this informal little Colegiales hideaway. Leave room for the lemon and passion fruit tart or the cardamom ice cream with coconut and coffee sauce. Closed lunch times and Sun.

Todos Contentos Arribeños 2177, Belgrano ☏011/4780-3437; Juramento subte. One of the best places to eat in Belgrano's Chinatown, a cheap and cheerful Chinese and Taiwanese establishment with a good selection of very filling noodle soups. Closed Mon.

Tuñín Av Rivadavia 3902, Almagro; Castro Barros subte. One of the city's best and most popular pizzerias, serving bargain huge *milanesas* as well as a tasty *fugazzeta* (pizza without tomato) and other classics among walls adorned by a curious mix of boxing photos and *filete* art.

Urondo Bar Beauchef 1207, and Estrada, Parque Chacabuco ☏011/4922-9671, Ⓦwww.urondobar .com.ar. This laidback family-run joint is an oasis of fine cuisine in an otherwise unremarkable barrio, just south of Chacarita (no subte nearby; it's best to take a taxi). Rabbit, tuna and *osso buco* are just some of the ingredients cooked with an unusual flair. Eve only, closed Sun & Mon.

Bars, live music and clubs

I f you've come to Buenos Aires eager to experience the city's renowned **after-dark attractions** you will not leave disappointed: there are opportunities galore for drinking, dancing or just chilling out from sunset to sunrise. You will, however, need to be prepared to lose some serious sleep to enjoy them – a typical night on the town doesn't begin until 10pm, when Porteños might meet friends for a meal, followed by an hour or so in a *confitería* or a bar. Not until at least 1am, and frequently an hour or two later, should you dream of hitting a club. Overall, nightlife in the city peaks between Thursday and Saturday (many nightclubs open only on these days), but you'll find plenty of places to go on Sunday and Wednesday, too (though Mondays and Tuesdays are more of a challenge).

The city's **bars** take in everything from dodgy dives, where both the *mozos* (waiters) and the wood panelling qualify as antiques, to sophisticated cocktail lounges where the baristas enjoy star status. There are also a few of those great imports from the British Isles, **pubs** – often of the (mock) Hibernian variety, they're the only venues in town where you may see someone in a suit looking a bit rough.

As for **nightclubs**, these can play host to some boisterous revelry, but many of them, true to Porteño style, are more places to show off and display fashion-model physiques than to really let down your hair – though there are some notorious exceptions. Another important component of a Porteño evening out is **live music**, of which options are plentiful and varied – rock, jazz, blues, folk and many more genres can be found on any given night.

Worthwhile nightspots are spread all over the city, but certain areas offer an especially intense selection of after-dinner diversions. The city's young and affluent head to **Palermo Viejo** to drink and strut their stuff year-round; in the summer the outdoor spots along the **Costanera Norte** come into their own for this crowd. **El Bajo**, in the microcentro, offers a walkable circuit of bars plus the odd Irish pub, while **San Telmo** harbours some eclectic bars among its tango spectacles. Live music venues are sprinkled city-wide, including some in neighbourhoods, like **Abasto** and **Boedo**, which you might not check out otherwise.

La Nación and *Clarín* both provide topical **listings**, as does the *Buenos Aires Herald*, while the tiny **magazine** *wipe*, given out in some bars or on sale in kiosks, is particularly good for trendy cultural events and nightlife; it has a very useful website, Ⓦ www.wipe.com.ar. Other websites with worthwhile listings include Ⓦ www.adondevamos.com and www.buenosaliens.com. For information and listings on **gay nightlife**, see pp.196–197. **Tango** is specifically dealt with in its own chapter (pp.191–194).

Bars and pubs

Just about every barrio has a selection of **bars** to suit all tastes: rough-and-ready drinking dens (mostly in **El Bajo**, and the other southern barrios); eminently cool places where the young and chic linger over a glass of wine, a cocktail or an imported lager (**Palermo** is prime hunting ground for these); and everything in between. Since Porteños seldom drink without eating – even if it's only olives (*aceitunas*) or peanuts (*maní*) – it can be hard to separate bars from cafés and *confiterías* (see Chapter 11); we have listed here places where people tend to come to drink and eat, in that order.

Buenos Aires also has some **pubs** (including the pseudo-Irish variety now found worldwide) but, as it does not have a heavy drinking culture, they tend to be frequented most by expats and tourists – though you can always find a smattering of locals propping up the bar, too. These establishments tend to cluster in **El Bajo**, **Retiro** and **San Telmo** and are the places to head for if you want to join in the city's increasingly boisterous **St Patrick's Day** celebrations (see p.220).

You must be 18 to purchase alcohol in Buenos Aires but you will never be asked for your ID unless you are obviously well under age; most Argentine teenagers usually stick to fizzy drinks (see box below). **Smoking** is banned in public spaces, including bars.

As most bars serve food, you will find they tend to be **open** when restaurants are – from around noon – though cocktail bars or less meal-oriented places may not open until 10pm or so; most bars, though, stay pretty empty until around midnight. The main exceptions are the so-called "after-office" evenings, often midweek in downtown bars, which begin at 6pm or so. Bars traditionally close when the last customer leaves – usually around 2am, a little later even on Fridays, Saturdays and on the eve of a public holiday.

Drink **prices** vary enormously – the swisher the surroundings, the more you pay. As a general rule, a glass of beer or wine costs around $10–20, a domestic

---

Drinking in Buenos Aires

Argentina doesn't really have its own national cocktail, though of course it does produce excellent **wine** (see box, p.165). Nonetheless, Buenos Aires does boast a number of **cocktail**-shaking wizards, who can produce an array of the usual international drinks. All manner of house specials may also tempt you and can be very innovative, but be warned that the Porteños like things sweet – you might tell the bar staff to go easy on the syrup. Don't be surprised to see home-grown variants (*nacionales*) of whisky, gin, brandy, port, sherry and rum, none of which is that good. It's far better to stick to *aguardientes* or fire-waters, some of which are deliciously grapey. A number of Italian-style vermouths and digestives are made locally – **Fernet Branca** is the most popular, a demonic-looking brew the colour of molasses with a rather medicinal taste, invariably combined with Coke.

Beer is more thirst-quenching than alcoholic, and mostly comes as fairly bland lager. The Quilmes brewery dominates the market with ales such as Cristal, while major international brands (Heineken, Guinness, Stella Artois and the like) can be found in pubs. Usually when you ask for a beer, it comes in 800ml bottles (*tres cuartos*), meant for sharing; a small bottle is known as a *porrón*, and a can is a *lata/latita*. If you want draught beer you must ask for a *chopp*. Home-brewed beer (*cerveza artesanal*) is increasingly available, often coming in a surprising array of hues and flavours, including Belgian-style fruity ales.

Fizzy drinks (*gaseosas*) are popular with people of all ages, and are also often drunk to accompany a meal. All the big-name brands are available, along with local varieties, such as Paso de los Toros, which makes tonic and fizzy grapefruit drinks (*pomelo*).

From Boca brawls to global passion

Tango in Buenos Aires is a whole world unto itself: *el mundo tanguero*. While nearly everyone associates it only with dance, in fact it is a complete art form. Part-seduction, part-performance, it's a combination of haunting music, melancholy poetry and scintillating footwork – sometimes brash, occasionally vulgar, but often elegant and always mesmerizing. Over the years Porteños have created, rejected, embraced and exported it. In the new millennium tango has seen a full revival at home, with flashy shows galore, spontaneous street displays and a huge influx of tango-hungry visitors from across the globe.

Out of the underworld

Tango mysteriously emerged from the bordellos of port-side, melting-pot Boca around the mid-nineteenth century, a blend of Neapolitan tarantella and Andalucían flamenco, with notes of polka, mazurka and African rhythms. The dance was initially performed by men only, giving it an aggressive feel – and its lowlife origins led to a decades-long boycott of tango by high society. During the 1920s, however, it captured the interest of Europe and North America, where it was adopted as an exotic ballroom form. Soon tango caught on at home too, with artistes like bandoneón-player Aníbal "Pichuco" Troilo captivating audiences in the 1930s. In the 1960s, tango again slumped into oblivion, too common for the bourgeoisie and too old-fashioned for the rock generation. Today, with Buenos Aires establishing a modern cultural identity, a full-blown tango renaissance has got under way and, in 2009, UNESCO granted tango international status on its new list of World Intangible Cultural Heritage. Still appreciated by Porteños mainly as

Tango musician, the Caminito ▲

Tango shoes ▼

Dancers performing the *gancho* move ▼

Stepping out

Generally recognized as one of the world's hardest dances, tango has many variations. **Tango orillero**, for example, introduced the scintillating acrobatics shown off at modern *tango cena* shows (see p.192). **Salón tango**, meanwhile, a product of the milonga (see p.193), is characterized by slow, smooth moves and lots of smooching. **Show tango**, or *fantasía*, is intricately choreographed and includes such spectacular moves as the *gancho* (where one partner hooks a leg around the other's) – definitely not one for beginners.

▲ Vocalist from the Gotan Project

▼ Bandoneón

▼ Ástor Piazzolla

music, the eight tricky steps remain integral to the city's complex fabric – you're bound to come across a street display or hear *La Comparsita*, tango's catchiest tune.

The sound of tango

Tango music gets its distinctive sound – the blood-curdling tone of longing – from the bandoneón, a German cousin of the accordion and the concertina; notoriously difficult to play, its melancholy groan, acidic timbre and sliding rhythm are perfect for tango. No orquesta típica (traditional tango orchestra) is complete without at least one *bandoneónista*. You'll undoubtedly hear compositions by Troilo, Ástor Piazzolla and José Libertella – great *bandoneónistas* of the past; among living legends, Dino Saluzzi, Rubén Juárez and Julio Pane loom large.

Most ensembles incorporate other instruments as well, such as the piano, violin, viola, cello, double-bass and even the guitar. Originally tango orchestras were trios, but they swelled into larger groups in the mid-twentieth century. Today's ensembles are smaller again, as *salón tango* has lost its popularity and venues

The tomb of Carlos Gardel ▼

have shrunk. Try and hear the Sexteto Mayor, one of the best such orchestras.

Tango songs first took off in the 1920s. The earliest used the language of the underworld – classic lyrics are almost all from the male perspective, portraying women as capricious heartbreakers. More recently, great female vocalists have begun to emerge; gravel-voiced Adriana Varela and more dulcet-toned Susana Rinaldi are just two of today's leading divas.

The godfather of tango

Of all the personalities associated with tango, one stands out: Carlos Gardel. Born either in France or Uruguay, when asked he would always state "I was born in Buenos Aires at the age of two and a half" – the age he arrived in the city. All that's really known of his early years is that he began his career in the Abasto district in 1912 singing folk songs. Blessed with silver-screen good looks and a mellifluous voice, his rise was meteoric. The Zorzal Criollo ("Criollo Songbird") went on to compose hundreds of songs, star in dozens of films and even sing for royalty. Worshipped as a heart-throb, he did more than anyone else to legitimize tango in Buenos Aires; indeed, the city's all-time favourite tango song has to be *Volver*, an ode to nostalgia by Gardel and his poet friend Alfredo Le Pera. Tragically, Gardel died young, in a plane crash in Colombia in 1935. Today the anniversary of his death, June 24, is a day of remembrance in Argentina (see p.221); his tomb, in Chacarita cemetery, is a place of pilgrimage (see p.142); and his name graces a street, a subte station and a museum in Balvanera (see p.141). Many Porteños believe Gardel to be immortal: if you ask their opinion of him, they have a stock answer, "He sings better every day".

spirit and mixer about the same and an imported version $20–30. The smartest bars charge as much as $50 for cocktails, but that really is as high as it gets; normally they are closer to $25–30.

The bars and pubs we've listed below are divided according to the barrio designations used in the Guide; you can find them plotted on the **maps** in each of the corresponding chapters.

San Nicolás

Celta Bar Sarmiento 1702. Popular with a friendly and relaxed crowd, this attractive bar with big wooden tables is a good place for an early-evening drink. There's often live music, including Argentine rock and Brazilian MPB, in the basement.

La Cigale 25 de Mayo 597. Bar with a vaguely French theme that is renowned for its long-running and lively Tues nights, when it offers French cocktails, such as kir royal, at ridiculously cheap prices. Popular with students.

San Telmo

647 Dinner Club Tacuarí 647. As the name indicates, this formerly exclusive club serves pricey dinners, but the main attraction is Tato and his cocktail shaker, and many people come for drinks only.

Bar Británico Defensa & Brasil. Long-established bohemian bar overlooking Parque Lezama, reopened in 2007 after a sustained neighbourhood campaign to save it from closure. Freshly renovated, it retains both the table where Ernesto Sábato wrote *On Heroes and Tombs* and its 24-hour opening policy.

Gibraltar Peru 895. Popular with both expats and locals who like to hang out with expats, *Gibraltar* is a British-style pub that's a bit more relaxed than *Kilkenny* (see p.179), with a friendly atmosphere, bar service and great bar food, including fish and chips and Thai curry.

Plaza Dorrego Bar Defensa 1098. The most traditional of the bars around Plaza Dorrego, a sober wood-panelled place where the names of countless customers have been etched on its wooden tables and walls, and piles of empty peanut shells adorn the tables.

Retiro and Recoleta

L'Abeille Arroyo 872, Retiro. White-coated barmen mix pricey but generally good cocktails in this smart new basement bar designed for showing off, with a leopard-skin staircase setting the tone (or

perhaps not). This being Buenos Aires you can have (overpriced) full-blown meals upstairs and nibble on tapas down below.

Bárbaro Tres Sargentos 415, Retiro. This cosy bar, a long-standing institution tucked down a side street, regularly puts on live jazz.

Buller Presidente Ortiz 1827, Recoleta. The shiny stainless-steel vats and whiff of malt here tell you that this brasserie brews its own excellent beer, which runs the gamut from pale ale to creamy stout, all served with hot and cold dishes.

Dadá San Martín 941, Retiro. Small, hip and attractive bar, playing jazz sound tracks, serving reasonable food and offering a laidback alternative to the nearby Irish joints.

Deep Blue Reconquista 920 & Ayacucho 1240, Retiro. A popular, modern bar, done out in vibrant blue, and with pool tables that look like they belong in an interior design magazine.

Gran Bar Danzón Libertad 1161, 1st floor, Retiro. Fashionable after-office bar (and restaurant) with sharply dressed staff and a very comprehensive wine list. Very popular, even mid week.

Kilkenny Reconquista & Paraguay, Retiro. Boisterous *Kilkenny* is one of the few pubs heaving well before midnight, and is an established favourite of both visiting foreigners and Guinness-drinking Porteños.

Milion Paraná 1048 ☎011/4815-9925, Recoleta. Cocktails and tiny portions of modern Argentine cuisine, served in a beautifully converted mansion with dozens of candlelit rooms. Singers and DJs play laid back dining grooves from 8pm, replaced by livelier dance music from midnight.

Shamrock Rodríguez Peña 1220, Recoleta. Mock-Irish bar with a marked Porteño touch (not much in the way of genuine beers) and a small club downstairs. A good place to meet foreigners – though plenty of locals hang out here, too.

Palermo

Antares Armenia 1447. Home-brewed Kölsch, porter, stout and barley beers, to name just a few, to accompany tapas and simple dishes, in a roomy, converted storehouse; jazz, blues and Irish music add to the ambience.

Bar Abierto J.L. Borges 1613. Pizzas, snacks, drinks and coffee come accompanied by live music, lectures and performances in this converted *almacén*, or corner shop, with contemporary paintings on the walls.

Carnal Niceto Vega 5511. This bar, right opposite *Niceto* (see p.184), has a large upstairs terrace that fills quickly during the warmer months, when a DJ plays dance music for a young, trendy crowd.

Congo Honduras 5329. A relatively new bar that has taken off quickly in popularity, not least for its massive garden area, which allows those wedded to their cigarettes to indulge and for everyone to enjoy the stars. Get there early – very early by local standards (around 8pm) – to get an outdoor booth, where you can sample the food, and expect to queue if you arrive after 10pm.

Malasartes Honduras 4999. Trendy Plaza Serrano hangout with avant-garde art on the walls and serving reasonably priced drinks and snacks.

Mundo Bizarro Serrano 1222. The name means "strange world" and this bar is definitely a bit different for Palermo; expect low lighting, good cocktails and a relaxed crowd.

El Taller Borges 1595 ☏011/4831-5501. This long-running place has the best outside seating in the Plaza Cortázar and hosts regular jazz events.

Tazz Armenia 1744. The refreshing yellows and oranges of *Tazz's* relaxing decor serve as a nice venue for the good cocktails – including a mean *mojito* – but stay away from the vaguely Tex-Mex fast food.

Único Honduras & Fitzroy. A lively crowd is always guaranteed at this well-known meeting-place at the very centre of Palermo Hollywood; it fills early but is more laid back – though still busy – after 1am or so.

The outer barrios

Bar Ocho7Ocho Thames 878, Villa Crespo. Located in a refitted wood workshop, this smart locale is the place to head if you are fond of a strong cocktail – anything whisky-based is a good bet. Some excellent food to accompany the drink, too, including fabulous beef fillet sandwiches with fried green tomatoes.

Live music

Nearly every night of the year you can listen to really good **live music** – including folk, jazz and rock – somewhere in Buenos Aires. Venues vary from intimate clubs (some of which serve food) to mammoth stadiums, and just about every barrio has at least one place that regularly stages concerts or gigs. Often the bars and cafés listed on pp.158–163 and the arts and cultural centres listed on pp.185–187 also feature musical entertainment. Tango is explored in its own chapter (Chapter 15), while classical music and opera are included in Chapter 14, "The arts and entertainment".

To learn about gigs by local bands, check the *S!* supplement in *Clarín* on Fridays (Ⓦwww.si.clarin.com) and the antonymically named *NO* in *Página 12* on Thursdays. Many international pop and rock stars include Argentina in their world tours, usually playing at the mega-venues, including the football stadiums, such as La Bombonera (see p.211) or El Monumental (see p.211). The website Ⓦwww.mundoteatral.com.ar is an excellent source of information about venues, gigs and shows in the city, though with a focus more on off beat stuff. If folk music is your thing, check out Ⓦwww.folkloreclub.com.ar.

Ticketek (☏011/5237-7200) sells tickets to many concerts and gigs, including the events held in stadiums. You can book over the phone or online, or visit one of their outlets; the most central is at Viamonte 560 (Mon–Sat 9am–8.30pm). You can also often get tickets at record stores such as Musimundo (see p.206) – posters or flyers advertising upcoming concerts give details. Smaller-scale venues where local artists play seldom charge more than $25–50 per person, but the combination of international stars and mega-venues can result in ticket prices well into several hundred pesos not specific enough to be "a mark".

Rock nacional

Followed passionately by a legion of fans in Buenos Aires and further afield, **rock nacional**, Argentina's home-grown rock music (ⓦ www.rock.com.ar), originally dates from the 1960s, though it only really started to become popular during the 1976–1982 military dictatorship (see p.257), when musicians such as **Charly García** performed songs with ambiguous references to the evils of the dictatorship right under the government's nose. As a result, *rock nacional* often has a political, anti-establishment bent, personified in acts like **Sumo**, whose Anglo-Italian frontman Luca Prodan wrote songs on his distaste for Porteño high society – a sentiment shared by many *rock nacional* fans, who tend to be lower middle class and proudly anti-fashion. Other contemporary big names – which you'll see emblazoned on T-shirts and school bags all over the city – include **Patricio Rey y sus Redonditas de Ricota**, **The Draytones**, **Los Fabulosos Cadillacs**, **Las Pelotas**, **Estelares** and **Babasónicos**. Musically, they're a mixed bag, though the tunes tend to be lively and more indie rock than heavy metal – think Talking Heads rather than Megadeth – and ska is often an influence. If you want to hear *rock nacional*, the best place is undoubtedly the massive Quilmes Rock (see p.220), though there are many smaller outlets too, including regular venues such as Mitos Argentinos (see below). To find other listings, look out around the city for flyers advertising gigs.

Larger venues

Estadio Luna Park Bouchard 465, San Nicolás, see map, p.73 ☏011/4311-5100, ⓦ www.lunapark.com.ar. Wonderful Art Deco construction whose huge capacity lends itself to big sell-out events like boxing fights, but also to concerts by big names, such as Tom Jones, Norah Jones and the Pet Shop Boys. Make sure you don't get a "poor visibility" seat: ask when you book.
Estadio Obras Sanitarias Av Libertador 73955, Núñez ☏011/4702-3223, ⓦ www.estadioobras .com. Seating over 5000, this leading venue for rock bands – both home-grown and world-famous – has seen the likes of Iggy Pop, the Red Hot Chili Peppers, Duran Duran and even the Sex Pistols grace its stage.
Teatro Gran Rex Av Corrientes 855, San Nicolás. Seating over 3000, this cavernous edifice is one of the major venues for musicals and gigs by national and international groups, such as Coldplay, plus theatre groups, such as the Black Theatre of Prague.

Rock, jazz, folk and eclectic

Blues Special Club Av Almirante Brown 102, Boca ☏011/4854-2338. The name says it all: special blues acts, including those from the US, perform Fri–Sun, while most Fridays there is also a *zapada blusera*, or jam session; you'll catch the occasional *rock nacional* gig here, too.

Boris Club de Jazz Gorriti 5568, Palermo ☏011/4777-0012. It may be new but this stylish jazz club in the thick of Palermo Hollywood is already attracting big local names like Adrián Iaies and international stars including blues and fusion guitarist Scott Henderson. You can also eat or have a drink here.

Clásica y Moderna Callao 892, Recoleta ⓦ www.clasicaymoderna.com. The interior of *Clásica y Moderna* was for many years a bookstore, but it was converted in the 1980s into a café/restaurant with live tango, jazz and flamenco acts, including many top names (daily from around 9 or 10pm). The classic Argentine food is very good, and there's an excellent bookshop at the back.

Mitos Argentinos Humberto 1° 489, San Telmo ☏011/4362-7810, ⓦ www.mitosargentinos .com.ar. The main attraction of this old mansion is the off-beat nature of the *rock nacional* bands that play Thurs–Sat; their names are offbeat, too: Los Melones and Camisa de Fuerza ("straitjacket"). You can also have dinner on Fri and Sat, and lunch on Sun (simple fare such as empanadas and steak).

ND/Ateneo Paraguay 918, Retiro ☏011/4328-2888, ⓦ www.ndateneo.com .ar. Folk, rock, tango, jazz, modern classical – all the big national and South American names play here at some point. The medium-sized theatre also hosts film screenings and recitals.

No Avestruz Humboldt 1857, Palermo ☏ 011/4771-1141, ⓦ www.noavestruz .com.ar. Outstanding venue – a cross between someone's garage and an informal cabaret – hosting emerging and established artists focusing on jazz and Latin sounds from Buenos Aires and further afield. Delicious food, too.

Notorious Av Callao 966, Recoleta ☏ 011/4816-2888, ⓦ www.notorious.com.ar. Friendly bar selling CDs that you can listen to on headphones. There's also a great garden at the back where you can chill out over a cold beer. Interesting small-scale concerts – blues, jazz, tango, Latin – are held throughout the year.

Pan y Teatro Muñiz & Las Casas, Boedo ☏ 011/4924-6920, ⓦ www.panyteatro.com.ar. Open every day except Mon for tango, classical music and jazz, this beautifully restored grocer's shop serves an original blend of Italian and *criollo* food.

Peña del Abasto Anchorena 571, Abasto ☏ 011/5076-0148. Another wonderful folk venue, with some of the country's leading performers, and a dancefloor; shows Wed–Sun 10pm.

Peña del Colorado Güemes 3657, Palermo ☏ 011/4822-1038, ⓦ www .delcolorado.com.ar. Famed for its past-midnight *guitarreadas* (bring your guitar, play and sing) that "finish when the candles burn out" (in practice 4am), the *Colorado* is the city's most traditional folk venue – there is also a *mate* bar, a restaurant and occasional folk and even tango shows.

Thelonious Club Salguero 1884, Palermo ☏ 011/4342-7650, ⓦ www.thelonious .com.ar. The odd soul or blues concert is given here, but, as the name implies, this is a jazz club, and generally regarded as the top; the music is always mesmerizing, the acoustics are faultless and the food isn't bad, but the barstools and metal chairs are not that comfortable – the only downside.

La Trastienda Balcarce 460, San Telmo, ☏ 011/4342-7650, ⓦ www.latrastienda.com. Trendy live music in a late nineteenth-century mansion, with a wide-ranging roster of acts including rock, jazz, salsa and tango.

Vaca Profana Lavalle 3683, Abasto ☏ 011/4867-0934, ⓦ www.vacaprofana.com.ar. This friendly little joint is known for its avant-garde music (and occasionally theatre) – mainly new South American sounds including neo-ethnic, modern versions of regional folk. It also serves a delicious vegetarian *picada* (cold platter) and all manner of food (good pizzas) and drinks.

Nightclubs

In terms of **nightclubs**, Buenos Aires stands head and shoulders above any other city in Argentina and, arguably, Latin America. Although quite a few clubs are in the city centre or **Puerto Madero**, the trendiest bits of **Palermo** (Soho, La Cañitas and, in summer, Costanera Norte) are home to the hippest venues. As always venues come and go, go up and down and change name, so check before you set out. It's always worth asking locals or checking websites such as ⓦ www .buenosaliens.com to find out what the flavour of the month is.

Music in clubs is usually either commercial dance or more cutting-edge, mixed by DJs of international standing. Although Buenos Aires has some great home-grown DJs, trends in dance music tend to follow those of Europe and the US. For something more local, there are also plenty of decidedly more low-brow places playing the tropical sounds you'll hear elsewhere in Latin America; specific to Buenos Aires, *cumbia villera* (see box opposite) can be heard at venues called *bailantas*. Cheap, alcoholic and rowdy, and normally found in poorer neighbourhoods, *bailantas* can be fun but are not really recommendable unless you go with a regular.

Admission prices range wildly from free (particularly for women) to $100 or more, with prices sometimes including a free drink. **Dress** at nightclubs tends towards the same mix of smart and quirky that you see around the world. Many clubs have VIP sections or long queues, but as a foreigner, you are unlikely to be turned away. Friday and Saturday are the big nights out, but some places are open in the week (especially Wed and Thurs) and Sunday, too. Places serving food

Cumbia

Classic *cumbia* hails from Colombia, though its roots go further back to *cumbe*, a music and dance brought by slaves from Guinea in Africa in colonial times; it was mixed with European and Amerindian instruments and rhythms to form *cumbia*. By the twentieth century it had evolved to create a style of music that is either irresistibly catchy or maddeningly repetitive, depending on your point of view. *Cumbia* is extremely popular all over Latin America, especially among the poorer sections of society. Different forms of *cumbia* have appeared in various parts of the region, and Buenos Aires' contribution to this cultural evolution is **cumbia villera**, which takes its name from *villas miserias*, or shantytowns (see p.98), from where it originated and where it is most popular. In some ways the Argentine equivalent of gangsta rap, *cumbia villera* glorifies drugs and crime, quite different from the slightly suggestive romantic lyrics of traditional *cumbia*. Bands generally consist of young men with waist-length hair, sports clothes and attitude, and revel in names such as Los Pibes Chorros (*lunfardo*, or Buenos Aires slang, for "young thieves") and Yerba Brava (ie strong *mate* – or marijuana). You can hear *cumbia* – both *villera* and otherwise – at a *bailanta* (see below).

usually open around 9pm, but don't get going until 10pm; otherwise disco doors seldom open before midnight and it is not cool to arrive much before 2am.

If you haven't had enough dancing by the time clubs finally close, you could go on to one of the popular **after-hours clubs** (referred to simply as *afters*), which principally operate on Sundays, usually from around 9am until noon.

Araoz Araoz 2424, Palermo. Gigantic restaurant-cum-nightclub best known for its Thursday "Lost Parties" for hip–hop.

Asia de Cuba Pierina Dealessi 750, Puerto Madero ⓦ www.asiadecuba.com.ar. Famous for its fashion model and VIP crowd, this place starts off the night as a sushi bar and then turns into an exclusive disco with cover charges to match.

Big One Alsina 940, Monserrat ⓦ www .bigoneclub.com.ar. A very lively crowd combined with its majestic setting in a converted nineteenth-century industrial building have made this club night deservedly popular. Less emphasis on posing and more on the music, which is mostly house and trance on Sat. The venue, Alsina, is usually gay/gay-friendly on Fri and (sometimes) Sun, with more commercial dance music.

Caix Costanera Norte ⓦ www.caix-ba.com.ar. For some years the most noteworthy after-hours club, attracting an inevitably motley bunch on Sun from 8am.

Le Click Rivadavia 1910, San Nicolás, ☏011/4543-4183. Slightly underground club holding up to a thousand revellers, with special nights (some gay) so call first to find out.

Crobar Paseo de la Infanta, Palermo ☏011/4778-1500, ⓦ www.crobar.com.ar.

This sleek disco is located inside the Palermo parks and its top DJs attract a smart crowd able to pay the high admission charge. Fri & Sat only

Fantástico Bailable Rivadavia & Sánchez de Loria, Once. The best-known *bailanta* – and a good place to try the heady mix of non-stop dancing and full-on flirting that goes with the territory.

Maluco Beleza Sarmiento 1728, San Nicolás ⓦ www.malucobeleza.com.ar. Long-running Brazilian club, playing a mix of lambada, afro, samba and reggae to a lively crowd of Brazilians and Brazilophiles. Wed is Brazilian music only, with a *feijoada* (heavy traditional stew) served; avoid it if you want to dance.

Mambo Báez 243, Las Cañitas ☏011/4778-0115. Extravagantly tropical Latino club with dinner-shows and disco – book ahead. Rather overpriced and limited menu. Runs Thurs–Sun. Salsa classes Wed, Fri & Sat 8.30pm.

Mint Complejo Punta Carrasco, Av Rafael Obligado s/n, Costanera Norte ⓦ www.puntacarrasco.com .ar. One of the biggest clubs along the Costanera that keeps coming back summer after summer with a DJ lineup packed with top domestic and international names playing trance and techno.

(13)

Niceto **Niceto Vega 5510, Palermo** Ⓦ**www .nicetoclub.com.** Varied rock and dance acts on Fri & Sat, but *Niceto* is most famous for Thursday's Club 69 "fiestas" – the ones to hit for a friendly, diverse crowd, outlandish podium dancers and house music played by the city's most acclaimed resident DJs (see Ⓦwww.club69.com.ar).

Pachá **Costanera Norte & La Pampa,** Ⓦ**www .pachabuenosaires.com.** The club scene in Buenos Aires changes fast but "Clubland" nights at *Pachá* just keep on going. Big and glitzy like its Ibiza namesake, *Pachá* attracts a lively mixed crowd, including a sprinkling of Argentine celebrities. DJs of international standing often play here. Shorts, caps and sandals are not allowed; relatively expensive. Sat from 1am.

The arts and entertainment

T here's a superb range of **cultural events** on offer in Buenos Aires: everything from avant-garde theatre and photography exhibitions to blockbuster films and grand opera, with a wealth of options in between: cabaret, chamber music, art house cinema – you name it. It is fairly easy to find out what is happening on any given day: a plethora of **listings** are given in the entertainment sections of both *Clarín* and *La Nación*. Numerous independent listings sheets are also available in bars, bookshops and kiosks throughout the city; it's always worth trying tourist kiosks for pamphlets and magazines, too. *Arte al Día* (☎011/5031-0023, ⓦwww.artealdia.com) is a monthly newspaper, available from newspaper stands, with details of exhibitions at galleries and arts centres.

In general, one of the best things about events in Buenos Aires is that ticket or entry **prices** tend to be low (by international standards), so even if an event turns out not to your liking, you won't have spent much on the gamble. In fact, there is even a strong tradition of **free** or subsidized cultural events. These include film showings and classical concerts at the city's museums and cultural centres and a series of outdoor events put on by the city government every **summer** – look out for posters and media announcements or ask at the tourist kiosks.

Though you can queue at the various venues for **tickets**, they are also available, and at discounted prices, for theatre, cinema and music events at the various *carteleras* (ticket agencies) in the centre, such as Cartelera Baires, Av Corrientes 1382, local 24 (Mon–Thurs 10am–10pm, Fri till 11pm, Sat till midnight, Sun 2–10pm; ☎011/4372-5058). Alternatively, Ticketek (☎011/5237-7200, ⓦwww.ticketek.com.ar) sells tickets to many concerts and plays, either over the phone or online, or at an outlet – try the one at Viamonte 560 (Mon–Sat 9am–8.30pm).

Cultural centres

Buenos Aires' numerous **cultural centres** are some of its greatest assets. Nearly every neighbourhood has its own modest centre – good places to find out about free tango classes or see art exhibitions and films and even have a snack – while the major institutions, such as the Centro Cultural Borges and the Centro Cultural Recoleta, regularly put on some of the city's best exhibitions. Various European countries also have their own arts centre in Buenos Aires.

British Arts Centre (BAC) Suipacha 1333, Retiro ☎011/4393-2004, ⊛www .britishartscentre.org.ar. This arts centre won prizes for its modern architecture, and was improved further by a 2007 refurbishment. It's the place to head for if you're nostalgic for a bit of Hitchcock or Monty Python – there are regular film and video showings, plus English-language plays by playwrights such as Harold Pinter, though it puts on drama in Spanish, too. Tues–Fri 3–9pm.

Carlos Regazzoni Sculpture Park Av Libertador 405, Retiro ☎011/4315-3663, ⊛www.regazzoniarts.com. Identifiable by the rusting iron giraffe outside, this sculpture collection is definitely different. Regazzoni works in Paris and Buenos Aires, recycling old railway junk and making it into figures of animals and vehicles, among other objects – one of his most impressive pieces is a full-scale twin-prop plane, complete with pilot. Most of the work is scattered inside a railway shed, which also holds occasional cultural events, mostly with a recycling theme. Mon–Fri 9am–6pm.

Centro Cultural Borges Viamonte & San Martín, Retiro ☎011/5555-5359, ⊛www .ccborges.org.ar. Large space above the Galerías Pacífico shopping centre. Several spacious galleries show a mixture of photography and painting – past exhibitions have included artists such as Toulouse-Lautrec and Andy Warhol. There's also a theatre and an art house cinema. Mon–Sat 10am–9pm, Sun noon–9pm; $15.

Centro Cultural Caras y Caretas (CCCyC) Venezuela 370, Monserrat ☎011/5354-6618, ⊛www.carasycaretas.org. Centre run by the publisher of a venerable society review with the ambition of acting as a cultural think tank. In practice, it puts on a variety of plays, art shows and folk, tango and jazz concerts, often of a very high quality. Mon–Sat 3–7.30pm.

Centro Cultural de España en Buenos Aires (CCEBA) Florida 943, Retiro. Other branches at Paraná 1159 and Balcarce 1150 (check website for venue details). ☎011/4313-3214, ⊛www.cceba.org.ar. Extremely active Spanish arts centre that puts on regular contemporary art exhibitions from the motherland, plus Argentine art, and organizes all manner of cultural events, such as video screenings. Mon–Fri 10.30am–8pm, Sat 10am–2pm.

Centro Cultural General San Martín Sarmiento 1551, San Nicolás ☎011/4374-1251, ⊛www .teatrosanmartin.com.ar. Tucked behind the Teatro General San Martín, with a varied selection of free painting, sculpture, craft and photography exhibitions and an art house cinema (see p.190). Box office daily 10am–10pm.

Centro Cultural Recoleta Junín 1930, Recoleta ☎011/4803-1040. One of the city's best cultural centres – see p.111.

Centro Cultural Ricardo Rojas Av Corrientes 2038, Balvanera ☎011/4954-5521, ⊛www .rojas.uba.ar. Affiliated with the University of Buenos Aires, this friendly cultural centre and gallery space offers free events including live music and bargain film showings, usually alternative/art house. Box office daily 10am–10pm. Closed Jan.

Central Cultural del Sur Caseros & Baigorri, Barracas ☎011/4305-6653, ⊛www.ccdelsur .blogspot.com. Wonderful arts centre housed in a well-preserved nineteenth-century stables and inn, with folklore, tango, children's theatre and puppet shows. Daily 11am–7pm.

Ciudad Cultural Konex Sarmiento 3131, Balvanera ⊛www.ciudadculturalkonex.org. Super cool, eclectic arts and culture centre in a large, converted factory. Most famous for its "bomba de tiempo" drumming circles on Monday evenings, there's something on every evening or weekend afternoon, from world dub nights to folk singers and architecture workshops for children. Box office opens daily at 5pm and closes after the shows begin.

Espacio Fundación Telefónica Arenales 1540, Recoleta ☎011/4333-1300, ⊛www.fundacion .telefonica.com.ar/espacio. A new, high-tech arts centre that lays emphasis on communications media, as you would expect for a foundation run by a telecom company. This sleek, modern space stages small, mostly avant-garde exhibitions of work by contemporary Argentine artists, and houses an excellent *mediateca* (media library). Mon–Sat 2–8.30pm.

Fundación Federico J. Klemm Marcelo T. de Alvear 626, Retiro ⊛www.fundacionfjklemm .org. The late Argentine maverick Federico Klemm was a larger-than-life collector of modern art, and there's a serious collection on display at this foundation; see p.99. Mon–Fri 11am–8pm.

Goethe Institut **Av world wide Corrientes 319, San Nicolás ☎011/4311-8964, ⓦwww.goethe .de/hs/bue.** This branch of the world wide German cultural institute has a good library for German and English books, as well as German movies and plays. Mon–Fri 9am–6pm; closed Jan & Feb.

Theatre

Theatre has a long and noble tradition in Buenos Aires, with Avenida Corrientes playing the local role of New York's Broadway or London's West End – although obviously almost all plays are in Spanish. In the major venues you'll find a good spread of international and Argentine works, both classic and contemporary, ranging from serious drama to musicals. Away from the conventional scene, the city is dotted with innumerable "underground" settings, with tiny auditoriums at the back of shopping centres and even stages in bars. You'll find that many press listings use the terms **"Off Corrientes"** and **"Off Off Corrientes"** to describe these independent theatres. The production standard at these smaller venues varies wildly, but they attract a loyal following and – if your Spanish is up to it – are a great way of tasting contemporary Argentine culture. You'll find many of them in the blocks around Corrientes and in San Telmo, well publicized by flyers given out in the street, in bars and in bookshops. The website ⓦwww.alternativateatral.com is a mine of information about independent shows throughout the metropolis. Prices vary quite a lot, usually from $25–45 for a seat at a marginal theatre to $60–200 at more mainstream venues.

Argentine playwrights to look out for include Roberto Cossa, whose plays deal with middle-class Porteño life and immigration; Griselda Gambaro, whose compelling dramas often focus on the power relations between victims and victimizers (with a clear reference to Argentina's past); and the idiosyncratic Roberto Arlt, whose work offers a darkly humorous and sometimes surreal vision of modernity. One of the leading contemporary playwrights is Javier Daulte (b.1963), who specializes in psychological thrillers with a touch of humour and larger-than-life characters – a kind of cross between Pedro Almodóvar and Harold Pinter.

Abasto Social Club Humahuaca 3649, Balvanera ☎011/4862-7205, ⓦwww.abastosocialclub .com.ar. Highly acclaimed Off Corrientes theatre with a café/bar and a programme of contemporary drama acted by up-and-coming local thespians.

Actors Studio Av Corrientes 3565, Balvanera ☎011/4867-6622, ⓦwww.actors-studio.org. Far north in Balvanera, this ebullient theatre, with its own restaurant, qualifies for Off Corrientes status. In a converted townhouse, it offers a varied diet of classics and headline-snatching provokers by contemporary playwrights; doubling as a drama school, the Studio tends to have young, promising casts.

Andamio 90 Paraná 660, San Nicolás ☎011/4373-5670, ⓦwww.andamio90.org. Long-established theatre school run by actress and director Alejandra Boero. Two auditoriums host a range of classics by playwrights such as Samuel Beckett.

El Camarín de las Musas Mario Bravo 960, Balvanera ☎011/4862-0655, ⓦwww .elcamarindelasmusas.com.ar. Simple food is on offer in the bar/restaurant but the main reason to come is for the underground (literally) theatre – lots of the works premiered are based on prize-winning pieces of Argentine literature. Small art exhibits add to the enjoyment.

Chacarerean Teatre Nicaragua 5565, Palermo ☎011/4775-9010, ⓦwww.chacarereanteatre .com.ar. Alternative theatre whose residence is a converted carpentry workshop in Palermo Hollywood. Plays – often on the impenetrable side – are by contemporary Argentines. One creation depicted the breakdown of a relationship in an Asian restaurant and featured a Tai-Chi-Chuan expert; the public drank green tea during the performance.

Espacio Callejón Humahuaca 3759, Balvanera ☎011/4862-1167, ⓦespaciocallejon.blogspot .com.** Another trendy Off Corrientes venue in

Balvanera, this one specializes in a contemporary home-grown repertory (a recent play was a comedy about a neighbourhood lacrosse team practising for the world championships in Hungary) – and striptease shows once a week. Make sure you check the programme first.

Teatro Astral Av Corrientes 1639, San Nicolás ☎011/4374-5707. The main revue theatre on Corrientes – it has titillated its audiences with cabaret, mainly leggy girls wearing very little, for years.

Teatro Belisario Av Corrientes 1624, San Nicolás ☎011/4373-3465. Consistently good theatre with emphasis on humorous works, including one-actor shows, plus musicals. Shows Thurs–Sun.

Teatro Concert Av Corrientes 1218, San Nicolás ☎011/4381-0345. An Off Corrientes theatre that puts on challenging, offbeat plays, such as the multimedia work of Alfredo Casero. Shows Fri & Sat only.

Teatro del Pueblo Av Roque Sáenz Peña 943, San Nicolás ☎011/4326-3606, ⓦwww .teatrodelpueblo.org.ar. This major theatre is one of the oldest non-state theatres in South America, having first opened its doors in 1930. Run in conjunction with the Fundación Carlos Somigliana, named after a leading playwright whose demanding plays it regularly stages, the theatre focuses on works by contemporary Argentine writers, such as Roberto Cossa and Griselda Gambaro.

Teatro General San Martín Av Corrientes 1500, San Nicolás ☎011/4371-0111, ⓦwww .teatrosanmartin.com.ar. Excellent modern venue with several auditoriums and a varied programme that usually includes one or two Argentine plays as well as international standards such as Pinter or Brecht. Also hosts contemporary dance events, ballet and a children's theatre, and there's an art

house cinema in the Sala Leopoldo Lugones (see p.190).

Teatro Gran Rex Av Corrientes 837, San Nicolás ☎011/4322-8000, Fabulous Art Deco building which, when it opened in 1937, was the largest moviehouse in South America. Similar on the inside to New York's Radio City Music Hall, it seats 3300 and for decades has been a major venue for cabaret plus frequent sell-out concerts by national and international stars. In recent years it has hosted Diana Krall, Caetano Veloso, Air Supply, Michael Buble and Björk, to name but five.

Teatro Maipo Esmeralda 443, San Nicolás ☎011/4322-4882, ⓦwww.maipo.com.ar. Over a century old, this historic theatre continues to pull in crowds to see blockbusters like *Sweeney Todd* or cabarets and tango shows. Upstairs the *Maipo Club* still puts on extravagant cabaret shows usually featuring the larger-than-life drag artist, Jean-François Casanovas, a Parisian who has been treading the local boards for years – expect sequins, feathers and an audience splitting their sides.

Teatro Nacional Cervantes Libertad 815, Retiro ⓦwww.teatrocervantes.gov.ar. This grand, old-fashioned theatre, superb inside and out (see p.70), presents a broad programme of old and new Argentine and foreign works.

Teatro Ópera Av Corrientes 860, San Nicolás ☎011/4326-1335. Fabulous Art Deco theatre, which in its heyday billed Edith Piaf and Josephine Baker, has undergone a recent revival focusing on a music and dance programme, usually of a very high quality.

Teatro El Vitral Rodríguez Peña 344, San Nicolás ☎011/4371-0948, ⓦwww.teatroelvitral.com.ar. An attractive old mansion literally off Corrientes is the setting for this small independent theatre that puts on alternative plays and some wacky musical comedies.

Classical music, opera and ballet

Argentina boasts a number of world-class classical performers, including **opera** singers such as tenors Marcelo Álvarez and José Cura and soprano María Cristina Kiehr, and the **classical music** on offer in the city has seen a recent revival. Some of the best concerts are small-scale affairs held at museums, churches and the like, in particular the **Museo de Arte Hispanoamericano Isaac Fernández Blanco** (see p.102). However, the larger venues are just as exciting, and more spectacular: an evening at the world-class **Teatro Colón** – the city's purpose-built opera house – is a memorable experience. Internationally renowned Argentine **ballet** star Julio Bocca retired in 2007; meanwhile, a younger Argentine has come to dominate world stages: La Plata-born Iñaki Urlezaga, a leading member of London's Royal Ballet, delights crowds in his native land from time to time. Perhaps the most famous Argentine classical musician alive is pianist and conductor Daniel Barenboim, who makes occasional visits to the city.

For **news** of concerts and performances, consult ⓦ www.musicaclasicaargentina .com, www.mozarteumargentino.org and www.festivalesmusicales.org.ar, all of which are packed with information. Many events, especially those in churches or institutional venues, are free. Otherwise the **price** of a ticket varies hugely from a handful of pesos for a small-scale recital to several hundred pesos for a VIP seat at the opera or ballet.

Casa de la Cultura Av de Mayo 575, Monserrat. Free classical concerts, mostly chamber music, are given from time to time in the marvellous Salón Dorado; look out for flyers and posters.

🏃 **Manufactura Papelera** Bolívar 1582, San Telmo ⓦ www.papeleracultural.8m.com. This fabulous recycled-paper factory in the heart of San Telmo puts on highly intellectual theatrical shows and, from time to time, classical music concerts – opera, chamber music and operetta.

🏃 **La Scala de San Telmo** Pasaje Giuffra 371 (Defensa 800), San Telmo ☏ 011/4362-1187, ⓦ www.lascala.com.ar. It may not be in Milan, but this sumptuous bijou theatre hosts tango, jazz and other music genres, plus some excellent operas and classical concerts, including ancient music.

Teatro Avenida Av de Mayo 1222, Monserrat ☏ 011/4381-0662, ⓦ www.balirica.org.ar. A stylish theatre, opened only a few months after the Colón in 1908, the Avenida is the home to Buenos Aires Lírica, which puts on a limited number of operas here every season.

Teatro Coliseo Marcelo T. de Alvear 1125, Retiro ☏ 011/4816-3789. The most important venue for ballet, musicals and classical music after the Colón; also offers occasional free recitals.

🏃 **Teatro Colón** Libertad 621, San Nicolás ☏ 011/4378-7344, ⓦ www.teatrocolon .org.ar. Buenos Aires' most glamorous night out and one of the world's great opera houses (especially since extensive renovation work in time for the 2010 bicentenary) – acoustically on a par with the very best, it showcases opera, ballet and classical music, including the Buenos Aires Philharmonic, from March to Dec. Tickets can be bought at the box office in person or online.

Teatro Margarita Xirgu Chacabuco 875, San Telmo ☏ 011/4300-8817, ⓦ www.margaritaxirgu .com. Named after the leading Catalan actress, this opulent theatre was opened by the city's Catalan community, and now stages spectacles that run the gamut from children's theatre to serious operas and classical recitals.

Cinemas

Porteños are keen and knowledgeable cinema-goers, and there are dozens of **cinemas** in the city showing everything from the latest Hollywood releases to Argentine films and foreign art house cinema (*arte y ensayo* or *cine de autor*). Cinemas showing mainstream stuff tend to concentrate on Calle Lavalle, while art house flicks are found on Avenida Corrientes. However, both are increasingly losing out to multiplex cinemas, most of which are inside the various shopping malls scattered around the city. Numerous free film showings are also held at the city's cultural centres and museums, often the best places nowadays to see something other than Hollywood hits.

For what's on, consult the listings sections of *Clarín* or *La Nación*, or visit ⓦ www .pantalla.com.ar, which features all the city's cinemas and all the movies showing, complete with reviews. Another excellent website is ⓦ www.cinesargentinos.com .ar. Once a year, usually in April, Buenos Aires holds an **International Festival of Independent Cinema** (ⓦ www.bafici.gov.ar; see p.221) with an excellent selection of national and foreign films. Outside festival times, the **price** of a cinema ticket ranges from $10 to $25 (Mon–Wed & Fri before 6pm is often cheaper).

Buenos Aires on screen

Since the introduction of sound in cinemas in the 1930s, Buenos Aires' **movie** output has been prolific, if sporadic. Tango was a major theme in those years – classic films of that time include *Tango* (1933) and a number of works featuring Carlos Gardel, such as *Luces de Buenos Aires*. The censorship of the Perón and Proceso administrations straitjacketed national movie-makers for much of the following three decades, but with the return to democracy a slew of interesting movies emerged examining the experience and legacy of those terrible years, notably 1985's Oscar-winning *La Historia Oficial* (The Official Story), where a middle-class Porteña begins to suspect her adopted child may have been taken from disappeared dissidents, and *Kiss of the Spider Woman*, an English-language film based on the novel by Manuel Puig that centres on two political prisoners. During the final years of the 1990s, a wave of social realism films, labelled New Argentine Cinema, began to appear on the silver screen. Many of these deal with the fallout of the economic crisis, though the serious subject matter is often leavened with a sharp wit. *Pizza, Birra, Faso* (Pizza, Beer, Cigarettes), the tale of marginalized Buenos Aires adolescents with a penchant for mugging folk, kicked it off. The excellent *Nueve Reinas* (Nine Queens) was a Porteño take on the heist movie; it starred Ricardo Darín, who also starred in the beguiling Oscar-nominated comedy *El Hijo de la Novia* (Son of the Bride); *XXY*, about a hermaphrodite and her family escaping Porteño society; and *Luna de Avellaneda* (Moon of Avellaneda), a story set in a community leisure club in the suburb of Avellaneda. Other recent films in this genre include *El Bonaerense*, a movie about corruption in Buenos Aires' police force, and *Buena Vida Delivery* (Good Life Delivery), a dark comedy on the different ways that people tried to cope with the economic crisis. Argentine cinema shot to international attention once more when *El Secreto de Sus Ojos*, directed by Juan José Campanella, won the Oscar for best foreign film in 2010. Combining romance and politics, and starring old favourite Ricardo Darín backed by an excellent cast, it no doubt won the Hollywood vote with its moral tone and tear-jerking tragedy, but it is well filmed, finely acted and worth seeing. Movie production in the city reached an all-time high around 2005–08 but then seemed to drop off somewhat – but you've still got a reasonable chance of bumping into a film set during your stay, with the city's relatively low costs and high expertise attracting film crews from outside the country.

Abasto Shopping Av Corrientes 3200, Balvanera. Enormous modern cinema at the Abasto shopping centre (see p.199), featuring a good mix of international and local movies.

Arteplex Centro Av Corrientes 1145, San Nicolás ☏011/4382-7934. One of the few art house cinemas still operating on Corrientes – mostly European films.

Cinemark Palermo Beruti 3399 & Bulnes, Palermo. Good-quality multiplex where Hollywood majors outnumber art house films.

Complejo Tita Merello Suipacha 442, San Nicolás ☏011/4322-1195. Another central art house cinema, named after a tango legend, Tita Merello (1904–2002), who appeared in Argentina's first talkie (*Tango*; 1933). Its programming focuses on home-grown cinema – mainstream and alternative. Its future hung in the balance at the time of writing.

Cosmos Av Corrientes 2046, Balvanera ☏011/4953-5405, ⊛cosmosuba.wordpress.com.

Despite the lack of comfort, many locals' favourite art house cinema, showing films from around the world. It closed in 2009 only to reopen a year later thanks to a rescue plan by the University of Buenos Aires.

Electric Lavalle 836, Balvanera ☏011/4322-1846. Another typical Lavalle cinema, showing anything popular churned out by Hollywood.

Gaumont Rivadavia 1633, Balvanera ☏011/4371-3050. One of several "Espacio INCAA" showcase cinemas run by the Instituto Nacional de Cine y Artes Audiovisuales, the Argentine cinema institute. If your Spanish is up to it, this is the place to catch the best examples of the country's national film industry.

Sala Leopoldo Lugones Av Corrientes 1530, San Nicolás. Part of the Teatro San Martín complex (see p.188), this pioneering screen puts on outstanding seasons dedicated to different directors, actors, countries or themes.

Tango

(15)

T ango is so strongly associated with Buenos Aires that a visit to the city really isn't complete unless you immerse yourself in it at least once. There are numerous ways of experiencing tango, the most accessible for visitors being *tango espectáculos*. Often referred to by locals as "tango for export" – since tango in the city is principally appreciated as a music form, with dance sometimes accompanying it – these generally expensive **cena shows** (dinner, *cena*, followed by a dance performance) are put on by skilled professionals. If you want to keep it simple and just see a polished show, one of these may be your best option. If, however, you seek something a bit less touristy, consider attending a music **recital**. These are usually excellent and authentic, but they don't normally include dancing. Your third main option is to try a **milonga** – not a show, but an event where people actually go to dance. Milongas are ideal if you want to take the plunge yourself, or if you are interested in seeing tango as a social event.

Failing all of the above, you're bound to come across **street tango** during your time in the city. The performance given every Sunday evening at the Plaza Dorrego in San Telmo (see p.82) is a good one, and the surrounding streets host a dozen or so dance teams, solo musicians, singers and even whole orchestras. Tango displays aimed at visitors are held on Calle Florida, near the Galerías Pacífico entrance, almost every afternoon, and around Boca's Caminito.

For serious fans, there are a number of **hotels** in Buenos Aires dedicated to tango and offering classes, shows and/or recitals; these include the *Moreno* (see p.151) and *Mansión Dandi Royal* (see p.156). Many hostels, such as *Milhouse* (p.157) or *Tango City Hostel Inn* (p.157), also put on classes and arrange evenings out to the more hip shows. If you're looking for some tango-related souvenirs, including music, instruments and attire, see p.207.

Buenos Aires also hosts regular **tango festivals**, which can be exciting – the biggest are the Buenos Aires Tango Festival in February or March (see p.222); the competitive World Tango Championships in August (see p.222); and the **Día del Tango**, celebrated on and around December 11, the birthday of *tango supremo* Carlos Gardel.

To find out what's on when you're in town, check the **websites** of the places listed below, or consult the specialist **magazine** *El Tangauta* (Ⓦ eltangauta.com), which can generally be picked up at tourist kiosks, hotels, cultural centres and record stores. Websites listing milongas come and go, rather like milongas themselves – try Ⓦ www.buenosairesmilongas.com.

For more on the history and background of tango in the city, see the "Tango" colour section.

Cena shows

The city's glitzy **cena shows** are most popular with tourists, though a smattering of locals usually attend as well. Concentrated in the southern barrios, particularly San Telmo, these shows cost in the region of $300–400, for which you get a three-course meal, a professional tango performance and transfers from and to your hotel; many places will allow you to skip the meal (seldom a gourmet experience anyway) and just watch the show for a discount. They rarely sell out, but it is worth booking in advance so you can request a table with a good view – hotels often do bookings, but you can always book direct.

Bar Sur Estados Unidos 299, San Telmo ☎011/4362-6086, ⊛www.bar-sur.com.ar. Long-running, traditional San Telmo tango show. The performance quality varies, but it's an intimate space where audience participation is encouraged towards the end of the evening. Daily 8pm–4am; $270 with dinner, $170 without.

Esquina Homero Manzi Av San Juan 3601, Boedo ☎011/4957-8488, ⊛www .esquinahomeromanzi.com.ar. Built in the 1920s, this classic *tanguería* (tango locale), named after one of the greatest and most prolific tango lyricists, has long been a hub of *tanguero* culture and puts on music/dance shows, preceded by dinner, at 10pm daily ($300).

Piazzolla Centro de Artes Galería Güemes, Florida 165, San Nicolás, ⊛www.piazzollatangoshow .com. In a renovated theatre in the lovely Galería Güemes, this is one of the most central tango shows, with an exciting programme daily at 8.30pm for US$100 with dinner, US$56 without.

El Querandí Perú 302 & Moreno, Monserrat ☎011/5199-1771, ⊛www.querandi.com.ar. A classy venue – a beautifully restored late nineteenth-century building – hosts gala dinners, milongas and tango classes. US$100 with dinner, US$65 without.

Señor Tango Vieytes 1655, Barracas ☎011/4303-0231, ⊛www.senortango.com.ar. Large, professional *cena* show in the quiet southern barrio of Barracas. Daily dinner and a real spectacle of a show that traces the history of tango and incorporates trapezes, 1980s tango fusion and even horses. From 8.30pm; $125 show only, $400 with dinner.

Taconeando Balcarce 725, San Telmo ☎011/4307-6696, ⊛www.taconeando.com. More informal *cena* show; a good choice if you want to see a show but avoid the larger, commercial options. Thurs–Sat; US$55 with dinner, US$35 show only.

El Viejo Almacén Av Independencia & Balcarce, San Telmo ☎011/4307-6689, ⊛www.viejo-almacen.com.ar. Probably the most famous of San Telmo's *tanguerías* (tango locales), in an attractive nineteenth-century building. It occasionally hosts nationally famous tango singers, but is usually home to slickly executed dinner and dance shows daily from 8pm. $400 with dinner, $220 show only.

Recitals

We've listed here a few venues where you can go to hear regular tango **recitals**, but lots of cafés, bars and cultural centres also occasionally host live acts, so check the places listed in chapters 11, 13 and 14 as well. The cost will depend on who's playing, but they are generally reasonable – anything from no charge at all to $100 or so.

Centro Cultural Caras y Caretas (CCCyC) Venezuela 370, Monserrat ☎011/5354-6618, ⊛www.carasycaretas.org. Cultural think-tank that puts on tango concerts – often of a very high quality – as well as other events (see p.186).

Centro Cultural Torquato Tasso Defensa 1575, San Telmo ☎011/4307-6506, ⊛www .torquatotasso.com.ar. Friendly San Telmo neighbourhood cultural centre with a top-class programme of recitals (Thurs–Sun). Every Dec the *Tasso* holds its own outstanding tango festival, with recitals every night featuring the leading musicians in the country.

El Chino Beazley 3566, Nueva Pompeya ☎011/4911-0215. This bar and *parrilla* in traditional Nueva Pompeya is probably the most authentic place to hear tango sung, with both the talented staff and a crowd of locals and regulars performing. It's even been the subject of a movie, *Bar El Chino*. Fri & Sat from 10pm.

Clásica y Moderna Callao 892, Recoleta Ⓦ www.clasicaymoderna.com. The dark, brick interior here was converted from a bookstore into a café/restaurant with great food, live tango and other acts, including many top names. Daily from around 9 or 10pm.

IFT Boulogne-sur-Mer 549, Balvanera ℡ 011/4962-9420. Down-at-heel Abasto neighbourhood theatre that stages the occasional tango recital of astounding quality, featuring the likes of Tata (Daddy) Cedrón and his famous quartet, or bandoneón demon Dino Saluzzi.

La Scala de San Telmo Pasaje Giuffra 371 (Defensa 800), San Telmo ℡ 011/4362-1187, Ⓦ www.lascala.com.ar. Sumptuous bijou theatre hosting tango and other music concerts (see p.189).

Milongas

Milonga venues can vary enormously, from stately mid-afternoon soirées in dusty tea salons to raunchy late-night bohemian affairs. These days, times and locations also change frequently – the term "milonga" has taken to meaning a moveable event, so always check times and places in advance with the city information desk (see p.40). Many of the best and most authentic milongas take place in the outer barrios, so if you're seriously on the tango trail, you should be prepared to travel (locations outside of downtown have their closest subte station listed if they are near the subte network; if not, a taxi is probably the best way of getting there). In many cases, classes are given first – you should definitely try to take part in these if you want to dance. Milongas are not expensive (usually $15–30), and some are completely free. For gay milongas, see p.196.

Milonga etiquette

Tango has gained a whole new audience in recent times, with an increasing number of young people filling the floors of social clubs, *confiterías* and traditional dancehalls for **milongas**. Even if you don't dance yourself, it's still worth going to one of these: the spectacle of many couples slipping, almost trance-like, around the dancefloor is a captivating sight. Apart from their understated skill and composure, one of the most appealing aspects of a milonga is the absence of class – and, especially, age – divisions; indeed, most younger dancers regard it as an honour to be partnered by older and more experienced dancers.

Protocol changes little from milonga to milonga. Once the event gets under way, it is divided into musical sets, known as **tandas**, which cover the three subgenres of tango: tango "proper"; *milonga* – a more up-tempo sound; and waltz. Each is danced differently. The invitation to dance comes from the man, who will nod towards the woman whom he wishes to partner. She signals her acceptance of the offer with an equally subtle gesture; only then will the man approach her table. Once on the dancefloor, the couple waits eight **compases**, or bars, and then begins to dance, circulating in an anti-clockwise direction around the floor. The woman follows the man's lead by responding to **marcas**, or signs, given by him to indicate the move he wishes her to make. The more competent she is, the greater number of personal touches she will add. The couple will normally dance until the end of a set, which lasts for four or five melodies. Once the set is finished, the woman should thank her partner who, if the experience has been successful and enjoyable, is likely to ask her to dance again. Note that although milonga dress should be smart, women in particular should not go dressed to kill if they are not intending to dance – do so and you are likely to spend the night turning down invitations from bemused-looking men. For the same reason, avoid making eye contact when possible.

La Calesita **Av Rivadavia 1350, Núñez** ☎011/4743-3631. Weather permitting, this popular weekly milonga takes place outdoors at a park on the Costañera Sur under strings of fairy lights. Sat 11pm, class at 9.30pm. Dec–March only.

Club Gricel La Rioja 1180, San Cristóbal ☎011/4957-7157; Urquiza subte. Small, friendly club holding milongas on Fri & Sat 11pm–4am, Sun 9pm–2am.

🏃 **Confitería Ideal Suipacha 384, 1st floor, San Nicolás** ☎011/5265-8069, ⓦ www .confiteriaideal.com. An oasis of elegance just a few blocks from busy Corrientes, the *Ideal* has a stunning salon, which is undoubtedly one of the most traditional and consistently popular places to dance. There is an exhaustive programme of classes and milongas every day, with shows at the weekend; see the website or call for details.

Glorieta at the Barrancas de Belgrano ⓦ www.glorietadebelgrano.com.ar. The Glorieta bandstand at the Barrancas is a perfect location for an alfresco milonga in the summer months. Sat & Sun classes at 4pm followed at 6pm by a milonga attended by up to 200 people.

Niño Bien Centro Región Leonesa, Humberto 1° 1462, Constitución ☎011/4147-8687; San José subte. Popular with both locals and foreign "tango tourists", and with a great atmosphere. Thurs from 10.30pm, with a class at 9pm.

Nuevo Salón La Argentina Bartolomé Mitre 1759, San Nicolás ☎011/4371-6767. Wonderful 1930s locale with classes most afternoons. Sometimes over 300 dancers are squeezed into a small floor, so deft steps are required. Mon & Tues 3–10pm, Fri & Sat 10pm–5am.

🏃 **Parakultural Salon Canning, Scalabrini Ortiz 1331, Palermo** ☎011/4832-6753, ⓦ www .parakultural.com.ar. Young, bohemian organization that puts on the coolest milongas and shows in town, moving to the Konex cultural centre on Wednesdays (see p.186). Classes also offered; see website for schedule.

🏃 **La Viruta Armenia 1366, Palermo** ☎011/4779-0030, ⓦ www.lavirutatango .com. Huge, long-running institution with regular overnight milongas that mix tango with folklore, salsa and even rock'n'roll. Fri & Sat midnight–6am, Sun 12.30pm–3am; classes also available.

Learning tango

Watching real tango danced often makes people long to do it themselves. Unfortunately, the dance is much harder than most people anticipate. If you can't bear the thought of attending a milonga without dancing, the answer is to take some **classes** – you should reckon on taking about six to be able to hold your own on the dancefloor.

There are innumerable places in Buenos Aires offering dance classes, including cultural centres, bars and *confiterías*, where they are often followed by a milonga (see p.193). These are often the best options for beginners. For the impatient or shy there are private teachers, who advertise in *El Tangauta*, and there are also schools dedicated to teaching tango, but they tend to be aimed at more advanced dancers. Note that if you're going to take classes, it's important to have a pair of **shoes** with a sole that allows you to swivel (rubber soles are useless). Women don't need to wear heels, but it is important to have shoes that support the instep. Lastly, if you're prepared to put the time in, you can also take lessons in the various musical instruments that appear in tango orchestras.

Escuela Argentina de Tango Centro Cultural Borges, Galerías Pacífico, Viamonte & San Martín, San Nicolás ☎011/4312-4990, ⓦ www .eatango.org. Comprehensive timetable of classes on all aspects of tango dance at various levels.

Escuela de Música y Artes TEMA Av Boedo 883, Boedo ☎011/4932-4237, ⓦ www.escuelatema .com.ar. For learning bandoneón and other instruments.

Gay and lesbian Buenos Aires

uenos Aires is now well established as the major urban **gay destination** in Latin America, mainly owing to an increasing open-mindedness on the part of the city's inhabitants and authorities. In 2002 it was the first place in the region to legalize gay civil unions; the national government pushed through legislation allowing same-sex marriage with full adoption rights in July 2010. Gay-bashing is thankfully a very rare occurrence – in fact most Porteños seem to apply the motto "live and let live". In September 2010, the Pink Point information centre opened its doors at Lavalle 669 (Mon–Sat 9am–8pm; ⓦ www.pinkpointbuenosaires.com) – it offers advice and supplies information on everything from gay tours to accommodation and shopping. However, for some unknown reason, there are fewer bars and nightclubs for gays and lesbians than in the 1990s, and the scene can be a disappointment for those looking for specifically gay and lesbian venues – the latter, in particular. For a lot of gay and lesbian travellers, though, this very lack of any "ghetto" is precisely the attraction of Buenos Aires; as in most Latin American cities, exclusively gay places are not the best places for gay patrons to go out, suggesting greater mainstreaming than in many other parts of the world.

As far as **publications** are concerned, news of events and venues can be gleaned from *La Otra Guía*, the main pink publication (ⓦ www.nexo.org), along with the monthly *Queer* newspaper. *Gay Buenos Aires* (ⓦ www.gay-ba.com) is a suitably pink booklet in English and Spanish, available at most bookshops; it carries comprehensive details of meeting points, clubs, restaurants, hotels, travel agencies, gay-friendly shops and so forth. The best **website** for the latest info is ⓦ www.gay-ba.com, which is especially good for nightlife listings. Most venues will also hand out a free gay city **map**, *BSASGay* (ⓦ www.mapabsasgay.com.ar), with all the popular spots plotted. **Lesbians** are less well catered for, but information about events and venues for gay women can be found online at ⓦ www.lafulana.org.ar. The city's **gay pride march** ("Marcha de Orgullo Gay"; see p.223) is held every November on a Saturday afternoon; after lots of political speechifying in the Plaza de Mayo, it trundles along Avenida de Mayo to Congreso.

Gay **venues** are spread throughout the city. One of the long-established focal points of the gay community in Buenos Aires is the nondescript (and not specifically gay) *Confitería El Olmo*, at the corner of avenidas Pueyrredón and Santa Fe, where people come on Fridays and Saturday evenings to pick up free entrance flyers, discount vouchers and the word on where to go. **Palermo** has increasingly become a gay hub, especially Palermo Hollywood, while some people see **San Telmo** as a potential Porteño "Village" (as in New York City), or the answer to Madrid's Chueca, but so far that has not been realized despite the existence of *Pride Café* (see p.162), a ground breaking gay-friendly café modelled on counterparts in San Francisco. Some of Buenos Aires' **parks and plazas** can be very cruisy – the Reserva Ecológica, Parque Las Heras and Jardín Botánico are all popular with gay men – making them likelier places to meet people than bars or nightclubs. While there are a few gay **restaurants**, fashionable eateries with a "mixed" crowd (such as *Empire Thai* or *Piola Pizzería*, see p.171) are much more interesting, especially if you want to eat well. **Tango** fans should head to *La Marshall*, Maipú 444 and Avenida Corrientes, where a gay milonga takes place every Saturday at 11.30pm, preceded by classes at 10pm, while there is also an annual gay tango festival (Ⓦwww.festivaltango queer.com.ar): usually held in late November it takes places at various venues around the city and includes classes and concerts. One more unusual option is provided by the occasional **gay cruise** parties on board a boat on the Río de la Plata – consult Ⓦwww.rainbowonboard.com for details and to sign up.

As far as **accommodation** is concerned, most places are tolerant or even outwardly gay-friendly (in any case discrimination is illegal) and are increasingly advertising themselves as such. The local media made a lot of fuss about the 2007 opening of Latin America's first specifically gay hotel – the super-sleek *Axel* (see p.151) – which we have reviewed in the main Accommodation chapter because it labels itself "heterofriendly". It has been followed by several more gay-specific lodgings, which can be found on the various gay and lesbian websites. Apartments are an excellent option and can be rented through the highly reliable website Ⓦwww.ba4uapartments.com.ar, which also contains useful information for gay and lesbian tourists.

Bars

Bach Bar Cabrera 4390, Palermo. Fairly mixed bar, with shows on Fri and Sat and karaoke on Sun, all starting very late (hardly ever before midnight), even though it is a pre-disco venue. Closed Mon.

Casa Brandon Luis María Drago 236, Villa Crespo ☏011/4858-0610, Ⓦwww.brandongayday.com. **ar.** Bar, restaurant and cultural centre rolled into one – best known for its regular "Tango Queer" evenings, with classes and single-sex milongas.

Flux Marcelo T. de Alvear 980, Retiro. Opens around 7pm every day, except Sun, and has a happy hour lasting until around 10pm – great cocktails and a cool ambience.

Inside Restobar Bartolomé Mitre 1571, San Nicolás. Located in the beautiful Pasaje de la Piedad, *Inside Restobar* functions as a restaurant, wine bar and show hall, hosting strippers, singers and dancers. Shows start around midnight.

Search Azcuénaga 1007, Recoleta. Owned by the same folk as *KM Zero* (see below), *Search* also puts on strip and drag shows – every night of the week.

Sitges Av Córdoba 4119 at Pringles, Palermo. Large, bright trendy bar, frequented by a mixed but invariably young crowd. Bursting at the seams from 11pm Wed–Sun, with late-night weekend shows.

Clubs

Alsina Buenos Aires Alsina 934, Monserrat. This palatial venue – the same converted industrial building that hosts the mixed "Big One" on Sat (see p.183) – stages gay nights on Fri and sometimes on Sun, attracting some of the most beautiful people in the city. Starting around midnight, all ages and tastes come to dance to varied music, everything from house to 1970s disco. The night occasionally switches to *Rheo* at

Paseo de la Infanta, Palermo – check the website ⓦ www.rheo.com.ar.

Amerika Gascón 1040, Almagro. One of the biggest and best-known gay discos, with three dancefloors playing house and Latin music Fri–Sun.

Angel's Viamonte 2168, Recoleta. Extremely popular club, frequented by drag queens Thurs–Sat.

Bahrein Lavalle 345, San Nicolás ⓦ www .bahreinba.com. This über-cool club in a beautifully renovated townhouse dripping with antique furnishings has gradually become increasingly gay since it opened a few years back. Opens well after midnight on Wed, Fri & Sat but around 10pm on Sun.

Contramano Rodríguez Peña 1082, Recoleta. One of the city's longest-running discos. The relatively early opening time on Sun (8pm) brings in an older crowd. Open Fri–Sun.

Human Club Av Costanera Norte & Av Sarmiento, Palermo. In 2010, at least, this was considered to be *the* gay club: two dance floors, one for trance and the other more pop. Keeps going until dawn. Open Sat.

KM Zero Av Santa Fe 2516, Palermo. Late-night weekend shows, including strippers and other raucous fun, but also other events during the week – check the gay websites for details. Daily from 11pm.

Sub Club Av Córdoba 543, Retiro ⓦ www .thesub.com.ar. Club with gay nights on Sat, on two floors (one for house and techno, the other for hip-hop, funk and drum'n'bass). You must first visit the website and subscribe to enter.

⑰

Shopping

S hopping in Buenos Aires is a pleasure unmatched elsewhere in South America. In general, designs are original and items mostly of high quality – although more "Western" than those you come across in neighbouring countries. You'll have no trouble finding interesting spots to give your wallet a workout, with the added bonus that many of these places are attractions in their own right, including Calle Florida's lovely covered arcades or **galerías**; shopping **malls** housed in converted turn-of-the-century marketplaces; lively **fairs** and markets; and independent designer **boutiques**. If you're on a budget, or just prefer less expensive gear without the designer label, head to Once (see p.139). For usual opening hours, see p.38.

Wherever you shop, you'll be spoilt for choice in terms of goods. Inventive fashion designers (*modistos*) make Buenos Aires a great place to expand your **wardrobe**, while interesting goods for the home can be found in the shape of both rural-style **crafts** and more modern designer items and **artwork**; traditionalists will want to spend time browsing the rows of **antique** shops. Certainly, no shopping trip in the city would be complete without a visit to its beautiful **bookshops**, or without the purchase of at least one tango **CD**. If you're looking for gifts for those at home, Buenos Aires' **comestibles** make excellent choices – few would turn up their noses at a bottle of quality Argentine wine or a jar of *dulce de leche*. And should you run out of space for all your purchases, the world-class **leatherware** for sale means you can even find a fine new bag in which to carry them home.

When it comes to **paying**, you'll have to use pesos in markets and smaller shops, and, even at the upper end, some shops do not accept plastic. If they do accept credit cards, they will often require you to confirm your identity with a passport, driving licence etc. A few establishments will take dollars, but this practice is not particularly widespread.

For visitors from the northern hemisphere, the seasonal difference really comes into its own at **sales** (*liquidación*) time – you get a summer sale in Buenos Aires just as the weather's warming up in the north and vice versa – although you never really see the savage discounting common in some other countries. You can get better bargains by claiming back **tax** on certain domestic goods as you leave the country – look out for the "Tax Free Shopping" signs, usually in luxury-goods shops, and ask for the relevant document when you spend the minimum amount (currently $70). The claims procedure is rather complicated, but you can get back cash for around fifteen percent of what you paid – at the airport, make sure you have the document given to you in the shop, the receipts and, before check-in, the goods themselves.

Shopping malls

Over the past decade or two, **shopping malls** (called *shoppings* in Buenos Aires) have partly superseded small shops and street markets, but those in Buenos Aires are among the most tastefully appointed in the world. Several of the malls, like Abasto and the Galerías Pacífico, are housed in revamped buildings of historical and architectural interest that qualify as sights of their own accord. On a practical level, the malls are air-conditioned and some of the only places in Buenos Aires to find public toilets.

Abasto Av Corrientes 3200, Balvanera. This grand building, dating from the 1880s, was once the city food market; now it's the daddy of all the central malls. As well as a ten-screen cinema, it has hundreds of designer and cheaper shops, an enormous food hall, an amusement arcade and the Museo de los Niños (see p.140).

Alto Palermo Av Santa Fe 3253, Palermo. Particularly strong on women's clothing stores, with most of the major Argentine chains and some international ones represented.

Bond Street Av Santa Fe 1670, Recoleta. The alternative mall, full of local teenagers skulking around skate stores and tattoo parlours; there are also a few surf shops in the surrounding streets. A good place to pick up flyers for live music and clubs.

Buenos Aires Design Center Plaza Intendente Alvear, Recoleta. Right next to the Centro Cultural de Recoleta, this mall is dedicated to shops selling the latest designs, mostly for the home, from Argentina and elsewhere.

Galerías Pacífico Florida 750, San Nicolás. Fashion boutiques and bookshops in a beautiful building decorated with murals by leading Argentine artists, plus the Centro Cultural Borges at the top and a food court, children's play area and baby-changing room in the basement. The most central mall (see p.66).

Paseo Alcorta Figueroa Alcorta & Salguero, Palermo. A huge shopping complex, with several cinemas and the large Carrefour supermarket.

Patio Bullrich Libertador 750, Retiro. Once a horse market (see p.105), this is one of the most exclusive malls, and a good place to find designer clothes and leather.

Antiques

Antiques (*antigüedades*) can be found in shops throughout Buenos Aires, but by far the biggest concentration is in **San Telmo**, particularly along Defensa between no. 800 and no. 1200. The barrio's Sunday antiques market in Plaza Dorrego makes for fascinating browsing, but is so crowded that any substantial buying can be difficult. Keep an eye out for old gaucho paraphernalia – few things look nicer on a mantle than a silver *mate*. Gilt-framed mirrors and altarpieces are also highly collectable, but won't be easy to transport. Antique clothing and jewellery will be easier to get home, and there are loads of dusty little shops dotted around the city for those whose tastes run that way.

Abraxas Defensa 1092, San Telmo. Lots of antique gems and some lovely silverwork.

Amir Cosas Viejas Defensa 961, San Telmo. Specializes in fascinating old brass scientific instruments.

Capítulo I Ayacucho 1206, Recoleta. Along with its other branch in the traditional gaucho town of San Antonio de Areco (see p.239), this second hand store sells Argentine books and pampas paraphernalia, such as original ponchos, saddlery, pictures and *boleadoras* (lassos).

Galería Cecil Defensa 839, San Telmo. This shopping arcade in a converted house hosts an antiques market during the week, worth browsing if you can't make it to the Sunday version in Plaza Dorrego or want to shop with fewer crowds.

Gil Antigüedades Humberto 1412, San Telmo. Gil Antigüedades specializes in luxury goods from the twentieth century. Make like a turn-of-the-century diva with silk parasols, leather suitcases, fans and lots of vintage clothes.

Guevara Gallery Defensa 982, San Telmo. With lots of Art Deco and Art Nouveau items, this large shop has lamps, glasswork, ceramics and furniture.

Art galleries

Contemporary **art**, including some intriguing landscapes and "gaucho art", is on display and for sale at scores of **commercial galleries** – *galerías de arte* – across the city. Elegant places targeting the city's affluent line Retiro's streets, particularly around **Plaza San Martín** and nearby Suipacha and Arenales, while more modern spaces are scattered across Recoleta, including several along **Avenida Alvear**. During May or early June, the **art fair** ARTE BA (see p.221) showcases work from Buenos Aires' most important galleries.

Aldo de Sousa Arroyo 858, Retiro ☎011/4393-0803, 🌐www.aldodesousa.com.ar. One of the leading galleries on a street that bristles with them, it rightly prides itself on picking Argentina's future artistic giants, such as Karin Godnic and Cecilia Picca.

Braga Menéndez Humboldt 1574, Palermo ☎011/4775-5577, 🌐www.galeriabm.com. Well-established artists like Marta Minujín have displayed their work at this Hollywood gallery, but it is better known for intro-ducing those fresh out of art school – a purchase here might be an investment in future masters.

Dabbah Torrejón El Salvador 5176, Palermo ☎011/4832-2332, 🌐www.dabbahtorrejon.com .ar. This gallery acts as a showcase for a select group of Argentine artists whose works go for a range of prices – an excellent place to find out who is at the cutting edge.

Daniel Abate Pasaje Bollini (between French and Peña), Recoleta ☎011/4804-8247, 🌐www .danielabategaleria.com.ar. One of the big names of the Porteño gallery world, Abate also stages exhibits at the Centro Cultural de Recoleta and elsewhere. This is a good place to check out up-and-coming painters and sculptors.

Daniel Maman Fine Arts Av del Libertador 2475, Palermo ☎011/4804-9700, 🌐www .danielmaman.com. This swish art space has a collection of works by the stars of Rioplatense art, all for sale, and stages exhibits by a more accessible set of contemporary artists.

Decastelli Chile 354, San Telmo ☎011/4307-7822, 🌐www.decastelli.com.ar. An unusual gallery mainly displaying and selling the works of its eponymous artist, whose playful and colourful toy sculptures – most in the shape of cartoon-like animals – are made of corrugated cardboard.

Elsi del Río Arévalo 1748, Palermo ☎011/4899-0171, 🌐www.elsidelrio.com.ar. Fernando Entin, this art gallery's director, has a sense of fun and high-camp,

something frequently reflected in the artwork – it often has an erotic or romantic theme, as in works by Silvina Der-Meguer ditchian and Celina Saubidet.

Galería Arroyo Arroyo 830, Retiro ☎011/4325-0947, 🌐www.galarroyo.com. Famed for its top-notch auctions (*subastas*), this is the place to pick up a Berni, a Valentín Thibon de Libian or a Quinquela Martín if you have US$100,000 or so to spare. If that sounds excessive, you can also purchase lesser-known artists' works for less than a tenth of that sum.

Galería del Viejo Hotel Balcarce 1053, San Telmo ☎011/4352-0086. Set in an 1890s building that was once a hotel, this *galería* has an attractive plant-lined courtyard, an art gallery and workshop for local painters and sculptors.

Rubbers Av Alvear 1595, Recoleta ☎011/4816-1864, 🌐www.rubbers.com.ar. This chic gallery on the city's smartest avenue started in the 1950s with a show dedicated to Xul Solar and has never looked back. A great place to come and browse, but if you have to ask the price you can't afford it.

Ruth Benzacar Gallery Florida 1000, Retiro ☎011/4313-8480, 🌐www.ruthbenzacar.com. Rather unexpectedly reached through an underground entrance at the end of Florida, this prestigious commercial gallery showcases both international and Argentine artists.

Sara García Uriburu Uruguay 1223, Recoleta ☎011/4813-0148, 🌐www.saragarciauriburu .com.ar. The building and, above all, the cheerful patio, are worth the visit alone. This bijou art gallery always has interesting, slightly offbeat exhibitions, and the welcome is always friendly.

VVV Gallery Aguirre 1153, 2nd floor, Villa Crespo 🌐www.vvvgallery.com. Highly promising young gallery promoting up-and-coming artists from Argentina and abroad, many of whom have their studios in the same building.

Wussmann Venezuela 570, San Telmo; Rodríguez Peña 1399, Recoleta

℡011/4343-4707 & 4811-2444, Ⓦwww
.wussmann.com. Excellent gallery focusing
on young artists and specializing in
photography as well as painting. The San
Telmo branch also includes a marvellous
art bookshop.

Books

Buenos Aires prides itself on being a literary city, and its dozens of **bookshops**
(*librerías*) are a real treat. Books – mostly in Spanish, though English and other
languages are not impossible to find – are sold at an astonishingly extensive range
of shops and markets throughout the city; new editions can be quite expensive,
but the trade in second-hand texts is flourishing. Antique books make for impressive souvenirs, and you can find some good ones in English about various aspects
of Argentina. **Avenida Corrientes** is the traditional place to head, and there are
also a number of fantastic antiquarian shops on **Avenida de Mayo** and in
Monserrat. Modern bookshops, with good foreign-language and glossy souvenir
book sections, can be found around **Florida**, **Córdoba** and **Santa Fe**. If you're in
town during April, don't miss Buenos Aires' hugely popular **Feria del Libro** (see
p.221), while Parque Rivadavia in Caballito hosts a second-hand book market that
is open daily but busiest on a Sunday.

Ateneo Grand Splendid Santa Fe 1860, Recoleta.
Easily the largest bookshop in Latin America,
the Ateneo is also a strong contender for the
most beautiful one in the world – it's housed
in a former cinema, built in 1919 and inspired
by the Opéra Garnier in Paris. A branch of
the Ateneo/Yenny chain, it is particularly
strong on art and architecture books, with an
array of collectable albums of photos of
Buenos Aires and the rest of the country.
There is a small café on the ground floor,
from where you can admire the sumptuousness of it all and browse before you buy.

**Kel Ediciones Marcelo T. de Alvear 1369,
Recoleta.** This all-English bookshop has
mostly fairly mainstream stock but it's big
enough for anyone to find that perfect
accompaniment to a long-distance bus
journey; they also stock Rough Guides.

Liberarte Av Corrientes 1555, San Nicolás. An
emporium of the assorted interests of the

Porteño left-wing intelligentsia. Loads of
offbeat periodicals.

Librería de Ávila Alsina 500, Monserrat.
Sprawling antique bookshop, well worth a
visit as much for the ambience as the
books, which include a great selection on
Argentina.

**Librería Hernández Av Corrientes 1436, San
Nicolás.** The helpful and well-informed staff
at this Corrientes institution make it a good
place to dip your toe into Argentine fiction.

Librería Platero Talcahuano 485, San Nicolás.
Decent selection of non-fiction about
Argentina and a big second-hand section.

**Walrus Books Estados Unidos 617,
San Telmo.** Excellent English-language
new and second-hand bookshop, with
the emphasis on quality literature and
non-fiction from around the world.
Closed Mon, restricted opening hours
during the summer.

Clothing and accessories

You can find everything from smart to jazzy to outrageous in Buenos Aires'
clothing shops (*boutiques* or *negocios de ropa*). Though the tendency is to echo
European fashion, albeit a season behind, you can also find shops offering some fairly
unique off-the-peg designs, both in the malls (see p.199 for a list) and the streets,
where they rub shoulders with shops selling more classic attire. We've included here
the most noteworthy Argentine shops and labels; you'll also see plenty of familiar
international names – Tommy Hilfiger, Adidas, Ralph Lauren and the like – but
these tend to be both expensive and not the latest styles. Argentine-made clothing is
cheaper, though it can be shoddier than you might expect for the increasingly high

Sizing you up

You don't need to be in Buenos Aires long to work out that Porteñas take staying slim very seriously indeed. While observable as a social phenomenon (see Contexts, p.260), female visitors will also understand this from a practical point of view as they peruse the rails in clothing shops and find they have been bumped up a **size** or two. Women who are a "medium" in Europe or the US will find themselves squeezing into "large" (either *grande* or the English term is used) here, and even sometimes an "extra large", while only the tiniest frame will fit a "small". Indeed, if you are more than about a UK 12/US 10 you will unfortunately struggle to find clothes to fit at all, at least in the fashionable shops. Tall or broad men will find the same problem. The sizing itself varies wildly from shop to shop and the only way to find the correct fit is to try it on. If you know your US or European size most sellers should be able to point you more or less in the right direction – even if it's out the door.

prices demanded. Fortunately, many labels have **outlet** stores selling last season's fashions at knock-down prices; we have listed some below, and you will find dozens more in the so-called "Palermo Queens" area (actually in neighbouring Villa Crespo), around the Aguirre and Gurruchaga cross streets.

An offshoot of the country's thriving beef industry is that the cattle of the Pampas also offer up their hides, which are turned into top-class **leather** shoes, jackets, bags, belts and wallets. The classy leatherware shops (called *talabarterías*) in the city centre will not disappoint when it comes to quality, but, again, prices are not necessarily low – try and track down factory outlets in further flung barrios.

Akiabara Abasto; Alto Palermo; Galerías Pacífico; Paseo Alcorta; Patio Bullrich; outlet Gurruchaga 772, Villa Crespo; ⓦwww.akiabara .com. Chic but wearable everyday casual clothes for women, in a somewhat similar vein to Spanish labels such as Zara and Mango; fans of Akiabara will also like fellow Argentine labels Uma and Ossira (found in the same malls).

Bokura Jeans El Salvador 4677, Palermo. Shop selling casual men's gear, including jeans, shirts and T-shirts. The look is colourful, with a nod to the Orient.

Bolivia Nicaragua & Thames, Palermo; Gurruchaga 1581, Palermo. Hip men's clothes, perfect for all-night clubbing sessions. Floral shirts, grungy tops, daft T-shirts and other clothes for guys who prefer not to take things too seriously.

Cardón Sante Fe 1399, Recoleta; Abasto; Alto Palermo; Galerías Pacífico; Paseo Alcorta; outlet Honduras 4755, Palermo; ⓦwww.cardon .com.ar. With the slogan "*cosas nuestras*" ("our things"), Cardón, beloved of the Argentine land-owning classes, sells smart khaki and white clothing and *carpincho* (capybara) leather shoes, jackets and belts. Perfect for polo matches or estancia stays – just don't get too muddy.

Carla Di Sí Gorriti 4660, Palermo. Nothing but the best for your eyesight – RayBan, Parada and Dolce & Gabbana frames make the nicest face furniture in town. Excellent service.

El Cid Gurruchaga 1732, Palermo; outlet Aráoz 1215, Palermo; ⓦwww.el-cid.com.ar. Wonderful smart-casual menswear, with a good selection of silk ties, linen suits, day-wear shirts and jeans, plus leather belts and bags.

Etiqueta Negra Patio Bullrich; Galerías Pacífico; Paseo Alcorta; outlet Gurruchaga 770, Villa Crespo. Sumptuous shops full of antique furniture and vintage automobiles, though these are not for sale – the equally sumptuous and expensive leather jackets, bags, shirts, suits and woollens designed by top couturier Federico Álvarez Castillo and Juan Cahen d'Anvers, however, are.

Falabella Florida 202, San Nicolás; ⓦwww .falabella.com.ar. Argentina's branch of a popular Chilean department store, selling cheap and cheerful men's and women's clothes, as well as electronic goods, over four floors. A second branch at Florida 343 has household appliances but also keenly priced children's clothing.

Giesso Santa Fe 1557, Recoleta; Florida 977, Retiro; Alto Palermo; Paseo Alcorta; @ www.giesso .com.ar. Originally opened by a Genoese milliner, Giesso has been providing classic European tailoring for the city's gents since the 1880s. Now providing smart women's wear, too, though it is still best known for its range of men's shirts, ties and suits.

Hermanos Estebecorena El Salvador 5960, Palermo. Top-quality cotton T-shirts, anoraks, trousers and shirts for men, for all weather, plus specially designed boxer shorts by brothers Javier and Alejo.

Isabel La Católica Gurruchaga 1509, Palermo; Alto Palermo. Funky urban and skate wear for men and women by international and local labels like Diesel, Vans, TresDe and Y Tu Quique?.

Jazmin Chebar El Salvador 4702, Palermo; Patio Bullrich; Paseo Alcorta; @ www.jazminchebar .com.ar. One of the country's best-known designers, creating clothes for women that are simultaneously voguish yet soft and feminine. Expensive, but top quality.

Kapush Gurruchaga 1867, Palermo. "Romantic boutique" selling attractive tops and dresses for women and girls in a pre-Raphaelite mood.

Kosiuko Santa Fe 1779, Recoleta, plus all the malls; outlet Córdoba 4299, Palermo; @ www .kosiuko.com.ar. Very cool national chain where affluent young Argentines go to get gear for the weekend's clubbing or hanging out. Lots of individual items made with a real flair – you're bound to find something irresistible. Men's, women's and children's ranges.

La Martina Paraguay 661, Retiro; Alto Palermo; Galerías Pacífico; outlet Aguirre 957, Villa Crespo; @ www.lamartina.com. Well-established Argentine polo brand that sponsors the national teams. As well as polo equipment (see p.206), shops carry the kind of clothes that people wear to matches (think pastel blouses and lozenge-patterned sweaters). The floor spaces are laid out beautifully, with the polo boots and piles of cashmere set off by dark wood fittings, leather sofas and stained-glass windows.

Rapsodia Alto Palermo; Galerías Pacífico; Paseo Alcorta; Patio Bullrich; @ www.rapsodia.com.ar. Although it markets a variety of clothes, many with a bohemian twist, Rapsodia is most famous for its range of jeans, which feature a unique wing design on the back pocket and are cut in ways that seem to flatter all shapes and sizes.

Seco Armenia 1646, Palermo. "Seco" means dry, and this small Palermo Viejo shop aims to shield you from the autumn rains, with a highly attractive selection of raincoats, wellington boots, hats and umbrellas.

Topper Santa Fe 1465, Recoleta; outlet Córdoba 4694, Palermo; also sold in general sportswear stores. Argentine sportswear brand beloved of *rock nacional* fans and anti-fashionistas who scorn the Porteño upper-class habit of wearing big international names on their trainers. Topper is best known for its white tennis shoes, though it also dabbles in most other sportswear.

Vision Express Florida 713, Retiro and many other branches. Best place to go if you want to have eyeglasses made fast – a good range of frames and reliable manufacture.

Leather goods

Casa López Marcelo T. de Alvear 640, Retiro; Patio Bullrich; Galerías Pacífico; @ www .casalopez.com.ar. Regarded as the city's very best exporter of classic leather goods, it has prices to match.

Centro del Cuero Murillo 500–700, Villa Crespo; Malabia subte. A three-block stretch known as the "Centro del Cuero" (leather centre), this is actually a clustering of around thirty warehouse shops and some boutiques selling leather clothing both wholesale and direct to the public. This is the place to go for a bargain, but prices are mostly unmarked so be prepared to haggle.

Charles Calfun Florida 918, Retiro @ www .charlescalfun.com. Purveyor of leather jackets and bags for half a century, along with the fur coats beloved by Recoleta's socialites.

Fortín Santa Fe 1245, Retiro. High-quality handmade leather goods, principally boots, jackets and bags.

JM Cueros Marcelo T. de Alvear 628, Retiro; Paraguay 616, Retiro; Santa Fe 1240, Retiro; @ www.jmcueros.com. Traditional *talabartería* selling shoes, bags and accessories, some leather and some made from the soft, attractively mottled skin of the capybara. Many items also feature the geometric designs characteristic of the Pampas region.

Peter Kent Av Alvear 1820, Recoleta. Peter Kent's handbags (*carteras*) are a favourite of Argentina's president – and she is not the only stylish woman in town who can't leave home without one.

Prüne Florida 961, Retiro, plus several branches around the city. If you want a great handbag but Peter Kent is above your price range, this the place for you – the umlaut on the "ü" tells you it's utterly fashionable, but the many branches make it less exclusive than it could be. The store also has an interesting shoe range.

Crafts and design

For **handicrafts**, try the city's markets and Sunday fairs (see box above). You can also sometimes find crafts from around Argentina at the *casas de provincia*, the tourist offices that represent each of the country's 23 provinces; these are scattered around the city centre. The best are: Catamarca, Av Córdoba 1080; Chaco, Av Callao 322; Jujuy, Av Santa Fe 967; Misiones, Av Santa Fe 989; Salta, Av Pte Roque S. Peña; and Tucumán, Suipacha 104. At these you'll often come across beautiful, unique ceramics, wooden masks or alpaca-wool items at far better value than the mass-produced alternatives sold in souvenir shops.

Buenos Aires is now producing exciting contemporary interior **design** pieces, too. Fairs are held regularly, notably the **Casa Foa**, an annual two-month interior-design exhibition (see p.222). Year-round, you can find interesting items in shops around Recoleta and Palermo, with the nerve centre being Buenos Aires Design (see p.111).

Arte Étnico Argentino El Salvador 4656, Palermo ⓦ www.arteetnicoargentino.com. Priceless (and mostly pricey) rugs and tapestries from the north, plus rustic furniture, all made from native woods. A fantastic shop – just go and look at the chairs hanging from the main ceiling like wooden bats – in every sense.

El Boyero Florida 953, Retiro. Leather and *campo* (countryside) creations, a miscellaneous mix of wine-bottle holders, horse whips, *mate* gourds and more. Many of Florida's souvenir shops can be on the gaudy side, but this has some more unusual pieces.

Elementos Argentinos Gurruchuga 1881, Palermo. Taking the colourful patterns of northern Argentina for their inspiration, this store creates textiles for the home, including blankets, throws, rugs and cushion covers.

El Gauchito Carabelas 306, San Nicolás. A stone's throw from the Obelisco, this reassuringly long-running store is an authentic vendor of gaucho clothing, artwork, antique and modern crafts for the home, as well as other goods from Argentina's pampas heartlands.

Tienda Diversia Humberto 580, San Telmo ⓦ www.tiendadiversia.com.ar. Various local designers sell their wares through this colourful San Telmo shop – including objects for the home, and gifts and clothing for men, women and children.

Food and drink

You might not be able to take much in the way of Argentine steaks back with you – although the duty-free shop at Ezeiza airport will pack certain cuts into a cooler for the plane – but there are other **foods** that can travel and allow you and your friends a taste of Buenos Aires at home. A box of widely available Havanna *alfajores* – a cookie sandwich filled with *dulce de leche* and coated in meringue or chocolate – makes a good present, as does a jar of *dulce de leche* itself. You can keep Argentine acquaintances and other *mate* drinkers sweet with a bag of their favourite brand of the local brew. If your tastes tend more towards alcoholic drinks, don't worry – there's plenty of Argentine **wine** to go around. Specialist shops (*vinotecas* or *enotecas*) are scattered around the city, and the bigger supermarkets (*supermercados*) also have a good range. Cheap plonk is best avoided – as a rule of thumb, give anything under $15 a miss.

Al Queso, Queso Uruguay 1276, Recoleta. The most central of a chain of shops specializing in Argentine and imported cheese (*queso*), hams and salamis. They'll put together a mean picnic basket, including bread and wine.

La Cava de la Brigada Bolívar1008, San Telmo. Run by a firm that owns one of the city's best *parrillas*, this wine shop has an impressive range of Argentine wines, some of which are priced well into triple figures.

Jumbo Av Int Bullrich 345, Palermo. Supermarket that stocks the city's widest range of food and drink, including a massive wine section, gourmet products and imported goods that are hard to find elsewhere – even peanut butter, on occasion.

Ligier Tte Gral Perón 1621, San Nicolás; Paraná & Corrientes, San Nicolás; Marcelo T. de Alvear & San Martín, Retiro; Callao & Santa Fe, Recoleta; plus several others. Chain of shops selling wines from all the major wineries, plus some smaller bodegas, with bottles ranging from a basic $10 *borgoña* to top of the range *vinos de autor* costing upwards of $400.

Terroir Buschiazzo 3040, Palermo ⓦwww .terroir.com.ar. Unpretentious *vinoteca* catering to Palermo's well-heeled denizens –

they stock wines from all over the country and elsewhere, along with a good selection of cigars and wine accessories.

Tikal Honduras 4890, Palermo; Galería Güemes. Chocolates are not usually that good in Buenos Aires, but this is an exception. They use Latin American and Ghanaian cocoa and all the best ingredients to produce fantastic looking and tasting truffles, liqueur chocolates and just simple bars.

Tonel Privado Suipacha 299, San Nicolás; Galerías Pacífico; Patio Bullrich; Paseo Alcorta ⓣ0810/321-8663. Well-established delicatessen chain that sells a good range of Argentine wine, as well as other drinks and gourmet delicacies. Will deliver Mon–Sat 9am–9pm.

Tutti Pani Guido & Montevideo, Recoleta. Wonderful local bakery with the softest freshly baked loaves (*pan del campo*), plus empanadas and other savoury and sweet nibbles – great for a picnic.

Winery Alem 880, Retiro ⓣ0810/777-9679 ⓦwww.winery.com.ar. As well as an interesting basement restaurant (see p.172), Winery does wine-tastings and sells bottles of some of the country's finest wines. Several branches around the city (see website), mostly without the eating option.

Buenos Aires for delivery

One of the most addictive – if somewhat calorific aspects of life in Buenos Aires is the way that you can get practically anything **delivered** to your hotel room or apartment, including ice cream, bottles of wine and sundry items from local shops, laundry, medicines from pharmacies, boxes of warm empanadas and, of course, pizzas. You can also get your **supermarket shopping** delivered; this latter often comes with a small charge unless the order is over a certain value, but most other delivery services are completely free, though a tip is appreciated. By the way, Argentine Spanish for "delivery" is... *delivery*.

Music

As with books, the best place in Buenos Aires to look for **music** – both recorded and sheet – is the city's cultural hub, **Avenida Corrientes**, between avenidas 9 de Julio and Callao. The shops (called *negocios de música* or *disquerías*) here carry plenty of Argentine music – tango, jazz, classical, folk and rock, among other genres – but also a good selection of music from the rest of Latin America, such as samba and *cumbia*. In addition to the places along Corrientes, you can also find music at shops dotted around the rest of microcentro, at the city's various markets, and at bookshops such as *Ateneo Grand Splendid* (see p.201), which often stock CDs, too.

El Coleccionista Esmeralda 562, San Nicolás ☎011/4322-0359. Small record and instrument shop with a dedicated staff. Their range includes tango, *rock nacional*, salsa, folk and world music.

Miles Honduras 4912, Palermo. Outstanding *disquería* with a varied range of national and international CDs and DVDs featuring *rock nacional*, pop, tango, jazz, punk and classical – and very helpful staff.

Musimundo Florida 267, San Nicolás; and branches throughout the city. Argentina's major record chain, stocking everything from techno to tango. Also carries DVDs and sometimes sells tickets for upcoming concerts.

Notorious J.L. Borges 1685, Palermo; Estados Unidos 488, San Telmo. These two branches of the leading music venue on Av Callao (see p.182) are fertile hunting grounds for the very latest jazz, tango and folk recordings, plus plenty of Latin sounds from Argentina and the rest of the continent. The expert staff are always willing to advise.

Zival's Av Callao 395, San Nicolás ⓦwww.tangostore.com. Small but well-stocked music shop, particularly good for tango. There's a strong selection of CDs and DVDs as well as books and sheet music, and the staff are most knowledgeable on the best tango recordings.

Sporting goods

There are plenty of general shops selling **sporting** clothing (*ropa deportiva*), such as trainers and T-shirts, in the city. These often also sell football tops, though you can find much cheaper replicas in markets and the little shops along the pedestrianized part of Lavalle, in Once (see p.139) and near the various stadiums. If after a few days of Buenos Aires' rich lifestyle, you suddenly find yourself hankering to do more than just take a jog around the parks, but find yourself ill equipped to do so, rest assured that there are plenty of camping and **outdoors** shops in the city. In addition to the outlets listed here, there is a whole row of camping and fishing stores along the 100 to 200 block of Calle Paraná, just off Corrientes.

Cristóbal Colón Rodríguez Peña 1127, Retiro; Gurruchaga & Soria, Palermo; Abasto; Alto Palermo; Paseo Alcorta. Surf and skatewear chain selling clothing for men and women, as well as boards, wetsuits and other paraphernalia. Stocks mostly international labels such as Ripcurl and Quiksilver but also has some local brands.

Deporcamping Santa Fe 4830, Palermo ☎011/4772-0534. Limited but decent-quality range of trekking clothes and boots, tents, mats and sleeping bags; also Maglites and stoves.

Ecrin Santa Fe 2723, Martinez, Zona Norte ☎011/4792-1935. The place for technical climbing and mountaineering gear,

including crampons and ropes, as well as outdoor jackets.

Explorer Lavalle 423, San Nicolás. Central shop stocking good-quality clothing and reasonable boots, along with an impressive range of penknives.

La Martina Paraguay 661, Retiro; Avenida Alvear; Alto Palermo; Galerías Pacífico. The place to go for polo equipment, including saddles, sticks, boots, helmets and protective wear. La Martina also sells clothes (see p.203) and runs its own polo ranch and school in the Pampas (ⓦwww.lamartinapolo.com.ar).

Stock Center Av Corrientes 590, San Nicolás; Alto Palermo, plus others. Comprehensive if rather garishly lit sportswear chain that sells all the big international names for trainers and workout gear, as well as Argentine label Topper (see p.203), and football kit for all the local teams plus the national squad.

Tango shopping

In addition to the music shops listed opposite, there are plenty of places in Buenos Aires specializing in **tango gear** – clothes, books, shoes and instruments – much of which might prove useful if you are looking for something quintessentially Porteño to take back, or something to wear if you plan on hitting a milonga. Many clothes shops for *tangueros* are clustered along the first couple of blocks of Suipacha, San Nicolás.

Almacén de Tangos Generales Don Anselmo Aieta 1067, San Telmo. Tango-related souvenirs, T-shirts, books and CDs pack the shelves of this shop near Plaza Dorrego.

Artesanal Susana Villarroel Anchorena 537, Balvanera. Elegant choice in tango wear, including slinky dresses and sling-back stilettos for the ladies, and felt hats and two-tone spats for the gents.

Bailarín Porteño Suipacha 251, San Nicolás. Everything a tango dancer needs, from head to toe – hats, shirts, jackets, shoes – plus books, CDs, DVDs and even jewellery, with a milonga touch.

Centro Artesanal de Tango Suipacha 256, San Nicolás. Shop selling traditional, high-quality, hand-stitched tango shoes for both sexes. Tango clothing also on offer.

Club de Tango Paraná 123, 5th floor, San Nicolás. Ancient tango recordings and the latest CDs sit side-by-side with a host of

tango memorabilia, publications, sheet music and quite a lot of junk.

Kiosko del Tango Av Corrientes 1512, San Nicolás. You'll find all sorts of books, magazines, sheet music, DVDs and tango souvenirs at this Corrientes landmark, declared part of the city's cultural heritage by the city authorities.

NeoTango Sarmiento 1938, Balvanera ⓦ www .neotangoshoes.com. Beautiful tango and other dance shoes for both men and women in a great range of colours with a modern twist, in a trendy boutique.

Vendoma Sarmiento 1459, San Nicolás ⓦ www .vendoma.com.ar. This venerable shop has been selling musical instruments for nearly a century and specializes in those for tango, particularly the bandoneón.

Victorio Montevideo 224, San Nicolás. One of the best places for investing in a pair of specially designed tango shoes or sandals.

Miscellaneous

There are also plenty of retail opportunities in Buenos Aires for those looking for something special – **silver** from national mines, **cigars**, artistic paper products, soaps, candles and more. **Jewellery** and other objects made from rhodochrosite, a red and pink stone mined only in Argentina (see box, p.208), makes an especially nice gift. Beauty and cosmetic products can be quite expensive, as most ranges are imported. **Bath products** tend to be very simple – fancy items such as bubble bath and shower gel are mostly espoused in favour of basic soap. All these products are generally sold behind the counter in pharmacies (see p.34), though there is the odd specialist.

Adrián Pallarols Marcelo T. de Alvear 462, Retiro. One of the country's most famous silversmiths uses Argentine silver to produce anything from spurs to trophies, jewellery to polo gear, plus tea services and the finishing for yacht interiors.

La Cigarrería Ko' E' Yu Galería Güemes, Florida 165, San Nicolás. Long-running cigar shop,

with the city's best selection. The owner has been advising local cigar aficionados of the best smoke for three generations.

Farmacity Lavalle 919, San Nicolás; Santa Fe 2830, Recoleta, plus many more; ⓦ www .farmacity.com.ar. Buenos Aires' main drug-store chain, selling a good range of bath products, make-up, nappies and similar

Rhodochrosite

Banded rhodochrosite (*rodocrosita* in Spanish) is a semi precious stone unique to Argentina, and its rarity has made it the country's unofficial national stone. Known popularly as the **Rosa del Inca** (Incan Rose), rhodochrosite is reminiscent of Florentine paper, with slightly blurred, marble-like veins of ruby-red and deep salmon pink, layered and rippled with paler shades of rose-pink and white. Thanks to its relative obscurity and softness, its market value is fairly low, and fakes are unheard of. Nonetheless, the stone does vary in quality and, therefore, in price: the redder and more translucent it is, the more it is worth. Such pieces are often sold in luscious blocks, suitable as paperweights or book-ends, or worked into fine jewellery or animal and bird figures. One of the best places in Argentina to purchase rhodochrosite is at the **Feria Plaza Francia** in Recoleta, where it is combined with silver to make some very attractive pieces.

goods. It's one of the few shops of its kind that allows you to browse, rather than selling over the counter.

Marcelo Toledo Humberto 1° 462, San Telmo ⓦwww.marcelotoledo.net. This elegant workshop opposite Plaza Dorrego showcases exquisite silverware by one of the great young silversmiths in the city. Do not expect low prices, but in view of the fabulous quality nothing is priced too excessively.

Papelera Palermo Honduras 4945, Palermo ⓦpapelera.eurofull.com/shop/index.asp. Paper for origami, writing or wrapping, in the form of diaries, albums, files or cardboard boxes and all kinds of stationery are sold at this beautiful shop.

Piedras Argentinas Florida 944, Retiro. This shop specializes in rhodochrosite jewellery and onyx pieces, mined mainly in San Luis, central Argentina. Try also *Rosa de Inca*, opposite at no. 969.

Plata Nativa Galería del Sol, Florida 860, Retiro. Jewellery and other items, including *mates* and gaucho accessories such as stirrups, all in silver and inspired by indigenous and colonial design.

Sabater Hermanos Gurruchaga 1821, Palermo. Choose from a huge variety of shapes, sizes, colours and, above all, perfumes, at this artisan soap-shop – its wares include golf-balls, floating cakes and soap petals to sprinkle in the bath.

Velas de la Ballena Soler 4802, Palermo. In addition to the rainbow range of home-made candles (hence the name, don't worry, they are not made from whales – *ballenas*), this vanguard shop also has soaps, hand creams and incense sticks galore.

Wussmann Venezuela 570, San Telmo. Not just a leading art gallery, Wussmann also produces fabulous paper articles, such as diaries, albums and the like, often bound in beautiful leather.

Sports and outdoor activities

Porteños, like all Argentines, suffer an incurable addiction to **sports**. Emotions are dominated by **football**, especially anything to do with either Boca Juniors or River Plate, but also a host of other major and minor club teams (with a total of 24, Buenos Aires has more professional clubs than any other city in the world), and support for the Argentine national squads, is passionate and vociferous. The country also pulls its weight in many other sports, though, and you will hear spirited debate in bars on topics as diverse as **rugby**, **hockey** and **tennis**, and the equestrian sports of **polo**, **horseracing** and uniquely Argentine **pato**. Horses have played an important role in national culture since early colonial times, and many Porteños still consider it a mark of *criollo* pride to be able to master them from a young age. **Basketball** (*básquetbol*) is extremely popular, too, and many Argentine players have had successful careers playing abroad, especially in the States.

For those interested in taking part themselves, there is also plenty of scope for **participatory activities** in or near the city. Within Buenos Aires proper you can jog or play tennis, and there's no shortage of gyms, while a day trip out to the Paraná Delta affords opportunities for watersports such as canoeing and wakeboarding (p.238). Go a bit further out and you can try galloping across the Pampas on horseback, or even have a go at playing polo (p.215).

Tickets for matches of all kinds are very affordable and generally easy to come by – in most cases you simply turn up at the venue. Some of the bigger games – mainly football matches – do sell out in advance, but you can usually get tickets for these by enquiring at the venue a few days beforehand; try also Ticketek (☏011/5237-7200, ⓦwww.ticketek.com.ar).

Football

Fútbol (football, or soccer) is, without a doubt, Buenos Aires' major sport, to the point of obsession. The top-flight **domestic league** includes teams from around Argentina, and is split into two main divisions, **Primera A** (the top division) and **Primera B** (the second). Primera A incorporates many teams from Buenos Aires, usually including the "big five": Boca Juniors, River Plate, San Lorenzo, Independiente and Racing Club. The year is split into two **seasons**, which allows for two champions and two sets of celebrations. The first season (*apertura* or "opening") runs from August to December while the second (*clausura* or "closure") goes from February to June; fixtures are mostly played on **Sunday** afternoons but there are midweek games too. In addition, there are two South American **club championships**, the Copa Toyota Libertadores and Copa Nissan Sudamérica, both dominated by teams from Argentina, as well as Brazil and Colombia, with a leg played in each country, usually midweek. If you're lucky, you may even get the chance to see the **national side** (*la selección*) strutting their stuff in a friendly or World Cup qualifier; they play at all the city's major stadiums.

Football in Buenos Aires is enthralling to watch – usually breathless, end-to-end stuff (goalless draws and defensive play are rare and loudly whistled). Derbies between any of the big five are referred to as **clásicos**, while those between Boca and River are denominated **superclásicos** and constitute one of the world's greatest sporting spectacles. Going for solo glory – frowned on in many other countries – is celebrated here: nimble dribbling and clever **goals** (called *golazos*, or, if you're a commentator, "*gooooooooolazos*") can be seen even at the lower levels. The tackling tends to be hard and dirty and the dives dramatic – but most people here consider it all part of the game. You can expect as many red cards as goals scored.

You can usually buy **tickets** at the venues listed below on match day, although the *clásico* derbies and twice-yearly top-of-the-table clashes between Boca and River (*superclásicos*) often sell out. For these, you can get tickets two days before the game at the stadium (be prepared for a scrum) or (more comfortably) from Ticketek (see above for details). **Prices** vary according to the importance of the match and where you are sitting – they can be anywhere from $20 to $200. Alternatively, for a premium, many tour agencies, hotels and hostels provide a ticket-and-transfer service. The Museo de la Pasión Boquense at Boca's Bombonera (see p.93) also arranges match visits – see its website, Ⓦwww.museoboquense.com.

The history of Argentine football

Football (soccer) was introduced to Buenos Aires by railworkers and other members of the **British** expatriate community in the late nineteenth century, with the preliminary version of the national Argentine league formed as early as 1891, the first such league outside the British Isles. In the early years, most players were from this community, a fact reflected in many club names to this day – it's "River Plate" (shortened to "River"), not Río de la Plata, for example. One of the oldest teams, Quilmes Atlético Club, founded in 1887 by one J.T. Stevenson, was originally called Quilmes Rovers and its first line-up was entirely British, but Perón made them take a more Hispanic name in 1950. In the early twentieth century **Italian** immigrants began to supplant the British, and the skill and popularity of the game rose fast. By 1930, South America had made its influence felt on the international pitch, with the Argentine national squad losing to Uruguay in the final of the first **World Cup**. In 1978, this tournament was held in Argentina – the Monumental (see p.146) was remodelled especially for the event, a cause of some controversy, as this was at the height of the Dirty War. Argentina won the cup that year, and again in 1986, thanks to some handy moves by **Diego Maradona** (see box, p.92). Players with abilities like Maradonas often emerge from the streets of Buenos Aires; their trajectory is usually: leisure club or school team, followed by a league team, then Boca or River and then Europe, where the money is, though some later return to manage in Buenos Aires. The city's teams continue to dominate the **national league** – a couple of teams from La Plata and Rosario are the only others who really get a look in – and the "big five" play their own mini-tournament each summer.

Tickets are always either for the *popular* or *platea*. The *popular* are the standing-only **terraces**, where the hardcore fans sing and swear their way through the match. This is the most colourful part of the stadium, but it's also the area where you're most likely to be pickpocketed, charged by police or faced with the wrath of the equally hardcore away fans (cooped in the *visitantes* section, where tickets are often cheapest, though standing-room only). Unless you're very confident (or downright brave), or with someone who is, you should head to the relative safety of the *platea* **seats**. Don't be surprised if someone's in the exact seat allocated to you – locals pay scant regard to official seating arrangements. Just sit wherever you want in your section – gate staff will direct you to the right area.

On match days, it's advisable to turn up forty minutes or so before the start time in order to avoid the rush, and not to hang around afterwards, when trouble sometimes brews. Dress down, avoid flaunting the colours of either side and take the minimum of valuables.

All football in Argentina is organized by the Argentine football association, the **AFA**. For the season's **fixture list** – including the women's, youth and national teams, in addition to the big clubs – check their website (Ⓦwww.afa.org.ar) or head to Ⓦwww.uol.com.ar/uolfutbol.

Teams and venues

Argentinos Juniors Estadio Diego Armando Maradona, Paternal Ⓦwww.argentinosjuniors.com.ar. The Argentinos stadium, in the small western barrio of Paternal, is named after Diego Maradona, its most famous player (see box, p.92). The team has a reputation for nurturing talent, hence its nickname "El Semillero" (the seed nursery); they were *clausura* champions in 2010. Note that despite the name it is a club team, and nothing to do with the Argentine national squad. Bus #133 from Constitución bus terminal gets you here.

Boca Juniors Estadio Alberto J. Armando, Brandsen 805, Boca Ⓦwww.bocajuniors.com.ar. The city's biggest and best-known team, blue-and-yellow Boca Juniors play at the stadium nicknamed "La Bombonera" (the chocolate box), which even has its own museum (see p.92). Originally an insult used by rival fans, "Los Bosteros" is a nickname Boca supporters now revel in – it means something like the "cow dung shovellers".

Huracán Estadio Tomás Adolfo Ducó, Parque Patricios Ⓦwww.clubahuracan.com.ar. Although it seesaws between Primera A and Primera B, Huracán has a long and fairly illustrious history. Its stadium is called "El Palacio" for its fine Art Deco details. Take bus #46 from Boca.

Independiente Estadio Libertadores de América, Avellaneda Ⓦwww.caindependiente.com. Way out in the working-class Gran Buenos Aires suburb of Avellaneda, Independiente is behind only Boca and River in terms of silverware won. Their big rival is nearby Racing; watching a derby between the two is well worth the journey beyond the city limits. You can take bus #95 from Plaza Italia, Palermo.

Racing Club Estadio Juan Domingo Perón, Avellaneda Ⓦwww.racingclub.com. One of the "big five", along with great rival and fellow Avellaneda-based club Independiente. Racing won the *apertura* championship in 2001, their first and so far only championship win since the 1960s. Also bus #95 from Plaza Italia, Palermo.

River Plate Estadio Monumental, Núñez, Ⓦwww.cariverplate.com.ar. Playing at the Monumental, on the Belgrano–Núñez border (see p.146), River Plate is Boca's great rival. Often referred to as "Los Millonarios" (as one of the richest teams they have seen some of the highest transfer fees in the country), they are known to rivals as "Las Gallinas" ("chickens").

San Lorenzo Estadio Pedro Bidegain, Nueva Pompeya, Ⓦwww.sanlorenzo.com.ar. Although the club headquarters are in Boedo, the original stadium is no longer there and the team now plays in Nueva Pompeya; its local derbies are against Huracán. The club is one of the "big five", though in recent years it has struggled to find its form. Bus #101 from Retiro terminal gets you here.

The barra brava

While most people in Buenos Aires are football fans to some extent, there are those who are truly fanatical; all the major teams have a set of these fully paid-up fans, known as the **barra brava**. You won't be able to miss them in the stadium – wrapped in flags and banging drums, they stand in the section of the terraces with the best view over the pitch. It's not a stretch to say that the *barra brava* are regarded with a certain awe and a little fear: in some respects tantamount to organized-crime outfits, they are often involved in extracurricular heavy duties for the club management. In turn, they have influence on matters such as player transfers, and receive free tickets to matches.

Hockey

Argentine women have recently found triumph in field sports, notably through their **hockey** team, the **Leonas** (Lionesses); they are ranked first in the world (according to the ABN AMRO league table) after beating their rivals, the Dutch, 3-1 in the 2010 World Championships final on their home turf in Rosario. The male team has often been in the world top dozen or so. Tournaments played on home soil include both club competitions and national trials, all of which are followed by an avid public. Argentine hockey has less of a Buenos Aires bias than football, but matches are played at various locales around the city; see the hockey federation website at ⓦ www.cahockey.org.ar for more details, including a list of upcoming fixtures. The main club tournament is the LNH Forbex, which runs from July to December.

Horseracing

One of Buenos Aires' three equestrian sports, **horseracing** attracts its fair share of spectators. The city has two main **hipódromos** (racecourses) where you can watch the country's top thoroughbreds: the evocative **Hipódromo Argentino de Palermo** (ⓦ www.palermo.com.ar; see p.136) and the **Hipódromo de San Isidro** (ⓦ www.hipodromosanisidro.com; see p.230). Races generally take place in the late afternoon and evening on weekdays – you can consult a calendar of race days on the websites. **Tickets** at both places are very cheap – the normal entrance is around $5–10, and women often get in free. The biggest event of the year is the Grand National, the Gran Premio Nacional (see p.223), held in November in Palermo.

Pato

The curious Argentine sport of **pato** – a fundamentally rural activity – can perhaps best be described as a cross between polo and basketball. Originally a **duck** was used instead of a ball (*pato* being Spanish for duck), and the sport basically consisted of two teams of men on horseback doing whatever they could to get the poor bird back to their "goal" (usually their home estancia). Without much in the way of actual rules, the whole affair often descended into violence. Banned repeatedly by the authorities, it finally won respectability in the 1930s when some rules were thrashed out, and modern pato emerged. The duck was replaced by a ball with handles, and the pitch given goal rings at either end. Players obtain the ball from the other side by standing in the stirrups and grabbing it by the handles.

As pato is still not embraced heartily by Porteños, who prefer the sophistication of polo if anything, most matches are played some way out of the city. If you are really curious, the best opportunity to see a match is during the national tournament held each year in November and December at the **Campo Argentino de Pato** in San Miguel, just outside the city limits (take a taxi). For more information, see the national federation's website, Ⓦ www.pato.org.ar. **Tickets** seldom cost more than a few pesos.

Polo

Most of the world's best **polo** ponies and players are from Argentina – the country hasn't lost a world championship since 1949 and the **Campeonato Argentino Abierto de Polo** (Argentine Open), held in Buenos Aires every year, is the biggest

Juan Manuel Fangio – the maestro of Formula One

Porteños love to drive fast – you will soon discover as a pedestrian that powerful engines exert a special fascination here. The world-class Dakar rally, transferred from North Africa for security reasons, now starts and ends in Buenos Aires, and over the years several Argentines have shone in the world of Formula One. Indeed 1953 saw the first ever F1 race held outside Europe, the Argentine Grand Prix, an event held on and off for the following 45 years until the money ran out at the purpose-built Autódromo, located in the southern reaches of the city.

Stars include the likes of José Froilán González (known as the Pampas Bull), who scored Ferrari's first win at the 1951 British Grand Prix, and Carlos "Lole" Reutemann, now a leading Peronist politician, who won several races in the 1970s. The king of them all, however, has to be Fangio: nicknamed "El Chueco" ("Bandy Legs"), but known more reverently as "El Maestro", Argentine **Juan Manuel Fangio** (1911–95) dominated the first decade of Formula One racing. He won five World Championship titles in the 1950s – a record broken only when Michael Schumacher took his sixth title in 2003 – with four different teams (Alfa Romeo, Ferrari, Mercedes-Benz and Maserati). For Argentines, Fangio is one of the greatest sportsmen ever, possibly second only to Diego Maradona.

Fangio began his career in 1934, driving a Ford Model T he rebuilt himself, and a few years later he won the marathon-like **Gran Premio del Norte**: a 10,000-kilometre route that began in Buenos Aires and wound through the Andes to Lima, Peru, and back again, taking nearly two weeks. He went on to win the Argentine National Championship twice in the early 1940s, and then travelled to Europe to race in 1949, sponsored by the Argentine Automobile Club and the Argentine government. He won his first **Grand Prix** the following year. In 1955 Fangio raced with **Mercedes**, driving the famous W196 Monoposto (known as the Silver Arrow). He won his fourth title in 1956 with Ferrari and his fifth in 1957 with Maserati. At the 1958 French Grand Prix he finished fourth, then retired. After the race Fangio stepped out of his car, famously said to his mechanic "It's over!", and never raced in another Grand Prix.

In 2005, four bronze **statues** of Fangio, sculpted by Catalan artist **Joaquim Ros Sabaté**, were erected around the world to commemorate the tenth anniversary of his death, with a fifth destined for Buenos Aires. City authorities, though, failed to agree on a location for the monument. In his heyday, Fangio had based himself in Barrio Norte, driving around the neighbourhood in his racing cars so often it was dubbed the "Fangiódromo". However, one proposed site for the statue, near **La Biela**, the *confitería* where Fangio and his fellow racers regularly hung out, was inexplicably rejected. In the end, the statue ended up at Boulevard Azucena Villaflor in Puerto Madero, a barrio he never frequented – many Porteños were scandalized. The statue is splendid, though – a life-size likeness of the Maestro standing next to his Silver Arrow, appropriately right opposite the Argentine HQ of Mercedes-Benz and its swish showroom.

international club competition. Even if the rules go over your head, the game is exciting and aesthetically pleasing to watch, accompanied by the sound of hooves galloping over impeccably trimmed grass and the thwack of the mallet on the ball. Most national tournaments are played at the **Campo de Polo** in Palermo (Ⓦwww .aapolo.com; see p.136) from March to May and September to December, on Saturdays and Sundays; the Argentine Open takes place in November and December. **Tickets** cost from around $25, rising sharply, depending on where you sit – there's no shade in the cheaper seats, so go prepared (stylish hats are de rigueur). There are a variety of Stalls selling food and drinks. You might even fancy having a go – see below under "Participatory activities".

Rugby

The first **rugby** league in Buenos Aires dates to the 1890s, when it was introduced by the British. Traditionally, it has been considered a somewhat elitist sport, so it is no surprise that the most successful **club teams** are based in the affluent Zona Norte: rivals **Club Atlético de San Isidro** (Ⓦwww.casi.org.ar) and **San Isidro Club** (Ⓦwww.sanisidroclub.com.ar). The main tournament runs from July to October, though there are others during the rest of the year.

However, virtually all the country's best players compete in Europe, so it's worth looking out for any matches involving Argentina's national men's rugby squad, the **Pumas**, currently ranked eighth in the world (according to the IRB) and by far the best in the Americas. At the time of writing, the Pumas had not yet been invited to take part in any major regional tournament, but after an impressive showing at the 2007 World Cup, where they came third, there was talk that they might be admitted to the southern hemisphere Tri Nations, though that still has to materialize; their 2011 result might prove decisive, especially as the hosts, New Zealand, are Tri Nations members. In the meantime, you can catch the burly Pumas at home playing test series or World Cup quali-fiers. These are played at stadiums all over the country; in Buenos Aires they have played at the Monumental (see p.146), but they more frequently appear at the stadium used by football team Vélez Sársfield in the western barrio of Liniers. The website of the **Unión Argentina de Rugby** (Ⓦwww.uar.com.ar) has a list of upcoming fixtures. For international matches, you should be able to get **tickets** through Ticketek (see p.219).

Tennis

Argentina has produced a number of successful **tennis** players in recent years, including Gastón Gaudio, Guillermo Coria, David Nalbandian, Mariano Puerta, Gabriela Sabatini and Paola Suárez, while Juan Martín del Potro won the US Open in 2010, becoming the tallest player ever to win a Grand Slam (he measures 1.98m/6ft 6in). Tennis in the country is regulated by the Argentine tennis association, the **AAT** (Ⓦwww.aat.com.ar). Quality tournaments played in the city include occasional **Davis Cup** matches (various locales; tickets available from Ticketek for around $150 and up); February's **Copa Telmex** (see p.220), held on the clay courts of Buenos Aires Lawn Tennis Club, at Olleros 1510 in Palermo (tickets from Ticketek for $100 and up); and December's **Peugeot Argentina Tennis Cup** (see p.224), also at the Lawn Tennis Club, but slightly cheaper ($80 and up).

Participatory activities

For a city that has so much green space, finding a piece of the great outdoors can sometimes be difficult, and if you're looking for a place to get up and moving, you may be best off heading to a gym (see below). This said, if you're just after a tranquil place for **jogging**, a popular and very pleasant spot is Parque 3 de Febrero in Palermo (see p.131); closer to the centre, you could also try Puerto Madero (see p.72). Note that on weekends, especially, except early in the morning, you'll probably find making progress hard at either place, as they get quite crowded.

Only those with a death wish would **bike** in the microcentro. Nonetheless, there are some good bike tours (see p.41), within the city; which usually take you along quieter thoroughfares, or to the parkland areas where there are increasing numbers of **cycle paths** (*bicisendas* or *ciclovías*) you could try renting the inexpensive bikes sometimes available in the much safer Reserva Costanera Sur (see p.79). There is also an excellent **cycle track** in the Zona Norte, running alongside the river from Estación Libertador on the Tren de la Costa line (see p.227) to San Isidro. You can rent bikes near Estación Barrancas, and there are stalls selling drinks and snacks along the route. **Fishing** can be undertaken along the Costanera Norte (see p.137 for details).

Gyms

Porteños like to look good, and the city has plenty of **gyms** and fitness centres catering for them, many of a high standard. Though you normally pay a monthly membership (from around $300), most places will also let you pay a reasonable fee for a one-off session ($80 or so). Buenos Aires' biggest **chain** is Megatlon (Ⓦwww.megatlon.com), which has branches all over the city – the most central are Reconquista 335, San Nicolás; Arenales 1930, Recoleta; Rodríguez Peña 1062, Recoleta; and Pasco 48, Balvanera.

Polo

Playing **polo** is at least as hard as it looks, but if you're confident on horseback and determined to have a go, some **estancias** outside the city offer lessons as part of their accommodation and activity packages (try the excellent Puesto Viejo near Cañuelas, south of Ezeiza international airport, Ⓦwww .puestoviejopoloclub.com.ar). Alternatively, contact the **Asociación Argentina de Polo** (Ⓣ011/4777-6444, Ⓦwww.aapolo.com), at Arévalo 3065 in Buenos Aires, which can also provide match information. As its name suggests Argentina Polo Day (Ⓦwww.argentinapoloday.com.ar) organizes days out, with lunch, a polo demo and a horse ride thrown in.

⑲

Kids' Buenos Aires

Argentines love **children**, and you will generally find them accommodating and understanding if you come to Buenos Aires as a family. There are few places where children (*niños*) aren't welcome, and indeed it is quite normal for Porteño children to stay out with their parents until late – you may well see families strolling home from a restaurant at 1 or 2am, especially in summer.

Practically speaking, international brands of **nappies** (*pañales*), **wipes** (*pañuelos*) and **baby formula** (*leche en polvo*) are widely available, as are dummies (*chupetines*); **baby food** is sold in the larger supermarkets (see p.205 for a list). Bring with you any children's medication you are likely to need, as working out the local equivalent can be difficult. Discreet breast-feeding in public is fine, and changing facilities can be found in most of the city's shopping malls.

For **accommodation**, a few hotels have a no-children rule; these are fairly few and far between, but check when you reserve. Otherwise, most places to stay have triple rooms or suites with connecting rooms to accommodate families, or will be able to provide a cot (*cuna*) if you have a small child (again, ask when you reserve).

When it comes to **eating** out, the city's Mediterranean-style café culture gives you great flexibility. There aren't many places aimed specifically at families, but only very exclusive restaurants will turn children away or look pained when you arrive. Pizzerias and places serving pasta are always good bets, and quite a few restaurants offer special **children's menus**. A highchair (*mesa para bebe* or *silla alta*) is sometimes, but not always, available.

In terms of **entertainment**, Buenos Aires' sophisticated attractions are perhaps more geared towards adults than children, but with a little lateral thinking you should find plenty in the city to keep youngsters amused. In addition to the suggestions here, keep in mind that during school holiday times (Dec–Feb, Easter and late July to early Aug) there are often extra **events**, sometimes referred to as "colonia de vacaciones" – plays, educational games, workshops and so on – laid on for children at city museums and art galleries; check newspapers and museum websites or ask at tourist kiosks for listings. The second Sunday in August is the **Día del Niño** (national children's day) – this is a mainly family-orientated event when children "rule" the home and receive presents, but there are also shows and other events around the city.

A few amusements are more suitable for children of certain ages rather than others. We've indicated those in the text below, though it's highly unlikely that you'll be turned away if you go with someone older or younger.

Museums and sights

Two **museums** in Buenos Aires are aimed specifically at children: the fun, if rather commercial, reconstruction of a town at the **Museo de los Niños** (ages 3–10; see p.140), in Shopping Abasto – where you'll also find fairground rides, children's cafés with colourful seating and a cinema – and the **Museo Participativo de Ciencias**, a hands-on science museum in the Centro Cultural Recoleta (ages 6–11; see p.111). Of other museums, children of all ages are bound to be awed by the dinosaur skeletons in Caballito's **Museo Argentino de Ciencias Naturales** (see p.141), but its tiny planetarium isn't that exciting – if they're interested in the heavens, take them instead to the larger and more impressive **Planetario Galileo Galilei** (ages 6 and up; see p.132) in Palermo's Parque 3 de Febrero, which has educational shows (in Spanish).

Budding transport buffs may enjoy Puerto Madero's two **museum boats**, both from the early twentieth century – though do warn them these vessels won't be moving. The boats can be a good place to take children interested in history, too, as they're loaded with pictures and other artefacts. If they don't find inspiration there, try going underground at the **Manzana de las Luces** (ages 7 and up; see p.52), where they can wander tunnels and hear tales of smuggling and pirates.

Of the city's many art museums, the best suited for youngsters are probably the modern **MALBA** (see p.125), which sometimes has guided visits and activities for kids, and **Museo Xul Solar** (see p.118), where they can admire the artist's vibrant, inventive and unusual works. The colourful **Caminito** (see p.89), with its painted buildings and papier-mâché murals, might also appeal to the artistically minded.

More traditional children's entertainment is provided by Tigre's **Parque de la Costa** (ages 4 and up; see p.235), which boasts rollercoasters and a pirate ship. Closer to the city centre, there's also a very decent **zoo** (see p.134) that's always a hit with children. Just outside the zoo, you can hire a horse and trap for a ride around Palermo's parks.

Natural attractions

One of Buenos Aires' greatest boons when it comes to young children is the number of **green spaces** it has in which they can run off their energy. Palermo's beautiful **Parque 3 de Febrero** (see p.131), in particular, is a wonderful place to take children, with loads of nooks and crannies to explore and a lake with pedalos to rent.

Nearby, there's a **botanical garden** with some very nice trees and flowers (see p.134) and a **Japanese garden** (see p.133), where children can feed some huge koi carp. More wildlife can be seen at the **Reserva Ecológica** (see p.79) in Puerto Madero, which has a bit of a rustic, untamed feel; you can explore it on a circuit of paths.

Out of the city, don't miss taking them on a boat trip on the lush green **Delta** (see p.238) – they'll probably enjoy the train trip there, too. An overnight stay at an estancia in the **Pampas** (see p.239) will provide the opportunity for some horseriding and the chance to help out with farm tasks.

You could also take them to visit the area's premier wildlife park, **Temaikén** (March–Nov Tues–Sun 10am–6pm; Dec–Feb same days till 7pm; $58, half-price on Tues; Ⓦ www.temaiken.com.ar), located about 50km northwest of the city at Km1 on RP-25, near the town of Escobar. Here you can see native species such as the capybara; the elegant guanaco, one of Argentina's four camelids; the dog-sized Patagonian hare (*mara*); the puma; and the long-nosed tapir. Though not quite their natural environments, the park still offers them more space to breathe than in the city's zoo. On-site attractions include an aquarium, a 360-degree cinema and an above-average playground. Avoid school holidays if at all possible, when it gets very busy. Bus #60, Escobar *ramal* (branch), is an express service that departs from Plaza Italia in Palermo and will take you via the Panamericana direct to Temaikén (frequent departures from 9am; 1hr 30min; $3.40).

Events

Other than the Día del Niño there aren't any major events aimed primarily at children in Buenos Aires, but many of the city's ferias and festivals contain plenty to keep them entertained amid the adult attractions. Among the best options in the city's calendar are April's **toy fair**, which also has circus performers and a mini-cinema, and the weekend **Feria de Mataderos** (see p.143), where you can spend a day watching displays of gaucho horsemanship and folk dancing in the eponymous western barrio. The **Predio La Rural** in Palermo (see p.135) does sometimes have exhibitions on themes such as babies or Christmas, with games and the like that may have appeal, though they are rather commercial and really aimed more at parting parents from their cash.

Sometimes theatres and cultural centres put on **shows** for children, particularly in the holidays, though of course they are in Spanish – check newspapers for listings if you and your brood speak the language. The **Centro Cultural del Sur** (see p.186) puts on regular puppet shows and plays for children. Alternatively, older children might appreciate the chance to go to a **football** match – see p.211 for information on attending – just make sure you get tickets for the seats, not the standing section. Likewise, **polo** (see p.213) may hold some appeal.

Shopping

Sadly, **toys** and **books** in Buenos Aires are often either poor-quality, locally made goods or expensive imports. There are exceptions, though, especially in **Palermo Viejo**, where independent shops sell more interesting selections. You can find some very cool **clothes** for children in Buenos Aires. As well as the stores listed below, you can get great little boho clothes at Recoleta's **Feria Hippy** (see p.112) and mini gaucho-style *bombachas* (trousers), alpaca sweaters and ponchos at the **Feria de Mataderos** (see p.143); these two fairs also have the distinct bonus of being entertaining destinations for your offspring – and you.

Kel Ediciones Marcelo T. de Alvear 1359, Recoleta. The city's best selection of English-language books for children (also stocks books for adults; see p.201).

Kosiuko Santa Fe 1779, Recoleta; Abasto; Alto Palermo; ⓦ www.kosiuko.com.ar. Hipper-than-thou clothes store with a children's range that mirrors the one for adults – the denim jackets and floral T-shirts are particularly nice.

Paula Cahen D'Anvers Abasto; Alto Palermo; Galerías Pacífico; Paseo Alberta. Designer collection of vibrantly coloured – and even black – clothes for everyone from babies to 12-year-olds, with nary a cartoon in sight.

Ufficio Borges 1733, Palermo. Lovely toys and gifts for children, including puppets, tea sets, musical instruments and a whole range of fairies.

Festivals and events

Here always seems to be something, or someone, to celebrate or commemorate in Buenos Aires – religious holidays, civil rights and all manner of revolutions provide the pretext for countless **festivals**, street parades and fun fiestas throughout the year. Porteños are especially crazy about sport, fashion, wine, music (including tango) and art, and many of the city's red-letter days relate to one of these deep-felt passions. We've included here all the city's major festivals, but there are certainly many more **events**, some specific to localities or minority interests, that happen throughout the year. Keep a look out for posters and flyers, check with the tourist kiosks or ask at your accommodation for the latest news. Where possible, we've tried to indicate when in the month an event occurs, but in many cases this changes from year to year – check the festival's website to get the most up-to-date information.

Recoleta's **Salas Nacionales de Cultura y Exposición** (see p.113), and Palermo's **Predio La Rural** (see p.135) and **Centro Costa Salguero**, at Avenida Costanera R. Obligado and J. Salguero (Ⓦwww.ccs.com.ar), are the city's main exhibition spaces; topics of exhibitions, fairs and salons held there range from medicine and art photography to regional tourism and gastronomy (see their websites for details). Obviously, outdoor happenings mostly take place in the warmer, brighter months (Sept–March), but heavy downpours are not infrequent in spring and summer, so don't be surprised if an event is washed out or postponed.

Many of these events are free, so you can just turn up and watch. **Tickets** for specific performance art festivals and sports events are on sale either at the venue or at a central office – check the website, where it exists, or call for information; sometimes you can buy a "season ticket" or tickets for several shows or concerts, or even the whole festival, often at a discount. Individual tickets seldom cost more than $20–50 per person, though some events, especially those attracting international stars, are much costlier. You can also buy tickets at the various centralized **carteleras** (ticket agencies) in the centre, such as Cartelera Baires, Av Corrientes 1382, local 24 (Mon–Thurs 10am–10pm, Fri 10am–11pm, Sat 10am–midnight, Sun 2–10pm; ℡011/4372-5058). Tickets for major events, including rock festivals and sports championships, are available through Ticketek, Viamonte 560 (Mon–Sat 9am–8.30pm; ℡011/5237-7200, Ⓦwww.ticketek.com.ar).

January

Aires Buenos Aires (mid-Jan to mid-Feb; Ⓦwww.airesbuenosaires.gob.ar): This popular government-run festival brings free culture to a number of outdoor venues for the height of summer. Events range from open-air cinema at the Rosedal in Palermo to rock and tango concerts at the Costanera Sur amphitheatre.

Chinese New Year (first full moon between Jan 21 and Feb 19; ⓦ www.mibelgrano.com.ar /barriochino.htm): A dragon parade, street fair and pyrotechnics, focused on the corner of Juramento and Arribeños, liven up Belgrano's Barrio Chino (Chinatown).

February

Copa Telmex (mid-Feb; ⓦ www.copatelmex .com): The world's two dozen top male tennis players – usually including a handful of local lads – compete before enthusiastic crowds on the outdoor clay courts of Palermo's prestigious Buenos Aires Lawn Tennis Club. The top prize is around US$100,000.

Carnival (late Feb): City employees get two days off to prepare for the *corso*, a lively festival held all round the metropolis, with the main parade on Avenida de Mayo. Multi-coloured *murgas* (carnival groups) try to outdo each other's decibel output (drums are big), much water and flour is chucked around and great fun is had by all.

March

South American Music Conference (variable; ⓦ www.samc.net): Not as academic as it sounds – in fact this is one of Latin America's major trance, techno and house festivals – though there are lectures and talks during the daytime. Attended in past years by an impressive list of national and international DJs, such as Nick Warren, Judge Jules, Ritchie Hawtin, Ferry Corsten and Tiesto.
Buenos Aires Moda (early March; ⓦ www .buenosairesmoda.com): Dozens of winter fashion collections presented on colourful catwalks and in exhibitions at the suitably glamorous *Buenos Aires Hilton* or at the Centro Costa Salguero (venues vary) serve as proof that few cities in Latin America take fashion as seriously as BA. A similar event, BAFWeek (ⓦ www.bafweek.com) is held at La Rural (usually) in Aug/Sept to show off the coming spring and summer vogues.

Fiesta de San Patricio (March 17) Not on the scale of celebrations in Dublin or New York, but the local Hibernian and Anglo communities, and all-comers, converge on the pubs in Retiro and San Nicolás and paint the town green in honour of St Patrick. It can get quite rowdy, as locals are often not used to downing more than half a pint of Guinness in one go.
Holy Week (Semana Santa; variable March–April; ⓦ www.buenosaires.gov.ar): During this week leading up to Easter many special events are put on throughout the city, so consult the city website and comb the press. Not as big as in most of Latin America, but important nonetheless.
Theatre and opera season (March–Dec): The arts season starts out with a bang – expect to see big names at the Colón and all other major theatres, on and off Corrientes.

April

Quilmes Rock (variable – in the past it has also taken place in March and in Oct/Nov): A major event on the international rock circuit – it's attended by over 200,000 – whose venue changes, though most recently it has been at the River Plate stadium and at other locales. Past line-ups have included Guns N' Roses, Iron Maiden, Kiss, Radiohead, Placebo, Aerosmith, Keane, Velvet Revolver and the Psychedelic Furs plus home-grown bands such as the Babasónicos, Los Piojos, Ratones Paranoicos and punk group Attaque 77. It has no website, so keep a lookout in the local press for details in the weeks leading up to it.
Autumn Wine Tour Urbano (all month; ⓦ www .winetoururbano.com.ar): Every Fri evening for three or four weeks various restaurants in a chosen barrio take part in this event to promote Argentine wine, celebrating the grape harvests from far away in the north, west and south of the country. Often specific wines are discounted or meals are concocted to match them. You can get a special ticket through Ticketek, entitling you to sample a given number of glasses.

Festival Internacional de Cine Independiente (early April; ⓦ www.bafici.gov.ar): Over a quarter of a million film buffs and curious visitors buy tickets for this annual film festival run by the city authorities. You can see a good mix of shorts and longs, Argentine and foreign films, including the odd premiere. BAFICI prizes are much coveted by domestic and foreign directors, producers and actors, and you might even see a star or two. The main venue and participating cinemas vary, so check out the website (in English and Spanish).

Código País (variable – in the past it has also taken place in Nov; ⓦ www.codigopais.com): This "creative trends" festival brings you up-to-date with all that is going on in the country, be it film, fashion, music or design. Venues are moveable – check the website for details.

Feria Internacional del Libro (late April to early May; ⓦ www.el-libro.org.ar): A festival devoted to the city's love of reading – Buenos Aires was chosen by UNESCO as 2011 World Book Capital. Attended by over one million people over three weeks, the annual Book Fair takes over the Predio La Rural's huge pavilions, with launches, discussions, workshops and professional meetings, but above all loads and loads of books free for browsing.

May

Aniversario de la Revolución de Mayo (May 24–25): At midnight on May 24 and in the evening of the next day, the national anthem is sung by patriotic crowds in front of the Cabildo (see p.50). Expect plenty of other celebrations – usually *asado*-centric – all over the city, with some alternative fiestas, too. Of course, it will be many years before there are such lavish celebrations as those held in the bicentenary year 2010.

ArteBA (late May – though in some years has been a month later; ⓦ www.arteba.org): Every afternoon and evening for five days you can admire displays of contemporary art – painting, sculpture and video – from both national and international galleries at the Predio La Rural. The "Premio Petrobras" is awarded to the best exhibits.

June

Ciudad Emergente (early June; ⓦ www .ciudademergente.gov.ar): Run by the city government, this five-day festival is based at the Centro Cultural Recoleta and is intended to introduce young talent in every stream of the arts world – including some from foreign countries – to a mass audience. The third event in 2010, was attended by over 130,000.

Día Carlos Gardel (June 24): The anniversary of Gardel's tragic death in 1935 is usually commemorated by concerts and other events, at various tango-linked venues, including the museum in Abasto.

July

Día de la Independencia (July 9): Traditionally city cafés, particularly those along Avenida de Mayo, serve hot chocolate and *churros* on this national holiday, though otherwise there's generally less pomp and celebration than you might expect for such an important historical event – the weather can be dreary and lots of people are away for their mid-winter break around this time.

Marcha del 26 de Julio (July 26): A number of events around the city mark the anniversary of the death of Eva Perón in 1952. Centres of activity include La Recoleta, the Museo Evita and the statue of the iconic heroine next to the national library, where ceremonies are usually held.

La Rural (late July; ⓦ www.exposicionrural .com.ar): An annual tribute to the role played by cattle and other livestock in Argentina's history, this highlight in the Predio La Rural's calendar is a gaucho fest, with blacksmith demos and rodeo extravaganzas, plus lots of cows.

August

Buenos Aires Tango Festival and World Tango Championships (mid-Aug; ⓦwww .mundialdetango.gob.ar): Coinciding (in recent years) with the city's major tango festival, the annual world championships are held at various venues around the city. There are two main categories in which dancers compete: *salón tango*, for which the evaluation criteria include good taste and popular dance guide-lines – unbroken embrace, style, movement around the floor, closeness to the floor, cadence and rhythm; and stage tango, for couples, in which skills are stylized for artistic display and the dancers are judged on chore-ographic composition, use of the stage, synchronicity, costumes and make-up.
Milongueando in Buenos Aires (mid-Aug; ⓦwww.milongueandoenba.com): Previously held in February, this serious highbrow

tango event is for the initiated only – a hefty registration fee gives you access to a set of multi-level classes with leading *milongueros*, exhibitions, live music and lectures on history, lyrics and the like. It is mostly held at the *Mansión Dandi Royal* (see p.156; ⓦwww.hotelmansiondandiroyal.com) and at *La Mariposita de San Telmo*, Carlos Calvo 950 (ⓦwww.mariposita.com.ar), both of which offer accommodation.
Festival of Light (Aug & Sept; ⓦwww .encuentrosabiertos.com.ar): Held at various venues and in conjunction with a number of other cities around the world, the Festival de Luz is a series of top-rate photography exhibitions and side events at which the work of artists from all over the country and abroad is showcased. There are competi-tions, lectures and guided tours galore.

September

Fiesta del Inmigrante (early Sept): Held on the weekend closest to Immigrants' Day (Sept 4), this festival gives the city's various immigrant communities the chance to show off their different artistic, musical and culinary skills and traditions. Recent fiestas have been held at the Rosedal in Palermo (see p.131).
Feria de Vinos y Bodegas (early Sept; ⓦwww.expovinosybodegas.com.ar): Repre-sentatives of over 100 Argentine bodegas (wineries) come together at the Predio La Rural to show off their best reds, whites, rosés and champagnes, giving the public a great opportunity to learn more about the different labels, grapes and *terroirs* – or just to taste a lot of wine.
Spring Wine Tour Urbano (starting mid-Sept; ⓦwww.winetoururbano.com.ar): On the third

Fri of Sept, Oct and Nov, the boutiques and fashion shops along calles Armenia and Honduras each represent a national winery and throw open their doors for the public to browse their collections while sipping the nominated grape of the night (usually malbec, cabernet or chardonnay/merlot).
Casa Foa (late Sept/early Oct to late Nov; ⓦwww.casafoa.com): Major design and architecture salon held in a different location each year – past venues have included Calle Lanín (Barracas), Calle Defensa and Palermo train station – with the idea of promoting creativity and reviving or kick-starting lesser-known localities, along with the latest in lighting, carpets or playroom designs, among other things.

October

Festival Internacional de Buenos Aires (FIBA) (mid-Sept/early Oct; ⓦwww.festivaldeteatroba .gov.ar): Every two years (in odd-numbered years) since 1997 this two-to-three-week-long event has been a major showcase for national and international theatre, dance, music and other performing arts groups. The FIBA is held at various theatres around BA – check the website for details.

Festival Buenos Aires Danza Contemporánea (early Oct – in the past it has also taken place in Dec; ⓦwww.buenosairesdanza.gob.ar): Held only in even-numbered years, this week-long festival demonstrates that tango is not the only dance to be found in the city. Usually takes place at the Teatro San Martín (see p.188) and a number of other venues.

Marathon (early Oct; ⓦ www.maratondebuenos aires.com): Held on the second Sun in Oct in 2010 but the first Sun of November (and other springtime dates) in the past, this international marathon normally starts and ends at the Obelisco and usually part of the route goes along Avenida 9 de Julio.

Alvear Fashion and Arts (late Oct): For the last week of the month, a red carpet is literally rolled out along the pavements of the city's most aristocratic thoroughfare for VIPs and top models alike, as the boutiques and galleries open late and promote Argentine and international fashion – the art on display in the elite shops' windows includes avant-garde painting, digital art and video.

Feria de Juguetes (variable – in the past it has also taken place in April; ⓦ www.caijuguete .com.ar): The national toy fair, featuring an exhibition of hundreds of different playthings, circus performers, stands with new toys and games and a mini-cinema showing cartoons. In recent years has been held at the Centro Costa Salguero.

November

Gay Pride (variable; ⓦ www.marchadelorgullo .org.ar): On a given Sat gay men, lesbians, transvestites, transgendered persons and anyone else join in the afternoon parade ("Marcha del Orgullo") from Plaza de Mayo to Congreso, with the usual colourful floats and lots of disco music – though there is always a political overtone, too, such as vocal demands for more protection from discrimination.

Creamfields Buenos Aires (early Nov; ⓦ www.creamfieldsba.com): Out of the dozen worldwide venues of this electronic music fest that originated in Liverpool, the Argentine edition regularly breaks all attendance records (over 60,000); it moved to the motor-racing tracks in Villa Riachuelo in 2007, when the line-up was headed by Britain's Chemical Brothers.

Día de la Tradición (early Nov): This annual celebration of gaucho customs and other *criollo* lore on the nearest weekend to Nov 10 is best observed either at the Feria de Mataderos (see p.143) or, better still, out in the province – say, at San Antonio de Areco (see p.239).

Gran Premio Nacional (early Nov; ⓦ www .palermo.com.ar): The kind of race where people are eyeing each other – and their fashion sense (think Ascot) – far more than the horses. Nevertheless, this is the biggest horse race of the year (usually the second Sat), held at the Hipódromo Argentino de Palermo, and the stables and jockeys, at least, take it seriously, as do the betters.

International Video Dance Festival (early Nov; ⓦ videodanzaba.com.ar): This festival has two categories: video-dance as an art form and documentaries on dance. Workshops, lectures and video-dance screenings with national and international participants – both amateur and professional – make up the programme.

Noche de los Museos (mid-Nov – in the past it has also taken place in Oct; ⓦ www .lanochedelosmuseos.com.ar): Over 100 museums and galleries stay open until 2am on this night (an international affair), with various *colectivos* and special minibuses, ferrying visitors between the various sites. Once the galleries finally close, a huge party is usually held in front of the Centro de Museos in Puerto Madero (see p.78).

Abierto Argentino de Polo (mid-Nov to mid-Dec; ⓦ www.aapolo.com): One of the world's oldest (it began in 1893) – and probably most prestigious – polo championships takes over its Palermo home (see p.136) every weekend for three to four weeks in the lead-up to Christmas. A good opportunity to find out what a chukka is.

December

Buenos Aires International Jazz Festival (early Dec; ⓦ www.buenosairesjazz.gov.ar): A moveable feast in terms of timing and venue, this international jazz festival truly lives up to its name – stars who have performed in the past include James Moody playing with the Dizzy Gillespie All Stars, the Terence Blanchard Quintet, Cuban pianist Gonzalo Rubalcaba and local favourite, trumpeter Roberto "Fats"

Fernández. The festival features jam sessions, interviews, jazz film screenings and plenty of concerts, some in the open, weather permitting.

Personal Fest (early Dec – in the past it has also taken place in late Nov; ⓦwww.personal .com.ar): An all-night pop, rock, tango, funk and electronic music festival usually held on the first weekend of the month (all night Sat to Sun) – past line-ups have featured Snoop Dogg, Gotan Project, Black Eyed Peas, Depeche Mode, Scissor Sisters, Massive Attack and Mika. Venues change from year to year.

Peugeot Argentina Tennis Cup (early Dec; ⓦwww.copapeugeotdetenis.com.ar): A dozen South American male players battle it out at the Buenos Aires Lawn Tennis Club for one of the last titles of the year, usually in the second week of the month.

Día del Tango (Dec 11): National tango day – expect plenty of special events at milongas, clubs, restaurants, theatres or plazas all over the city. Check the press for details.

Cambalache Festival (early to mid-Dec; ⓦwww .festivalcambalache.com.ar): Taking its name

from a famous 1930s tango, this cerebral festival, held at the Teatro El Cubo in Abasto, combines dance and drama with tango music, live performances, videos and very serious workshops.

Christmas and New Year's Eve (Dec 25–Jan 1): Both these holidays (Navidad and Año Nuevo) and the week between them (jointly known as *"las fiestas (del fin del año)"* are fairly low-key in Buenos Aires, though the tradition of cribs (*pesebres*) is quite strong. As with many Catholic countries, Christmas Eve (*Noche Buena*) is a bigger celebration than Christmas Day: families gather to eat and give presents and the Catedral Metropolitana and other city churches hold midnight masses, though without much in the way of carols.

Villancicos – Hispanic yuletide songs – are sung at services (or by groups in the streets), but if you are yearning for "While shepherds watched their flocks" and the like, check the *Buenos Aires Herald* for details of Anglican advent services. Don't miss the impressive fireworks held at midnight on Dec 31 in the Palermo parks.

Out from the city

Out from the city

㉑ San Isidro 227

㉒ Tigre and the Paraná Delta 232

㉓ The Pampas 239

㉔ Colonia del Sacramento (Uruguay) 245

San Isidro

T he city's northern suburbs, known as "Zona Norte", extend for several leisurely kilometres beyond the city limits and offer a more relaxed feel and pace of life – with the whirring of lawnmowers and chirping of kiskadees a frequent soundtrack. Of these suburbs, **San Isidro** holds the greatest allure: a delightful, prosperous place, its cobbled streets are lined with lush trees and exuberant bougainvilleas, pretty villas and well-tended gardens, none of which are far from the Río de la Plata. In San Isidro's central **Casco Histórico** you'll find the Neo-Gothic **cathedral** near a viewpoint looking out on the river, while down by the water itself you can enjoy the natural delights of a **beach** and an **ecological reserve**. The main attractions are a trio of restored nineteenth-century villas, each of which evokes a pleasing mood of tropical languor: the immaculate **Quinta Los Ombúes**, the historic **Casa del General Pueyrredón** and, the highlight of them all, the ultra-refined **Villa Ocampo**. Reached by train in about half an hour from the city centre, San Isidro has a

The Tren de la Costa – a train ride through Zona Norte

The **Tren de la Costa** (daily, approx. every 20min 7am–11pm; $15 for a *boleto turístico* one-way, allowing you to get off and on as many times as you like – tickets can be bought onboard or at some of the stations; ☏011/4002-6000) runs north from the Zona Norte suburb of Olivos all the way to Tigre, a 25-minute trip if you do it in one go. It runs parallel to the waterfront, mostly through green parkland and past grandiose suburban mansions and villas; at each of the eleven stop-offs is a restored or purpose-built station, many of them done in a red-brick British Victorian style. Originally part of the state-run Tren del Bajo line, which was built in 1891, the service fell into disuse in the 1960s. In 1995 the northernmost section reopened as this privately run scenic railway, with luxurious mock-Victorian carriages running smoothly and silently along electrified tracks. There have been problems, though, with the service suspended for a while in 2010.

The train's southernmost Olivos terminus, known as **Estación Maipú**, is reached via a walkway over Avenida Maipú from Estación Mitre, which is on the **Retiro** commuter train line (not the same line that goes to San Isidro and Tigre). It is not far from the suburb's best-known place of interest, the **Quinta de Olivos**, a villa built in 1854 by Prilidiano Pueyrredón (also responsible for the Casa Pueyrredón in San Isidro; see p.229) and now the Argentine president's official residence; it's not open to the public and is hidden behind high brick walls in a large garden. Two stops along the line are in San Isidro: **Estación Barrancas**, which hosts an **antiques fair** (Sat & Sun 10am–6pm) and is close to the riverside parks and nature reserve; and **Estación San Isidro**, with its **shopping mall**, near the suburb's historic quarter. The line's northern terminus is at **Estación Delta**, in Tigre (see p.234).

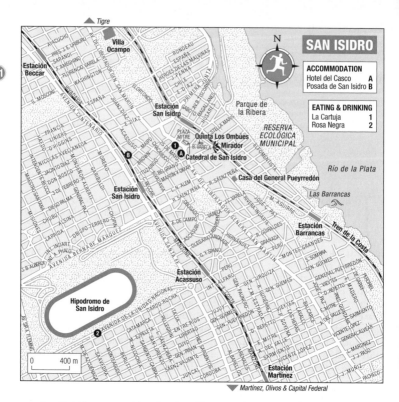

San Isidro map showing ACCOMMODATION (Hotel del Casco A, Posada de San Isidro B) and EATING & DRINKING (La Cartuja 1, Rosa Negra 2).

couple of well-appointed hotels, ideal if you want to escape Buenos Aires for a few days, and some excellent shops, cafés and restaurants, some of which skirt the **Hipódromo de San Isidro**, a huge racecourse, also used for concerts.

Arrival and information

San Isidro is served by the commuter **train link** from the Estación Retiro (Mitre branch) in downtown Buenos Aires to Tigre, which passes by the racecourse and stops at Acasusso, San Isidro and Beccar stations; there is also the touristic Tren de la Costa (see box, p.227), though it is rather more expensive and, starting in the suburb of Olivos, not very convenient if you are coming from the city. **Buses** #60 (take one displaying *bajo* on the front as these are more direct) from Constitución, via Avenida Callao, and #168 all the way from Boca, go to San Isidro but take rather longer. The **tourist office** in the Casco Histórico (Mon–Fri 8am–5pm, Sat & Sun 10am–6pm; ☎011/4512-3209, ⊛www.sanisidroturismo.gov.ar) hands out plenty of maps and information on places of interest.

Accommodation

Should you wish to take a few days' break from the city centre's hustle and bustle, there are some limited **accommodation** options in San Isidro. In front of the cathedral, the smart *Hotel del Casco*, Av del Libertador 16170 (☎011/4732-3993, ⊛www.hoteldelcasco.com.ar; US$200), is in a late nineteenth-century mansion, which has been renovated but retains many of its original features, including an elegant central patio. Less expensive is the *Posada de San Isidro* (☎011/4732-1221, ⓦwww.posadasanisidro.com.ar; $370), which has modern, slightly characterless rooms with basic cooking facilities, three blocks from the main train station at Maipú 66.

Casco Histórico

San Isidro's most appealing section is the leafy **Casco Histórico**, or historic quarter, around the main square – the stepped **Plaza Mitre** – which slopes towards the river. On the upper level of its steps, the soaring Neo-Gothic **Catedral de San Isidro** (Mon–Sat 7.30am–8pm, Sun 8am–10pm), built in 1898, merits a quick visit for its striking French stained-glass windows; every May 15, a procession headed by an image of San Isidro Labrador sets out from here.

Behind the cathedral, villa-lined Beccar Varela street curls round to the viewpoint **Mirador Los 3 Ombúes**, where you can glimpse the tan-hued waters of the Río de la Plata steadily being swallowed up by the ever-expanding islands of the Paraná Delta. Opposite the mirador is the lovely pink and green facade of a nineteenth-century villa, **Quinta Los Naranjos**.

Quinta Los Ombúes

Quinta Los Ombúes, a short walk from the viewpoint at Beccar Varela 774, is a simple whitewashed building with a red-tiled roof and green shutters, open to the public as the **Museo Municipal de San Isidro Dr Horacio Beccar Varela** (Dec, Feb & March Tues & Thurs 10am–6pm, Sat & Sun 3–7pm; April–Nov Tues & Thurs 10am–6pm, Sat & Sun 2–6pm; free; ☎011/4575-4038). The well-preserved nineteenth-century house is filled with the wealthy Beccar Varela family's art and furniture. You will notice many red-coloured items on display, evidence of the family's allegiance to Rosas and the Federalists (see p.254). An attractive tiled Andalucían-style patio and a garden in the back hum with birdsong and there are fine tree-framed views of the river.

Casa del General Pueyrredón

Claiming the title of the oldest house in Zona Norte, the **Casa del General Pueyrredón**, Rivera Indarte 48 (Tues & Thurs 10am–6pm, Sat & Sun 2–6pm; free; ☎011/4512-3131), was built in 1790 and bought by General Juan Martín de Pueyrredón, a hero of the Reconquista (see p.253) and Supreme Director of the United Provinces of the Río de la Plata (as post-independence Argentina was initially called) from 1816 to 1820. His son, Prilidiano Pueyrredón, a painter and architect, inherited it and added the beautiful gallery that runs along its northern side and the marble fireplaces inside.

Now a national historic monument and housing San Isidro's **Museo Histórico Municipal**, the building's classic colonial lines are enhanced by its splendid location: there are fantastic views of the river estuary from the garden. Under the garden's enormous native carob tree (known as the *algarrobo histórico*) Pueyrredón famously discussed Latin American independence with General San Martín. The museum has a display of historical documents relating to the general's achievements but also features a series of rooms handsomely furnished in period style. Occasional exhibitions focus on the country's colonial past.

To get here, follow Avenida del Libertador past the cathedral and turn left into Roque Sáenz Peña, some five blocks away. The villa is in a short street to the right, just where the street begins to dip down towards the riverside.

Villa Ocampo

Villa Ocampo, at Elortondo 1837 (Thurs–Sun 12.30–6pm; $10 Thurs & Fri, $15 Sat & Sun; excellent guided visits at 2pm; ⓦwww.villaocampo.org), is a wonderful late nineteenth-century mansion, the family home of the wealthy and influential Ocampo family and occupied on a permanent basis from 1942 onwards by Argentina's doyenne of letters, **Victoria Ocampo** (1890–1979). The author of several books and a proto-feminist whose friends included Virginia Woolf, she is most famous in Argentina for founding the literary magazine *Sur*, which popularized the names of many important Latin American writers, not least among them Jorge Luis Borges. She hosted no end of prestigious lectures and talks at the house, attended by many contemporary cultural icons, including Chilean Nobel laureate Gabriela Mistral, Rabindranath Tagore, Graham Greene, Borges, Victoria's sister Silvina and her brother-in-law, Adolfo Bioy Casares. Indira Gandhi even visited the villa in 1968 to award Victoria an honorary doctorate (you can see the photos).

The peach-coloured Italianate residence, which features a large veranda looking out over pristine gardens (planted with giant palms and delicate gingkos) and elegant, airy rooms filled with refined period furniture and fine portraits, was immaculately restored and opened to the public in 2005, thanks to assistance from UNESCO and private benefactors. Among other things you can see a handsome grand piano played by Igor Stravinsky, García Lorca and the great Arthur Rubinstein, while one of the highlights is the **library**, with its twelve thousand tomes, including works signed by the likes of Albert Camus.

An excellent **cafeteria** serves refreshments, brunch and light meals, while a small **shop** sells books (of course) and designer jewellery. Occasional **cultural events** of a suitably highbrow nature take place in the villa, such as piano recitals, plays, dances and art exhibitions. To get there, follow Avenida del Libertador about ten blocks north from the centre of San Isidro to the corner of Uriburu, and turn right; Villa Ocampo is about one block away, to the right. The nearest train station (on the Tigre line from Retiro; see p.234) is Beccar, a few blocks to the west.

Parque de la Ribera

Down on the riverfront east of the Casco Histórico, the **Parque de la Ribera** is where San Isidro's affluent go to talk politics, drink *mate* and take in the view of the city from deckchairs under palm trees. There's a small **ecological reserve** here (Mon–Fri 9am–6pm, Sat & Sun till 7pm; free; guided visits Sat & Sun at 4pm) home to five dozen bird species, along with turtles, lizards and frogs. Just south of the reserve you'll find a riverside **beach** and restaurant area.

Hipódromo de San Isidro

Inland and south of the Casco Histórico, the prestigious **Hipódromo de San Isidro** (ⓦwww.hipodromosanisidro.com) is one of the largest racecourses on the continent, with an area of 1.5 square kilometres, a grass track nearly 3km long allowing for thousand-metre races without turns, and stands holding up to 100,000 spectators. In December it hosts the Gran Premio Carlos Pellegrini, arguably the most important horse race in Argentina. It is easily accessed from San Isidro train station.

Eating

Good **food**, with an emphasis on fish, can be found upstairs at *La Cartuja*, on the corner of Plaza Mitre, which also boasts a gourmet ice-cream parlour and patisserie (*Gaudí*) downstairs. You might also try one of the many cafés, pubs and eateries at the Tren de la Costa complex. On Boulevard Dardo Rocha, which runs alongside the Hipódromo, parallel to Avenida de la Unidad Nacional, are a selection of upmarket *parrillas* and other, mainly evening, restaurants – *Rosa Negra* at no. 1918 is particularly good.

Tigre and the Paraná Delta

One of the world's most beautiful and unusual suburban landscapes, the exotic **Paraná Delta** is located just a few kilometres north of Buenos Aires' Avenida General Paz, the boundary between city and province. Constantly expanding owing to sediment deposited by the Río Paraná, the lush delta region (covering over 15,000 square kilometres) is a wonderfully seductive maze of lush, green islands separated by rivers and streams. Divided into three administrative sections, most of the delta is uninhabited, but the first section, closest to Buenos Aires, is a favourite weekend getaway for Porteños. It's also home to around three thousand islanders who (or whose forbears) fled the rat race more permanently, mainly living in wooden houses on stilts with their own docks and boats. The main settlement here – and the lower delta's transportation hub – is the picturesque town of **(El) Tigre**, around 10km northwest of San Isidro. Mostly used as a base for exploring the other sections of the delta, it also offers attractions in its own right, including a wonderful modern art museum and a riverine fruit and wicker market. Past Tigre, as you head into the more isolated and harder-to-access places in the second administrative section, the wild charm of the delta really shines through. Travelling along the Río Paraná de las Palmas you may be forgiven for thinking that you've stumbled onto a tributary of the Amazon (after all, the Paraná is South America's second longest river): the delta widens, amenities are much more dispersed and *isleños* rely on electric generators and kerosene lamps for power. Tigre can be visited on a day-trip from the city, but to get a real feel for the place and the depths of the delta, in particular, you might plan for at least an overnight break.

Tigre and around

Tigre owes its poetic name to the jaguars that once inhabited the delta region. Until the late nineteenth century it was a thriving, if unremarkable, farming town, but the yellow fever epidemics in the capital in the 1870s led to the arrival of the Porteño elite, who built sumptuous mansions and palatial rowing clubs here while escaping infection – many of these were retained as summer houses once the epidemics ended. Social life, meanwhile, revolved around events at the **Tigre**

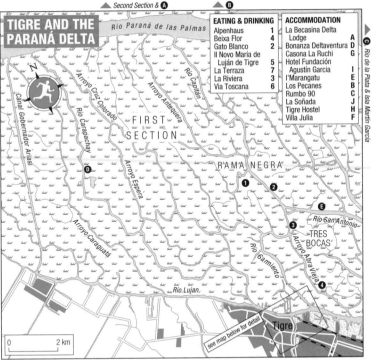

Second Section & Ⓐ   Ⓑ

TIGRE AND THE PARANÁ DELTA

Río Paraná de las Palmas

Río de la Plata & Isla Martín García

EATING & DRINKING		ACCOMMODATION	
Alpenhaus	1	La Becasina Delta	
Beixa Flor	4	Lodge	A
Gato Blanco	2	Bonanza Deltaventura	D
Il Novo María de		Casona La Ruchi	G
Luján de Tigre	5	Hotel Fundación	
La Terraza	7	Agustín Garcia	I
La Riviera	3	I'Marangatu	E
Via Toscana	6	Los Pecanes	B
		Rumbo 90	C
		La Soñada	J
		Tigre Hostel	H
		Villa Julia	F

Canal Gobernador Arias

N

Río Carapachay

Arroyo Cruz Colorado

Arroyo Espera

Arroyo Antequera

Río Capitán

F I R S T
S E C T I O N

Arroyo Caraguatá

R A M A   N E G R A

Ⓓ

Ⓔ

Ⓘ

Ⓩ

Ⓔ

Río San Antonio

TRES
BOCAS

Río Sarmiento

Arroyo Abra Vieja

Ⓓ

Río Luján

0   2 km

see map below for detail

Tigre

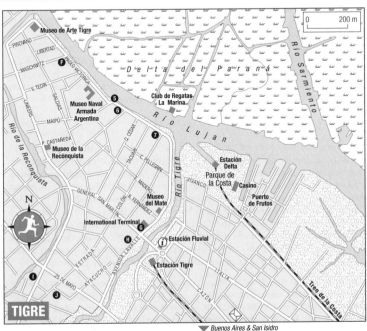

TIGRE

0   200 m

Museo de Arte Tigre

PIROVANO

LIBERTAD

MASCHWITZ

PASEO VICTORICA

V. TEDIN

SALDIAS

LINIERS

MAIPÚ

Ⓕ

D e l t a   d e l   P a r a n á

Río Sarmiento

Museo Naval
Armada
Argentina

Ⓔ

Ⓢ

Club de Regatas
La Marina

Río Luján

P. CASTAÑEDA

Museo de la
Reconquista

Río de la Reconquista

O. CÉSAR

TACUARÍ

C. PELLEGRINI

MADERO

COLÓN

R. FERNÁNDEZ

Ⓩ

GENERAL SAN MARTÍN

N

Museo
del Mate

Río Tigre

VIVANCO

Estación
Delta

Parque de
la Costa

Casino

Puerto
de Frutos

International Terminal

Ⓖ

Ⓗ

Estación Fluvial

ESTRADA

AVENIDA LAVALLE

AYACUCHO

Ⓘ

25 DE MAYO

Ⓙ

Estación Tigre

ITALIA

TAZON

Tren de la Costa

Buenos Aires & San Isidro

Club, home to Argentina's first casino (now a marvellous art gallery), and the grand **Tigre Hotel**, whose clientele included Enrico Caruso and the Prince of Wales. The closing of the casino in 1933 and the demolition of the Tigre Hotel in 1940 signalled an end to the glamour days.

As a departure point for excursions into the delta the town itself might be easily overlooked; at first glance (especially around the station) it's a bit of a hodgepodge, with recent constructions having been carried out with little regard to the existing architecture. Don't be put off by initial impressions, however: Tigre offers an appealing mix of faded glamour and cultural diversions – including a very sophisticated museum – and the bars and restaurants around its refurbished riverside provide perfect vantage points for an unhurried contemplation of the comings and goings of delta life.

Arrival and information

To get to Tigre, take the **train** from Retiro station (Línea Mitre); the hour's journey, stopping at several stations including Lisandro de la Torre, in Palermo, and Belgrano "C", costs $1.35 and terminates in Tigre's main train station, Estación Tigre. There is also the **Tren de la Costa** (see box, p.227), a picturesque alternative but costing ten times more and with the inconvenience of starting in Olivos, already in the city suburbs. **Bus** #60 starts at Constitución, passing through the microcentro, Recoleta, Palermo, Belgrano and San Isidro; take the one with a green sign bearing the word "Panamericana" (this bus has about twenty slightly different routes and not all go to Tigre, so ask the driver). Eventually reaching the same destination as the train (but terminating in Escobar), it takes up to ninety minutes from downtown Buenos Aires even in good traffic and costs $2. A *remise* (radio taxi) from the city centre would set you back $90–100, taking thirty to forty minutes in good traffic (but you risk a much longer journey at rush hour).

Getting to most destinations around the delta from Tigre requires a bit of forward planning; the excellent **tourist office** (daily 8am–6pm; ☎011/4512-4498, ⓦwww.tigre.gov.ar/www.vivitigre.gov.ar) in Tigre's Estación Fluvial, across the large roundabout from Estación Tigre, is very helpful, but can be very busy at weekends. It's worth the wait, though, as they have good maps and can help guide you through the labyrinth of available delta trips and the booking process. Lots of water and a warm climate unfortunately mean that mosquitoes are a real problem around here, so arm yourself with repellent.

Accommodation

If you want to base yourself in **Tigre** and visit the delta on day-trips – with the advantage of greater flexibility and a bigger choice of restaurants and other amenities than staying on the delta itself – you have a wide range of good **accommodation** options. If, however, you ache to replace urban racket with the gentle tinkling of water and hiss of cicadas at least for a night or two, do consider staying on the **delta**. There are a couple of hotels in the area known as Tres Bocas, a thirty-minute boat trip from the Estación Fluvial, and one or two others (more luxurious) scattered in the less developed parts of the delta. In all cases, reservations are essential and the individual hotels will be able to provide you with transport details (or even private transfers). Often weekends see prices increase by as much as fifty percent.

La Becasina Delta Lodge ☎011/4328-2687, ⓦwww.labecasina.com. Luxury complex of 15 wooden bungalows, each with its own deck, scattered through luxuriant forest in the quieter second section of the delta; there is a spa, an outdoor pool and you have the opportunity to use kayaks or go on guided walks. They have their own motor-launch. US$240–330.

Bonanza Deltaventura ☎011/4728-1674, 🌐www.deltaventura.com. At an isolated spot on the Río Carapachay, *Deltaventura* is *the* place to go for serious peace and quiet, with only three rooms and around 6km worth of trails, where you can trek, bird-watch and canoe. It can also be visited as a day-trip ($215, including lunch). $730, two nights minimum, full board.

Casona La Ruchi Lavalle 557 ☎011/4749-2499, 🌐www.casonalaruchi.com.ar. Fabulous old family house with enormous wood-floored bedrooms, huge balconies, a swimming pool in the garden and exceptionally friendly owners, though only shared bathrooms are available. $240.

Hotel Fundación Agustín García Av Liniers 1547 ☎011/4749-0140, 📧fundaciongarcia @yahoo.com.ar. A decent budget option in the southern end of town, with fine views over the river. $150.

l'Marangatu ☎011/4728-0752, 🌐www .i-marangatu.com.ar. Well-known place on the Río San Antonio close to Tres Bocas, complete with swimming pool, sports pitches and even a heliport. $500.

Los Pecanes ☎011/4728-1932, 🌐www .hosterialospecanes.com. An appealing, family-run *hostería* out on the Arroyo Felicaria in the second section of the delta, away from the roar of the jet skis. From $250. No credit cards.

Rumbo 90 ☎011/15-5483-9454, 🌐www .rumbo90.com.ar. Well-appointed lodge and spa on the Canal del Este, a 40min journey from Tigre in the lodge's private boats. The plush rooms have their own decks overlooking the river or gardens, while the spa offers jacuzzi, sauna, massages etc. Incredibly – given the location – the place even has wi-fi. US$150–250.

La Soñada Anastacio El Pollo 1786 ☎011/4749-0800, 🌐www.bybtigre.com.ar. Slightly old-fashioned but very pleasant family B&B in a fairly quiet residential street – there's a large garden with a pool and deck, and a car park. $240–590.

Tigre Hostel Avenida San Martín 137 ☎011/4749-4034, 🌐www.tigrehostel.com.ar. Friendly and well-run hostel, with a nearby annex (*Posada del 1860* at no. 190; it is named after the date of construction) offering slightly superior lodgings (US$65–90). There are some double rooms for US$45 but these face the street so don't expect a totally quiet night. US$20.

Villa Julia Paseo Victorica 800 ☎011/4749-0242, 🌐www.villajuliaresort.com.ar. This 1910 house, many of the original floors, fittings and furniture, alongside modern comforts such as luxury pillows and air-conditioning. The rooms' wide balconies look out over the river, and the hotel has its own elegant restaurant, the *Acacia*. $500–700.

Tigre

Tigre lies on an **island** positioned along the western bank of the Río Luján, one of the delta's main arteries, and is divided in half by the smaller Río Tigre, which runs north–south through its centre. Busy riverside avenues flank both sides of the Río Tigre, while the broad Paseo Victorica runs along the Río Luján in the more attractive western half of town. The best place to begin a tour is the **Estación Fluvial**, just north of the bridge over the Río Tigre.

Estación Fluvial

The neat **Estación Fluvial** (River Station) is sandwiched between the mainline Estación Tigre and the Tren de la Costa's Estación Delta. Since the 1990s this development has been the point of contact between island and mainland life, and is the place to head for before undertaking any trip on the delta – the companies that operate river launches (see p.238) all have their offices here, as does the tourist office (see opposite), while a row of kiosks advertise hotels and *cabaña* outfits. There are also cafés and some shops where you can stock up on provisions before heading out into the watery wilds.

Parque de la Costa

On the same side of the Río Tigre as the Estación Fluvial, and overlooking the Río Luján, you'll find the **Parque de la Costa** at Vivanco 1509 (March–Nov Fri–Sun

11am–7pm; Dec–Feb Tues–Sun till 7.30pm; $70; ☎011/4002-6000, ⓦwww
.parquedelacosta.com.ar). This is one of Latin America's largest amusement parks,
and as popular with local families as you would expect. Attractions include
"Aconcagua", which has a climbing wall; South America's biggest fountain, the
focus of a *son-et-lumière* show; "El Faro" ("the lighthouse"), with great views of
the delta; and a whole clutch of rollercoasters and other rides.

Puerto de Frutos

A couple of blocks west of the Parque de la Costa, also alongside the Río Luján,
the serene **Puerto de Frutos** (daily 10am–6pm) – or fruit port – dates from the
early twentieth century, when fruit cultivation was the region's main source of
income. It remains a working port where you can watch boats being unloaded
with fruit, wood, wicker – which grows in abundance in the delta – and other
goods. However, the port is principally known these days for operating more as a
craft market – country-style furniture and wickerwork are the chief products.

Avenida Lavalle and the Museo del Mate

Tigre's genteel past is somewhat more in evidence on the western side of the Río
Tigre, making it an enjoyable area to explore on foot. Get there by crossing the
main bridge over the river, near the Estación Fluvial, then follow **Avenida Lavalle**
north, past a miscellany of villas and bungalows, smart rowing and yacht clubs and
a curious double-sided fuel station, servicing both road and water transport. At
no. 289 you'll find the **Museo del Mate** (Wed–Sun winter 10am–6pm; summer
11am–7pm; $10; ⓦwww.elmuseodelmate.com), where half a dozen rooms trace
the history of Argentina's national beverage (see p.30) and explain the customs
surrounding it. You can try some of the herby brew on the premises.

Paseo Victorica and the Museo Naval de la Nación

Keep going north to the confluence with the wide Río Luján, where Lavalle turns
into **Paseo Victorica**. At the corner, an imposing bronze statue pays tribute to the
glories of Argentine rowers, while across the river you can see the mock-Tudor
wonder that is the headquarters of the highly exclusive **Club de Regatas La
Marina**, founded in 1867; the present building was opened in 1927 by President
Marcelo T. de Alvear. The *paseo* itself is a delightful riverside walk, partly closed
to motor traffic at weekends, with plenty of cafés, ice cream parlours and restaurants to choose from and benches from which to gaze at the aquatic goings-on.

At Paseo Victorica 602 the **Museo Naval de la Nación** (Mon–Fri 8.30am–
5.30pm, Sat & Sun 10.30am–6.30pm; $3; ⓦwww.histarmar.com.ar) is housed
in an attractive mid-nineteenth-century building (formerly a naval workshop)
with a pristine white Neoclassical facade, adorned with a bas relief of Neptune.
The museum, operated by the Argentine navy, tells the story of maritime
history and navigation – both national and worldwide – through scale models of
boats and navigational instruments. In the grounds are numerous planes and
other military hardware.

Museo de Arte Tigre

Right at the end of Paseo Victorica, set among immaculate gardens with fabulous
river views, is the stunning **Museo de Arte Tigre** or **MAT** (Wed–Fri 9am–7pm,
Sat & Sun noon–7pm; guided tours Wed–Fri 11am & 5pm, Sat & Sun 1pm, 3pm
& 6pm; $5; ⓦwww.mat.gov.ar), opened in 2006 following some sixteen years of
restoration work. The vast turreted and balustraded structure, built in the early
twentieth century by French architects, began life as the Tigre Club. Outside, the

building presents a majestic combination of Neoclassical columns and intricate carvings, culminating in a fabulous hexagonal **belvedere** linked to the mansion by a raised walkway. Inside, the incredibly opulent edifice – with its marble staircase, wrought-iron banisters, gigantic chandeliers and delicate ceiling frescoes – is a setting to rival any of the capital's art museums.

The art itself is more impressive than you might imagine from a suburban museum, and has the added benefit of being mostly by Argentines or on Argentine subjects. The rooms are arranged thematically; the largest salon – previously the ballroom – focuses on ports, with works by **Quinquela Martín** (see p.91) and Oscar Vaz, who uses light to great effect in his busy Boca scenes. In the landscapes room, look out for two pampas scenes by the wonderful Florencio Molino Campos, a noted cartoonist whose colourful countryside illustrations for almanacs are found on hotel walls the length and breadth of the country. Part of the museum is given over to **temporary exhibitions**, which in the past have focused on eminent Argentine artists such as Alfredo Hlito and Miguel Ocampo, on contemporary Panamanian art and works by the late Spanish sculptor Eduardo Chillida.

Museo de la Reconquista

From the end of Victorica, the road curves round, merging with Avenida Liniers, which leads back towards the town centre, via Avenida General San Martín. The avenue is flanked by fine, if sometimes slightly decaying, examples of the town's grand nineteenth-century mansions, interspersed with luxurious modern residences. Almost as impressive as the street's architecture are its giant plane trees whose powerful roots have turned the narrow pavement into a kind of pedestrian rollercoaster. At no. 818 (but with its entrance at the side in Padre Castañeda) you'll find reconstructed colonial Casa de Goyechea, housing the **Museo de la Reconquista** (Wed–Sun 10am–6pm; free; call for a guided visit ☏011/4512-4496). General Liniers and his troops used the original building as a base before they launched their counterattack against the British invasions in 1806. The museum contains an interesting display of documents and objects relating to the recapture of Buenos Aires, as well as a section devoted to local history.

Eating and drinking

There is no shortage of **restaurants in Tigre**. The pick of them are along Paseo Victorica, including *La Terraza* at no. 135, a classy modern *parrilla* with an outside seating area, and *Il Novo María de Luján de Tigre* at no. 611, Tigre's smartest restaurant, situated in an elegant dining room right on the river bank. *Via Toscana*, nearby at no. 470, has a lovely Victorian-style garden area from where you can enjoy its ice cream and observe river life. There are lots of cheap and cheerful *parrillas* near the entrance to the Parque de la Costa, while the above-average **café** at the Estación Fluvial prepares good sandwiches for eating in or takeaway.

Most hotels located **in the delta** itself have their own **restaurants** and, unless you have a private boat, it's difficult to escape elsewhere. The Tres Bocas area has a few, including the rather swanky *Gato Blanco*, on the Río Capitán (☏011/4728-0390), which does a mean *lenguado a la citron vert* (sole in a lime sauce), and the simple and pretty *La Riviera* (☏011/4728-0177) just by the jetty, which is one of the delta's oldest restaurants, with a typical *parrilla* menu. *Beixa Flor* (🌐www.beixaflor.com.ar) on Arroyo Abra Vieja, closer to Tigre, offers a whole day's entertainment, with its own beach, hammocks, tropical music and a bar, plus a very decent restaurant; check the website for transfers and packages. In the Rama Negra district, to the northwest of Tres Bocas, lurks the Germanic *Alpenhaus*

(☎011/4728-0422), with a spa, tearoom and bar, as well as comfortable bungalows to stay the night. Some restaurants, including *La Riviera*, double up as a **bar** if you just fancy a contemplative beer or two.

Boat trips and other activities

There are myriad ways to explore the river delta from Tigre. Several companies offer *paseos*, or **round-trip tours**, generally lasting an hour or two, inevitably without venturing far into the delta; if you're pressed for time and don't have anything booked they will give you a taste of river life. Rather touristy catamarans as well as the more authentic but smaller *lanchas* (launches) run regular *paseos* (11am–5 or 6pm; $25–60), some from Tigre's Estación Fluvial and others from the international terminal opposite at Lavalle 520 (which also serves Uruguay, hence its name). Many of the tours include a lunch stop and a visit to the **Museo Sarmiento**, home to a prominent nineteenth-century president – located on the banks of the river bearing his name, curiously it is encased in a glass cage.

A couple of **specialized outfits** offer more memorable trips into the delta: Navegando por el Delta (⊛ www.navegandoporeldelta.com.ar), a company based in nearby San Fernando, offers excellent trips around the delta in handsome craft with *asados* thrown in, while outstanding DeltaSur (⊛ www.deltasurecoturismo .com.ar) offer scheduled and tailor-made rides lasting anything from three hours to two days.

Alternatively do what the locals do and use the frequent **passenger services**, known as *lanchas colectivas*, run by three companies – Delta (⊛ www.lineasdelta.com .ar), Interisleña and Jilgüero (⊛ www.lanchasjilguero.com.ar). For timetables phone or visit the tourist office (rather than the companies themselves) or consult the company websites. Most routes are one-way, but all three companies also do return trips as far as the **Paraná de las Palmas**, where the second section begins, lasting about four hours (Delta 10.30am; Jilgüero 12.30pm; Interisleña 2.15pm & 3.30pm; all around $30–40; at weekends the boats are often packed and journeys can take much longer). If you want to do some **walking**, take one of the regular services to Rama Negra and/or Tres Bocas (about $20 return) and wander along the public riverside path and over the wooden footbridges that cross from island to island.

There are also various places where you can practise **watersports** without being the member of a prestigious Tigre club. Parana Ecoturismo (☎011/4797-1143) does guided tours in kayaks, while Puro Remo, Lavalle 945 (☎011/4731-2924, ⊛ www .puroremo.com.ar), gives you the choice of kayaks or more old-fashioned rowing boats with wooden oars. There's also a **wakeboarding** school run by South American champion Gabriela Díaz (☎011/4728-0031, ⊛ www.wakeschool.com.ar).

The Pampas

S outh, west or northwest of Buenos Aires, past its mostly unremarkable residential suburbs, you strike right into the archetypal Argentine landscape of the **Pampas**. This vast expanse of flat grassland, dotted with cattle ranches and agricultural towns, is one of the country's most famous features, and understanding its character is crucial to getting to grips with what makes Argentines tick. Scratch the surface of most Porteños, and you'll find the proud and indomitable spirit of the **gauchos** underneath (Argentine cowboys; see box, p.242), never more at home than when warming their feet by the fire and sharing a *mate*.

The major destination to head for is attractive **San Antonio de Areco**, to the capital's northwest. A centre of pampas tradition and with a remarkably authentic feel despite its popularity, the town has a well-preserved centre, a thriving artisan community, and a clutch of estancias in its environs. Even further off the gringo trail, tranquil **Mercedes** is a quiet pampas town with a particularly well-preserved *pulpería* – a traditional store-cum-bar.

San Antonio de Areco

San Antonio de Areco is considered the home of gaucho traditions and hosts the annual **Fiesta de la Tradición**, the country's most important festival celebrating pampas culture (see p.223). Despite its modest promotion as a tourist destination, the town has retained a surprisingly genuine feel, augmented by its setting on the banks of a tranquil river, the Río Areco. You may not find the place full of galloping gauchos outside festival week (the first or second week of Nov), but you still have a good chance of spotting estancia workers on horseback, sporting traditional berets and rakishly knotted scarves, or of coming across *paisanos* propping up the bar of a traditional *boliche* establishment.

The town's only real sights are a couple of museums, including one devoted to gaucho culture (closed temporarily; see p.242); you're more likely to be impressed by the harmonious architectural character of the town's centre: all cobbled streets and faded Italianate and colonial facades punctuated by elaborate wrought-iron grilles and delicately arching lamps. There are also some excellent silversmiths, weavers and tanners working in *talleres* (workshops).

SAN ANTONIO
DE ARECO

Museo
Gauchesco
Ricardo
Güiraldes

Parque Criollo

Río Areco

Puente
Viejo

ZERBONI

Zoo

MATHEU

Centro Cultural
Usina Vieja

LAVALLE

MITRE

Los Principios

G. PAZ

SAN MARTIN

ALEM

ALVEAR

Puente
Gabino
Tapia

Centro Cultural
y Taller Draghi

PLAZA
RUIZ DE
ARELLANO

SEGUNDO SOMBRA

Iglesia Parroquial
San Antonio de Padua

Chevallier
Bus Terminal

ACCOMMODATION
Los Abuelos .... A
Antigua Casona ...... D
La Cinacina C
Hostal de Areco ..... B
Patio de Moreno ..... E

EATING & DRINKING
Almacén de
  Ramos Generales ... 5
Bar San Martín 9
Barril 990 8
Café de las Artes 4
La Costa 2
La Esquina de Merti . 6
La Olla de Cobre 3
Puesto La Lechuza ... 1
La Vieja Sodería 7

El Ombú, La Bamba & ▲ Buenos Aires

0   200 m

Arrival and information

Plenty of **buses** ply the four-hour journey from Buenos Aires' Retiro station to San Antonio de Areco (driving yourself only takes about half the time). The two main bus companies operating this route are Nueva Chevallier (☎011/4000-5255) and Pullman General Belgrano (☎011/4315-6522); call ahead or visit the companies' Retiro kiosks in person to check the timetable – there's a service every hour or two – and book tickets. Buses stop at the pink Chevallier terminal at General Paz and Avenida Dr Smith, six blocks east of Areco's town centre. It's an easy stroll into town along Calle Segundo Sombra, which brings you to Areco's main square, Plaza Ruiz de Arellano. If you're carrying a lot of luggage – or heading for an estancia – take a *remise* (☎02326/456225).

The **tourist office** on the corner of Arellano and Zerboni (daily 8am–7pm; ☎02326/453165, ⓦwww.areco.mun.gba.gov.ar) has useful information, including maps and lists of hotels and artisan workshops.

Accommodation

San Antonio de Areco can potentially be visited as a day trip from Buenos Aires, but staying overnight gives you the chance to explore at a more leisurely pace and enjoy Areco as its best, in the morning and evening. In addition to the recommendations below, the Draghi family (see p.242) has elegant rooms available in a *parador* (inn) on Matheu, a block from their workshop – enquire at the workshop in person (☎02326/454219).

Los Abuelos Zapiola & Zerboni
☎02326/456390, ⓦwww.losabueloshotel.com.
A reasonable deal for a somewhat modern hotel – there is a television and fan in each room, and some rooms

have balconies with views over the Río Areco. $180.

Antigua Casona Segunda Sombra 495
☎02326/456600, ⓦwww.antiguacasona.com.
A rustic B&B with a lovely tiled patio where

a good breakfast is served, and a large garden that ensures you hear crickets and birdsong rather than traffic. $300.

Hostal de Areco Zapiola 25 ☎02326/456118, ⓦwww.hostaldeareco.com.ar. Relatively simple but very attractive, this friendly hotel is in a traditional rose-coloured building with farmhouse-style decor. $200.

Patio de Moreno Moreno 251 ☎02326/455197, ⓦwww.patiodemoreno.com. The most luxurious option in town, this classily converted house with a cool tiled floor has a garden, pool and comfortable rooms decked out in neutral furnishings, with touches such as wi-fi and safeboxes that are hard to find in the town's otherwise more rustic hotels. US$160.

The Town

Areco's main square, the leafy **Plaza Ruiz de Arellano**, is named after José Ruiz de Arellano, whose estancia stood on the site now occupied by the town and who built Areco's founding chapel, the **Iglesia Parroquial San Antonio de Padua**, on the south side of the square. The original chapel was declared a parish church in 1730, and was rebuilt in 1792 and then again in 1870 in keeping with the town's growing importance. Of no great architectural note, the current version is nonetheless a pleasingly simple white construction, with clear Italian influences. The exterior is dominated by a sculpture of San Antonio himself, who stands within a niche clad with blue and white tiles that echo those of the church's small bell-shaped dome. The inside is impressive, with a high vaulted ceiling.

Staying at an estancia

The province of Buenos Aires has dozens of **estancias** (ranches) that allow you a taste of country life in style; many are authentic working farms that have rooms for visitors in the *casco* (homestead) or outlying buildings and provide quality meals on a full-board basis and activities such as swimming and riding on the premises. Though it's best to stay a night or two if you can, most can also be visited as day-trips; in all cases, advance reservation is essential. Estancias will give you directions if you are driving, or for an extra charge will usually be able to pick you up from a nearby town or even provide a direct transfer from Buenos Aires. We've listed "a few" below, but there is a plethora of others available, too – many city-based tour agencies can advise or you could try websites such as ⓦwww.estanciasargentinas.com.

La Cinacina San Antonio de Areco: follow Bartolomé Mitre five blocks west of the main plaza to the end of the street ☎02326/452045, ⓦwww.lacinacina.com.ar. Offers a full day of *asado*, horseriding and a display of gaucho skills for $160, or $240 as a day-trip from Buenos Aires with transport included (Tues, Fri, Sat & Sun). You can also stay the night in pretty, country-style rooms (US$160).

El Ombú Ruta 31 Cuartel VI, near San Antonio de Areco ☎011/4710-2795, ⓦwww.estanciaelombu.com. Sumptuously decorated rooms, with a lovely tiled and ivy-covered veranda running round the exterior of the building. As well as offering horseriding, the estancia has a small but well-maintained swimming pool and a games room. Other activities include helping out with – or at least observing – farm tasks such as cattle herding and, of course, eating delicious *asados*, sometimes served under the shade of the large ombú tree that gives the estancia its name. US$160 per person per night full board or US$70 as a day visit with lunch.

La Margarita Tapalque ☎11/49510638, ⓦwww.estancialamargarita.com. Five hours from Buenos Aires' Retiro bus station, *La Margarita* is a homey estancia to the southwest of the city, worth the journey for its authentic feel, outstandingly friendly staff and excellent food. It offers a range of gaucho-led horse rides, fishing and hunting (Dec–May), swimming and cycling. Fully catered en-suite rooms US$175, self-catered studios in the beautiful gardens US$68 per person; rates include free pick-up from Tapalque bus terminal.

Among the elegant *fin-de-siècle* residences that flank the plaza, there is the Italianate **municipalidad**, to the north; originally a private residence, it is painted a particularly delicate version of the pink that characterizes so many of Areco's buildings. Right opposite the church, at Lavalle 387, one of San Antonio's most renowned silversmiths runs the **Centro Cultural y Taller Draghi** (Mon–Sat 9am–1pm & 3.30–7.30pm, Sun 10am–1pm; free guided visits 11am, 5pm & 6pm; $10). The centre displays pieces made in the style of *platería criolla*, which first emerged around 1750 when local craftsmen, who had previously been working according to Spanish and Portuguese tradition, began to develop their own style. Fantastically ornate yet sturdy, in keeping with the practical use to which the items are – at least in theory – put, the style is still commonly used to produce gaucho knives (*facones*), belts (*rastras*), *mates* and stirrups. The museum/workshop mixes the creations of the late Juan José Draghi with a collection of nineteenth-century silver spurs, bridles and swords that were his inspiration. Acknowledged as one of San Antonio's finest silversmiths, Draghi produced pieces for various international figures, including the king and queen of Spain. His finest work, and that of his equally talented sons, who now run the business, includes decorative *mates*, which come in their original chalice shape (based on those used in churches) with finely wrought silver stems of cherubs and flowers.

A block north of Plaza Ruiz de Arellano, at Alsina 66, the **Centro Cultural Usina Vieja** (Tues–Sun 11am–5pm; $1.50) originally housed Areco's first electrical generator but is now a cultural centre and contains the Museo de la Ciudad, an eclectic collection of everyday items, from clothing to record players and even the town's old telephone switchboard. There's also a good display of the famous gaucho cartoons of Florencia Molino Campos, first published in almanacs.

Museo Gauchesco Ricardo Güiraldes

Beyond the cultural centre, wide Calle Zerboni separates the town centre from the grassy banks of the Río Areco, popular for picnics and *asados* during good weather. Crossing the simple brick Puente Viejo opposite the zoo on Zerboni leads to the rather scrubby **Parque Criollo**, which houses the **Museo Gauchesco Ricardo Güiraldes** (closed due to floods at time of writing, due to reopen late 2011). Both

Gauchos

The **gaucho** who once roamed the Pampas on horseback, knife clenched between his teeth, leaving a trail of broken hearts and gnawed steak bones behind him, is as important a part of Argentina's collective romantic imagination as the Wild West cowboy is in the US. He emerged as a distinct figure in the nineteenth century, with roots in indigenous and Spanish culture and an evolution suited to the specific conditions of the Pampas. The gaucho was totally self-sufficient, highly skilled on horseback and devilishly fast with that knife. Despised by both the rural landowning elite and the urban intelligentsia as barbaric and dangerous, gauchos lived outside society's strictures, moving wherever they could find work. Historians estimate that they probably numbered 80,000 at their peak in the 1870s, but large-scale immigration, urbanization and technological progress sounded the death knell for the gaucho not long after. The freedoms represented by the lifestyle came to embody a sense of what it was to be a true Argentine – an image makeover heavily influenced by Ricardo Güiraldes' 1926 novel *Don Segundo Sombra*, partially set in San Antonio, and José Hernández' epic 1872 poem *Martín Fierro*. These attributes – compulsive *mate* drinking, sharing an *asado* (barbecue) with friends around the fire, a defiantly macho attitude coupled with a proud independence – all went to form the basis of *Argentinidad*, or Argentine identity.

park and museum are entered via the Pulpería La Blanqueada, once a staging post on the old Camino Real, which linked Buenos Aires with Alto Perú. It was the setting for the first encounter between Fabio – a sort of South American Huckleberry Finn and the young hero of Güiraldes' famed novel *Don Segundo Sombra* – and his mentor, the book's namesake. The *pulpería* was closed in the 1930s but its original features have been retained, including the traditional grille that separated the owner from his customers and their knives and light fingers. For a *pulpería* that's still serving, head to Moreno and Mitre, where you'll find *Los Principios*, an authentic store that also sells groceries to locals from its high wooden shelves.

The museum, a short distance away across the park, is housed in a 1930s reproduction of an old estancia. Its collection mixes gaucho paraphernalia – *mate* gourds, silverware and *boleadoras* (lasso balls) – with objects deemed to be interesting largely because of their famous owners: General Rosas' bed, W.H. Hudson's books and so on. Of particular interest are the photos of the original gauchos who were the inspiration for Güiraldes, and the branding irons they used – each landowner had his own, somewhat cabalistic symbol, worn in various forms as a badge of pride by his men as well as his cattle. At the end is an impressive collection of works by Uruguayan artist Pedro Figari; his paintings capture the almost hypnotic quality of the pampas landscape perfectly.

Eating, drinking and nightlife

San Antonio de Areco has an excellent selection of **restaurants**, cafés and bars that ooze character. *La Esquina de Merti*, on the main plaza at Lavalle and Arellano, has walls adorned with old signs, ads and bottles and is a tasteful recreation of a *pulpería* serving straightforward Argentine classics. A similar ambience is found at *Almacén de Ramos Generales*, Zapiola 143, with *parrilla*, *picadas* and specials such as trout in Roquefort sauce. The owners also run the wonderful ✦ *La Vieja Sodería* café/bar at Bolívar and General Paz, whose walls are lined with coloured soda bottles; it does a wide range of teas and beers. At Bolívar 68, the pretty *Café de las Artes* cooks up tasty home-made pasta, while the length of Calle Zerboni, which skirts the park, is thick with the smoke of *parrillas* – *La Costa*, on the corner of Zerboni and Belgrano, is especially popular with locals. If you've got a sweet tooth, don't miss *La Olla de Cobre*, a small chocolate factory and sweet shop at Matheu 433, where you can try handmade chocolates and particularly delicious *alfajores* before buying.

The best **bars** in Areco are *boliches* – traditional places where estancia workers drink Fernet and play cards. These include *Bar San Martín*, at Moreno and Alvear, and *Puesto La Lechuza*, near the river at Victorino Althaparro 423, which can also be good places to catch folklore music and dancing. *Barril 990*, San Martín 381, is a more modern pub, where there is occasional live music.

Mercedes

Tranquil and cultured **mercedes**, about 100km southwest of Buenos Aires along the RN-5, was founded in 1752 as a fortress to protect nearby Luján from attacks by indigenous tribes. It's a well-preserved provincial town and easy to find your way around – the main drag is Avenida 29, which crosses central Plaza San Martín. The plaza houses a large cathedral and is a real hub of activity – especially in the evening, when locals fill the tables that spill out of its various cafés.

Mercedes' main draw is its unmissable **pulpería**, over twenty blocks north of Plaza San Martín, at the end of Avenida 29. *Pulperías*, essentially provisions stores with a bar attached, performed an important social role in rural Argentina and enjoy an almost mythical status in gaucho folklore. *Lo de Cacho* (Cacho's Place) claims to be the last one left standing. It's easy to believe that the gloomy interior has hardly changed since the *pulpería* opened its doors in 1850, with a collection of dusty bottles, handwritten notices – including an original poster for the biggest gaucho outlaw of them all, Juan Moreira – and gaucho paraphernalia. Musicians frequently drop in for a drink and some impromptu singing and guitar playing, much of it dedicated to Cacho himself, who passed away in 2009. To get to the *pulpería*, best visited in the evening for a beer and some of the renowned local salami, take the local bus that runs towards the park from Avenida 29.

Practicalities

Mercedes' **bus terminal**, served by regular buses (2hr 30min) from Retiro bus station in the capital, is south of the town centre, from where it's a twenty-minute walk to Plaza San Martín, or you could take a taxi (℡02324/420651). The **tourist office**, on the corner of Avenida 29 and Calle 26 (Mon 7am–1pm, Tues–Fri till 6pm, Sat & Sun 10am–5pm; ℡02324/421080, ⓦwww.mercedes.gba.gov.ar), doesn't have much in the way of printed information, but the staff are enthusiastic and knowledgeable, and can provide you with a map of the town.

Accommodation is not plentiful, and what exists is rather lacking in character. The best option is the *Hostal del Sol*, on the western edge of town at avenidas 2 and 3 (℡02324/433400, ⓦwww.hotelhostaldelsol.com; $265), which has large rooms in a tranquil setting. **Eating and drinking** options in the centre include *La Vieja Esquina*, a charming traditional bar on the corner of calles 25 and 28, which also sells delicatessen produce.

Colonia del Sacramento (Uruguay)

erched on a promontory jutting into the Río de la Plata, the historic Uruguayan town of **Colonia del Sacramento**, with its blend of colonial history, museums and laidback ambience, feels a universe apart from Buenos Aires. In fact, it's only a short boat ride across the river. The Portuguese founded Nova Colonia do Sacramento in 1680 and, although it was officially ceded to Spain in 1750, its Portuguese settlers resisted the transfer of power and the Spanish took possession only in 1777, destroying part of the town in the process. Meanwhile, Colonia was established as a smuggling centre, exploited mainly by the British. A stop was put to this when Uruguay was created in 1828.

Getting to Colonia

From Buenos Aires, fast **catamarans** (1hr) and more leisurely **ferryboats** (3hr) to Colonia depart from the ferry **terminal** at Dársena Norte, Av Antártida Argentina 821, at the bottom of Avenida Córdoba. Buquebus (℡011/4316-6500, ⊛www.buquebus .com) is the main **company**, with offices at the terminal, at Av Córdoba 867, at Posadas 1452 and at the Retiro bus terminal. Their rival, Colonia Express (℡011/4317-4100, ⊛www.coloniaexpress.com.ar), has offices at the terminal and at Ave Córdoba 753.

There are several crossings daily in summer, but only a couple in winter. The return passenger **fare** starts at about $200 for the ferry or $300 for the catamaran, but rockets in the summer at weekends and holidays. Ask about **packages** (*paquetes*), comprising ferry tickets, a tour of Colonia, lunch and/or a night in a hotel there. Book tickets well in advance (especially from late Dec to late Feb), either directly at the terminal, offices or by phone/online.

On the catamarans, your **luggage** is checked in. With this procedure and double customs to clear, you should arrive at least 1 hour before departure time; have your passport with you both when buying tickets and checking in. Uruguay is usually an **hour ahead** of Argentina – worth remembering to avoid missing the boat back.

Arguably over-restored, Colonia has in fact managed to cling to its charisma thanks in part to the quality of its architecture, both old and modern. A few other assets help: immaculate parks and gardens, a lovely historic centre, quiet cobbled streets and miles of nearby beaches. Well-preserved vintage cars are still a relatively common sight around the town's streets, and *mate*-drinking on this side of the river is done rather obsessively, even more so than in Argentina.

Arrival and information

Colonia boasts a new, cavernous ferry terminal to rival that of Buenos Aires: you will find a **national tourist office** here, and a bureau de change, although you'll really only need Uruguayan pesos to buy stamps, make a telephone call or use the buses – elsewhere you can pay with Argentine pesos or US dollars. The **city tourist office** is at the corner of General Flores and Rivera (Mon–Fri 8am–7pm, Sat & Sun 10am–6pm; ☎598/452-26886, ⓦwww.coloriaturismo.com), with a second branch at the entry to the old town, by the **Portón de Campo** (see p.247). Ask them for the booklet *güear*, in Spanish and English; it is packed full with all manner of useful data about the town.

Accommodation

There's a good range of mostly high-quality accommodation, including some boutique hotels that ooze charm; prices are not that friendly, though, especially at weekends in the high season (as much as 50 percent more than the prices quoted).

Real de San Carlos (5km), Campsite & Beaches

ACCOMMODATION
Hostel Colonial	B
Hotel Italiano	D
Posada del Virrey	A
Posada Plaza Mayor	C

Río de la Plata

N

BARRIO HISTÓRICO

EATING & DRINKING
Blanco y Negro	1
La Bodeguita	2
El Drugstore	3
La Pulpería de los Faroles	4

COLONIA DEL SACRAMENTO

0   100 m

Montevideo (180km) ▶
Playa Ferrando (2km) ▶

Docks

▼ Buenos Aires (50km)

Hostel Colonial General Flores 440 ☎598/052-30347, ✉hostelling_colonial@hotmail.com. With two storeys of rooms looking out onto a courtyard, Colonia's very decent youth hostel resembles an old inn. It charges UR$250 a night for a bed, with free internet and bike rental. There are also doubles for UR$300.

Hotel Italiano Intendente Suarez & Manuel Lobo ☎598/052-22103, ⓦwww.hotelitaliano.com.uy. This laid back family-run hotel is handily located between the port, Plaza 25 de Agosto and the historic town. The rooms are small, but there is a swimming pool, garage and restaurant. US$88.

Posada del Virrey España 217 ☎598/052-22223, ⓦwww.posadadelvirrey.com. Elegant place with all modern conveniences – a/c, cable TV, and jacuzzis in some rooms, plus great river and bay views and a delicious buffet breakfast. US$88.

Posada Plaza Mayor Calle del Comercio 111 ☎598/052-23193, ⓦwww.posadaplazamayor.com. Housed in a colonial-style building, the *Plaza Mayor* combines atmosphere with comfort, plus sea views from upstairs rooms, and an attractive fountain-cooled patio. It's a favourite with Argentine honeymooners. US$110–190.

The Town

It's not difficult to find your way around Colonia's **Barrio Histórico**, confined to the far western end of the headland. It is best seen early in the morning, before the day-trippers arrive, or at dusk, especially when there's a good sunset (arm yourself with mosquito repellent). Out of Colonia, in either direction, are sandy **beaches**; the best one is 2km east at **Playa Ferrando**.

Barrio Histórico

The best approach to the **Barrio Histórico** from the port and the nineteenth-century "new" town – focused on Plaza 25 de Agosto – is via Calle Manoel Lobo, which steers you through the ornate **Portón de Campo**, the only remaining colonial gateway in the fortified walls. Just beyond lies the **Plaza Mayor**, the heart of the Barrio Histórico. Since Colonia started out as a Portuguese settlement, it's logical to begin with the **Museo Portugués** (daily 11am–4.45pm, closed Wed; UR$50, which will allow access to all Colonia's museums), housed in an early eighteenth-century house on the southern side of the square, at the corner of the picturesque Calle de los Suspiros ("Street of Sighs"). Inside the museum an early colonial ambience has been recreated, with a modest display of domestic items, clothes and jewellery. Overlooking Colonia, the pristine white lighthouse, **El Faro** (daily 1pm–dusk; UR$15), a few metres towards the waterfront from the plaza, has views from the top that take in the whole town.

The two well-restored colonial buildings on the west side of the plaza are the **Casa Nacarello**, on the corner of San Francisco (daily 11am–4.45pm, closed Tues), which transports you to seventeenth-century Portugal, and the **Museo Municipal** (daily 11am–4.45pm, closed Tues), home to an eclectic collection ranging from dinosaur remains to an array of lace fans. In the northwest corner of the plaza is the flinty facade of the **Archivo Regional** (Mon–Fri 11am–4.45pm, closed Wed), with a small but informative collection of maps and parchments. A discreetly restored colonial building at the far western end of Calle Misiones de los Tapes houses the **Museo de los Azulejos** (daily 11am–4.45pm, closed Thurs). *Azulejos*, decorative glazed wall-tiles inspired by Moorish designs, are incorporated into Colonia's street signs and some of its facades.

From the eastern end of the Plaza Mayor, Calle San Antonio leads to the **Plaza de Armas** (or Plaza Manoel Lobo), dominated by the gleaming white **Iglesia Matriz**, which dates from 1680 and is Uruguay's oldest church. Next to the church, the ruins of the Portuguese Governor's house have been landscaped into a garden, with a walkway and signs explaining the original positions of the rooms.

Eating and drinking

There are plenty of restaurants to suit all budgets and tastes in Colonia. While the **food** here is mainly the traditional Uruguayan fare of *parrilladas*, pasta or pizza – the same familiar trio you find in Argentina – more adventurous new places are cropping up all the time.

Blanco y Negro General Flores & Ituzaingó. Stylish wooden interior and live music form the backdrop to a menu of home-made pastas, plus the standard beef dishes. Closed Wed.

La Bodeguita Del Comercio 167. The town's best pizzeria – try the broccoli and mushroom, and drink the local Pilsen. Evenings only.

El Drugstore Vasconcellos 179. Funky decor, smiling waitresses, live music at weekends and fresh food at decent prices – with a view of the Iglesia Matriz thrown in. A couple of surprises on the menu include sushi and glazed chilli chicken.

La Pulpería de los Faroles Misiones de los Tapes 101. The surroundings are pleasant and the staff friendly at this place, which, in addition to the customary Río de la Plata fare, has some more unusual veggie dishes, such as gratinated palm hearts on spinach.

Contexts

Contexts

History...251

Art 262

Books...265

History

For a place that didn't even exist until the late sixteenth century, **Buenos Aires** is laden with history. A product of colonialism and, later, immigration from all corners of Europe plus the Middle East (present-day Syria and Lebanon), the city has been at the heart of Argentina's politics, culture and economy since the Spanish were thrown out of the region in the early nineteenth century. Over the years, Buenos Aires' presence on the international scene has run in cycles – periods of quiet followed by intense attention, either for the behaviour of its icons, such as Evita and Maradona, for the terrible dictatorships based there or for massive economic meltdowns, such as the last one that occurred in 2001. Through it all, though, Porteños' resilience and entrepreneurship has shone through, and this, along with the increasing number of foreign visitors who come to enjoy its manifold attractions, has helped revive its economy quickly in the twenty-first century.

Early settlement

Unlike much of Latin America, the area encompassing modern-day Buenos Aires was home to relatively few pre-Columbian civilizations. Hunter-gatherer tribes who did live in what is now Buenos Aires Province were what the Spanish referred to as Pampas Indians – mostly the Taluhet, Didiuhet and Chechehet, collectively called Het or **Querandí**. There were also some **Tehuelche** and **Mapuche** tribes, mainly living farther west and south.

The first recorded visit by Europeans was in 1516, when **Juan (or João) Díaz de Solís**, a Portuguese mariner in the employ of the Spanish Crown, landed with a small crew while searching for a trade route to the Far East. This first incursion ended ignominiously – Solís was murdered by either the Querandí or the Charrúa, who inhabited what is now Uruguay. Ten years later, **Sebastian Cabot** arrived, christening the area's principal river the Río de la Plata ("River of Silver"), after he found silver bullion among the indigenous groups of Paraguay and assumed there must be deposits nearby. The silver actually probably came from an earlier Portuguese adventurer, but the name stuck, and Cabot's discovery also led to the word "**Argentina**", which derives from the metal's Latin name, *argentum*.

One effect of this "discovery", though, is that the Spanish Crown – in search of treasure – authorized **Pedro de Mendoza** to colonize the Río de la Plata, in an effort to pre-empt the Portuguese conquest of the region. In February 1536, Mendoza founded **Buenos Aires**, originally named Puerto Nuestra Señora Santa María del Buen Ayre ("Port of our Lady the Blessed Maria of fair wind") after Italian sailors' favourite saint, la Madonna di Bonaria – hence Porteño, from *puerto*, the name given to anyone born in the city. The site of this first founding is thought to be the current Parque Lezama (see p.85).

But Mendoza found it impossible to subjugate the Querandí, and there was little food available; a mere eighteen months after its arrival, the party's size had been reduced by two-thirds. Shifting upstream, the Spanish discovered a more amenable indigenous population in the **Guaraní**, founded Asunción, and evacuated the failed Buenos Aires settlement.

In 1580, another expedition was sent from Asunción under the command of **Juan de Garay** down the River Paraná to **resettle Buenos Aires**. No longer dependent on having to secure its own indigenous labour force or food supplies, as it could be assisted from Asunción, it flourished. There was also one vital legacy of the first Mendoza settlement – the **horses and cattle** brought with that expedition had multiplied incredibly in the fertile Pampas. The cattle provided food and income and the horses a means of transport for both the new settlers and local nomadic groups.

Colonial developments

Expansion was slow. With its focus on what is now modern-day Peru – where there was plenty of silver and gold to fill Spain's hungry coffers – the area known as the Governorship of the River Plate, which encompassed Buenos Aires, was ignored as a backwater by the royal authority in Spain. The Viceroyalty of Peru was given authority over southern Spanish South America and direct trade with Europe was prohibited, with all goods meant to be exchanged via Lima. This trade rule both restricted the growth of Buenos Aires as a port and, inevitably, encouraged **contraband**. The fledgling economy was dependent on round-ups of wild cattle (*vaquerías*) for its **hide and tallow industries**, frequently coming into conflict with groups of Tehuelche and Mapuche, who relied on the same feral cattle and horses. The importance of cattle saw the emergence in the seventeenth century of **gauchos** (see box, p.242), nomadic horsemen who roamed in small bands and lived off the wild herds of livestock.

The sixteenth to eighteenth centuries were also the zenith of the **Jesuit missions**. Although these were mostly concentrated in the upper Paraná area, a number of Jesuits settled in Buenos Aires, building churches and convents, including the Manzana de las Luces (see p.52) and the Basílica del Pilar (see p.110). In 1767 King Charles III ordered the **Jesuits' expulsion** from all Spanish territories – because, among other reasons, he viewed them as a threat to royal authority. The Jesuit missions and churches were uniformly abandoned; those in Buenos Aires were soon adopted by other religious orders.

The Viceroyalty of the River Plate

By the late eighteenth century, the British were blocking the Lima sea lanes, and for the Spanish the establishment of a new route to the silver mines of **Potosí** in modern-day Bolivia became imperative. The Río de la Plata was the logical choice. The Crown, recognizing the growing value of Buenos Aires both as a market and a staging post along the river, named the nascent city the capital of the new **Viceroyalty of the River Plate** in 1776. Overseeing an area that reached as far as modern Bolivia, Paraguay and Montevideo, Buenos Aires came, increasingly, to dominate the interior. The Spanish Crown's commercial restrictions were gradually relaxed as, unable to guarantee a steady supply of manufactured goods to its empire, it was forced to allow its colonies to trade with neutral countries. Cheap goods began flowing into the city courtesy of contraband merchants, who used neutral ships to import items from enemy countries. Once restrictions had been lifted, it became increasingly difficult to reinstate them, and attempts to do so caused anger among those, such as merchant **Manuel Belgrano**, who argued for free trade. The progressive ideas of the American and French revolutions circulated among Buenos Aires' elite, and resentment was building.

Afro-Argentines

In the second half of the eighteenth century, demand for labour in the viceroyalty led to the importing of **black slave labour**. Though the numbers of slaves brought to the region were nothing like that seen in the US or Brazil, by the time slavery was officially abolished in 1813 around a third of the population of Buenos Aires was Afro-Argentine. Nowadays, however, the city is considered one of the most "white" of all world capitals – and it's something of a historical mystery what happened to the black community. Historians point out that the entire city population was only 100,000 back in the early nineteenth century – so the community was soon lost in the massive wave of European immigration that hit the city later in the century. The natural process of assimilation was accelerated by a disproportionate ratio of men to women, while the mostly impoverished Afro-Argentine community was also heavily hit by the city's yellow fever epidemics and the country's nineteenth-century wars. Experts estimate that, excepting recent immigrants (from Cuba, Colombia, Brazil and Senegal), there are around 3000 Afro-Argentines living in and around Buenos Aires today. The influence of this community can be seen in various aspects of local culture, notably tango and carnival celebrations.

The other major change in the economy of Buenos Aires at this time was the growth of **livestock farms** in the surrounding province. By the end of the eighteenth century, these **estancias** had become highly profitable and Buenos Aires' numbers were swelled by immigration from Spaniards and native-born Spanish Americans from the interior. In the mid-eighteenth century, Buenos Aires had 12,000 inhabitants, already twice as many as any city in the continent's interior, and by 1810 it had reached over 42,000.

The British invasions

When the British heard of the commercial tensions in Buenos Aires, they took it as a sign that revolution was on its way – and seized the perceived opportunity. In June 1806, a force of 1600 men led by **General William Beresford** stormed into the city, hoping to eventually gain control of the entire viceroyalty. The viceroy, the **Marqués de Sobremonte**, fled the city, and the remaining Spanish authorities reluctantly swore allegiance to the British Crown.

But the British had underestimated the city. The people of Buenos Aires regrouped under a new commander-in-chief, French-born **Santiago Liniers**, and ousted their invaders during the reconquest, or **Reconquista**, of August 12. Undaunted, the British captured Montevideo, from where they launched a second assault on Buenos Aires in July 1807. Again, they were defeated, surrendering in what came to be known as **La Defensa**, during which the militia peppered the enemy with cannon and musket fire, while women poured boiling oil and water on the hapless British soldiers from the tops of the city's buildings – Defensa, the main street running through Monserrat and San Telmo, is named after this event.

One consequence of the victory over the British was to make the people of Buenos Aires aware of the extent to which they could manage their own affairs. This was the first time that they had fought in unison against a foreign invader and the feeling of pride carried over into a stance of defiance in certain sectors against the monarchy.

The May revolution

Following the British invasions, a new viceroy, **Viscount Balthasar de Cisneros**, arrived to replace the disgraced Sobremonte. Foolishly, Cisneros scrapped free-trade initiatives Liniers had issued in the interim, and a ban on trading in silver was reinstated. It was then that free-trade proponents such as Belgrano began to plan a revolution. Coincidentally, Spain was in the throes of its own revolution: in 1810, news reached Buenos Aires that Napoleon had captured Seville, the last outpost hanging on in the face of a French invasion. This led to an extraordinary meeting of Buenos Aires notables. On **May 25** (now a national holiday, celebrated in a host of ways in 2010, the bicentenary year, see p.47), the people of Buenos Aires gathered in front of the Cabildo (see p.50) wearing rosettes made from sky-blue and white ribbons, the colours that later made up the **Argentine flag**. Inside, Viceroy Cisneros was ousted after it was agreed that the Spanish administration in the motherland had effectively ceased to exist, and the **Primera Junta** was sworn in to become the first independent government of the region. However, many still proclaimed loyalty to Ferdinand VII, imprisoned heir to the Spanish throne. Thus began two decades of turbulence, involving **independence struggles** with Spain and **civil war** between Buenos Aires and the interior provinces of the old viceroyalty.

Independence and early battles

The Primera Junta was headed by **Cornelio Saavedra**, who believed in sharing power between Buenos Aires and the provinces of the viceroyalty, and insisted on proclaiming a token loyalty to the Spanish Crown. The other members of the Junta, including Belgrano and Mariano Moreno, were less moderate, intent on bringing the rest of the territory under the control of Buenos Aires. Over time Moreno's views came to represent the position of the **Unitarists** (the "Blues") who favoured centralism, while Saavedra's contained the first seeds of the ideas of later **Federalists** (the "Reds"), promoting the autonomy of the provinces within the framework of a loose confederation. This dispute was to dominate Argentine politics of the nineteenth century, causing bitter division and repeated civil war, and the tension between the provinces and Buenos Aires is still a feature of life in Argentina today. The 1810s and 1820s saw the old viceroyalty break up, as authorities in its further reaches were unwilling to submit to Buenos Aires, and Paraguay, Bolivia and Uruguay were formed.

The royalist factions in Buenos Aires had, by 1812, effectively been crushed, and a front led by **José de San Martín**, who replaced Manuel Belgrano as head of the independence forces, essentially finished them off. San Martín became known as the "Great Liberator", and the "Grandfather of the Nation" – you won't be able to go far in Buenos Aires without seeing something named in his honour. **Independence** from Spain was formally declared on July 9, 1816, at a congress in the city of Tucumán, and the **United Provinces of the River Plate** came into existence. However, Unitarists and Federalists continued to battle for control of the capital, and struggles with pro-royalist forces flared up across the old viceroyalty.

The power struggle between Buenos Aires and the provinces continued over the next few decades, as the former proved unwilling to renounce its privileged trading terms. This culminated in Buenos Aires refusing to approve the **1853 constitution** and seceding to form its own republic for seven years, until it was forced to ratify and rejoin the republic. In 1880 the city was formally **federalized** and made the nation's capital, separated from the province of Buenos Aires (whose capital became the city of La Plata). Buenos Aires was given its own **mayor** – to be appointed by the president – and the Casa Rosada (see p.48) became the president's seat of office.

The first mayor of Buenos Aires was **Torcuato de Alvear** (see box, p.110), who, during his term in the 1880s, made significant improvements to city infrastructure. His modernizing attitude echoed that of the president at the time, **Domingo Sarmiento**, the man most identified with the drive to "Europeanize" Argentina, who was responsible for the city's public parks, such as Parque 3 de Febrero.

Immigration and expansion

Few cities in the world have experienced the kind of astonishing growth that Buenos Aires did between 1870 and 1914. Finally the city was able to exploit and export the Pampas' great riches, thanks to **technological advances** such as the steamship, the railway and, above all, refrigeration – which enabled Europeans to dine on Argentine beef for the first time. Massive foreign investment – most notably from the British – soon poured into the city, and Buenos Aires' stature leapt accordingly. Most of the old town was razed and an eclectic range of new buildings went up in a huge grid pattern, a perfect implementation of the orderly, square *urbs americana* city plan. The standard of living of the city's growing middle class equalled or surpassed that of many European countries, while the wealth of its elite was almost unparalleled. When a series of yellow fever epidemics swept through Buenos Aires in the 1870s, the affluent moved from the south of the city to the relatively undeveloped north – many of Retiro's and Recoleta's decadent *palacios* date from these years.

Encouraged by leaders like Sarmiento, an astounding six million **immigrants** came to Argentina during this time – almost all passed through Buenos Aires, and many stayed. Half of these were Italians, a quarter were Spaniards, while other groups included the French, Portuguese, Basques, Russians, Ottomans, Irish and Welsh. The city's total population doubled between 1880 and 1890, and by 1895 foreigners represented nearly one-third of this number. By 1900 it was the largest city in Latin America, with a population nearing a million. Generally, immigrants were welcomed as part of the drive towards economic expansion, though they did not all share in the city's amazing wealth – many endured appalling conditions in the city's overcrowded *conventillos* or tenement buildings in places like San Telmo.

By the time of Argentina's **centenary** in 1910, Buenos Aires had little cause to envy the capitals of the old continent, and the anniversary of the country's formation was a time of great celebration.

The Perón years

By the mid-twentieth century the breakneck development had come to a close: Buenos Aires' growth ground to a halt as the country slid into a long stretch of political turmoil and economic crisis. The first character to emerge in this period was **Juan Domingo Perón**, a charismatic military man of modest origins. Appointed Secretary for Labour, he used this post to cultivate links

Evita Perón began life humbly – a fact emphasized like a mantra in the fascinating museum in Palermo dedicated to her life, work and death (see p.135). She was born **María Eva Duarte** in 1919, the fifth illegitimate child of a landowner in the rural interior of Buenos Aires Province. She was raised in poverty by her mother, her father having abandoned the family when Eva was still a baby. At age 15, she headed to the capital to pursue her dream of becoming an actress, and managed to scrape a living from several minor roles in radio and TV before working her way to a leading role in the cinema through the influence of well-connected lovers. Her life changed dramatically in 1944, when she met Juan Domingo Perón at a charity event held at Luna Park (see p.181). She became his mistress and married him a year later, shortly before his election to the presidency.

As First Lady, Evita was in her element. She championed the rights of the working classes and underprivileged poor, whom she named the **descamisados** ("shirtless ones"), and immersed herself in populist politics and programmes of social aid. She received petitions in person from the public, distributing favours on a massive scale through her Social Aid Foundation. She played the role of the devoted wife, but was, in her own way, a pioneering feminist, credited with assuring that women were granted suffrage in 1947.

Another role she revelled in was that of **ambassador** for her country, captivating the press and public during a 1948 tour of Europe. Dressed in Dior and Balenciaga, hers was the international face of Argentina, which assuredly compounded the jealousy of Europhile upper-class women at home – she was detested by the Argentine elite as a vulgar upstart. They painted her as a whore and as someone who was more interested in feeding her own personality cult than assisting the *descamisados*. Evita, for her part, seemed to delight in antagonizing the oligarchic establishment, whipping up popular resentment towards an "anti-Argentine" class.

Stricken by cervical **cancer**, she died aged only 33 in 1952. Her death was greeted with outpourings of grief never seen in Argentina, before or since. Eight people were crushed to death in the crowds of mourners that gathered, and over two thousand needed treatment for injuries. In death, Evita led an even more rarefied existence than she had in life; society was polarized, though, and some of the most tasteless political graffiti ever seen ("Long Live Cancer!") was daubed on walls all over Buenos Aires. After the military coup of 1955, the palace where the Peróns had lived was razed to the ground – under Menem the site was chosen as the location of the new national library and, renamed Plaza Evita, of a statue of the lady herself. The ruling officers even had decoy copies of her **embalmed corpse** made, and spirited the original away to Europe, all too aware of its power as an icon. There followed a truly bizarre series of burials and reburials and even allegations of necrophilia, before she was repatriated in 1974. She was then finally afforded a decent burial in Recoleta Cemetery (see p.108). To this day, Evita retains saint-like status among many working-class Peronists. Protests and furious graffiti greeted the casting of Madonna, fresh from a series of pornographic photo shoots, to portray her in the Alan Parker film musical, *Evita*. For many, this was sacrilege – an insult to the memory of the most important woman in Argentine history.

with trade unions, generating a political presence by combining dynamic personal leadership with well-orchestrated mass rallies. Perón's popularity alarmed his military superiors, who arrested him in 1945. However, this move backfired when Perón's iconic wife, **Evita** (see box above), organized **mass demonstrations** in the **Plaza de Mayo** to protest his imprisonment. Shortly thereafter, Perón was released, and swept to the presidency in 1946 on a tide of public popular sentiment. Rallies of almost religious fervour in support of Perón and Evita, who came out onto the balcony of the **Casa Rosada** to deliver their speeches, followed at regular intervals.

As Perón faced dissent within the army, alongside the wrath of the Church and wealthy sections of society, political violence erupted in the city. In 1953 a pro-Perón rally was bombed by upper-class anti-Peronists, which led to arson attacks by pro-Peronists on places such as the Jockey Club, a perceived seat of privilege (see p.104). More devastating was the massacre that occurred in June 1955, when the armed forces, planning a coup, bombed a pro-Perón demonstration in the Plaza de Mayo, killing some three hundred people but leaving Perón untouched. The demonstration had been called by Peronists to show their support for the president in his struggle against the Catholic Church, and led to angry protestors going on the rampage, setting fire to a number of important historical churches in the city. Losing control of the country and its people, in 1955 Perón resigned and went into exile in Spain.

There followed eighteen years of short-lived civilian and military regimes, economic stagnation, strikes, wage freezes and a growing disillusionment with the institutions of government. **Guerrilla** organizations, principally the **Montoneros**, emerged, targeting multinationals, landed oligarchies and the security forces. In 1973, with the economy continuing to splutter into recession and guerrilla violence spreading, a reluctant military allowed Perón to return to stand in new elections.

By this time, Perón had come to represent all things to all men. Radical left-wing Montoneros saw themselves as true Peronists – the natural upholders of the type of Peronism that championed the rights of the *descamisados* and freedom from imperialist domination. Likewise, conservative landed groups saw him as a symbol of stability in the face of anarchy. Any illusion that Perón was going to be the cure-all balm for the nation's ills dissipated before he touched down at Ezeiza airport: his welcoming party dissolved into a violent melee, with rival groups in the crowd of 500,000 shooting at each other.

Perón died in July 1974, and power devolved to his third wife, Isabelita. Out of her depth, the unelected Isabelita clung to the advice of José López Rega, who has been compared to Rasputin and was the figure behind the forming of notorious right-wing **death squads**. The only boom industry, it seemed, was corruption in government, and, with hyperinflation and spiralling violence, Buenos Aires was gripped by paralysis.

The Dirty War

The long-expected **military coup** finally came in March 1976. Under **General Jorge Videla**, a military junta initiated what it termed the Process of National Reorganization (usually known as the **Proceso**), which is more often referred to as the Guerra Sucia, or **Dirty War**. The Constitution was suspended, and a campaign of systematic state violence was unleashed. As well as guerrillas, their families and anyone suspected of harbouring guerrilla sympathies, those who were targeted included liberal intellectuals, journalists, psychologists, Jews, Marxists, trade unionists and atheists. The most notorious tactic was to send hit squads to make people "disappear". Once seized, these **desaparecidos** simply ceased to exist – no one knew who abducted them or where they were. In fact, the *desaparecidos* were taken to secret detention camps – places like the infamous **Navy Mechanics School** (ESMA) in the northern suburb of Núñez (see p.146) – where they were subjected to torture, rape and, usually, execution.

In the midst of this, the armed forces had the opportunity to demonstrate the "success" of their regime to the world, by hosting the **1978 World Cup**; many matches were played in River Plate's **Monumental** stadium, which was expanded especially for the event (see p.146). Though Argentina's victory in the final stoked nationalist pride, few observers were fooled – indeed, the event backfired on the military in other ways. It provided a forum for human rights advocates, including the **Madres de Plaza de Mayo** (see box, p.49), to bring the issue of the *desaparecidos* to the attention of the international media.

With the military's grip increasingly shaky, it chose in April 1982 to invade the **Falkland Islands**, or the Islas Malvinas. The Argentine population reacted with delight; Buenos Aires' city centre saw massive demonstrations of support. This joy, however, soon turned to dismay when people realized that the British government was prepared to go to war for the islands, and Argentine forces were defeated by mid-June (a major monument on Plaza San Martín commemorates the Argentine fallen; see p.97). One positive thing did come out of the debacle, though: it proved to be the nail in the coffin for the regime.

The return to stability

Democracy was finally restored with the elections of October 1983, which were won by **Raúl Alfonsín**. He was unable to control runaway inflation, and many of Buenos Aires' shops closed, preferring to keep their stock rather than selling it for a currency with no value. Bad as it was in the city during this period, it was worse elsewhere, and immigrants began flowing to Buenos Aires again, this time from Argentina's poorer provinces and neighbouring countries – Peru, Bolivia and Paraguay. Many newcomers settled in the capital's growing number of shantytowns, now known as *villas miseria* (see box, p.98).

The 1990s were dominated by **Carlos Menem**, who became president of Argentina and embarked on a series of sweeping **neo-Liberal reforms**. The peso was pegged to the US dollar and inflation was held flat or in single digits throughout the 1990s – thereby temporarily stabilizing the economy. Massive **public spending cuts** accompanied swift **privatization**, causing seismic reverberations throughout Porteño society. On the one hand, the strength of the currency brought a new upsurge in spending by those who could afford it – and an infrastructure to match. Smart new shopping malls, restaurants and cinema complexes sprung up around the city, changing the way many Porteños lived. But for those who had no pesos to spend, the downsizing of newly privatized industries and the removal of protective tariffs caused unemployment rates to rise to eighteen percent, and acute financial hardship resulted in strikes and sporadic civil unrest, as more and more people fell beneath the poverty line. Federal railway subsidies were ceased in 1993 – the main reason for the decrepit state of Buenos Aires' overland trains.

In 1994, Menem reformed the Constitution, granting Buenos Aires autonomy – although it is still often referred to as the *Capital Federal*, its actual title is **Ciudad Autónoma de Buenos Aires**. Since then, instead of a mayor appointed by the president, the head of the city government, a powerful political position, has been voted for in local elections. Its first incumbent was **Fernando de la Rúa**, who garnered a reputation for being dull but efficient, and in 1999 went on to become President of Argentina.

Crisis and recovery

Much of Argentina's new-found prosperity was built on the shakiest of foundations – huge **loans** from the IMF that it never really had a hope of paying off. As the country lurched further into recession and nervous citizens began to withdraw cash from the banks, in December 2001 de la Rúa announced restrictions limiting access to private deposits.

A general strike was staged by the Peronist-controlled unions and, within days, acts of looting were reported throughout Greater Buenos Aires. De la Rúa announced a curfew, ignored by thousands of protestors bashing pots and pans (the first of many noisy **"cacerolazos"**, or saucepan protests) who marched on the Plaza de Mayo. Brutal efforts by the police to clear the plaza ended in a bloodbath, with protestors shot dead in the street. De la Rúa finally left office, ignominiously departing the Casa Rosada by helicopter.

By January, the new caretaker government had **devalued the peso**. These were troubled times in Buenos Aires: *cacerolazos* occurred daily, angry graffiti appeared everywhere, vouchers (*patacones*) were issued by the government to pay wages and those whose cash had been frozen traded goods and services directly with others similarly affected. The head of the city government at this time was Aníbal Ibarra, a political ally of the man elected president in 2003, **Néstor Kirchner**. The left-leaning Kirchner repealed the amnesty laws that had made it impossible to prosecute members of the military guilty of human rights atrocities in the Dirty War; in December 2010 General Jorge Videla was sentenced to life in prison for the torture and murder of prisoners. He also closed the ESMA so it could be turned into a monument to the disappeared, leading the Madres of the Plaza de Mayo (see box, p.49) to call off their weekly vigil after the best part of thirty years.

Street politics

Buenos Aires is a city where politics are fought out on the streets, as well as, and sometimes more than, at the ballot box. Demonstrations (*manifestaciones*) are frequent happenings in the city, be they striking workers or people angry about the pollution from paper-pulp plants across the Río Uruguay. These days they're seldom violent, but they can be noisy and disruptive, and are likely to occur at any time in the vicinity of Congreso or the Plaza de Mayo. The specific phenomenon of *piqueteros* – from the English "pickers" – first came to the attention of the world around the time of the 2001 crisis. They are principally leftist militants, from the extreme wings of trade unions and anarchist groups; they can occasionally turn nasty, staging violent protests outside the houses of former junta members or banks and businesses, blockading major roads and access points in order to draw notice to social injustices such as hospital closures or poor factory conditions. The most notorious groups of *piqueteros* belong to the Movimiento Patriótico Revolucionario, better known as Quebracho, whose stated goal is to abolish poverty and all forms of ownership within it. They deliberately attack forces of law and order and hold confrontational demonstrations when foreign dignitaries come to Buenos Aires, and the Peronist government has been reluctant to confront them. The number of incidents involving them has decreased of late, but steer well clear if you hear they are in action. Another similar phenomenon is the *barra brava* (see p.212) – these are football fanatics in the pay of several football clubs, whose noisy presence at matches can be extremely threatening. Some of them are paid-up members of rent-a-mob outfits.

Although the cheaper peso supported economic growth and recovery, a large and visible underclass did not immediately benefit and demonstrations by unemployed Porteños became part of the fabric of everyday life in Buenos Aires; even now, you'll come across the sad sight of *cartoneros* (see box below) rooting through rubbish in search of scrap paper and cardboard. In keeping with a global trend, disparity of wealth became more acute than ever and crime rose fast in a city once considered by far Latin America's safest, leading to a media-fuelled obsession among the middle classes over *la inseguridad* (lack of security). Ibarra was forced to leave office after a fire at a rock concert in December 2004 left 194 dead, taking the blame for poor safety checks that also cost many bars and nightclubs their licences in the disaster's wake.

On the positive side, the favourable exchange rate led to a rocketing number of international visitors (2010 was a record year, with over five million foreign tourists in Argentina, compared with barely two million in 2002, most of whom spent at least a day or two in the capital). Dozens of new restaurants and boutique

BA today

Buenos Aires' three million or so inhabitants, plus the ten million who live in its suburbs (officially known as Bonaerenses – natives of Buenos Aires Province) are fiercely and justifiably proud of their city, *La Reina del Plata*, or "Queen of the River Plate".

Highly individualistic (watch how they drive), the people of Buenos Aires nonetheless have a special sense of community and a strong **social conscience** – in few such big cities do citizens give as generously to buskers and beggars or queue so patiently for buses. However, there is a definite **class system** here, and members of each class live in different parts of the city, leading to pronounced postcode snobbery. The new *clase alta* (upper class), the nouveau riche jet-setters, dwell in penthouses and villas in select parts of Palermo, Puerto Madero and San Isidro, while the more conservative middle classes (or *burguesía*), the ones living off older money, still congregate in Recoleta. Some have fled the perceived crime of the centre to live in *countries* (from "country house") and *barrios cerrados* (gated communities) in the city's hinterland. Golf courses, swimming pools and stables of polo ponies are all part of this scene, but most important are the armed guards who control entry and exit. Buenos Aires' large lower middle class (*clase media baja*) lives mostly in the western barrios, such as Balvanera, Almagro and Caballito, with a large Jewish community living and trading cheek-by-jowl with Peruvians and other Latin immigrants in Once. As has traditionally been the case, in Boca and the other southern barrios and suburbs you'll still find the *clase obrera*, or working class, whose daily occupations keep the city going. At the bottom of the pile, the city's poorest are often immigrants from the provinces or less prosperous South American nations, who live in the primitive homes that make up the *villas miseria*. Some eke out a living by begging or by working as *cartoneros*, people – often whole families – who act as semi-official rubbish recyclers.

Across the social spectrum, people spend a good deal of time and income on their **appearances**, in extreme cases shelling out small fortunes on cosmetic surgery, a thriving industry in the city that is also supported by tourists. A sad side of this focus on the body beautiful is the emphasis on staying slim, which hits young females particularly hard in the form of anorexia and other eating-related conditions. On the other hand obesity, as in many other parts of the world, is also a serious problem, especially since international fast-food and coffee chains have become highly popular. Yet every barrio has a variety of much-frequented gyms and Pilates parlours. Smart attire (though that doesn't necessarily mean jacket and tie for men) is de rigueur in most places when going out – dress up rather than down if you don't want to look like a tourist.

hotels sprung up, the world's biggest **cruise liners** dropped anchor offshore during the warmer months; and Buenos Aires became the self-proclaimed leading **gay and lesbian** destination in Latin America. Right-leaning **Mauricio Macri** triumphed in 2007's city elections, a win that was considered a vote of no confidence in Kirchner, who was succeeded soon after by his wife, Cristina Kirchner, the country's first elected female president. Cristina Kirchner's administration has been involved in a series of bruising political battles, and she was forced to back down in a dispute with farmers over export taxes after thousands of rural workers descended on the capital and erected a semi-permanent protest camp in the Plaza del Congreso.

Also the boss of Boca football club, Macri's plans for a more modern city, with improved transport and less pollution, have been constrained by a huge financial deficit, while spying and corruption scandals have tarnished his own image. However, in preparation for the 2010 bicentenary celebrations – and with some parts looking a little the worse for wear after years of economic misery – the city government embarked on a significant programme of public works. An expansion of the subte network began, Buenos Aires' many parks and plazas were tidied up, and millions were spent on refurbishing the landmark Colón opera house, which reopened in May 2010 (see p.69). This programme stepped up a gear in early 2011, as candidates of varied political stripes, including the incumbent Macri, jockeyed for positions in the popularity stakes, with municipal elections due later in the year. At least there is a positive side to this: the city has not looked this good since the heyday of the first centenary in 1910.

Art

One of the delights of Buenos Aires is visiting its fine art collections. There are a number of small galleries and other establishments, but the pick of the assembled works can be found in the **Museo Nacional de Bellas Artes** (MNBA; see p.113), the **MALBA** (see p.125), the new **Fortabat foundation** (see p.74) and the recently reopened **MAMBA** (see p.85), all four of which contain pieces by major Argentine masters and contemporary artists. Buenos Aires is one big open-air art museum, too, with dozens of works, mainly monumental sculptures, scattered around its parks, gardens and plazas. You can find all the works discussed below at the MNBA unless otherwise noted.

In colonial times Buenos Aires relied on two main sources to satisfy the city's growing demand for artwork: Peruvian and Bolivian craftsmen, especially those of the **Cusco School**; and artisans from Brazil. As a gaucho identity began to emerge, a more specific creativity appeared, in the form of mostly silver and leather "*motivos*" – *mate* vessels, saddles, knives. A major collection of these objects is at the **Museo Hernández** in Palermo (see p.127). But as a middle class and wealthy landowning aristocracy became firmly established, they scorned this "vulgar sub-culture", wanting nothing in their homes but European and European-style art. Not until 1799 did Buenos Aires have its own **art school**, but it was shut down by King Charles IV three years later. After independence, an academy of fine art was founded, but all the teachers came from Europe and it too was closed, for lack of funding, in the 1830s.

Carlos Morel (1813–94), one of the first recognized Argentine artists, had trained at the academy; firmly entrenched in the Romantic tradition of early nineteenth-century France, his oils are exquisite. A particularly fine example is his *Carga de Caballería del Ejército Federal* (exact date unknown). Other artists from the first century of Argentine art include portraitist **Prilidiano Pueyrredón** (1823–70); landscape painter **Eduardo Sívori** (1847–1918), who has a Palermo museum named after him; expressionist **Fernando Fader** (1882–1935); and **Valentín Thibon de Libian** (1889–1931), influenced by Degas. One of the few women to come to the fore in the nineteenth century was Dolores Mora Vega de Hernández – better known as **Lola Mora**. Born in 1866, in Salta Province, she studied in Tucumán, but completed her studies in Italy, where she took to working in marble, a medium used for much of her prolific oeuvre of statues and monuments. One of her finest works is the magnificent Nereidas fountain adorning the Costanera Sur (see p.78). Beginning at the turn of the twentieth century, another Argentine sculptor, **Rogelio Yrurtia**, also figured prominently in the city, with such public works as *Canto al Trabajo*; Yrurtia has a museum housed in his former residence (see p.145).

Argentina's artistic creativity was not "decolonized" until the **1920s**, when its painters and sculptors, at least momentarily, stopped drawing inspiration exclusively from Europe. Of all the early "post-colonial" artists, **Xul Solar**, born Oscar Solari (1887–1963), stands out, both technically and for his originality; he deservedly has a museum to himself, the fantastic **Museo Xul Solar** (see p.118). Solar was an eccentric polymath, who experimented with new influences and in 1939, fascinated by astrology and Buddhism, founded the **Pan Klub**, a group of artists and intellectuals sharing his Utopian credo. The wonderful watercolour *Pupo* is one of his earlier works. *Arlequín* (1928) is a key work by Solar's friend and contemporary, **Emilio Pettoruti** (1892–1971), whose major exhibition in 1924 sent ripples across conservative Buenos Aires. Pettoruti transferred into painting and collage his personal and, for some, Argentine, vision of Cubism. This event is widely interpreted as the beginning of the modern era in Argentine painting.

Despite the developments of the 1920s, most of Argentina's artists continued to fix their gaze on Europe, and increasingly the US. Two of the greatest Argentine artists in that period were **Antonio Berni** (1905–81) – look out for his *Primeros pasos* (1937) – and **Lino Enea Spilimbergo** (1896–1964) – seek out his *Figura* (1937). Their paintings aimed to depict the social reality of Argentina in economic and political turmoil without espousing any political cause – Berni was hailed as the leader of the so-called *Arte Político*. His incredibly moving *La Torre Eiffel en la Pampa* (1930) single-handedly seems to sum up the continuing dilemma among Argentine artists – are they nostalgic for Paris while in Argentina or for Buenos Aires when in Europe?

A second big break with European artistic traditions came towards the end of World War II. Just after Perón came to power, a number of groundbreaking exhibitions were staged in Buenos Aires. Three major art **manifestos** were also published: the Manifiesto Intervencionista, by Tomás Maldonado and his friends; the Manifiesto Blanco, issued by members of the Academia Altamira, which wanted to create a new art form based on "matter, colour and sound in perpetual movement"; and the Manifiesto Madí, signed by Hungarian-born **Gyula Kosice** (born 1924).

Madí, probably a nonsense word like Dada, but sometimes said to be derived from "*materialismo dialéctico*", was decidedly political. In 1946 Kosice, one of the movement's leaders, produced a series of works using neon-lighting, thought to be the first of their kind, and he later experimented with plexiglass, acrylic, cork, aluminium and bone – his *Dispersión del aire* (1967) is one such work. **Rhod Rothfuss** (1920–69) was the Uruguayan leader of Madí, and his enamel paintings on wood were highly influential in Argentina.

Rivals of the Madí group, the Asociación Arte Concreto-Invención or **Intervencionistas**, were far more radical, espousing solidarity with the Soviet Union largely as a means of protesting against US interference in Latin America. Artistically, though, they were more conventional than the Madí lot, and tended to produce paintings in traditional frames; they drew much of their inspiration from artists like Mondrian, Van Doesburg and Malevich. Members included leading theorist **Tomás Maldonado** (born 1922), but the most acclaimed artists in the movement are **Enio Iommi** (born 1926), **Alfredo Hlito** (1923–93) and **Raúl Lozza** (1911–2007). The first of the three is generally regarded as one of Argentina's greatest-ever artists. His sculptures in stainless steel – such as *Torsión de planos* (1964), wood, bronze and aluminium – express his personal "spatialist" credo. Iommi underwent an about turn in the 1970s and began producing objects with emphasis on the material, using industrial and household refuse – his 1977 Retiro exhibition entitled *Adiós a una época* marked his switch to Arte Povera, after decades of using "noble" materials. Hlito was a more "mainstream" Intervencionista – a very typical work of his is *Líneas tangentes* (1955). Lozza, on the other hand, became so obsessed with the intricacies of colour, form and representation in art that he formed his own movement in 1949, called **Perceptismo**, according to which paintings must be sketched obeying certain architectural rules before the colour can be filled in. His work *Pintura Numero 153* (1948) was executed just before he left the Intervencionistas.

The 1950s, 1960s and 1970s were once again times of turmoil in Argentina. **Raquel Forner** (1902–87) came to the fore in the 1950s, mainly because she was unmistakeably influenced by Picasso. This comes through in her style – in which human figures are amalgamated with symbolic images – and subject matter. She painted two series of haunting oils about the Spanish Civil War and World War II: *España* (1937–39) and *El drama* (1939–46); the spine-chilling *Retablo de dolor* (1944), which belongs to the second group, also reveals her interest in the religious paintings of El Greco. She set herself apart in the 1960s by concentrating on the theme of the human conquest of space, as exemplified by her 1968 *Conquest of Moon Rock*.

Italian-born sculptor **Libero Badii** (1916–2001), some of whose work, including later paintings, is displayed at the Fundación Banco Francés, won a national prize in 1953 with a sensually organic marble figure, *Torrente*.

A number of young artists dominated Argentine painting in the 1960s. **Ernesto Deira** (1928–86), **Jorge de la Vega** (1930–71), **Rómulo Macció** (born 1931) and **Luis Felipe Noé** (born 1933) all produced acclaimed work, though Vega is usually regarded as the most original. Heavy neofigurative shades of Francis Bacon are detectable in Macció's *Vivir un poco cada día* (1963); while Noé's Ensoresque masterpiece *Introducción a la esperanza* (1963) illustrates his theory of "*cuadro dividido*", in which several paintings are chaotically assembled to make one work. Vega's *Intimidades de un tímido* (1960s) is typical of his vast canvases, brimming with vitality but largely mysterious in their imagery. **Alberto Heredia** (1924–2000) had a lot in common with both Surrealism and Pop Art. His now-famous *Camembert Boxes* (1961–63), filled with day-to-day junk, are seen as a breakthrough in Argentine sculpture.

Worldwide, the 1960s were marked by the new artistic phenomenon of Happenings, and what Argentine artists called **Ambientaciones**; despite their often massive scale and laborious preparations, they were by nature ephemeral events, and all we have left now are photographic documents. **Marta Minujín** (born 1941), Argentina's answer to Andy Warhol, has been a leading exponent. Her two key works in 1965, *La menesunda* and *El batacazo*, both staged at the Centro de Artes Visuales, were labyrinths meant to excite, delight, disturb and attack the visitor's five senses. She continued to perform into the 1970s, poking fun at national icons like Carlos Gardel; in 1979 she constructed a 30m-high *Obelisco de pan dulce*, a half-scale model of Buenos Aires' famous symbol clad with thousands of plastic-wrapped raisin breads, erected at the cattle-raisers' temple, the Sociedad Rural in Palermo. To celebrate the return to democracy in 1983, her *Partenón de libros* was a massive monument covered in books – many publications had been banned or burned under the junta – in the capital.

The 1970s and early 1980s saw many artists leave the country, but some preferred to stay, using indirect means of criticizing the government. Two figures stand out during this period: **Pablo Suárez** (1937–2006), whose *La terraza* (1983) is typical of his black humour and anti-Argentinidad credo, being a sardonically cruel pastiche of the Sunday *asado*; and his contemporary **Víctor Grippo** (1936–2002), whose *Analogía I* (1970–71) comprises forty potatoes in pigeonholes with electrodes attached, seen retrospectively as a horrific premonition of the military's torture chambers. Another contemporary of theirs, **Antonio Seguí** (born 1934), is also out on an artistic limb: his comic-like paintings on display at various venues around the city depict a somewhat sinister, behatted figure in countless different poses, representing urban alienation (according to the artist himself). The style of **Ricardo Cinalli** (born 1948) has been described as postmodern Neoclassicism, and his *Blue Box* (1990) is a prime example of his original use of layers of tissue paper on which he colours in pastel.

Guillermo Kuitca (born 1961) is without a doubt Argentina's most successful contemporary artist, and in many ways he encapsulates what Argentine art has become. It is no coincidence that his series of maps, such as those printed onto a triptych of mattresses (1989), are largely of Germany and central Europe, where his own roots are. Argentine artists seem finally to have given up trying to forge the Argentinidad that Borges and his colleagues were set on inventing in the 1920s, and have acknowledged instead that, in the global village of constant interaction, personal styles and talent are more important than an attempt to create an artificial national identity through art.

Books

uenos Aires is a city with both a fine literary heritage and a very high literacy rate, and its many splendidly monumental bookshops are a reflection of the considerable interest in what is written in both Argentina and the outside world. If you can read Spanish you will be spoilt for choice, but even without it you will find there are a fair number of books relating to Buenos Aires available in English – either Argentine writers in translation or travelogues and other works written by English-language authors. You can track down most of the works listed below fairly easily via the internet – Amazon (ⓦwww.amazon.co.uk or www.amazon.com) is a good starting point. In Buenos Aires itself, there are many coffee-table books produced that focus on the city, as well as on subjects such as gauchos and estancias. They vary in quality, although generally speaking they consist of dubious text interspersed with good, glossy photos.

The term "o/p" denotes that a book is currently out of print, but is still generally available through second-hand bookstores or the internet; similarly, if a book is currently only published in the UK or US that fact is indicated in parentheses after the title.

🜋 preceding a title denotes that it is highly recommended.

Travel and specialist guides

Dereck Foster & Richard Tripp *Food and Drink in Argentina*. The *Buenos Aires Herald*'s food and drink columnist Foster co-authors this slim and useful guide, providing both general information to whet the appetite of first-time visitors and a detailed pictorial glossary to enable veteran travellers to tell *medialunas* from *moñitos*.

Miranda France *Bad Times in Buenos Aires*. Despite the title and the critical (some might say patronizing) tone, this journal penned during the height of the Menem era brings Porteños to life, and you can't help feeling the author secretly loves the place. Highlights include a near-miss with Menem's toupée.

Che Guevara *The Motorcycle Diaries*. Ernesto "Che" Guevara's own account of his epic motorcycle tour around Latin America, beginning in Buenos Aires and heading south to Patagonia and then up through Chile. Che undertook the tour when he was just 23 and the resulting diary is an intriguing blend of travel anecdotes and an insight into the mind of a nascent revolutionary, filmed in 2004 with Gael García Bernal playing the part of Che.

Paul Theroux *The Old Patagonian Express*. Tales about trains by the tireless cynic. In the four chapters on Argentina, which he passed through just before the 1978 World Cup, he waxes lyrical about cathedral-like Retiro station and has a surreal dialogue with Borges.

Jason Wilson *Buenos Aires: A Cultural and Literary History*. Described by the author as a "sort of literary arm-chair stroll", this text illuminates the streets of the city with extensive quotes from authors and travellers, as well as historical anecdotes.

History, politics and society

CONTEXTS | Books

Rita Arditti *Searching for Life*. The story of the *abuelas* (grandmothers) of the Plaza de Mayo and their long-running investigation into the whereabouts of hundreds of children who disappeared during the military dictatorship – many of whom were abducted with their parents and then raised by military families. A moving yet positive account of the grandmothers' ongoing search, which remains a controversial issue in the country.

Samuel L. Baily *Immigrants in the Land of Promise: Italians in Buenos Aires and New York City, 1870–1914*. The fascinating topic of migration is examined here by looking at the different experiences of the many Italians who left their country at the turn of the twentieth century, some going north to New York and some south to Buenos Aires. Baily concludes that the latter group found a more welcoming environment and a culture easier for them to identify with, and progressed and integrated faster than those who went to the US.

Paul Blustein *And the Money Kept Rolling In (and Out); Wall Street, the IMF, and the Bankrupting of Argentina*. The definitive account of the Argentine economic crisis of 2001. *Washington Post* journalist Blustein contends that, though Argentina's fate was always in the hands of its own politicians, the IMF worsened the situation by indulging their emerging market "poster child" long beyond the point when the debt burden had become unsustainable, while the unrestricted flows of the global finance market had their role to play, too. Authoritative, and a cracking read.

Ian Fletcher *The Waters of Oblivion: the British Invasion of the Rio de la Plata 1806–07*. The only dedicated account in English of the abortive attempt by the British to invade Buenos Aires in 1807, explaining how the mighty British army was routed by a local militia. One for fans of military history.

Uki Goñi *The Real Odessa*. This is the authoritative account of the aid given by Perón (and the Vatican) to Nazi war criminals; hundreds settled in Argentina. The Argentine government and Peronist party in particular has done little to address its sheltering of these men – indeed, Goñi finds evidence that incriminating documents were being burned as late as 1996.

Nunca Más (o/p). The 1984 report by CONADEP, Argentina's National Commission on the Disappeared, headed by novelist Ernesto Sabato, which was appointed to investigate the fate of those who disappeared during the 1976–83 military dictatorship. Not comfortable reading, but essential for anyone who wishes to understand more about what happened in those years; if you can't stomach the firsthand accounts, at least read the excellent prologue by Sabato.

Michael McCaughan *True Crimes: Rodolfo Walsh* (UK; o/p). The life and work of journalist Rodolfo Walsh, assassinated by the military government in Buenos Aires in 1977 for his involvement with the Montoneros guerrillas and his continued criticism of the dictatorship. The text alternates Walsh's own work, including his acclaimed short stories, with a biography that illuminates the period from a left-wing perspective.

Gabriella Nouzeilles and Graciela Montaldo (eds) *The Argentina Reader*. Compendium of essays and stories on Argentina's history and culture, with the majority of the pieces written by Argentines. An excellent starting point for further reading, though a bit hefty for lugging around.

Domingo F. Sarmiento *Facundo, or Civilization and Barbarism*. Probably the most influential of all books written in Latin America in the nineteenth century, this essay defines one of Argentina's major cultural peculiarities – the battle between the provinces seeking decentralized power and a sophisticated metropolis more interested in what is going on abroad than in its vast hinterland.

Jacobo Timerman *Prisoner Without A Name, Cell Without A Number* (US). A gruelling tale of detention under the 1976–83 military dictatorship, as endured by Timerman, then the editor of leading liberal newspaper of the time, *La Opinión*. The author is Jewish, and his experiences lead to a

wider consideration of anti-Semitism and the nature of totalitarian regimes.

Horacio Verbitsky *The Flight: Confessions of an Argentine Dirty Warrior*. A respected investigative journalist, Verbitsky tells the story of a junior naval officer who was involved in the horrific practice of pushing drugged prisoners out of airplanes over the Río de la Plata during the Dirty War. A meticulously researched account of a dark episode in Argentina's history. See also *Buenos Aires Herald* editor Andrew Graham Yool's account of this dark period as seen through the eyes of someone living through and reporting on it, *State of Fear*.

The arts

Simon Collier (ed) (o/p) *Tango! The Dance, the Song, the Story*. A glossy coffee-table book with a lively account of the history of tango and its key protagonists, well illustrated with colour and black-and-white photos.

David Elliott (ed) *Art from Argentina: 1920–1994* (UK). Comprehensive illustrated account of the development of twentieth-century Argentine art, composed of a series of focused essays and monographs of major figures. Indispensable to anyone with a serious interest in the subject.

John King and Nissa Torrents (eds) *Garden of the Forking Paths: Argentine Cinema* (o/p). Authoritative collection of essays on Argentine cinema, compiled by two experts in the field. An excellent introduction to Argentina's film industry.

Alberto Manguel *With Borges*. Accomplished Argentine writer Manguel recounts the time as a young man he spent reading to Borges. Absolutely charming essay, with the kind of gentle humour, subtle poetry and sharp insights into Buenos Aires life that characterize the great man's own work.

Fiction

Roberto Arlt *The Seven Madmen* (o/p). Until his tragically early death, Roberto Arlt captured the lot of the poor immigrant with his gripping, if idiosyncratic, novels about anarchists, whores and other marginal characters in 1920s Buenos Aires. *The Seven Madmen* is the pick of his works.

Jorge Luis Borges *Labyrinths*. Not only Argentina's greatest

writer, but one of the world's finest and most influential. His prose is highly original, witty and concise; rather than novels, he introduces his ideas through short stories and essays – ideal for dipping into – and *Labyrinths* is a good introduction to these, with selections from his major collections. It includes many of his best-known and most enigmatic tales, including

Library of Babel, an analogy of the world as a never-ending library.

Julio Cortázar *Hopscotch* (o/p) and *The Winners*. Cortázar is probably second only to Borges in the canon of Argentine writers and *Hopscotch* is a major work, considered by some as the first "hypertext" novel. *The Winners* begins in Buenos Aires, with a group of people from diverse parts of Porteño society meeting at the café *London City* (see p.159), before embarking on a cruise they have won as a prize in a mysterious lottery. Cortázar is also well regarded for his enigmatic short stories – try *Blow Up and Other Stories*.

Nathan Englander *The Ministry of Special Cases*. US writer Englander set his 2007 novel in 1970s Buenos Aires, with the backdrop of the Dirty War and the plot centring on the disappearance of a teenage son from a middle-class Jewish family. The observations of Argentine society are astute, and the story is wry, compelling and tragic in equal measures.

Ricardo Güiraldes *Don Segundo Sombra*. A tender and nostalgic evocation of past life on the pampas, chronicling the relationship between a young boy and his mentor, the novel's eponymous gaucho. Written in 1926, some decades after the gaucho era had come to a close, it was a key text in changing the image of the Argentine cowboy from that of a violent undesirable to a strong, independent man with simple tastes, at the heart of Argentina's national identity.

José Hernández *Martín Fierro*. The classic gaucho novel – actually a verse of epic proportions, traditionally learned by heart by many Argentines. Written as a protest against the corrupt authorities, it features a highly likeable gaucho outlaw on the run, who rails against the country's weak institutional structures and dictatorial rulers. Its rhyming verse and liberal use of gaucho lingo make translation difficult; one version is the classic Walter Owen translation from the 1930s, available in Argentine bookshops.

Tomás Eloy Martínez *The Perón Novel*, *Santa Evita* (both o/p) and *The Tango Singer*. One of the country's best contemporary writers, Tomás Eloy Martínez darts between fact and fiction in his brace of novels on the Peróns. *The Perón Novel* intersperses his account of the events surrounding Perón's return to Argentina in 1973 with anecdotes from his past, while *Santa Evita* recounts the fascinating, morbid and at times farcical story of Evita's life and – more importantly – afterlife. Martínez' latest work is *The Tango Singer*, an evocative tale set in the milongas of Buenos Aires, as a New Yorker trawls the city looking for the mysterious tango singer Julio Martel.

Manuel Puig *Kiss of the Spiderwoman* (US; o/p). Arguably the finest book by one of Argentina's most original twentieth-century writers, distinguished by a style that mixes film dialogue and popular culture with more traditional narrative. Set during the 1970s dictatorship, this is an absorbing tale of two cellmates, worlds apart on the outside but drawn together by gay protagonist Molina's recounting of films to his companion, left-wing guerrilla Valentín.

Ernesto Sabato *The Tunnel*. Existential angst, obsession and madness are the themes of this supremely accomplished novella, which tells the story of tormented painter Castel's destructive fixation with the sad and beautiful María Iribarne.

Colm Tóibin *The Story of the Night*. A moving tale of a young Anglo-Argentine trying to come to terms both with his sexuality and existential dilemmas in the wake of the South Atlantic conflict, and getting caught up in an undercover plot by the CIA to get Carlos Menem elected president.

Language

Language

Argentine Spanish...271

Pronunciation...271

Useful expressions and vocabulary...272

An Argentine menu reader...276

A glossary of terms and acronyms..279

Argentine Spanish

t's very useful to have at least a decent smattering of Spanish in Buenos Aires. Even though you'll frequently come across English-speakers, especially in the central barrios, you can't rely on someone being there when you need them, and, in general, Porteños are appreciative of visitors who make the effort to communicate in **castellano** (as Spanish is nearly always called here, rather than *español*). Any basic Spanish course will give you a good grounding before you go. A good pocket **dictionary**, such as Collins, is a vital accessory – make sure your choice covers Latin American usage.

Porteño Spanish is one of the most distinctive varieties of the language, characterized by an expressive, almost drawling intonation, and peppered with colloquialisms. If you've learnt Spanish in **Spain**, the most obvious difference you will encounter is the absence of the lisping "th" sound in words like *cielo* ("sky"; pronounced SYE-lo in Argentina) and *zorro* ("fox"; it sounds like the English word "sorrow" but with a Scottish-style trilled r). You will also be struck by the strong "zh" or "j" pronunciation of both "y" and "ll", as in *yo* and *calle* (see p.272). Another notable difference is the use of *vos* as the second-person pronoun, in place of *tú*, with correspondingly different verb endings (see box, p.271). *Ustedes* is used as the second-person pronoun, never *vosotros*, and it takes the third-person plural (*ellos*) form of the verb. A good guideline is that *vos* is always used for children and friends and usually between strangers under about 50 – otherwise use the more formal *usted*. The Porteño **vocabulary** is often quite different from other forms of Spanish, too (see box, pp.274–275).

Pronunciation

The Spanish **pronunciation** system is remarkably straightforward, with only five pure vowel sounds. Just a few consonant sounds tend to cause problems for English-speakers, most notably the rolled double (or initial) R and the single R which, though not rolled, is trilled more than in English.

L is pronounced as in the English "leaf" but not the swallowed English sound in "will" or "bell".

The voseo

Using *vos* as the second-person pronoun, a usage known as the *voseo*, is specific to Buenos Aires but is also found in the rest of Argentina and in some other parts of Latin America. Though you will be understood perfectly if you use the *tú* form, you might familiarize yourself with the *vos* form, if only in order to understand what is being said to you.

The easiest way to form the present-tense verb endings employed with *vos* is to take the infinitive and replace the final -r with an -s, adding an accent to the final vowel to retain final stress. Thus, *venir* (you come) becomes *vos venís*; the main exception to this rule is the verb *ser* (to be) – *vos sos*. The imperative is formed by dropping the final -s: *¡vení!* – the only exception being *¡andá!*, from *ir* (to go). Past, conditional, subjunctive and future forms used with *vos* are the same as the *tú* forms.

LL is pronounced rather like the "j" in French *jour*, or the "g" in beige, or the "s" in pleasure; some people make a softer sound, almost like "sh", but this may be considered vulgar; thus *calle* (street) is pronounced "KA-je".

Q only occurs before UE and UI, and is pronounced like English "k" (as in "Kenneth" and "kilt" rather than "quell" or "quilt").

R is pronounced in one of two ways. At the beginning of a word, and after L, N or S it is rolled as for RR, below. Between vowels, or at the end of a word it is a single "flapped" R, produced by a single tap of the tongue on the roof of the mouth immediately behind the teeth.

RR is written "rr", or "r" in the positions detailed above, and is a strongly trilled sound, produced in the same way as R, but with several rapid taps of the tongue. It is important for differentiating words such as *pero* (but) and *perro* (dog), or the potentially embarrassing *foro* (forum) and *forro* (slang for "condom", or "idiot").

V (*ve corta*, in Argentine Spanish) sounds just like the letter "b" (*be larga*, in Argentine Spanish), i.e. like the "b" in "bed", though it softens to sound more like the English "v" between vowels, as in *breve* (meaning "brief").

Y (*i griega*, in Spanish) between vowels (*playa*, beach) or at the beginning of a word (*yo*, I) is pronounced as LL (see above). Otherwise it is pronounced as I, as in *y*, the Spanish word for "and".

Z is pronounced the same as S, and is never lisped (as it is in most of Spain) or hard like the English "z".

Useful expressions and vocabulary

Basics

yes, no	sí, no
please, thank you	por favor, gracias
where, when	dónde, cuándo
what, how much	qué, cuánto
here, there	acá, allá
this, that	esto, eso
now, later	ahora, más tarde/luego
open, closed	abierto/a, cerrado/a
with, without	con, sin
good, bad	buen(o)/a, mal(o)/a
big	gran(de)
small	chico/a
more, less	más, menos
a little, a lot	poco, mucho
very	muy
today, tomorrow, yesterday	hoy, mañana, ayer
nothing, never	nada, nunca
but	pero
entrance, exit	entrada, salida
pull, push	tire, empuje
Australia	Australia
Canada	Canadá
Ireland	Irlanda
New Zealand	Nueva Zelanda
South Africa	Sudáfrica
United Kingdom	Reino Unido
United States	Estados Unidos

Greetings and responses

hello, goodbye	hola, chau
good morning	buen día
good afternoon	buenas tardes
good night	buenas noches
see you later	hasta luego
how are you?	¿cómo está(s)? ¿cómo anda/andás?
(very) well, thanks, and you?	(muy) bien gracias, ¿y vos/usted?
not at all	de nada
excuse me	(con) permiso
sorry	perdón, disculpe (me)
cheers!	¡salud!

Useful phrases and expressions

Note that when two verb forms are given, the first corresponds to the familiar *vos* form and the second to the formal *usted* form.

I (don't) understand	(no) entiendo
Do you speak English?	¿hablás inglés or (usted) habla inglés?
I (don't) speak Spanish	(No) hablo castellano
My name is ...	Me llamo ...
What's your name?	¿Cómo te llamás /Cómo se llama (usted)?
I'm British	Soy británico/a
... English	inglés(a)
... American	... estadounidense norteamericano/a
... Australian	... australiano/a
... Canadian	... canadiense
... Irish	... irlandés(a)
... a New Zealander	... neocelandés/a
... South African	... sudafricano(a)
What's the Spanish for this?	¿Cómo se dice en castellano?
I'm hungry	Tengo hambre
I'm thirsty	Tengo sed
I'm tired	Tengo sueño
I'm ill	No me siento bien
What's up?	¿Qué pasa?
I don't know	No (lo) sé
What's the time?	¿Qué hora es?

Hotels and transport

Is there a hotel /bank nearby?	¿Hay un hotel/banco cerca?
How do I get to...?	¿Cómo hago para llegar a...?
Turn left/right, on the left/right	Doblá/doble a la izquierda/derecha, a la izquierda/derecha
Go straight on	Seguí/siga derecho
one block/two blocks	una cuadra, dos cuadras
Where is... ?	¿Dónde está... ?
...the toilet	...el baño
Where does the bus for ... leave from?	¿De dónde sale el colectivo para...?
Do you go past... ?	¿Usted pasa por... ?
far, near	lejos, cerca
slow, quick	lento, rápido
I want/would like...	Quiero/quería...
There is (is there a discount for students?)	Hay (¿hay descuento para estudiantes?)

Is there hot water available?	¿Hay agua caliente?
Do you know... ?	¿Sabe/conoce...?
Do you have... ?	¿Tenés/tiene... ?
... a (single, double) room	...una habitación (single/doble)
... with two beds	... con dos camas
... with a double bed	... con cama matrimonial
... with a private bathroom	... con baño privado
... with breakfast	... con desayuno
How much is it?	¿Cuánto es/cuánto sale?
It's fine	Está bien

Numbers, days and months

0	cero
1	uno/una
2	dos
3	tres
4	cuatro
5	cinco
6	seis
7	siete
8	ocho
9	nueve
10	diez
11	once
12	doce
13	trece
14	catorce
15	quince
16	dieciséis
17	diecisiete
18	dieciocho
19	diecinueve
20	veinte
21	veintiuno/a
30	treinta
31	treinta y uno/una
40	cuarenta
50	cincuenta
60	sesenta
70	setenta
80	ochenta
90	noventa

Local vocabulary

Those who have learnt Spanish elsewhere will need to become accustomed to some different vocabulary in Buenos Aires. In general, Peninsular Spanish terms are recognized, but a familiarity with Porteño expressions will smooth things along. Few terms used in Spain are actually rejected in Argentina, with one major exception: the verb *coger*, used in Spain for everything from "to pick up" or "fetch" to "to catch (a bus)" is never used in this way in Latin America, where it is the equivalent of "to fuck". This catch-all Spanish verb is replaced by terms such as *tomar* (to take) as in *tomar el colectivo* (to catch the bus) and *agarrar* (to take hold of or grab) as in *agarrá la llave* (take the key). Less likely to cause problems, but still one to watch is *concha*, which in Spain means seashell but in Argentina is usually used to refer to the female genitals. The words *caracol* or *almeja* are used instead to refer to shells.

el auto	car	**la manteca**	butter
la birome	biro/ballpoint pen	**las medias**	socks
el boliche	nightclub; also sometimes bar/ store/shop in rural areas	**el negocio**	shop (in general)
		el nene/la nena	child
		la palta	avocado
		la papa	potato
las bombachas	knickers	**la pollera**	skirt
la cartera	handbag/purse	**el pomelo**	grapefruit
la carpa	tent	**la remera**	T-shirt
chico/a	small (also boy/girl)	**el suéter**	sweater
el colectivo	bus	**el tapado**	coat (usually woman's)
el durazno	peach		
estacionar	park to	**la vereda**	pavement
la lapicera	pen	**la vidriera**	shop window
el living	living room		

Colloquial speech and *lunfardo*

Colloquial speech in Buenos Aires is extremely colourful, and it's good fun to learn a bit of the local lingo. There's a clear Italian influence in some words. Many colloquial expressions and words also derive from a form of slang known as *lunfardo*, originally the language of the underworld. *Lunfardo* is also an important part of the repertoire of tango lyrics. Another feature to listen for is the widespread use of the prefix "re-", to mean "really" or "totally". *Re-lindo/a* means "really good-looking", *re-malo/a* is "really bad".

Words that are marked with an asterisk (*) should be used with some caution; those marked with a double asterisk (**) are best avoided until you are really familiar with local customs and language.

100	cien/ciento	Tuesday	martes
101	ciento uno/una	Wednesday	miércoles
200	doscientos/as	Thursday	jueves
1000	mil	Friday	viernes
2000	dos mil	Saturday	sábado
Monday	lunes	Sunday	domingo

afanar	to rob	**una maza**	something cool, as in *es una maza* "it's/he's/she's really cool"
bancar	to put up with; *no me lo banco* "I can't stand it/him"		
		el milico	member of the military*
bárbaro/a	great!		
la barra brava	hardcore football supporters	**la mina**	woman/girl
		morfar	to eat
la birra	beer	**onda**	atmosphere/character, as in *tiene buena onda*, "it's got a good atmosphere" or "she's good-natured"
el boludo/ pelotudo	idiot (equivalent to prat, jerk, etc)**		
el bondi	bus		
la bronca	rage, as in *me da bronca*, "he/she/it makes me angry"		
		el palo	one million (pesos); *un palo verde* is a million US dollars
el cana	police officer (cop)*		
canchero	sharp-witted, (over)confident		
		la patota	gang
el chabón	boy/lad	**el pendejo**	kid (mostly used derogatorily)**
el chamuyo	conversation/chat		
el chancho	ticket inspector*	**petiso**	small, also small person
el chanta	braggart, unreliable person*		
		el pibe	kid
el chorro	thief	**pinta**	"it looks good"
chupar	to drink (alcohol)*	**la pinta**	appearance, as in *tiene pinta* or *tiene buena pinta*
copado	cool, good		
el despelote	mess		
estar en pedo	to be drunk*	**piola**	cool, smart
el faso	cigarette	**el pucho**	cigarette
la fiaca	tiredness/laziness, eg *tengo fiaca*	**el quilombo**	mess*
		el tacho	taxi (*tachero* is taxi driver)
el forro	condom/idiot**		
el gil	idiot*	**el tano/la tana**	Italian*
la guita/la plata	money*	**el telo**	short-stay hotel where couples go to have sex*
el hinchapelotas	irritating person**		
laburar	to work		
la luca	one thousand (pesos)		
mamado	drunk* (*un mamado*** means a blow-job)	**trucho**	fake, phoney
		la vieja/el viejo	mum/dad
el mango	peso/monetary unit	**zafar**	to get away with*
manyar	to eat		

January	enero	**July**	julio
February	febrero	**August**	agosto
March	marzo	**September**	se(p)tiembre
April	abril	**October**	octubre
May	mayo	**November**	noviembre
June	junio	**December**	diciembre

An Argentine menu reader

Basics

aceite de maíz	corn oil
aceite de oliva	olive oil
ajo	garlic
ají	chilli
almuerzo	lunch
arroz	rice
azúcar	sugar
carta/menú	menu
cena	dinner
comedor	diner or dining room
copa	glass (for wine)
cuchara	spoon
cuchillo	knife
cuenta	bill
desayuno	breakfast
harina	flour
huevos	eggs
manteca	butter
mayonesa	mayonnaise
medialuna	kind of croissant
mermelada/dulce	jam
mostaza	mustard
pan (francés)	bread (baguette)
pebete	sandwich in a bun
pimienta	pepper
pimentón dulce	paprika
plato	plate or dish
queso	cheese
sal	salt
sandwich/sanduich	sandwich
servilleta	napkin
taza	cup
tenedor	fork
vaso	glass (for water)
vegetariano	vegetarian
vinagre	vinegar

Culinary terms

parrilla	barbecue
asado	roasted or barbecued
a la plancha	grilled
ahumado	smoked
al horno	baked/roasted
al natural	canned (of fruit)
al vapor	steamed
crudo	raw
frito	fried
picante	hot (spicy)
relleno	stuffed

Meat (*carne*) and poultry (*aves*)

bife	steak
bife de chorizo	prize steak cut
cabrito	goat (kid)
carne vacuna	beef
cerdo	pork
ciervo	venison
conejo	rabbit
cordero	lamb
chivito	kid or goat
chuleta	chop
churrasco	grilled beef
fiambres	cured meats
filete	fillet steak
jamón	ham
lomo	tenderloin steak
pato	duck
pavo	turkey
pollo	chicken
tocino/beicon	bacon

Offal (*achuras*)

bofes	lights (lungs)
corazón	heart
criadillas	testicles
chinchulines	small intestine
chorizo (blanco)	meaty sausage
hígado	liver
lengua	tongue
mollejas	sweetbreads
mondongo	cow's stomach
morcilla	blood sausage
orejas	ears
patas	feet or trotters
riñones	kidneys
sesos	brains
tripa gorda	tripe (large intestine)
ubre	udder

Typical dishes (*platos*)

arroz con pollo risotto	chicken with rice
bife a caballo	steak with a fried egg on top
bife a la criolla	steaks braised with onions, peppers and herbs
brochetas	kebabs
carbonada	meat stew
cazuela de marisco	a seafood casserole
cerdo a la riojana	pork cooked with fruit
fainá	baked chickpea dough
guiso	basic meat stew
locro	stew based on maize
matambre relleno	cold stuffed flank steak
matambrito	pork, often simmered in milk until soft
milanesa napolitana	breaded veal escalope topped with ham, tomato and melted cheese
milanesa de pollo	breaded chicken breast
provoletta	provolone cheese grilled on a barbecue
puchero	stew, usually of chicken (*puchero de gallina*), made with potatoes and maize
vittel tonné	slices of cold roast beef in mayonnaise mixed with tuna

Fish (*pescado*)

abadejo	cod
atún	tuna
boga	large, flavoursome fish caught in the Río de la Plata
caballa	mackerel
corvina	sea bass
dorado	a large freshwater fish
lenguado	sole
merluza	hake
pacú	firm-fleshed river fish
pejerrey	popular inland-water fish
salmón	salmon
surubí	kind of catfish
trucha (arco iris)	(rainbow) trout

Seafood (*mariscos*)

camarones	shrimps or prawns
cangrejo	crab
centolla	king crab
mejillones	mussels
ostras	oysters
vieira	scallop

Vegetables (*verduras*)

aceitunas	olives
acelga	chard
albahaca	basil
alcauciles	artichokes
apio	celery
arvejas	peas
aspárragos	asparagus
berenjena	aubergine/eggplant
berro	watercress
cebolla	onion
champiñon	mushroom
choclo	maize or sweetcorn
coliflor	cauliflower
ensalada	salad
espinaca	spinach
garbanzo	chickpea
habas	broad beans
lechuga	lettuce
lentejas	lentils
morrón	pepper
palmito	palm heart
palta	avocado
papa	potato
papas fritas	chips/French fries
perejil	parsley
pimiento	green pepper
poroto	bean
tomate	tomato
tomillo	thyme
zanahoria	carrot
zapallo	pumpkin

Fruit and nuts (*fruta y frutos secos*)

almendra	almond
almíbar	syrup
ananá	pineapple
arándano	cranberry/blueberry
avellana	hazelnut
banana	banana
batata	sweet potato
castaña	chestnut
cereza	cherry
ciruela (seca)	plum (prune)
dátiles	dates
damasco	apricot
durazno	peach
frambuesa	raspberry
frutilla	strawberry
higo	fig
lima	lime
limón	lemon
maní	peanut
manzana	apple
melón	melon
naranja	orange
nuez	walnut
pasa (de uva)	dried fruit (raisin)
pera	pear
pomelo (rosado)	(pink) grapefruit
sandía	watermelon
uva	grape(s)
zarza mora	blackberry

Desserts (*postres*)

arroz con leche	rice pudding
budín de pan	bread pudding
crema	custard or cream
dulce de leche	thick caramel made from milk and sugar
dulce	sweet in general
ensalada de fruta	fruit salad
flan	crème caramel
helado	ice cream

miel (de abeja)	honey
miel (de caña)	molasses
panqueque/crepe	pancake
sambayón	zabaglione (Marsala-flavoured custard) – popular ice cream flavour
torta	tart or cake
tortilla/tortita	breakfast pastry

Drinks (*bebidas*)

agua	water
agua mineral (con gas/sin gas)	mineral water (sparkling/still)
aguardiente	brandy-like spirit
botella	bottle
café (con leche)	coffee (with milk)
cerveza	beer
champán	sparkling wine or champagne
chocolate caliente	hot chocolate
chopp	draught beer
clericó	sangria
cortado	espresso coffee "cut" with a little steaming milk
Fernet (branca)	Italian-style digestive drink, popularly mixed with Coke
gaseosa	fizzy drink
jugo (de naranja)	(orange) juice
lata	can
leche	milk
licuados	juice-based drinks or milkshakes
mate cocido	infusion made with *mate*
sidra	cider
soda	fizzy water
té	tea
vino (tinto/blanco/rosado)	wine (red/white/rosé)

A glossary of terms and acronyms

ACA (Automóvil Club Argentino) National motoring organization (pronounced A-ka).

Arroba The @ sign.

Autopista Motorway.

Bailanta Dance club, where the predominant sound is *cumbia* (see below).

Barrio Neighbourhood.

Boletaría Ticket office.

Boleto Travel ticket.

Bombilla Straw-like implement, usually of metal, used for drinking *mate* from a gourd.

Bonaerense Adjective relating to or person from Buenos Aires Province.

Bondi Colloquial term in Buenos Aires for a bus.

C/ The abbreviation of *calle* (street); only rarely used.

Cabildo Colonial town hall; now replaced by Municipalidad.

Cabina telefónica Phone booth.

Cajero automático Cashpoint machine (ATM).

Cambio Change or exchange.

Cancha Football stadium.

Cantina Traditional restaurant, usually Italian.

Característica Telephone code.

Cartelera Agency for buying discounted tickets for cinemas, theatres and concerts.

Cartonero Scrap paper collector.

Casco Main building of estancia; the homestead.

Caudillo Regional military or political leader, usually with authoritarian overtones.

Cebar (mate) To brew (*mate*).

Ceibo Tropical tree with a twisted trunk, whose bright-red or pink blossom is the national flower of Argentina.

Chamamé Music and dance form originating in the Litoral (north of Buenos Aires).

Churro Strip of fried dough, somewhat similar to a doughnut, often filled with *dulce de leche*.

Colectivo Urban bus.

Confitería Café and tearoom, often with patisserie attached.

Conventillo Tenement building.

Costanera Riverside avenue.

Country Term for exclusive out-of-town residential compound or sports and social club.

Criollo Historically an Argentine-born person of Spanish descent. Used today in two ways: as a general term for Argentine (as in *comida criolla*, traditional Argentine food) and used by indigenous people to refer to those of non-indigenous descent.

Cuadra The distance from one street corner to the next, usually 100 metres (see also *manzana*); often used as a measure, as in 10 cuadras.

Cumbia Popular Argentine "tropical" rhythm, inspired by Colombian *cumbia*.

Enoteca Wine shop.

Entrada Ticket (for football match, theatre etc).

Estancia Argentine farm, traditionally with huge areas of land.

Estanciero Owner of an estancia.

Federalist Nineteenth-century term for person in favour of autonomous power being given to the provinces; opponent of Unitarist (see p.254).

Feria artesanal/de artesanías Craft fair.

Ferrocarril Railway.

Ficha Token.

Fonda Simple restaurant.

Galería Small shopping arcade.

Gaseosa Fizzy drink.

Gaucho The typical Argentine "cowboy", or rural estancia worker.

Gomero Rubber tree.

Gringo Any white foreigner, though often specifically those from English-speaking countries; historically European immigrants to Argentina (as opposed to *criollos*), as in *pampa gringa*, the part of pampas settled by European immigrants.

Guardaequipaje Left-luggage office.

Intendente Mayor.

Interno Telephone extension number.

IVA (*impuesto de valor agregado*) Value-added tax or sales tax.

Junta Military government coalition.

Kiosko Newspaper stand or small store selling cigarettes, confectionery and some foodstuffs.

Lapacho Native tree with colourful pink or yellow blooms.

Locutorio Call centre, where phone calls are made from cabins and the caller is charged after the call is made.

Manzana City block; the square bounded by four *cuadras* (see p.279).

Marcha Commercial dance music.

Mate Strictly the *mate* gourd or receptacle, but used generally to describe the national "tea" drink.

Menú del día Standard set menu.

Menú ejecutivo Set menu. Tends to be more expensive than the *menú del día*, though not always that executive.

Milonga Style of folk-guitar music usually associated with the Pampas region; also a tango dance and a subgenre of tango, more uptempo than tango proper. Also tango dancing event, often with tuition (see p.193).

Ombú Large shade tree associated with the Pampas.

Pampa(s) The broad flat grasslands of central Argentina.

Parquímetro Parking meter.

Parrillada The meat barbecued on a *parrilla*.

Pasaje Narrow street.

Paseaperro Professional dog walker.

Peatonal Pedestrianized street.

Peña Circle or group (usually of artists or musicians); a *peña folklórica* is a folk-music club.

Picada Plate of small snacks eaten before a meal, particularly cheese, ham or smoked meats.

Planta baja Ground floor (US first floor).

Playa Beach.

Playa (de estacionamiento) Car park; garage.

Porteño Someone from Buenos Aires city.

Pulpería Traditional general-provisions store that doubles up as a bar and rural meeting point.

Querandí Original indigenous inhabitants of the Pampas region.

Recargo Surcharge on credit cards.

Remise/Remís Taxi or chauffeur-driven rental car.

Río River.

Rioplatense Referring to people or things (including language) from the region around the Río de la Plata, and slightly further afield.

RN (Ruta Nacional) Major route, usually paved.

Ruta Route or road.

S/N Used in addresses to indicate that there's no house number (*sin número*).

Subte Underground railway.

Talabartería Leather store (especially horseriding goods).

Tanguería Tango club.

Taxímetro Taxi meter.

Tenedor libre All-you-can-eat buffet.

Tipa Acacia-like tree.

Truco Argentina's national card game, in which the ability to outbluff your opponents is of major importance.

Unitarists Nineteenth-century centralists, in favour of power being centralized in Buenos Aires and usually more progressive; opponents of Federalists (see p.254).

Villa Short for *villa miseria*, a shantytown; "town" in general.

YPF (Yacimientos Petroleros Fiscales) The principal Argentine petroleum company, now privatized and owned by Spanish firm REPSOL.

Travel store

Travel

Andorra The Pyrenees, Pyrenees & Andorra Map, Spain
Antigua The Caribbean
Argentina Argentina, Argentina Map, Buenos Aires, South America on a Budget
Aruba The Caribbean
Australia Australia, Australia Map, East Coast Australia, Melbourne, Sydney, Tasmania
Austria Austria, Europe on a Budget, Vienna
Bahamas The Bahamas, The Caribbean
Barbados Barbados DIR, The Caribbean
Belgium Belgium & Luxembourg, Bruges DIR, Brussels, Brussels Map, Europe on a Budget
Belize Belize, Central America on a Budget, Guatemala & Belize Map
Benin West Africa
Bolivia Bolivia, South America on a Budget
Brazil Brazil, Rio, South America on a Budget
British Virgin Islands The Caribbean
Brunei Malaysia, Singapore & Brunei [1 title], Southeast Asia on a Budget
Bulgaria Bulgaria, Europe on a Budget
Burkina Faso West Africa
Cambodia Cambodia, Southeast Asia on a Budget, Vietnam, Laos & Cambodia Map [1 Map]
Cameroon West Africa
Canada Canada, Pacific Northwest, Toronto, Toronto Map, Vancouver
Cape Verde West Africa
Cayman Islands The Caribbean
Chile Chile, Chile Map, South America on a Budget
China Beijing, China,

Hong Kong & Macau, Hong Kong & Macau DIR, Shanghai
Colombia South America on a Budget
Costa Rica Central America on a Budget, Costa Rica, Costa Rica & Panama Map
Croatia Croatia, Croatia Map, Europe on a Budget
Cuba Cuba, Cuba Map, The Caribbean, Havana
Cyprus Cyprus, Cyprus Map
Czech Republic The Czech Republic, Czech & Slovak Republics, Europe on a Budget, Prague, Prague DIR, Prague Map
Denmark Copenhagen, Denmark, Europe on a Budget, Scandinavia
Dominica The Caribbean
Dominican Republic Dominican Republic, The Caribbean
Ecuador Ecuador, South America on a Budget
Egypt Egypt, Egypt Map
El Salvador Central America on a Budget
England Britain, Camping in Britain, Devon & Cornwall, Dorset, Hampshire and The Isle of Wight [1 title], England, Europe on a Budget, The Lake District, London, London DIR, London Map, London Mini Guide, Walks In London & Southeast England
Estonia The Baltic States, Europe on a Budget
Fiji Fiji
Finland Europe on a Budget, Finland, Scandinavia
France Brittany & Normandy, Corsica, Corsica Map, The Dordogne & the Lot, Europe on a Budget, France, France Map, Languedoc & Roussillon, The Loire, Paris, Paris DIR,

Paris Map, Paris Mini Guide, Provence & the Côte d'Azur, The Pyrenees, Pyrenees & Andorra Map
French Guiana South America on a Budget
Gambia The Gambia, West Africa
Germany Berlin, Berlin Map, Europe on a Budget, Germany, Germany Map
Ghana West Africa
Gibraltar Spain
Greece Athens Map, Crete, Crete Map, Europe on a Budget, Greece, Greece Map, Greek Islands, Ionian Islands
Guadeloupe The Caribbean
Guatemala Central America on a Budget, Guatemala, Guatemala & Belize Map
Guinea West Africa
Guinea-Bissau West Africa
Guyana South America on a Budget
Holland see The Netherlands
Honduras Central America on a Budget
Hungary Budapest, Europe on a Budget, Hungary
Iceland Iceland, Iceland Map
India Goa, India, India Map, Kerala, Rajasthan, Delhi & Agra [1 title], South India, South India Map
Indonesia Bali & Lombok, Southeast Asia on a Budget
Ireland Dublin DIR, Dublin Map, Europe on a Budget, Ireland, Ireland Map
Israel Jerusalem
Italy Europe on a Budget, Florence DIR, Florence & Siena Map, Florence & the best of Tuscany, Italy, The Italian Lakes, Naples & the Amalfi Coast, Rome, Rome DIR, Rome Map, Sardinia, Sicily, Sicily Map, Tuscany & Umbria, Tuscany Map,

Venice, Venice DIR, Venice Map
Jamaica Jamaica, The Caribbean
Japan Japan, Tokyo
Jordan Jordan
Kenya Kenya, Kenya Map
Korea Korea
Laos Laos, Southeast Asia on a Budget, Vietnam, Laos & Cambodia Map [1 Map]
Latvia The Baltic States, Europe on a Budget
Lithuania The Baltic States, Europe on a Budget
Luxembourg Belgium & Luxembourg, Europe on a Budget
Malaysia Malaysia Map, Malaysia, Singapore & Brunei [1 title], Southeast Asia on a Budget
Mali West Africa
Malta Malta & Gozo DIR
Martinique The Caribbean
Mauritania West Africa
Mexico Baja California, Baja California, Cancún & Cozumel DIR, Mexico, Mexico Map, Yucatán, Yucatán Peninsula Map
Monaco France, Provence & the Côte d'Azur
Montenegro Montenegro
Morocco Europe on a Budget, Marrakesh DIR, Marrakesh Map, Morocco, Morocco Map,
Nepal Nepal
Netherlands Amsterdam, Amsterdam DIR, Amsterdam Map, Europe on a Budget, The Netherlands
Netherlands Antilles The Caribbean
New Zealand New Zealand, New Zealand Map

DIR: Rough Guide **DIRECTIONS** for short breaks

Available from all good bookstores

Nicaragua Central America on a Budget

Niger West Africa

Nigeria West Africa

Norway Europe on a Budget, Norway, Scandinavia

Panama Central America on a Budget, Costa Rica & Panama Map, Panama

Paraguay South America on a Budget

Peru Peru, Peru Map, South America on a Budget

Philippines The Philippines, Southeast Asia on a Budget,

Poland Europe on a Budget, Poland

Portugal Algarve DIR, The Algarve Map, Europe on a Budget, Lisbon DIR, Lisbon Map, Madeira DIR, Portugal, Portugal Map, Spain & Portugal Map

Puerto Rico The Caribbean, Puerto Rico

Romania Europe on a Budget, Romania

Russia Europe on a Budget, Moscow, St Petersburg

St Kitts & Nevis The Caribbean

St Lucia The Caribbean

St Vincent & the Grenadines The Caribbean

Scotland Britain, Camping in Britain, Edinburgh DIR, Europe on a Budget, Scotland, Scottish Highlands & Islands

Senegal West Africa

Serbia Montenegro Europe on a Budget

Sierra Leone West Africa

Singapore Malaysia, Singapore & Brunei [1 title], Singapore, Singapore DIR, Southeast Asia on a Budget

Slovakia Czech & Slovak Republics, Europe on a Budget

Slovenia Europe on a Budget, Slovenia

South Africa Cape Town & the Garden Route, South Africa, South Africa Map

Spain Andalucía, Andalucía Map, Barcelona, Barcelona DIR, Barcelona Map, Europe on a Budget, Ibiza & Formentera DIR, Gran Canaria DIR, Madrid DIR, Lanzarote & Fuerteventura DIR Madrid Map, Mallorca & Menorca, Mallorca DIR, Mallorca Map, The Pyrenees, Pyrenees & Andorra Map, Spain, Spain & Portugal Map, Tenerife & La Gomera DIR

Sri Lanka Sri Lanka, Sri Lanka Map

Suriname South America on a Budget

Sweden Europe on a Budget, Scandinavia, Sweden

Switzerland Europe on a Budget, Switzerland

Taiwan Taiwan

Tanzania Tanzania, Zanzibar

Thailand Bangkok, Southeast Asia on a Budget, Thailand, Thailand Map, Thailand Beaches & Islands

Togo West Africa

Trinidad & Tobago The Caribbean, Trinidad & Tobago

Tunisia Tunisia, Tunisia Map

Turkey Europe on a Budget, Istanbul, Turkey, Turkey Map

Turks and Caicos Islands The Bahamas, The Caribbean

United Arab Emirates Dubai DIR, Dubai & UAE Map [1 title]

United Kingdom Britain, Devon & Cornwall, Edinburgh DIR England, Europe on a Budget, The Lake District, London, London DIR, London Map, London Mini Guide, Scotland, Scottish Highlands

& Islands, Wales, Walks In London & Southeast England

United States Alaska, Boston, California, California Map, Chicago, Colorado, Florida, Florida Map, The Grand Canyon, Hawaii, Los Angeles, Los Angeles Map, Los Angeles and Southern California, Maui DIR, Miami & South Florida, New England, New England Map, New Orleans & Cajun Country, New Orleans DIR, New York City, NYC DIR, NYC Map, New York City Mini Guide, Oregon & Washington, Orlando & Walt Disney World® DIR, San Francisco, San Francisco DIR, San Francisco Map, Seattle, Southwest USA, USA, Washington DC, Yellowstone & the Grand Tetons National Park, Yosemite National Park

Uruguay South America on a Budget

US Virgin Islands The Bahamas, The Caribbean

Venezuela South America on a Budget

Vietnam Southeast Asia on a Budget, Vietnam, Vietnam, Laos & Cambodia Map [1 Map],

Wales Britain, Camping in Britain, Europe on a Budget, Wales

First-Time Series FT Africa, FT Around the World, FT Asia, FT Europe, FT Latin America

Inspirational guides Earthbound, Clean Breaks, Make the Most of Your Time on Earth, Ultimate Adventures, World Party

Travel Specials Camping in Britain, Travel with Babies & Young Children, Walks in London & SE England

For more information go to www.roughguides.com

Small print and
Index

A Rough Guide to Rough Guides

Published in 1982, the first Rough Guide – to Greece – was a student scheme that became a publishing phenomenon. Mark Ellingham, a recent graduate in English from Bristol University, had been travelling in Greece the previous summer and couldn't find the right guidebook. With a small group of friends he wrote his own guide, combining a highly contemporary, journalistic style with a thoroughly practical approach to travellers' needs.

The immediate success of the book spawned a series that rapidly covered dozens of destinations. And, in addition to impecunious backpackers, Rough Guides soon acquired a much broader and older readership that relished the guides' wit and inquisitiveness as much as their enthusiastic, critical approach and value-for-money ethos.

These days, Rough Guides include recommendations from shoestring to luxury and cover more than 200 destinations around the globe, including almost every country in the Americas and Europe, more than half of Africa and most of Asia and Australasia. Our ever-growing team of authors and photographers is spread all over the world, particularly in Europe, the US and Australia.

In the early 1990s, Rough Guides branched out of travel, with the publication of Rough Guides to World Music, Classical Music and the Internet. All three have become benchmark titles in their fields, spearheading the publication of a wide range of books under the Rough Guide name.

Including the travel series, Rough Guides now number more than 350 titles, covering: phrasebooks, waterproof maps, music guides from Opera to Heavy Metal, reference works as diverse as Conspiracy Theories and Shakespeare, and popular culture books from iPods to Poker. Rough Guides also produce a series of more than 120 World Music CDs in partnership with World Music Network.

Visit www.roughguides.com to see our latest publications.

Rough Guide credits

Text editor: Alison Roberts
Layout: Sachin Gupta
Cartography: Swati Handoo
Picture editor: Mark Thomas
Production: Louise Minihane
Proofreader: Kate Berens
Cover design: Nicole Newman, Dan May
Photographer: Greg Roden
Editorial: London Andy Turner, Keith Drew, Edward Aves, Alice Park, Lucy White, Jo Kirby, James Smart, Natasha Foges, James Rice, Emma Beatson, Emma Gibbs, Kathryn Lane, Monica Woods, Mani Ramaswamy, Harry Wilson, Lucy Cowie, Lara Kavanagh, Eleanor Aldridge, Ian Blenkinsop, Charlotte Melville, Joe Staines, Matthew Milton, Tracy Hopkins; **Delhi** Madhavi Singh, Jalpreen Kaur Chhatwal
Design & Pictures: London Scott Stickland, Dan May, Diana Jarvis, Nicole Newman,

Sarah Cummins; **Delhi** Umesh Aggarwal, Ajay Verma, Jessica Subramanian, Ankur Guha, Pradeep Thapliyal, Sachin Tanwar, Anita Singh, Nikhil Agarwal
Production: Rebecca Short, Liz Cherry, Erika Pepe
Cartography: London Ed Wright, Katie Lloyd-Jones; **Delhi** Rajesh Chhibber, Ashutosh Bharti, Rajesh Mishra, Animesh Pathak, Jasbir Sandhu, Deshpal Dabas, Lokamata Sahu
Marketing, Publicity & roughguides.com: Liz Statham
Digital Travel Publisher: Peter Buckley
Reference Director: Andrew Lockett
Operations Coordinator: Becky Doyle
Operations Assistant: Johanna Wurm
Publishing Director (Travel): Clare Currie
Commercial Manager: Gino Magnotta
Managing Director: John Duhigg

Publishing information

This second edition published August 2011 by
Rough Guides Ltd,
80 Strand, London WC2R 0RL
11, Community Centre, Panchsheel Park, New Delhi 110017, India
Distributed by the Penguin Group
Penguin Books Ltd,
80 Strand, London WC2R 0RL
Penguin Group (USA)
375 Hudson Street, NY 10014, USA
Penguin Group (Australia)
250 Camberwell Road, Camberwell, Victoria 3124, Australia
Penguin Group (NZ)
67 Apollo Drive, Mairangi Bay, Auckland 1310, New Zealand
Rough Guides is represented in Canada by Tourmaline Editions Inc. 662 King Street West, Suite 304, Toronto, Ontario M5V 1M7
Cover concept by Peter Dyer.
Typeset in Bembo and Helvetica to an original design by Henry Iles.

Printed in Singapore
© Andrew Benson and Rosalba O'Brien 2011
Maps © Rough Guides
No part of this book may be reproduced in any form without permission from the publisher except for the quotation of brief passages in reviews.
296pp includes index
A catalogue record for this book is available from the British Library
ISBN: 978-1-84836-891-0
The publishers and authors have done their best to ensure the accuracy and currency of all the information in **The Rough Guide to Buenos Aires**, however, they can accept no responsibility for any loss, injury, or inconvenience sustained by any traveller as a result of information or advice contained in the guide.

1   3   5   7   9   8   6   4   2

Help us update

We've gone to a lot of effort to ensure that the second edition of **The Rough Guide to Buenos Aires** is accurate and up-to-date. However, things change – places get "discovered", opening hours are notoriously fickle, restaurants and rooms raise prices or lower standards. If you feel we've got it wrong or left something out, we'd like to know, and if you can remember the address, the price, the hours, the phone number, so much the better.

Please send your comments with the subject line "**Rough Guide Buenos Aires Update**" to mail@uk.roughguides.com. We'll credit all contributions and send a copy of the next edition (or any other Rough Guide if you prefer) for the very best emails.

Find more travel information, connect with fellow travellers and book your trip on www.roughguides.com

Acknowledgements

Andrew Benson wishes to thank: all his friends in Buenos Aires for their support: in particular (*espero no olvidar a nadie*) Marta Susana, Gustavo, Fernando M., Dorita, Eduardo, Mirta, Rubén and Gastón. Special thanks to Isobel and Julie for their impeccable efficiency and charming helpfulness. Thanks, too, to the Salaún twins and to Bettiana. Total gratitude to Rosalba for being supportive, professional and dedicated, as always. Many thanks to Alison for patient and diligent editing. And finally special *saludos* for Fernando F: always be a clown!

Rosalba O'Brien would like to thank Esteban, Mimi, Amalia & Sebastian for love and support, Estelares for the soundtrack, Andrew and Alison for wise words, and most of all Arwen, my constant companion.

Readers' letters

Thanks to all the readers who have taken the time to write in with comments and suggestions (and apologies if we've inadvertently omitted or misspelt anyone's name):

Gabriel Bagdadi, Alex Bernhardt, Jim Berry, Elizabeth, Eugenia Calviño, Mayra Decastelli, Alvaro Diaz, Daniel Duarte, Hannah Fox, Richard Jabs, Callie Johnson, Maddy King, Joachim Körner, Rosalind Lester, Rebecca Losange, Mary Massolo, Lara Misculin, Nad Mylvaganam, Linda Neilson, Sergio Novikov, Yann Poulhazan, Margaret Ransdell, Peque Saavedra, Melina Saccal, BC Slais.

Photo credits

All photography by Greg Roden © Rough Guides except the following:

Introduction
Boys playing table football © Jenny Acheson/Axiom
Puente de la Mujer © Anothony Arendt/Alamy
Caryatid, San Telmo © Aido Sessa/Getty Images
The Obelisco in Plaza de la República © Bao Bao/Photolibrary
Men playing chess © photononstop/Superstock
Mural of Carlos Gardel © Jordi Cami/Alamy
Subway © Hemis/Superstock
Busy crossing © JTB/Superstock

Things not to miss
01 Plaza de Mayo © Robert Frerck/Getty Images
03 Feria de San Pedro Telmo © Andrew Benson
05 Tigre riverside © Harriet Cummings
06 MALBA © image courtesy of MALBA
07 Reserva Ecológica Costanera © Jon Arnold images/Alamy
08 Recoleta Cemetery © Anthony Arendt/Alamy
09 Bandoneón player © cusp/Superstock
10 Parrillas © Food and Drink/Superstock
11 Palacio de las Aguas © Hemis/Alamy
12 San Antonio de Areco © Apeiron Photo/Alamy
13 Leather boots © Aurora Photos/Alamy
17 Estudiantes footballer celebrating © AFP/Getty Images

Architecture colour section
Basílica Nuestra Señora del Pilar © Bernardo Galmarini/Alamy
Basilica de Nuestra Señora de la Merced © Jon Arnold Images/Alamy
Congreso Nacional © Hemis/Alamy
Abasto shopping mall © Ron Giling/Photolibrary
Puerto Madero © Chris der Grosse/Photolibrary

Tango colour section
Tango dancers © Altrendo/Getty Images
Musician © Peter M Wilson/Axiom
Tango shoes © Andrew Benson
Dancers performing the *gancho* move © Juan Mabromata/Getty Images
Gotan Project © Matt Cardy/Getty Images
Astor Piazzolla © Interfoto/Alamy
The tomb of Carlos Gardel © Hemis/Alamy

Index

Map entries are in colour.

A

Abasto 140, 199
accommodation .. 149–157
addresses 27
Aeroparque Jorge
  Newbery 22
Afro-Argentines 253
airlines 21
airports 21
Alvear family 69, 91, 109,
  110
Anchorena family ... 99, 113,
  144
antiques shops 199
architecture ... see *Building
  Buenos Aires* colour
  section
arrival 21
art 262–264
art galleries 200
ATMs 38
Avenida 9 de Julio 57, 68
Avenida Alvear 112
Avenida Corrientes 67
Avenida de Mayo 55

B

ballet 188
Balvanera 139–141
Balvanera 140
Banco Central 64
Banco de Boston 63
Barracas 138
Barrio Parque 125
bars (by area)
  outer barrios, the 180
  Palermo 179
  Recoleta 179
  Retiro 179
  San Nicolás 179
  San Telmo 179
bars (by name)
  647 Dinner Club 179
  L'Abeille 179
  Antares 179
  Bar Abierto 180
  Bar Británico 179
  Bar Ocho7Ocho 180
  Bárbaro 179
  Buller 179
  Carnal 180

Celta Bar 179
La Cigale 179
Congo 180
Dadá 179
Deep Blue 179
Gibraltar 179
Gran Bar Danzón 179
Kilkenny 179
Malasartes 180
Milion 179
Mundo Bizarro 180
Plaza Dorrego Bar 179
Shamrock 179
El Taller 180
Tazz 180
Único 180
Basílica de Nuestra
  Señora de la Merced ... 64
Basílica de San
  Francisco 51
Basílica de Santo
  Domingo 54
Basílica del Santísimo
  Sacramento 98
Basílica Nuestra Señora del
  Pilar 110
bed and breakfasts 155
  1890 156
  Babel 155
  Bed and Baires Hostel 156
  Calden Guesthouse 155
  Mansión Dandy Royal 156
  La Otra Orilla 156
  Posada de la Luna 155
  Posada Histórica Gotan .. 156
  Posada Palermo 156
  Rooney's 155
  Soco 156
Belgrano 144–146
Belgrano 145
Belgrano, Manuel 252
Biblioteca Nacional 54,
  117
Bicentenary 47
boats 47, 76, 131, 238
Boca 88–92
Boca 89
Boca Juniors 91, 211
Boedo 138
Bolsa de Comercio 64
books 265–268
bookshops 201
Borges, Jorge Luis 54,
  55, 56, 80, 108, 119, 128,
  129, 130, 131, 134, 138
Bosques de Palermo
  130–136

Brown, Admiral William
  .... 93, 109
Buenos Aires Design ... 111,
  199
buses 22, 24, 26

C

Caballito 141
Caballito & Almagro 142
Cabildo 50
cafés (by area)
  Monserrat 159
  outer barrios, the 161
  Puerto Madero 160
  Recoleta 160
  Retiro 160
  San Nicolás 159
  San Telmo 160
cafés (by name)
  A222 159
  Abuela Pan 162
  La Americana 162
  Los Angelitos 161
  Le Bar 162
  La Biela 160
  California Burrito Company
  162
  Carlitos 162
  Le Caravelle 159
  La Casa del Queso 163
  El Club de la Milanesa 162
  Como en Casa 160
  Confitería Ideal 159
  Confitería El Vesuvio 159
  Costumbres Criollas 162
  Cumaná 162
  Del Limonero 160
  Farinelli 162
  Florencio 162
  Florida Garden 160
  "i" Fresh Market 160
  La Giralda 160
  London City 56, 159
  Mark's Deli 162
  Martínez 159
  Medio y Medio 162
  Molière 162
  New Brighton 160
  Paulin 159
  La Paz 160
  Persicco 163
  La Poesia 160
  PostData 161
  Pride Café 162
  La Puerto Rico 159
  Retiro 160

Richmond..................66, 159
Siga La Vaca...................160
Tea Connection...............161
Tortoni.......................56, 159
Ugi's...............................162
Viva Victoria...................163
Las Violetas.....................161
Calle Defensa....51, 52, 54,
  81, 85, 86
Calle Florida............65–67
Calle Lavalle...................66
Caminito.........................89
Campo Argentino de
  Polo...................136, 214
car rental........................27
cartoneros....................260
Casa Amarilla.................93
Casa Atucha..................104
Casa de la Cultura..........55
Casa de la Moneda........54
Casa del General
  Pueyrredón.................229
Casa Nacarello...............247
Casa Rosada...................48
casino flotante..............77
Catedral Anglicana de San
  Juan Bautista...............65
Catedral Metropolitana...50
Cementerio de Chacarita
 142
Cementerio de Recoleta
 108–110
Centro Cultural Borges..67,
  186
Centro Cultural Recoleta
  ....111, 186
Centro Cultural Usina
  Vieja............................242
Centro Cultural y Taller
  Draghi.........................242
Centro Nacional de la
  Música...........................54
Centro Naval...................99
Chacarita.......................142
Chacarita cemetery......142
Chinatown......................146
cinema...........................189
classical music............188
clothes shops.....202–204
Club de Pescadores.....137
clubs...................182–184
Colegio Nacional...........53
Colonia del Sacramento
 245–248
Colonia del Sacramento
 246
Congreso Nacional.........58
Constitución.................138
Convento de San
  Francisco.....................51

Convento San Ramón....64
Correo Central................37
Costanera Norte...........137
Costanera Sur................78
costs..............................31
  accommodation...............150
  eating......................158, 164
  drinking...........................178
  entertainment..................187
crafts.............................204
credit cards....................38
crime..............................32
cuisines........................166
cultural centres...185–187
cumbia..........................183
currency exchange.........38
cycling...........................215

D

discount agents..............21
drinks......................30, 278
driving............................26
dual pricing....................31
dulce de leche..............163

E

Edificio Barolo................57
Edificio Kavanagh..........97
El Bajo............................65
El Zanjón de Granados
 84
electricity........................33
embassies......................33
emergencies..................32
entry requirements.........33
ESMA....................146, 211
Estadio Monumental....146
estancias......................241
etiquette.........................29
Evita.......48, 109, 118, 135,
  256, 257
Ezeiza airport..................21

F

Falklands/Malvinas........49,
  92, 97, 101, 258
Fangio, Juan Manuel...111,
  213
Fería de Mataderos......143
Feria de San Pedro
  Telmo...........................82
Feria Hippy...................112

Fernández de Kirchner,
  Cristina................59, 261
ferries............................245
festivals..............219–224
filete art..........................82
fishing...........................215
flights..............................19
Floralis Genérica...........117
food.....................276–278
food shops...................205
football.................209–211
Fundación Federico Jorge
  Klemm..........................99
Fundación Proa..............90

G

Galería Mitre...................66
galerías..........................66
Galerías Pacífico....66, 199
Gardel, Carlos...141, 142 &
  Tango colour section
gauchos.......117, 124, 127,
  135, 239, 242
**gay and lesbian Buenos
  Aires**..................195–197
  accommodation...............196
  bars.................................196
  clubs...............................196
  information.......................195
  pride march......................223
  tango...............................196
gyms.............................215

H

Harrods............................99
health..............................34
Hipódromo Argentino...136
Hipódromo de San Isidro
 230
history..................251–261
hockey...........................212
horse-racing.................212
hospitals........................34
hostels
  Buenos Ayres Hostel.......157
  Che Lagarto Youth Hostel
   156
  Circus Hostel...................157
  Colonial...........................157
  Eco Pampa.......................157
  El Hostal de San Telmo....157
  Limehouse Youth Hostel
   156
  Milhouse..........................157
  Ostinatto Hostel...............157
  Recoleta Youth Hostel.....157

So Hostel 157
Tango City Hostel Inn....... 157
V&S Youth Hostel............. 157
hotels (by area)
Monserrat..................... 151
Palermo............................. 154
Puerto Madero 152
Recoleta............................. 153
Retiro................................. 152
San Nicolás...................... 151
San Telmo 152
hotels (by name)
725 Buenos Aires............. 151
1551 Palermo Boutique
    Hotel 154
Algodón Mansión............. 153
Alvear Palace Hotel.......... 153
Art Hotel........................... 153
Axel 151
Bel Air............................... 153
Bo Bo 154
Casa Calma 152
Casa Las Cañitas.............. 154
Castelar............................ 151
La Cayetana..................... 151
City Hotel 151
Claridge............................ 151
Craft 154
Crillon............................... 152
Design Suites and Towers
    153
Elevage............................. 152
Etoile 153
Facón Grande 152
Faena Hotel & Universe ... 152
Finisterra 154
Five Cool Rooms 154
Four Seasons................... 153
Gran Hotel España........... 151
Hilton................................ 152
Home 154
Hotel de los Dos Congresos
    151
Intercontinental 151
Jousten 152
Krista................................ 154
Lancaster 153
Legado Mítico 154
Lion d'Or 153
LoiSuites Recoleta 153
Madero 152
Magnolia 154
Malabia 1555 154
Mansión Vitraux 152
Marriott Plaza Hotel 153
Moreno.............................. 151
Nuss 155
Obelisco Center 152
Palacio Duhau-Park Hyatt
    154
Regal Pacific 152
Rendezvous 155
Rochester Concept Hotel
    152
Roma................................. 151
Sofitel 153
Madero 152

Sportsman........................ 151
Tailor Made Hotel............. 155
Los Tres Reyes................. 152
Vain 155
Vitrum............................... 155

I

ice cream........................ 163
Iglesia de San Juan
    Bautista 53
Iglesia de San Pedro
    Telmo 83
Iglesia Dinamarquesa 84
Iglesia Ortodoxa Rusa.... 87
immigration.................... 255
indigenous groups ... 54, 251
insurance......................... 35
internet 35

J

Jardín Botánico Carlos
    Thays 133
Jardín Japonés............. 133
Jardín Zoológico........... 134
Jewish community ... 70, 71,
    139, 144
Jockey Club 104
jogging............................ 215

K

kids' Buenos Aires
    216–218
events.............................. 218
natural attractions 217
shopping 218
sights.............................. 217
Kirchner, Néstor............. 59

L

La Bombonera................ 91
La City 63
La Inmobilaria................ 58
La Prensa 55
language.............. 269–280
laundry............................ 35
leather goods 203
live music venues
    180–182
living in Buenos Aires..... 36
lost property 37

M

Macri, Mauricio.......91, 261
Madres de Plaza de
    Mayo..............49, 75, 259
magazines 28
mail 37
Malvinas Falklands........ 49,
    92, 97, 101, 258
Mansión Alzaga Unzué... 104
Manzana de las Luces ... 52
Manzana Franciscana 51
maps................................ 37
Maradona, Diego......48, 92
markets.......................... 204
Mataderos 143
mate 30
media.............................. 28
Menem, Carlos............. 258
Mercado de Pulgas 204
Mercado Municipal......... 83
Mercedes....................... 243
Mitre, Bartolomé........... 118
money.............................. 37
Monserrat............... 45–60
Monserrat....................... 46
Montoneros 257
Monumental stadium.... 146
Monumento a los Dos
    Congresos 60
Monumento a los Héroes
    de la Guerra de las
    Malvinas 97
Monumento de los
    Españoles.................. 133
museums
Armas de la Nación 100
Arte Decorativo 121
Arte Español.................... 144
Arte Hispanoamericano Isaac
    Fernández Blanco 102
Arte Latinoamericano de
    Buenos Aires (MALBA)... 125
Arte Moderno de Buenos
    Aires (MAMBA) 85
Arte Popular José
    Hernández 121
Arte Tigre 236
Artes Plásticas Eduardo
    Sívori............................. 132
Azulejos............................ 247
Bellas Artes de la Boca 91
Buque Corbeta ARA
    Uruguay 76
Buque Fragata ARA
    Presidente Sarmiento 76
Cabildo.............................. 50
Casa Carlos Gardel......... 141
Casa de Yrurtia 145
Casa Rosada 49
Centro de Museos de
    Buenos Aires 78

INDEX

I

291

Ciencias Naturales 141
Ciudad................................. 52
Colección de Arte Amalia
Lacroze de Fortabat 74
Español 284
Etnográfico Juan Bautista
Ambrosetti 53
Evita 135
Gauchesco Ricardo
Güiraldes 242
Historia del Traje 55
Histórico Municipal
(San Isidro).................... 229
Histórico Nacional............... 86
Judío Dr Salvador Kibrick... 70
Mate................................. 236
Monseñor Fray José María
Bottaro........................... 52
Mundial del Tango............... 57
Municipal de Colonia 247
Municipal de San Isidro ... 229
Nacional de Bellas Artes
.................................113–117
Nacional de Bellas Artes... 114
Niños 140
Participativo de Ciencias ... 111
Pasión Boquense.............. 93
Portugués......................... 247
Reconquista.................... 237
Shoá................................. 71
Xul Solar........................... 118
music shops 206
music venues 180–182

N

newspapers 28
Núñez 146

O

Obelisco 68
Once 139
Once station 139
opening hours 38
opera 188
outer barrios, the
.... 138–146

P

Pabellón de la Bellas
Artes 76
Palacio Celedonio Pereda
.... 104
Palacio de Justicia 70
Palacio de las Aguas
Corrientes 141

Palacio Estrugamou 101
Palacio Nacional de las
Artes 113
Palacio Ortiz Basualdo
.... 104
Palacio Paz................... 100
Palacio Retiro 100
Palacio San Martín 101
Palacio Unzué de Casares
.... 104
Palais de Glace 113
Palermo 120–137
Palermo............... 122–123
Costanera Norte.............. 137
Palermo Chico 121–128
Palermo Hollywood.......... 130
Palermo Soho 128–130
Palermo Viejo 128–130
Pampas................ 239–244
Parque 3 de Febrero 131
Parque Chacabuco 124
Parque Colón 49
Parque de la Costa 235
Parque de la Ribera...... 230
Parque Lezama 85
parrillas......................... 167
Pasaje de la Defensa...... 85
Pasaje San Lorenzo 84
pato 212
Perón, Eva 48, 109, 118,
135, 256, 257
Perón, Isabel 68
Perón, Juan Domingo ... 48,
59, 71, 135, 255, 257
Peronism 59
Perú station 56
pharmacies.................... 34
Pirámide de Mayo 50
Planetario Galileo Galilei
.... 132
Plaza Carlos Pellegrini
.... 104
Plaza de Mayo............... 45
Plaza del Congreso 58
Plaza Dorrego................ 82
Plaza Embajada de Israel
.... 103
Plaza Evita................... 118
Plaza Francia............... 112
Plaza Italia 131
Plaza Lavalle................. 69
Plaza Mitre................... 118
Plaza San Martín 96
Plaza San Martín de Tours
.... 111
Plaza Serrano 128
politics 59
polo 213
Predio La Rural....135, 218,
221

Proceso 257
public holidays 38
pubs 178–180
Puente de la Mujer 76
Puerto de Frutos 236
Puerto Madero 72–79
Puerto Madero.............. 73

Q

Querandí........................ 251
Quinquela Martín, Benito
........75, 89, 91, 117, 142,
237
Quinta Los Ombúes 230

R

radio 29
Recoleta 106–119
Recoleta....................... 107
Recoleta cemetery
.... 108–110
Remises......................... 27
Reserva Ecológica
Costanera Sur 79
restaurants (by area)
Boca.................................. 171
Monserrat.................166–168
outer barrios, the 175
Palermo....................173–175
Puerto Madero 170
Recoleta........................... 172
Retiro................................ 171
San Nicolás 168
San Telmo 170
restaurants (by name)
Amici Miei 170
Les Anciens Combattants
.... 175
Artemisia 173
Arturito 168
Azema Exotic Bistro......... 173
Banchero 171
El Baqueano...................... 170
Bengal 171
Bereber 173
Bice 170
Bio.................................... 173
Bi Won.............................. 175
Bodega Campo................. 168
Brasserie Berry 169
El Buen Sabor.................. 175
Cabaña Las Lilas 170
La Cabrera 174
Café Margot 175
Café San Juan 170
Casa Cruz 174
El Caserío......................... 167
La Catédra 174

Chan Chan 167
Chez Juanito 174
Chila 170
Chiquilín 169
Chori & Wine 174
El Claustro...................... 169
Club Danés 171
Club Sirio 172
Cluny.............................. 174
Las Cuartetas................. 169
El Cuartito 171
Dashi 172
Demuru 174
Due................................. 172
Empire Thai..................... 171
El Establo 171
El Estrebe....................... 172
Filo 171
La Fondue 174
Francesco 174
Garbis............................. 174
El Globo 167
La Gran Taberna 175
Granix............................. 169
Guerrin 169
Guido 174
Hsiang Ting Tang 175
Iñaki............................... 167
Juana M 172
Katmandu........................ 176
Keum Kang Sang............. 176
Laurak-Bat 167
El Manto.......................... 174
Masamadre es con M 176
Il Matterello 171
Miramar........................... 176
Moche 174
Naturaleza Sabia............. 170
Nectarine........................ 172
El Obrero 171
Olsen.............................. 174
Oviedo............................ 172
Parrilla Peña.................... 169
El Patio de Aldo 176
Il Piccolo Vapore 171
Piola Pizzería.................. 172
Pippo.............................. 169
Las Pizarras 174
Plaza Mayor 168
El Pobre Luis................... 176
El Primo.......................... 175
Prosciutto....................... 168
Reconquista 169
La Reina Kunti................. 176
Restó.............................. 173
Rodi Bar.......................... 173
Romario Pizza 173
Sabot.............................. 169
El Sanjuanino 173
Los Sabios 176
Sarkis............................. 175
Sifones y Dragones.......... 176
Sipan.............................. 172
Social Paraíso 175
Sottovoce........................ 173
Status............................. 168
Sudestada....................... 175

Tancat............................. 172
Todos Contentos............. 176
Tomo 1 169
Tuñín.............................. 176
Urondo Bar 176
Vera Cruz 175
La Vinería de Gualterio
    Bolívar........................ 170
Winery 172
Yoko's............................. 175
Retiro 94–105
Retiro.............................. 95
Retiro station 97
rhodochrosite 208
River Plate 146, 211
rock nacional 181
Rosas, Juan Manuel de
    ...65, 101, 109, 117, 121,
131
rugby 214

S

safety............................. 32
San Antonio de Areco
    239–243
San Antonio de Areco
    240
San Ignacio church 53
San Isidro 227–231
San Isidro...................... 228
San Martín, José de 48,
51, 86, 96, 109, 254
San Nicolás 61–71
San Nicolás.................... 62
San Telmo............... 80–87
San Telmo 81
Sarmiento, Domingo 48,
76, 109, 115, 131, 255
shopping malls 199
shops
    Abasto............................ 199
    Abraxas 199
    Adrián Pallarols 207
    Akiabara 202
    Al Queso, Queso.............. 205
    Aldo de Sousa 200
    Almacén de Tangos
        Generales..................... 207
    Alto Palermo 199
    Amir Cosas Viejas........... 199
    Arte Étnico Argentino....... 204
    Ateneo Grand Splendid ... 201
    Artesanal Susana Villaroel
        207
    Bailarin Porteño 207
    Bond Street..................... 199
    Bokura Jeans.................. 202
    Bolivia 202
    El Boyero........................ 204
    Braga Menéndez............. 200

Buenos Aires Design........ 199
Capitulo I......................... 199
Cardón 202
Carla Di Sí....................... 202
Casa López 203
La Cava de la Brigada 205
Centro Artesanal de Tango
    207
Centro del Cuero............. 203
Charles Calfun 203
El Cid.............................. 202
La Cigarreria Ko' E' Yu..... 207
Club de Tango.................. 207
El Coleccionista 206
Cristóbal Colón 206
Dabbah Torréjon.............. 200
Daniel Abate.................... 200
Daniel Maman Fine Arts... 200
Decastelli......................... 200
Deporcamping 206
Ecrin 206
Elementos Argentinos...... 204
Elsi del Rio 200
Etiqueta Negra 202
Explorer........................... 206
Falabella.......................... 202
Farmacity 207
Fortin.............................. 203
Galería Arroyo 200
Galería Cecil.................... 199
Galería del Viejo 200
Galerías Pacifico 199
El Gauchito 204
Giesso 203
Gil Antiguedades............. 199
Guevara Gallery 199
Hermanos Estebecorena
    203
Isabel La Católica 203
Jazmin Chebar................. 203
JM Cueros........................ 203
Jumbo............................. 205
Kapush............................ 203
Kel Ediciones 201
Kiosko del Tango 207
Kosiuko........................... 203
Liberarte.......................... 201
Libreria de Ávila 201
Librería Hernández.......... 201
Libreria Platero................ 201
Librerías ABC.................. 234
Ligier 205
Marcelo Toledo 208
La Martina 203, 206
Miles............................... 206
Musimundo 206
NeoTango......................... 207
Notorious 206
Papelera.......................... 208
Paseo Alcorta................... 199
Patio Bullrich................... 199
Peter Kent 203
Piedras Argentinas.......... 208
Plata Nativa..................... 208
Prune.............................. 204
Rapsodia......................... 203
Rubbers........................... 200

Ruth Benzacar Gallery 200
Sabater Hermanos...........208
Sara García Uriburu 200
Seco...................................203
Stock Center....................206
Terroir 205
Tienda Diversia 204
Tikal.................................205
Tonel Privado 205
Topper 203
Tucci................................236
Tutti Pani 205
Velas de la Ballena...........208
Vendoma 207
Victorio 207
Vision Express..................203
VVV Gallery 200
Walrus Books...................201
Winery 205
Wussmann 200, 208
Zival's 206
Sinagoga Central............70
sizes (clothes)...............202
slang...............................274
smoking..........................30
society, modern............260
Solar de French..............83
Solar, Xul 75, 117, 118,
    126, 262
sporting goods 206
sports....................209–215
student cards 32
study programmes 36
subte...............................24

tango.......................56, 89,
    111, 113, 127, 131, 135,
    138, 141, 143, 191–194 &
    Tango colour section
    accommodation 191
    cena shows 192
    festivals 222
    information 191
    lessons 194
    milongas..........................193
    museum 57
    recitals............................192
    shopping 207
taxes.................................31
taxis 27
Teatro Colón 69
Teatro Nacional
    Cervantes 70
telephones.......................39
television 28
Temaikén 217
tennis.............................214
Thays, Charles.......96, 112,
    121, 125, 131, 133, 134
theatre 187
tickets............................185
**Tigre and the Paraná
    Delta**.................232–238
Tigre and the Paraná
    Delta 233
Tigre station..................236

time...................................40
tipping 31
Torre de los Ingleses 97
Torre Monumental 97
tourist information 40
tours 41
trains....................228, 234
Tranvía del Este 74
travellers' cheques 38
travellers with disabilities
   40
trees...............................124
Tren de la Costa 227

vegetarians 168
Villa Ocampo 230
villas miseria..................98
volunteering in Buenos
    Aires............................36

wine 165
women travellers 41
working in Buenos Aires...36
Yrurtia, Rogelio............145,
    262

T

V

W

So now we've told you about the things not to miss, the best places to stay, the top restaurants, the liveliest bars and the most spectacular sights, it only seems fair to tell you about the best travel insurance around

Map symbols

maps are listed in the full index using coloured text

—·—	Provincial boundary	☉	Statue
═══	Major road	↯	Viewpoint
───	Minor road	⍭	Fountain
▬▬	Pedestrianized street	ⓘ	Information office
)(	Bridge	✉	Post office
■—■—	Railway	ℂ	Telephone
Ⓜ	Metro station (Subte)	@	Internet point
—Ⓣ—	Tram stop & line (Tranvía)	⊠—⊠	Gateway
⚓	Ferry port	♜	Mosque
— —	Ferry route	✡	Synagogue
───	Waterway	⬯	Stadium
⬥	Point of interest	▬	Building
✈	International airport	⊞	Church/cathedral
✗	Domestic airport	▨	Park
🗻	Cliff	⊹	Cemetery
〜	Surf area	⌐ᵂ	Swamp

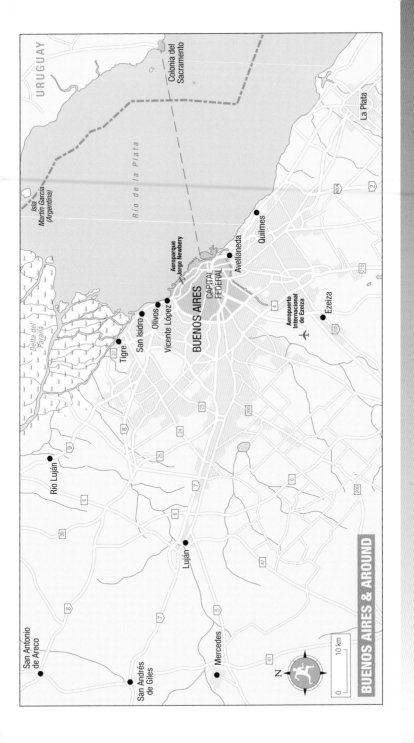

BUENOS AIRES & AROUND

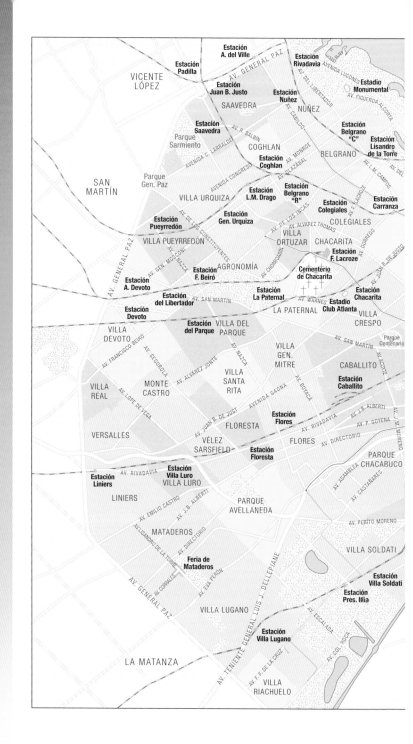

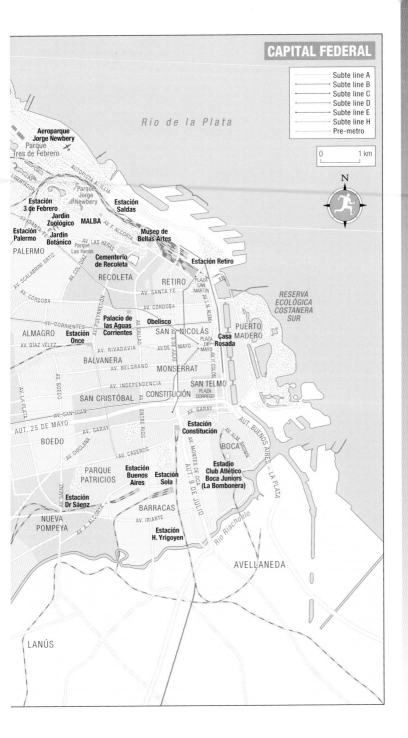

CAPITAL FEDERAL

- Subte line A
- Subte line B
- Subte line C
- Subte line D
- Subte line E
- Subte line H
- Pre-metro

0   1 km

N

Río de la Plata

Aeroparque
Jorge Newbery
Parque
Tres de Febrero

AUTOPISTA A. ILLIA

LIBERTADOR

Parque
Jorge
Newbery

Estación
3 de Febrero

Jardín
Zoológico

Estación
Saldas

MALBA

AV. F. ALCORTA

Estación
Palermo

Jardín
Botánico

Museo de
Bellas Artes

AV. SANTA FE

AV. LAS HERAS

Parque
Las Heras

PALERMO

AV. COL. DÍAZ

Cementerio
de Recoleta

Estación Retiro

RECOLETA

RETIRO

PLAZA
SAN
MARTÍN

AV. SCALABRINI ORTIZ

AV. SANTA FE

AV. CÓRDOBA

AV. CÓRDOBA

RESERVA
ECOLÓGICA
COSTANERA
SUR

AV. PUEYRREDÓN

Palacio de
las Aguas
Corrientes

Obelisco

AV-GORRIENTES

AV. L. ALEM

ALMAGRO

Estación
Once

SAN NICOLÁS

PUERTO
MADERO

AV. DÍAZ VÉLEZ

AV. RIVADAVIA

AV. 9 DE MAYO

Casa
Rosada

PLAZA
DE
MAYO

AV. F. COLÓN

BALVANERA

AV. BELGRANO

MONSERRAT

AV. BOEDO

AV. INDEPENDENCIA

SAN TELMO

SAN CRISTÓBAL

CONSTITUCIÓN

PLAZA
DORREGO

AV. LA PLATA

AV-SAN-JUAN

ENTRE RÍOS

AV. GARAY

AUT. 25 DE MAYO

AV. GARAY

Estación
Constitución

AV. ALM. BROWN

AUT. BUENOS AIRES — LA PLATA

BOEDO

AV. CHICLANA

AV. CASEROS

BOCA

PARQUE
PATRICIOS

Estación
Buenos
Aires

Estación
Sola

AV. MONTES DE OCA

Estadio
Club Atlético
Boca Juniors
(La Bombonera)

AUT. 9 DE JULIO

AV. SÁENZ

Estación
Dr Sáenz

BARRACAS

AV. A. ALCORTA

AV. IRIARTE

NUEVA
POMPEYA

Estación
H. Yrigoyen

Río Riachuelo

AVELLANEDA

LANÚS

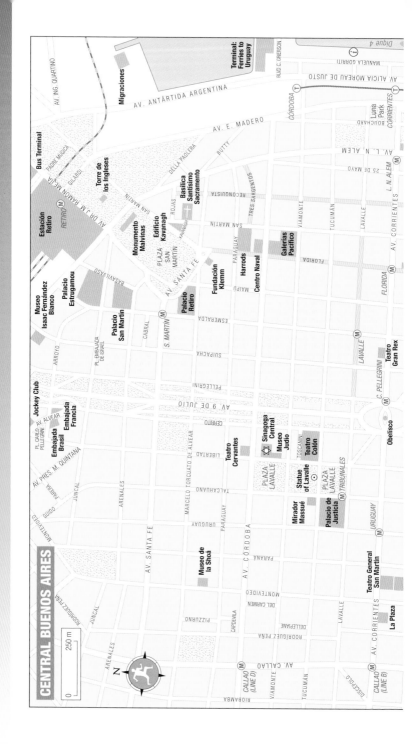

CENTRAL BUENOS AIRES

0 — 250 m

N

Terminal: Ferries to Uruguay
Migraciones
AV. ANTÁRTIDA ARGENTINA
AV. ING. QUARTINO
Bus Terminal
PADRE MÚGICA
GILARDI
Torre de los Ingleses
Estación Retiro
RETIRO Ⓜ
AV. DR JM RAMÓN MEJÍA
SAN MARTÍN
Museo Isaac Fernández Blanco
Palacio Estrugamou
BASAVILBASO
Palacio San Martín
ARROYO
PL. EMBAJADA DE ISRAEL
Jockey Club
PL. CARLO PELLEGRINI
AV. ALVEAR
Embajada Brasil
Embajada Francia
PL. PRES. M. QUINTANA
PABRA
JUNCAL
GUIDO
ARENALES
MONTEVIDEO
JUNCAL
RODRÍGUEZ PEÑA
ARENALES

Monumento Malvinas
PLAZA SAN MARTÍN
Edificio Kavanagh
ROJAS
PARAGUAY
DELLA PAOLERA
Basílica Santísimo Sacramento
AV. E. MADERO
BUTTY
CÓRDOBA
AV. ALICIA MOREAU DE JUSTO
Dique 4
MANUELA GORRITI
BLVD. C. GRIERSON
CORRIENTES Ⓣ
Luna Park
BOUCHARD
AV. L. N. ALEM
25 DE MAYO Ⓜ
L. N. ALEM

Fundación Klemm
Palacio Retiro
AV. SANTA FE
S. MARTÍN Ⓜ
CABRAL
SUIPACHA
ESMERALDA
Harrods
Centro Naval
MAIPÚ
PARAGUAY
SAN MARTÍN
TRES SARGENTOS
RECONQUISTA
VIAMONTE
TUCUMAN
LAVALLE
AV. CORRIENTES
Galerías Pacífico
FLORIDA

PELLEGRINI
AV. 9 DE JULIO
CERRITO
Teatro Cervantes
LIBERTAD
Sinagoga Central ✡
Museo Judío
PLAZA LAVALLE
Statue of Lavalle ☉
PLAZA LAVALLE
TOSCANINI
Teatro Colón
TRIBUNALES Ⓜ
C. PELLEGRINI Ⓜ
Teatro Gran Rex
LAVALLE Ⓜ
Obelisco

Museo de la Shoá
AV. SANTA FE
AV. CÓRDOBA
MARCELO TORCUATO DE ALVEAR
TALCAHUANO
URUGUAY
PARAGUAY
AV. CÓRDOBA
PARANÁ
MONTEVIDEO
DEL CARMEN
CAPDEVILA
PIZZURNO
DELLEPIANE
Mirador Massué
Palacio de Justicia
URUGUAY Ⓜ

CALLAO Ⓜ (LINE D)
AV. CALLAO
RIOBAMBA
RODRÍGUEZ PEÑA
VIAMONTE
TUCUMAN
LAVALLE
AV. CORRIENTES
Teatro General San Martín
La Plaza
CALLAO Ⓜ (LINE B)
DISCÉPOLO

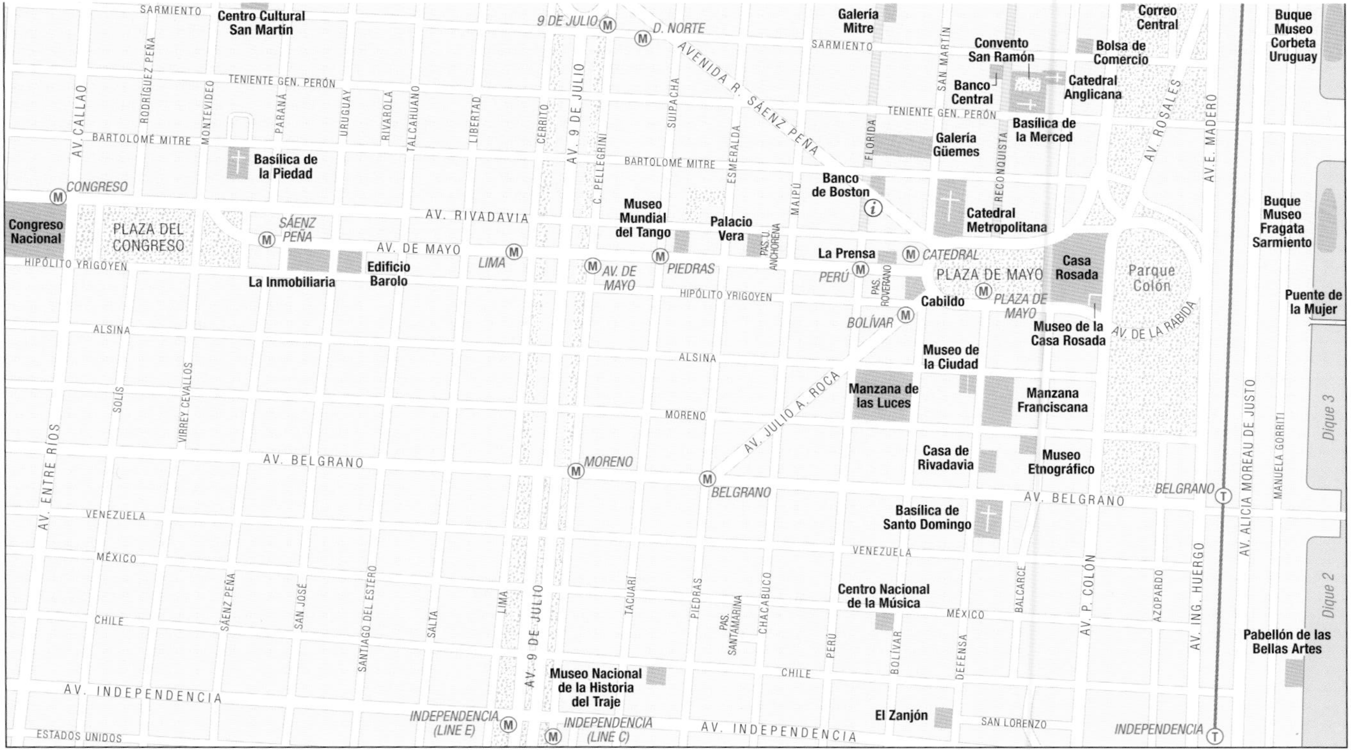
Congreso Nacional
Centro Cultural San Martín
Basílica de la Piedad
PLAZA DEL CONGRESO
La Inmobiliaria
Edificio Barolo
Museo Mundial del Tango
Palacio Vera
Banco de Boston
La Prensa
Galería Mitre
Galería Güemes
Convento San Ramón
Banco Central
Basílica de la Merced
Catedral Anglicana
Bolsa de Comercio
Correo Central
Catedral Metropolitana
Casa Rosada
PLAZA DE MAYO
Cabildo
Museo de la Casa Rosada
Parque Colón
Museo de la Ciudad
Manzana de las Luces
Manzana Franciscana
Casa de Rivadavia
Museo Etnográfico
Basílica de Santo Domingo
Centro Nacional de la Música
Museo Nacional de la Historia del Traje
El Zanjón
Buque Museo Corbeta Uruguay
Buque Museo Fragata Sarmiento
Puente de la Mujer
Dique 3
Dique 2
Pabellón de las Bellas Artes
CONGRESO
SÁENZ PEÑA
LIMA
AV. DE MAYO
PIEDRAS
9 DE JULIO
D. NORTE
PERÚ
CATEDRAL
PLAZA DE MAYO
BOLÍVAR
MORENO
BELGRANO
INDEPENDENCIA (LINE E)
INDEPENDENCIA (LINE C)
INDEPENDENCIA
AV. CALLAO
AV. ENTRE RÍOS
AV. RIVADAVIA
AV. DE MAYO
HIPÓLITO YRIGOYEN
ALSINA
MORENO
AV. BELGRANO
VENEZUELA
MÉXICO
CHILE
AV. INDEPENDENCIA
ESTADOS UNIDOS
SARMIENTO
TENIENTE GEN. PERÓN
BARTOLOMÉ MITRE
RODRÍGUEZ PEÑA
MONTEVIDEO
PARANÁ
URUGUAY
RIVAROLA
TALCAHUANO
LIBERTAD
CERRITO
AV. 9 DE JULIO
C. PELLEGRINI
SUIPACHA
ESMERALDA
PAS. U. ANCHORENA
MAIPÚ
FLORIDA
SAN MARTÍN
RECONQUISTA
PAS. ROVERANO
AVENIDA R. SÁENZ PEÑA
AV. JULIO A. ROCA
AV. ROSALES
AV. DE LA RÁBIDA
AV. E. MADERO
AV. ALICIA MOREAU DE JUSTO
MANUELA GORRITI
AV. ING. HUERGO
AZOPARDO
AV. P. COLÓN
BALCARCE
DEFENSA
BOLÍVAR
PERÚ
CHACABUCO
PAS. SANTAMARINA
PIEDRAS
TACUARÍ
LIMA
SALTA
SANTIAGO DEL ESTERO
SAN JOSÉ
SÁENZ PEÑA
VIRREY CEVALLOS
SOLÍS
SAN LORENZO

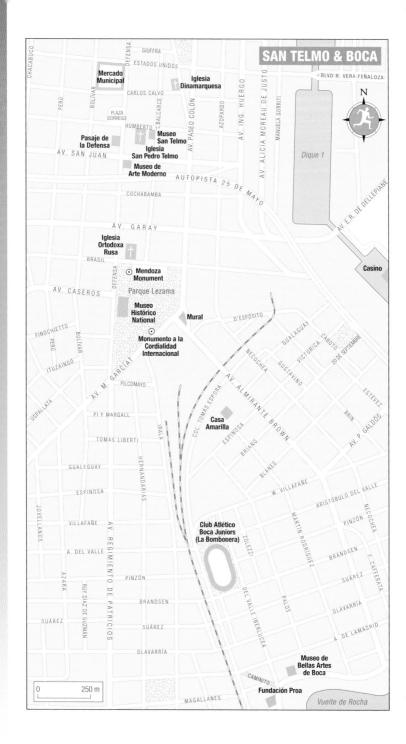

SAN TELMO & BOCA

CHACABUCO
GIUFFRA
ESTADOS UNIDOS
DEFENSA
BLVD R. VERA PEÑALOZA

N

Mercado
Municipal

Iglesia
Dinamarquesa

CARLOS CALVO

AV. ALICIA MOREAU DE JUSTO

MANUELA GORRITI

AV. ING. HUERGO

AZOPARDO

AV. PASEO COLÓN

PERÚ
BOLÍVAR
BALCARCE

PLAZA
DORREGO

HUMBERTO 1º

Dique 1

Pasaje de
la Defensa

Museo
San Telmo

Iglesia
San Pedro Telmo

AV. SAN JUAN

AV. E.R. DE DELLEPIANE

Museo de
Arte Moderno

AUTOPISTA 25 DE MAYO

COCHABAMBA

AV. GARAY

Iglesia
Ortodoxa
Rusa

Casino

BRASIL

DEFENSA

Mendoza
Monument

AV. CASEROS

Parque Lezama

Museo
Histórico
National

Mural

D'ESPÓSITO

FINOCHIETTO

PERÚ
BOLÍVAR

Monumento a la
Cordialidad
Internacional

GUALAGUAY

VICTORICA

CABOTO

20 DE SEPTIEMBRE

ITUZAINGÓ

NECOCHEA

GUSTAVINO

USPALLATA

AV. M. GARCÍAT

PILCOMAYO

AV. ALMIRANTE BROWN

ESTEVEZ

PI Y MARGALL

IRALA

COL. TOMÁS ESPORA

Casa
Amarilla

ESPINOSA

BRIN

AV. P. GALDÓS

TOMÁS LIBERTI

BRIANO

GUALEGUAY

HERNANDARIAS

BLANES

ESPINOSA

W. VILLAFAÑE

JOVELLANOS

VILLAFAÑE

AV. REGIMIENTO DE PATRICIOS

ARISTÓBULO DEL VALLE

PINZÓN

NECOCHEA

A. DEL VALLE

MARTÍN RODRÍGUEZ

AZARA

RUY DÍAZ DE GUZMAN

PINZÓN

Club Atlético
Boca Juniors
(La Bombonera)

ZOLEZZI

BRANDSEN

F. CAFFERATA

SUÁREZ

BRANDSEN

DEL VALLE IBERLUCEA

PALOS

SUÁREZ

OLAVARRÍA

SUÁREZ

SUÁREZ

A. DE LAMADRID

OLAVARRÍA

Museo de
Bellas Artes
de Boca

0   250 m

CAMINITO

MAGALLANES

Fundación Proa

Vuelte de Rocha

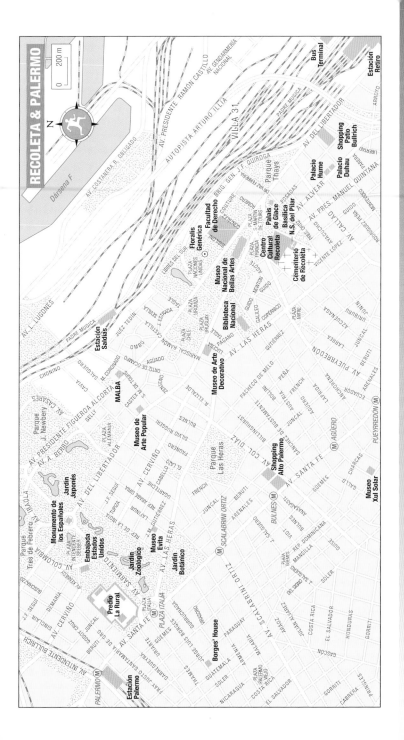
RECOLETA & PALERMO

0   200 m

N

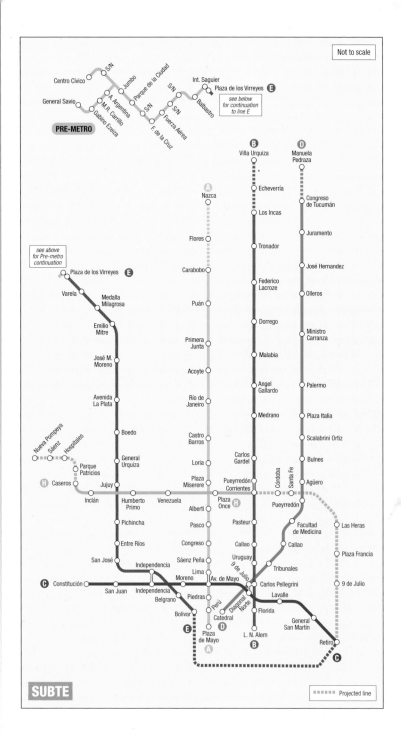